ISLAM and REVOLUTION

ISLAM and REVOLUTION

Writings and Declarations
Imam Khomeini

Translated and
Annotated by Hamid Algar

KPI

London, Melbourne and Henley

This edition first published in 1985 by KPI Limited,
14 Leicester Square, London WC2H 7PH, England

Distributed by
Routledge & Kegan Paul plc
14 Leicester Square, London WC2H 7PH, England

Routledge & Kegan Paul
464 St Kilda Road, Melbourne,
Victoria 3004, Australia and

Routledge & Kegan Paul plc
Broadway House, Newtown Road,
Henley-on-Thames, Oxon RG9 1EN, England

Printed in Great Britain

ISBN 0-7103-0098-0

CONTENTS

FOREWORD

The present anthology is designed to serve as a detailed and reliable introduction to the ideas and pronouncements of Imam Khomeini for those who have no access to the original Persian texts. Imam Khomeini has been a prolific writer and frequent speaker, and this volume represents only a fraction of his total output. We have excluded writings that deal with technical aspects of Islamic jurisprudence and philosophy, although passing reference to such matters inevitably does occur in some of the texts we have translated.

We begin with the best-known work of Imam Khomeini, his lectures on Islamic Government, and then proceed to offer a selection of his speeches and declarations, which, chronologically arranged, form an outline documentary history of the Islamic Revolution. These are followed by two interviews that Imam Khomeini granted me and two items indicating the lasting concern of Imam Khomeini with moral purification and spiritual realization as the ultimate purpose of all correctly guided human activity. The first of these items is an extract from lectures given at Najaf in 1970, and the second, a series of lectures given in late 1979 and early 1980 on the opening chapter of the Qur'an. Finally, some of the most significant legal rulings of the Imam are presented in the appendix.

In the introduction, I have made no attempt to document my summary biography of Imam Khomeini, because I am engaged in writing a comprehensive and fully documented account of the Imam's life and achievements, to which this anthology is intended as a companion volume. Those who desire further information on the Imam are urged to consult this forthcoming work.

The notes accompanying the texts are addressed to two separate sets of readers: those whose acquaintance with Islam is minimal, and who would never have thought of reading a book on the subject had it not been for the Islamic Revolution of Iran; and those with a previous and specialized interest in the subject. I hope each type of reader will be easily able to identify the notes intended to benefit him and overlook the rest.

The reader will notice that the title of Imam is consistently used in this book before the name of Khomeini. This contravenes the stubborn practice of the Western press, which insists on designating him Ayatullah ("Sign of God"), but conforms to current Iranian usage. The title "Ayatullah" in Shi'i Islam is generally bestowed on high-ranking religious scholars, and has also been applied to Imam Khomeini. However, since his role has been unique among the religious scholars of Iran and has exceeded what is implied in the title "Ayatullah," he has received the designation of Imam in recent years. It is important to note that the word *imam* applied to Khomeini has its general and original sense of leader, and not the particular and technical sense it has acquired when applied to the Twelve Imams believed by Shi'i Muslims to be the successors of the Prophet. Concerning the difference between the two applications of the word, see pp. 80 and 83.

As for the transliteration of Persian and Arabic names and terms, those whom the subject interests will understand how I have proceeded; those whom it does not, will not care. It is necessary only to add that I have consciously departed from the system of transliteration adopted in this volume in the case of well-known proper names for which a different orthography has become established in English usage, above all the name of Imam Khomeini himself.

Acknowledgments are due to the friends who made it possible for me to spend a week at the headquarters of Imam Khomeini at Neauphle-le-Chateau in December 1978; to all those who extended assistance and hospitality to me during my visit to Iran in December 1979, especially Ahmad Ajall-Lu'iyan and Mustafa

Safavi; to Husayn 'Abbasi, who supplied the photograph on the back cover; and to Javad Larijani, who assisted me in the understanding of several passages in this book.

Hamid Algar

Berkeley
18 Rabi' al-Awwal 1401/5 Bahman 1359/
January 25, 1981

INTRODUCTION BY
THE TRANSLATOR

IMAM RUHULLAH AL-MUSAVI AL-KHOMEINI was born on September 24, 1902 into a family of strong religious traditions in Khumayn, a small town some hundred kilometers to the southwest of Tehran.[1] Both his grandfather and father were religious scholars. The former, Sayyid Ahmad, was known as al-Hindi because of a period he had spent in India, where a distant branch of the family is said still to exist. The latter, Ayatullah Mustafa, was murdered by bandits only five months after the birth of Ruhullah, so that his mother and an aunt were responsible for his early upbringing. At the age of sixteen, he lost both mother and aunt in the course of a single year, and the task of supervising his education then fell to an elder brother, Sayyid Murtaza (better known, in later years, as Ayatullah Pasandida). Ayatullah Pasandida recalls that even in his youth, Imam Khomeini showed great piety, seriousness, and determination. It was the general consensus in Khumayn that a significant if turbulent career awaited him.[2]

At the age of nineteen, the young Khomeini was sent to study the religious sciences in the nearby town of Arak under the guidance of Shaykh 'Abd al-Karim Ha'iri,[3] who had been a pupil of great scholars at the Shi'i teaching centers in Iraq, most notably Mirza Hasan Shirazi.[4] His studies under Ha'iri made Khomeini an heir to the traditions established by the great figures of the nineteenth century, traditions that included political activism as well as learning.

The following year, Ha'iri accepted an invitation from the people and scholars of Qum to settle there. Qum had always been a center of learning as well as pilgrimage, but Ha'iri's arrival there, followed by his reorganization of the religious teaching institution, was the first in a series of developments that elevated Qum to the status of spiritual capital of Islamic Iran. The final and decisive development would be the movement of nationwide opposition to the Pahlavi monarchy that Imam Khomeini was to initiate in Qum in 1962.

Indications of Imam Khomeini's future role were already present in those early years. He attained prominence among the numerous students of Ha'iri, excelling in a wide variety of subjects, but especially ethics and the variety of spiritual philosophy known in Iran as 'irfan. At the early age of twenty-seven, he wrote a treatise in Arabic on these subjects, *Misbah al-Hidaya,* which was well received by his teachers.[5] Many of Imam Khomeini's important associates who came to be well known during the Revolution years—e.g., Ayatullah Muntaziri[6]—recall that they were first attracted to him by his proficiency in ethics and philosophy and that the classes he taught on them twice a week in Qum were frequently attended by hundreds of people.[7]

Given the current fame of Imam Khomeini as a revolutionary leader who has achieved a rare degree of success in the purely political sphere, it may appear surprising that he first gained fame as a writer and teacher concerned with devotional and even mystical matters. For Imam Khomeini, however, spirituality and mysticism have never implied social withdrawal or political quietism, but rather the building up of a fund of energy that finds its natural expression on the socio-political plane. The life of Imam Khomeini is a clear indication that the Revolution wrought by Islam necessarily begins in the moral and spiritual realm.[8] The classes he taught at Qum in the 1930's bore witness to this; topics of an ethical and spiritual nature were constantly interwoven with evocations of the problems of the day and exhortations to his listeners to devote themselves to solving them as part of their religious duty.

The early years of Imam Khomeini's activity in Qum coincided with the establishment of the Pahlavi state by Riza Khan. Riza Khan transformed the Iranian monarchy into a dictatorship of the modern, totalitarian kind and made its chief internal aim the elimination of Islam as a political, social, and cultural force.

Efforts directed toward this aim were directly witnessed by Imam Khomeini in Qum, and reports reached him regularly from other cities such as Mashhad, Isfahan, and Tabriz. What he saw and heard in those years left a deep impression on him; the repressive measures directed against the religious institution in later years by the second and last of the Pahlavi shahs, Muhammad Riza, were for him a natural and direct continuation of what he had experienced in the period of Riza Shah; father and son were of a piece.

Imam Khomeini's first public statement of a political nature came in a book published in 1943, *Kashf al-Asrar.*[9] The book is essentially a detailed, systematic critique of an anti-religious tract, but it also contains numerous passages that are overtly political and critical of the Pahlavi rule.

In 1937, Ha'iri died, and the religious institution was temporarily headed by a triumvirate of his closest senior associates: Ayatullahs Sadr, Hujjat, and Khwansari. Soon, however, a single leader succeeded to the role of Ha'iri, Ayatullah Burujirdi. Imam Khomeini was active in promoting the candidacy of Burujirdi, whom he expected to utilize the potentialities of the position of supreme religious authority in order to combat Pahlavi rule. He remained close to Burujirdi until his death in 1962, but other influences prevailed on Burujirdi; history regards him as a religious leader of great piety and administrative ability, but almost totally inactive in political matters.[10]

After the death of Burujirdi, no single successor to his position emerged. Khomeini was reluctant to allow his own name to be canvassed, but he ultimately yielded to the urgings of close associates that a collection of his rulings on matters of religious practice be published, thus implicitly declaring his availability as leader and authority. It was not, however, primarily through technical procedures such as this that the prominence of Imam Khomeini spread first within Qum, and then throughout the country. Of greater importance was his willingness to confront the Shah's regime at a time when few dared to do so. For example, he was alone among the major religious scholars of Qum in extending support publicly to the students at the religious institution who were campaigning against the opening of liquor stores in the city.

Soon his attention was devoted to matters of greater significance. The first step came in October 1962, when the Shah promulgated a law abolishing the requirement that candidates for
election to local assemblies be Muslim and male. Imam Khomeini,
joined by religious leaders elsewhere in the country, protested
vigorously against the measure; it was ultimately repealed.[11] The
measure itself was not intrinsically important, because elections
to local assemblies were invariably corrupt and their functions
were purely formal. But the campaign against it provided a point
of departure for more comprehensive agitation against the regime as well as an opportunity to build a coalition of religious
scholars that might be mobilized for more fundamental aims in
the future.

The next step was taken in 1963, when the Shah began to
promulgate a series of measures for reshaping the political, social,
and economic life of Iran that were collectively designated the
"White Revolution." The appearance of popular approval was
obtained by a fraudulent referendum held on January 26, 1963.
However, the measures in question were correctly perceived by
a large segment of Iranian society as being imposed on the country
by the United States and designed to bring about augmentation
of the Shah's power and wealth, as well as intensification of
United States dominance, which had been instituted with the CIA
coup d'etat against Prime Minister Muhammad Musaddiq in
August 1953. Imam Khomeini moved immediately to denounce
the fraudulent "revolution" and to expose the motives that under-
lay it, preaching a series of sermons from Fayziya Madrasa[12] in
Qum that had a nationwide impact.

The Shah's regime responded by sending paratroopers to
attack Fayziya Madrasa on March 22, 1963. A number of students
were killed and the madrasa was ransacked. Far from intimidating
Imam Khomeini, this event marked the beginning of a new period
of determined struggle that was directed not only against the errors and excesses of the regime, but against its very existence.
The attack on the madrasa had an almost symbolic value, exem-
plifying as it did both the hostility of the regime to Islam and
Islamic institutions and the ruthless, barbaric manner in which
it expressed that hostility.

Throughout the spring of 1963, Imam Khomeini continued to denounce the Shah's regime. He concentrated his attacks on its tyrannical nature, its subordination to the United States, and its expanding collaboration with Israel. The confrontation reached a new peak in June with the onset of Muharram, the month in the Muslim calendar when the martyrdom of Imam Husayn, the grandson of the Prophet, is commemorated and aspirations to emulate his example, by struggling against contemporary manifestations of tyranny, are awakened. On the tenth day of the month, Imam Khomeini delivered a historic speech in Qum, repeating his denunciations of the Shah's regime and warning the Shah not to behave in such a way that the people would rejoice when he should ultimately be forced to leave the country.[13] Two days later, he was arrested at his residence and taken to confinement in Tehran.

The arrest of Imam Khomeini brought popular disgust with the Shah's regime to a climax, and a major uprising shook the throne. In Qum, Tehran, Shiraz, Mashhad, Isfahan, Kashan and other cities, unarmed demonstrators confronted the Shah's U.S.-trained and -equipped army, which, upon the command to shoot to kill, slaughtered not less than 15,000 people in the space of a few days. The date on which this uprising began, Khurdad 15 according to the solar calendar used in Iran, marked a turning point in the modern history of Iran. It established Imam Khomeini as national leader and spokesman for popular aspirations, provided the struggle against the Shah and his foreign patrons with a coherent ideological basis in Islam, and introduced a period of mass political activity under the guidance of the religious leadership instead of the secular parties that had been discredited with the overthrow of Musaddiq. In all of these ways, the uprising of Khurdad 15 foreshadowed the Islamic Revolution of 1978-1979.

The uprising was suppressed, but the general public and the religious scholars refused to tolerate the imprisonment of Imam Khomeini. Agitation persisted throughout the country, and numerous religious leaders converged on Tehran to press for Imam Khomeini's release. It finally came on April 6, 1964, accompanied by a statement in the government-controlled press that Imam Khomeini had agreed to refrain from political activity as a condition for his release. This was immediately refuted by the Imam,[14] who resumed his denunciations of the regime with undiminished vigor.

If further proof were needed of the Shah's tutelage to the U.S., it came in October 1964, when legal immunity was granted to American personnel for all offenses committed in Iranian territory. After learning that the Iranian rubber-stamp Majlis had agreed to this measure, Imam Khomeini spent a sleepless night, and the next day, October 27, he furiously denounced this open violation of Iranian sovereignty and independence.[15] It had by now become apparent to the Shah and his foreign overlords that Imam Khomeini could not be intimidated into silence, and it was decided to exile him, in the vain hope of destroying his influence. Accordingly, on November 4, 1964, Imam Khomeini was arrested again and sent into exile in Turkey, accompanied by agents of the Shah's secret police.

After a brief stay in Ankara, Imam Khomeini was obliged to take up residence in Bursa, a city in the west of Turkey. Continual pressure was brought on the Shah's regime to permit Imam Khomeini to leave Turkey for a more favorable place of exile, Najaf, one of the Shi'i shrine cities of Iraq. In October 1965, consent was given, and Imam Khomeini proceeded to Najaf, which was to be his home for thirteen years.

In agreeing to this move, the Shah's regime had been motivated not only by the desire to free itself from popular pressure, but also by the assumption that Imam Khomeini would be overshadowed in Najaf by the religious authorities resident there. This assumption proved false. Imam Khomeini established himself as a major presence in Najaf. More importantly, he maintained his influence and popularity in Iran. He issued periodic proclamations concerning developments in Iran that were smuggled into the country and clandestinely circulated at great risk. In addition, his messages addressed to the Muslim world at large were distributed several times in Mecca during the pilgrimage season of the year. In Najaf itself, he received visits during the long years of his exile from a number of important Iranian and other Muslim personalities.

The name and person of Imam Khomeini and the cause that he embodied were never forgotten in Iran. His example inspired a number of religious scholars and groups, which continued to build on the foundations laid in 1963 and 1964, and unnoticed by most foreign observers, an Islamic movement of unparalleled breadth and profundity came into being.

It was, then, entirely natural that Imam Khomeini should swiftly emerge as the leader and guide of the Islamic Revolution of 1978-1979. Notwithstanding his physical absence from the country, he was present in the hearts of his countrymen and infinitely more in tune with their aspirations than politicians who had suffered neither exile nor imprisonment.

On November 23, 1977, the elder son of Imam Khomeini, Hajj Mustafa, died suddenly in Najaf, assassinated by the Shah's U.S.-instituted security police, SAVAK. Imam Khomeini bore this blow stoically, but the tragedy inflamed the public in Iran. Massive social corruption and economic dislocation as well as continuing political repression had already aroused universal discontent in Iran, and when the regime aimed its next blow against Imam Khomeini, discontent overflowed into rebellion, and rebellion, in turn, matured into revolution.

On January 8, 1978, one week after President Carter had been in Tehran lauding the Shah as a wise statesman beloved of his people,[16] the government-controlled press printed an article supplied by the Ministry of the Court attacking Imam Khomeini as an agent of foreign powers. The public reaction was immediate outrage. The following day in Qum, demonstrations broke out that were suppressed with heavy loss of life. This was the first of a series of demonstrations that progressively unfurled across the country, until in the end, barely a single region remained untouched by revolutionary fervor. Throughout the spring and summer of 1978, Imam Khomeini issued a series of proclamations and directives congratulating the people on their steadfastness and encouraging them to persist until the attainment of the final objective—overthrow of the monarchy and institution of an Islamic republic.

The centrality of the Imam in the revolutionary movement was obvious from the beginning. His name was constantly repeated in the slogans that were devised and chanted in the demonstrations; his portrait served as a revolutionary banner; and his return from exile to supervise the installation of an Islamic government was insistently demanded. Acting under another of its erroneous assumptions, the Shah's regime requested the Baathist government of Iraq, in September 1978, to expel Imam Khomeini from its territory, in the hope of depriving him of his base of operations and robbing the Revolution of its leadership. Imam Khomeini had never enjoyed cordial relations with the various governments that had ruled Iraq since his arrival there in 1965, and he now informed the Baathists that he would be happy to leave Iraq for a country that was not subject to the Shah's dictates. Syria and Algeria were considered as possible destinations, but in the end, as Imam Khomeini testifies himself, no Muslim country offered him refuge with the assurance of his being able to continue his activity freely.[17] So he went to France, taking up residence at the hamlet of Neauphle-le-Chateau near Paris in early October 1978.

The move to France proved beneficial. Paradoxically, communication with Iran was easier from France than it had been from Iraq. The declarations and directives that were now being issued with increasing frequency were telephoned directly to Tehran, for further dissemination to a number of centers in the provinces. A never-ending stream of Iranians, from Europe and the United States as well as Iran itself, came to visit and pay homage to the Imam and to consult with him. The world's media also descended on the modest residence of the Imam at Neauphle-le-Chateau, and his words began to reach a global audience.

The month of Muharram that coincided with December 1978 witnessed vast and repeated demonstrations in Tehran and other Iranian cities demanding the abolition of the monarchy and the establishment of an Islamic republic under the leadership of Imam Khomeini. Despite all the savagery the Shah had employed, including the slaughter of thousands of unarmed demonstrators, the torture and abuse of detainees, and massacres of the wounded in their hospital beds, and despite the unstinting support he had received from the United States and other foreign powers, the corrupt and murderous rule of the Shah was approaching its end. His masters decided it was politic for him to leave, and when preparations had been made for the installation of a surrogate administration under Shahpur Bakhtiar, the Shah left Iran for the last time on January 16, 1979. The outburst of joy that followed his departure was a fulfillment of the prophecy Imam Khomeini had made sixteen years earlier.

Once the Shah left Iran, Imam Khomeini prepared to return to his homeland. When he did, on February 1, he was met with a tumultuous welcome. With his renewed presence in Iran, the fate of the Bakhtiar government was sealed. After a final outburst of savagery on February 10 and 11, the old regime collapsed in disgrace, and the Islamic Republic of Iran was born.

In the six eventful years that have elapsed since the triumph of the Revolution, Imam Khomeini has played a central role in confronting the crises that have assailed the Islamic Republic — war, the decimation of the leadership, the continuing dislocation of society and the economy. Soon after his return to Iran in February 1979, he took up residence in Qum, with the evident intention of exercising only general supervision over the affairs of the Islamic Republic. But early in 1980 he came to Tehran for treatment of a heart problem, and after his release from hospital he installed himself in the north Tehran suburb of Jamaran instead of returning to Qum. The main reason for this was, no doubt, the perceived need to stay in the capital and remain in close touch with post-revolutionary affairs, which were proving more tempestuous than had, perhaps, been anticipated.

In a formal sense, the role of Imam Khomeini has been defined by Articles 107 to 112 of the Constitution of the Islamic Republic of Iran,[18] which incorporate the key political principle of the "governance of the *faqih*" (*vilayat-i faqih*).[19] In a more general sense, however, his countless addresses and proclamations have mirrored as well as directed the flow of events in Iran.

The present anthology of Imam Khomeini's writings and declarations—which first appeared in the United States in 1981—has, as its most recent statement by Khomeini, the message that he sent to the pilgrims to Mecca in September 1980. It would have been desirable to include representative statements made by him during the past four years, but this did not prove feasible. However, the volume has continuing value as a record of the world-view and career of Imam Khomeini, containing as it does all the statements he made during the formative and decisive years of the Revolution.

Now his role—although still central—is no longer of paramount daily importance, as the political institutions created by the Revolution settle down to smooth functioning; and his greatest legacy to Iran will be seen to have founded a new order capable of outliving his passing.

Pages 13-21

Notes

1. Some information about the early life of Imam Khomeini is to be found in the opening sections of two books that concern themselves chiefly with the events of 1962-1964: S.H.R., *Barrasi va Tahlili az Nihzat-i Imam Khomeini* (Najaf? n.d.); and anon., *Biyugrafi-yi Pishva*, n.p., n.d.

2. Interview of the translator with Ayatullah Pasandida, Qum, December 19, 1979.

3. For detailed accounts of the life and achievements of Shaykh 'Abd al-Karim Ha'iri, see Muhammad Sharif Razi, *Asar al-Hujja* (Qum, 1332 Sh./1953), I, 22-90, and *Ganjina-yi Danishmandan* (Tehran, 1352 Sh./1973), I, 283-304. His relations with Riza Shah are discussed briefly in Abdul-Hadi Ha'iri, *Shi'ism and Constitutionalism in Iran* (Leiden, 1977), pp. 135-139.

4. Concerning Mirza Hasan Shirazi, see p. 124 and p. 162, n. 155.

5. For lists of Imam Khomeini's writings, published and unpublished, see S.H.R., *Barrasi va Tahlili az Nihzat-i Imam Khomeini*, pp. 55-61, and anon., *Biyugrafi-yi Pishva*, I, 52-53.

6. Ayatullah Muntaziri, born to a family of peasant stock in Najafabad in 1301/1884, has for many years been closely associated with Imam Khomeini, who has described him as "the product of my life." Not only a master of both law and philosophy, but also a militant leader, Ayatullah Muntaziri played an important role in sustaining the struggle against the Shah during Imam Khomeini's years in exile.

7. Razi, *Asar al-Hujja*, II, 45.

8. See Imam Khomeini's own remarks on the connection between spirituality and socio-political activity on pp. 399-400.

9. For an extract from this book, see pp. 169-173.

10. For a brief account of the achievements of Ayatullah Burujirdi, see Murtaza Mutahhari, "Mazaya va Khadamat-i Marhum Ayatullah Burujirdi," *Bahsi dar bara-yi Marja'iyat va Ruhaniyat* (Tehran, n.d.), pp. 233-249.

11. See p. 118 and p. 161, n. 151.

12. Fayziya Madrasa, founded in Safavid times, has acquired particular fame among the teaching institutions in Qum because of the role it has played in the Islamic movement. Closed down in 1975 by the Shah's regime, it was ceremonially reopened after the triumph of the Revolution.

13. For the text of this speech, see pp. 177-180.

14. See p. 139.

15. For the text of this speech, see pp. 181-188.

16. Carter told the Shah in Tehran on January 1, 1978: "Iran is an island of stability in one of the more troubled areas of the world. This is a great tribute to you, Your Majesty, and to your leadership and to the respect, admiration and love which your people give to you." *New York Times,* January 2, 1978.

17. See p. 238.

18. See Hamid Algar, trans., *The Constitution of the Islamic Republic of Iran* (Berkeley, 1980), pp. 66-69.

19. This principle forms the central topic of the first section of this anthology. See especially pp. 62-125.

I

Islamic Government

√Probably the best known of Imam Khomeini's works, the book Islamic Government originated in a series of lectures given at Najaf between January 21 and February 8, 1970. The lectures were recorded and transcribed by a student, and then published in book form.

"Islamic Government" is an exact translation of the original Persian title, Hukumat-i Islami. However, the reader should bear in mind that the book does not purport to offer either a complete scheme of Islamic political philosophy or a detailed plan for the establishment and functioning of an Islamic state. Its purpose is narrower and more specific, and geared to the audience to whom the lectures were delivered: students of the religious sciences, who might be expected later to assume positions of influence in Muslim society.

Three major points emerge from the lectures. The first is the necessity for the establishment and maintenance of Islamic political institutions, or to put it differently, the need for subordinating political power to Islamic goals, precepts, and criteria. The second is the duty of the religious scholars (the fuqaha) to bring about an Islamic state, and to assume legislative, executive, and judicial positions within it—in short, the doctrine of "the governance of the faqih" (vilayat-i faqih). The various texts that support this second point are subjected to lengthy review and examination. Finally, Imam Khomeini sets out a program of action for the establishment of an Islamic state, including various measures for self-reform by the religious establishment. All three themes are expounded against a backdrop of particular concern with Iran; hence the occurrence of numerous references to Iran in the course of the general and theoretical discussion.

Accurate translations of Hukumat-i Islami exist in French, Arabic, Turkish, and Urdu. In the fall of 1978, the Joint Publications and Research Service, the translation branch of the U.S. Central Intelligence

Agency, commissioned an English translation, not of the original Persian text, but of the translation in Arabic. The resulting version, crude and unreliable, was subsequently published in a vulgar and sensational format by Manor Books, a commercial publisher in New York. What follows is an integral and faithful translation of the third edition of the Persian text, published at Najaf in 1391/1971.

1

INTRODUCTION

THE SUBJECT OF THE GOVERNANCE OF THE FAQIH *(vilayat-i faqih¹)* provides us with the opportunity to discuss certain related matters and questions. The governance of the *faqih* is a subject that in itself elicits immediate assent and has little need of demonstration, for anyone who has some general awareness of the beliefs and ordinances of Islam will unhesitatingly give his assent to the principle of the governance of the *faqih* as soon as he encounters it; he will recognize it as necessary and self-evident. If little attention is paid to this principle today, so that it has come to require demonstration, it is because of the social circumstances prevailing among the Muslims in general, and in the teaching institution in particular. These circumstances, in turn, have certain historical roots to which I will now briefly refer.

From the very beginning, the historical movement of Islam has had to contend with the Jews, for it was they who first established anti-Islamic propaganda and engaged in various stratagems, and as you can see, this activity continues down to the present. Later they were joined by other groups, who were in certain respects more satanic than they. These new groups began their imperialist penetration of the Muslim countries about three hundred years ago, and they regarded it as necessary to work for the extirpation of Islam in order to attain their ultimate goals. It was not their aim to alienate the people from Islam in order to promote Christianity among them, for the imperialists really have no religious belief, Christian or Islamic. Rather, throughout this long historical period, and going back to the Crusades,

27

they felt that the major obstacle in the path of their materialistic ambitions and the chief threat to their political power was nothing but Islam and its ordinances, and the belief of the people in Islam. They therefore plotted and campaigned against Islam by various means.

The preachers they planted in the religious teaching institution, the agents they employed in the universities, government educational institutions, and publishing houses, and the orientalists who work in the service of the imperialist states—all these people have pooled their energies in an effort to distort the principles of Islam. As a result, many persons, particularly the educated, have formed misguided and incorrect notions of Islam.

Islam is the religion of militant individuals who are committed to truth and justice. It is the religion of those who desire freedom and independence. It is the school of those who struggle against imperialism. But the servants of imperialism have presented Islam in a totally different light. They have created in men's minds a false notion of Islam. The defective version of Islam, which they have presented in the religious teaching institution, is intended to deprive Islam of its vital, revolutionary aspect and to prevent Muslims from arousing themselves in order to gain their freedom, fulfill the ordinances of Islam, and create a government that will assure their happiness and allow them to live lives worthy of human beings.

For example, the servants of imperialism declared that Islam is not a comprehensive religion providing for every aspect of human life and has no laws or ordinances pertaining to society. It has no particular form of government. Islam concerns itself only with rules of ritual purity after menstruation and parturition. It may have a few ethical principles, but it certainly has nothing to say about human life in general and the ordering of society.

This kind of evil propaganda has unfortunately had an effect. Quite apart from the masses, the educated class—university students and also many students at the religious teaching institutions —have failed to understand Islam correctly and have erroneous notions. Just as people may, in general, be unacquainted with a stranger, so too they are unacquainted with Islam; Islam lives among the people of this world as if it were a stranger.[2] If somebody were to present Islam as it truly is, he would find it difficult

28

to make people believe him. In fact, the agents of imperialism in the religious teaching institutions would raise a hue and cry against him.

In order to demonstrate to some degree how great the difference is between Islam and what is presented as Islam, I would like to draw your attention to the difference between the Qur'an and the books of *hadith*,[3] on the one hand, and the practical treatises of jurisprudence, on the other. The Qur'an and the books of *hadith*, which represent the sources for the commands and ordinances of Islam, are completely different from the treatises written by the *mujtahids*[4] of the present age both in breadth of scope and in the effect they are capable of exerting on the life of society. The ratio of Qur'anic verses concerned with the affairs of society to those concerned with ritual worship is greater than a hundred to one. Of the approximately fifty sections of the corpus of *hadith* containing all the ordinances of Islam, not more than three or four sections relate to matters of ritual worship and the duties of man toward his Creator and Sustainer. A few more are concerned with questions of ethics, and all the rest are concerned with social, economic, legal, and political questions—in short, the gestation of society.

You who represent the younger generation and who, God willing, will be of service to Islam in the future must strive diligently all your lives to pursue the aims I will now set forth and to impart the laws and ordinances of Islam. In whatever way you deem most beneficial, in writing or in speech, instruct the people about the problems Islam has had to contend with since its inception and about the enemies and afflictions that now threaten it. Do not allow the true nature of Islam to remain hidden, or people will imagine that Islam is like Christianity (nominal, not true Christianity), a collection of injunctions pertaining to man's relation to God, and the mosque will be equated with the church.

At a time when the West was a realm of darkness and obscurity —with its inhabitants living in a state of barbarism and America still peopled by half-savage redskins—and the two vast empires of Iran and Byzantium were under the rule of tyranny, class privilege, and discrimination, and the powerful dominated all without any trace of law or popular government, God, Exalted and Almighty, by means of the Most Noble Messenger (peace and blessings be upon him), sent laws that astound us with their magnitude. He instituted laws and practices for all human affairs and laid down injunctions for man extending from even before the embryo is formed until after he is placed in the tomb. In just the same way that there are laws setting forth the duties of worship for man, so too there are laws, practices, and norms for the affairs of society and government. Islamic law is a progressive, evolving, and comprehensive system of law. All the voluminous books that have been compiled from the earliest times on different areas of law, such as judicial procedure, social transactions, penal law, retribution, international relations, regulations pertaining to peace and war, private and public law—taken together, these contain a mere sample of the laws and injunctions of Islam. There is not a single topic in human life for which Islam has not provided instruction and established a norm.

In order to make the Muslims, especially the intellectuals and the younger generation, deviate from the path of Islam, foreign agents have constantly insinuated that Islam has nothing to offer, that Islam consists of a few ordinances concerning menstruation and parturition, and that this is the proper field of study for the *akhunds*.[5]

There is something of truth here, for it is fitting that those *akhunds* who have no intention of expounding the theories, injunctions, and world-view of Islam and who spend most of their time on precisely such matters, forgetting all the other topics of Islamic law, be attacked and accused in this manner. They too are at fault; foreigners are not the only ones to be blamed. For several centuries, as might be expected, the foreigners laid certain plans to realize their political and economic ambitions, and the neglect that has overtaken the religious teaching institution has made it possible for them to succeed. There have been individuals among us, the *'ulama*,[6] who have unwittingly contributed to the fulfillment of those aims, with the result that you now see.

It is sometimes insinuated that the injunctions of Islam are defective, and said that the laws of judicial procedure, for example, are not all that they should be. In keeping with this insinuation and propaganda, agents of Britain were instructed by their masters to take advantage of the idea of constitutionalism in order to deceive the people and conceal the true nature of their political crimes (the pertinent proofs and documents are now available). At the beginning of the constitutional movement, when people wanted to write laws and draw up a constitution, a copy of the Belgian legal code was borrowed from the Belgian embassy and a handful of individuals (whose names I do not wish to mention here) used it as the basis for the constitution they then wrote, supplementing its deficiencies with borrowings from the French and British legal codes.[7] True, they added some of the ordinances of Islam in order to deceive the people, but the basis of the laws that were now thrust upon the people was alien and borrowed.

What connection do all the various articles of the Constitution, as well as the body of Supplementary Law[8] concerning the monarchy, the succession, and so forth, have with Islam? They are all opposed to Islam; they violate the system of government and the laws of Islam.

Islam proclaims monarchy and hereditary succession wrong and invalid. When Islam first appeared in Iran, the Byzantine Empire, Egypt, and the Yemen, the entire institution of monarchy was abolished. In the blessed letters that the Most Noble Messenger (peace and blessings be upon him) wrote to the Byzantine Emperor Heraclius and the Shahanshah of Iran,[9] he called upon them to abandon the monarchical and imperial form of government, to cease compelling the servants of God to worship them with absolute obedience, and to permit men to worship God, Who has no partner and is the True Monarch. Monarchy and hereditary succession represent the same sinister, evil system of government that prompted the Lord of the Martyrs[10] (peace be upon him) to rise up in revolt and seek martyrdom in an effort to prevent its establishment. He revolted in repudiation of the hereditary succession of Yazid,[11] to refuse it his recognition.

Islam, then, does not recognize monarchy and hereditary succession; they have no place in Islam. If that is what is meant by the so-called deficiency of Islam, then Islam is indeed deficient. Islam has laid down no laws for the practice of usury, for banking on the basis of usury, for the consumption of alcohol, or for the cultivation of sexual vice, having radically prohibited all of these. The ruling cliques, therefore, which are the puppets of imperialism and wish to promote these vices in the Islamic world, will naturally regard Islam as defective. They must import the appro-

31

priate laws from Britain, France, Belgium, and most recently, America. The fact that Islam makes no provision for the orderly pursuit of these illicit activities, far from being a deficiency, is a sign of perfection and a source of pride.

The conspiracy worked out by the imperialist government of Britain at the beginning of the constitutional movement had two purposes. The first, which was already known at that time, was to eliminate the influence of Tsarist Russia in Iran, and the second was to take the laws of Islam out of force and operation by introducing Western laws.[12]

The imposition of foreign laws on our Islamic society has been the source of numerous problems and difficulties. Knowledgeable people working in our judicial system have many complaints concerning the existing laws and their mode of operation. If a person becomes caught up in the judicial system of Iran or that of analogous countries, he may have to spend a whole lifetime trying to prove his case. In my youth I once encountered a learned lawyer who said, "I can spend my whole life following a litigation back and forth through the judicial machinery, and then bequeath it to my son for him to do the same thing!" That is the situation that now prevails, except, of course, when one of the parties has influence, in which case the matter is examined and settled swiftly, albeit unjustly.

Our present judicial laws have brought our people nothing but trouble, causing them to neglect their daily tasks and providing the occasion for all kinds of misuse. Very few people are able to obtain their legitimate rights. In the adjudication of cases it is necessary not only that everyone should obtain his rights, but also that correct procedure be followed. People's time must be considered, as well as the way of life and profession of both parties, so that matters are resolved as swiftly and simply as possible.

A case that a *shari'a*[13] judge in earlier times settled in one or two days cannot be settled now in twenty years. The needy, young and old alike, must spend the entire day at the Ministry of Justice, from morning to night, wasting their time in corridors or standing in front of some official's desk, and in the end they will still not know what has transpired. Anyone who is more cunning, and more willing and able to give bribes, has his case settled expeditiously, but at the cost of justice. Others must wait in frustration and perplexity until their entire lives are gone.

The agents of imperialism sometimes write in their books and their newspapers that the legal provisions of Islam are too harsh. One person was even so impudent as to write that the laws of Islam are harsh because they originated with the Arabs, so that the "harshness" of the Arabs is reflected in the "harshness" of Islamic law!

I am amazed at the way these people think. They kill people for possessing ten grams of heroin and say, "That is the law" (I have been informed that ten people were put to death some time ago, and another person more recently, for possession of ten grams of heroin).[14] Inhuman laws like this are concocted in the name of a campaign against corruption, and they are not to be regarded as harsh. (I am not saying it is permissible to sell heroin, but this is not the appropriate punishment. The sale of heroin must indeed be prohibited, but the punishment must be in proportion to the crime.) When Islam, however, stipulates that the drinker of alcohol should receive eighty lashes, they consider it "too harsh." They can *execute* someone for possessing ten grams of heroin and the question of harshness does not even arise!

Many forms of corruption that have appeared in society derive from alcohol. The collisions that take place on our roads, and the murders and suicides, are very often caused by the consumption of alcohol. Indeed, even the use of heroin is said to derive from addiction to alcohol. But still, some say, it is quite unobjectionable for someone to drink alcohol (after all, they do it in the West); so let alcohol be bought and sold freely.

But when Islam wishes to prevent the consumption of alcohol—one of the major evils—stipulating that the drinker should receive eighty lashes, or sexual vice, decreeing that the fornicator be given one hundred lashes (and the married man or woman be stoned), then they start wailing and lamenting: "What a harsh law that is, reflecting the harshness of the Arabs!" They are not aware that these penal provisions of Islam are intended to keep great nations from being destroyed by corruption. Sexual vice has now reached such proportions that it is destroying entire generations, corrupting our youth, and causing them to neglect all forms of work. They are all rushing to enjoy the various forms of vice that have become so freely available and so enthusiastically promoted. Why should it be regarded as harsh if Islam stipulates that an offender should be publicly flogged in order to protect the younger generation from corruption?

At the same time, we see the masters of this ruling class of ours enacting slaughters in Vietnam over fifteen years, devoting enormous budgets to this business of bloodshed, and no one has the right to object! But if Islam commands its followers to engage in warfare or defense in order to make men submit to laws that are beneficial for them, and kills a few corrupt people or instigators of corruption, then they ask: "What's the purpose for that war?"

All of the foregoing represent plans drawn up several centuries ago that are now being implemented and bearing fruit.

First, they opened a school in a certain place,[15] and we overlooked the matter and said nothing. Our colleagues also were negligent in the matter and failed to prevent it from being established so that now, as you can observe, these schools have multiplied, and their missionaries have gone out into the provinces and villages, turning our children into Christians or unbelievers.

Their plan is to keep us backward, to keep us in our present miserable state so they can exploit our riches, our underground wealth, our lands, and our human resources. They want us to remain afflicted and wretched, and our poor to be trapped in their misery. Instead of surrendering to the injunctions of Islam, which provide a solution for the problem of poverty, they and their agents wish to go on living in huge palaces and enjoying lives of abominable luxury.

These plans of theirs are so broad in scope that they have even touched the institutions of religious learning. If someone wishes to speak about Islamic government and the establishment of Islamic government, he must observe the principle of *taqiya*[16] and count upon the opposition of those who have sold themselves to imperialism. When this book was first printed, the agents of the embassy undertook certain desperate measures to prevent its dissemination,[17] which succeeded only in disgracing them more than before.

Matters have now come to the point where some people consider the apparel of a soldier incompatible with true manliness and justice, even though the leaders of our religion were all soldiers, commanders, and warriors. They put on military dress and went into battle in the wars that are described for us in our history; they killed and they were killed. The Commander of the Faithful[18] himself (upon whom be peace) would place a helmet on his blessed head, don his coat of chain mail, and gird on a sword. Imam Hasan[19] and the Lord of the Martyrs (peace be upon them) acted likewise. The later Imams did not have the opportunity to go into battle, even though Imam Baqir[20] (peace be upon him) was also a warrior by nature. But now the wearing of military apparel is thought to detract from a man's quality of justice,[21] and it is said that one should not wear military dress. If we want to form an Islamic government, then we must do it in our cloaks and turbans; otherwise, we commit an offense against decency and justice!

This is all the result of the wave of propaganda that has now reached the religious teaching institution and imposed on us the duty of proving that Islam also possesses rules of government.

That is our situation then—created for us by the foreigners through their propaganda and their agents. They have removed from operation all the judicial processes and political laws of Islam and replaced them with European importations, thus diminishing the scope of Islam and ousting it from Islamic society. For the sake of exploitation they have installed their agents in power.

So far, we have sketched the subversive and corrupting plan of imperialism. We must now take into consideration as well certain internal factors, notably the dazzling effect that the material progress of the imperialist countries has had on some members of our society. As the imperialist countries attained a high degree of wealth and affluence—the result both of scientific and technical progress and of their plunder of the nations of Asia and Africa—these individuals lost all self-confidence and imagined that the only way to achieve technical progress was to abandon their own laws and beliefs. When the moon landings took place, for instance, they concluded that Muslims should jettison their laws! But what is the connection between going to the moon and the laws of Islam? Do they not see that countries having opposing laws and social systems compete with each other in technical and scientific progress and the conquest of space? Let them go all the way to Mars or beyond the Milky Way; they will still be deprived of true happiness, moral virtue, and spiritual advancement and be unable to solve their own social problems. For the solution of social problems and the relief of human misery require foundations in faith and morals; merely acquiring material power and wealth, conquering nature and space, have no effect in this regard. They must be supplemented by, and balanced with, the faith, the conviction, and the morality of Islam in order truly to serve humanity instead of endangering it. This conviction, this morality, these laws that are needed, *we* already possess. So as soon as someone goes somewhere or invents something, we should not hurry to abandon our religion and its laws, which regulate the life of man and provide for his well-being in this world and the hereafter.

The same applies to the propaganda of the imperialists. Unfortunately, some members of our society have been influenced by their hostile propaganda, although they should not have been. The imperialists have propagated among us the view that Islam does not have a specific form of government or governmental institutions. They say further that even if Islam does have certain laws, it has no method for enforcing them, so that its function is purely legislative. This kind of propaganda forms part of the overall plan of the imperialists to prevent the Muslims from becoming involved in political activity and establishing an Islamic government. It is in total contradiction with our fundamental beliefs.

We believe in government and believe that the Prophet (upon whom be peace) was bound to appoint a successor, as he indeed did. Was a successor designated purely for the sake of expounding law? The expounding of law did not require a successor to the Prophet. He himself, after all, had expounded the laws; it would have been enough for the laws to be written down in a book and put into the people's hands to guide them in their actions. It was logically necessary for a successor to be appointed for the sake of exercising government. Law requires a person to execute it. The same holds true in all countries of the world, for the establishment of a law is of little benefit in itself and cannot secure the happiness of man. After a law is established, it is necessary also to create an executive power. If a system of law or government lacks an executive power, it is clearly deficient. Thus Islam, just as it established laws, also brought into being an executive power.

There was still a further question: who was to hold the executive power? If the Prophet (upon whom be peace and blessings) had not appointed a successor to assume the executive power, he would have failed to complete his mission, as the Qur'an testifies.[22] The necessity for the implementation of divine law, the need for an executive power, and the importance of that power in fulfilling the goals of the prophetic mission and establishing a just order that would result in the happiness of mankind—all of this made the appointment of a successor synonymous with the completion of the prophetic mission. In the time of the Prophet, laws were not merely expounded and promulgated; they were also implemented. The Messenger of God was an executor of the law. For example, he implemented the penal provisions of Islam: he cut off the hand of the thief and administered lashings and stonings. The successor to the Prophet must do the same; his task is not legislation, but the implementation of the divine laws that the Prophet has promulgated. It is for this reason that the formation of a government and the establishment of executive organs are necessary. Belief in the necessity for these is part of the general belief in the Imamate, as are, too, exertion and struggle for the sake of establishing them.

Pay close attention. Whereas hostility toward you has led them to misrepresent Islam, it is necessary for you to present Islam and the doctrine of the Imamate correctly. You must tell people: "We believe in the Imamate; we believe that the Prophet (upon whom be peace) appointed a successor to assume responsibility for the affairs of the Muslims, and that he did so in conformity with the divine will. Therefore, we must also believe in the necessity for the establishment of government, and we must strive to establish organs for the execution of law and the administration of affairs." Write and publish books concerning the laws of Islam and their beneficial effects on society. Improve your style and method of preaching and related activity. *Know that it is your duty to establish an Islamic government.* Have confidence in yourselves and know that you are capable of fulfilling this task.

The imperialists began laying their plans three or four centuries ago; they started out with nothing, but see where they are now! We too will begin with nothing, and we will pay no attention to the uproar created by a few "xenomaniacs"[23] and devoted servants of imperialism.

Present Islam to the people in its true form, so that our youth do not picture the *akhunds* as sitting in some corner in Najaf or Qum, studying the questions of menstruation and parturition instead of concerning themselves with politics, and draw the conclusion that religion must be separate from politics. This slogan of the separation of religion and politics and the demand that Islamic scholars not intervene in social and political affairs have been formulated and propagated by the imperialists; it is only the irreligious who repeat them. Were religion and politics separate in the time of the Prophet (peace and blessings be upon him)? Did there exist, on one side, a group of clerics, and opposite it, a group of politicians and leaders? Were religion and politics separate in the time of the caliphs—even if they were not legitimate—or in the time of the Commander of the Faithful (upon whom be peace)? Did two separate authorities exist? These slogans and claims have been advanced by the imperialists and their political agents in order to prevent religion from ordering the affairs of this world and shaping Muslim society, and at the same time to create a rift between the scholars of Islam, on the one hand, and the masses and those struggling for freedom and independence, on the other. They have thus been able to gain dominance over our people and plunder our resources, for such has always been their ultimate goal.

If we Muslims do nothing but engage in the canonical prayer, petition God, and invoke His name, the imperialists and the oppressive governments allied with them will leave us alone. If we were to say, "Let us concentrate on calling the *azan*[24] and saying our prayers. Let them come rob us of everything we own—God will take care of them! There is no power or recourse except in Him, and God willing, we will be rewarded in the hereafter!"—if this were our logic, they would not disturb us.

Once, during the occupation of Iraq, a certain British officer asked: "Is the *azan* I hear being called now from the minaret harmful to British policy?" When he was told that it was harmless, he said: "Then let him call for prayer as much as he wants!"

If you pay no attention to the policies of the imperialists, and consider Islam to be simply the few topics you are always studying and never go beyond them, then the imperialists will leave you alone. Pray as much as you like; it is your oil they are after—why should they worry about your prayers? They are after our minerals, and want to turn our country into a market for their goods. That is the reason the puppet governments they have installed prevent us from industrializing, and instead, establish only assembly plants and industry that is dependent on the outside world.

They do not want us to be true human beings, for they are afraid of true human beings. Even if only one true human being appears, they fear him, because others will follow him and he will have an impact that can destroy the whole foundation of tyranny, imperialism, and government by puppets. So whenever some true human being has appeared, they have either killed him or imprisoned and exiled him, and tried to defame him by saying: "This is a political *akhund!*" Now the Prophet (peace and blessings be upon him) was also a political person. This evil propaganda is undertaken by the political agents of imperialism only to make you shun politics, to prevent you from intervening in the affairs of society and struggling against treacherous governments and their anti-national and anti-Islamic policies. They want to work their will as they please, with no one to bar their way.

2

THE NECESSITY FOR ISLAMIC GOVERNMENT

A BODY OF LAWS ALONE is not sufficient for a society to be reformed. In order for law to ensure the reform and happiness of man, there must be an executive power and an executor. For this reason, God Almighty, in addition to revealing a body of law (i.e., the ordinances of the *shari'a*), has laid down a particular form of government together with executive and administrative institutions.

The Most Noble Messenger (peace and blessings be upon him) headed the executive and administrative institutions of Muslim society. In addition to conveying the revelation and expounding and interpreting the articles of faith and the ordinances and institutions of Islam, he undertook the implementation of law and the establishment of the ordinances of Islam, thereby bringing into being the Islamic state. He did not content himself with the promulgation of law; rather, he implemented it at the same time, cutting off hands and administering lashings and stonings. After the Most Noble Messenger, his successor had the same duty and function. When the Prophet appointed a successor, it was not for the purpose of expounding articles of faith and law; it was for the implementation of law and the execution of God's ordinances. It was this function—the execution of law and the establishment of Islamic institutions—that made the appointment of a successor such an important matter that the Prophet would have failed to fulfill his mission if he had neglected it. For after the Prophet, the Muslims still needed someone to execute laws and establish the institutions of Islam in society, so that they might attain happiness in this world and the hereafter.

By their very nature, in fact, law and social institutions require the existence of an executor. It has always and everywhere been the case that legislation alone has little benefit: legislation by itself cannot assure the well-being of man. After the establishment of legislation, an executive power must come into being, a power that implements the laws and the verdicts given by the courts, thus allowing people to benefit from the laws and the just sentences the courts deliver. Islam has therefore established an executive power in the same way that it has brought laws into being. The person who holds this executive power is known as the *vali amr.*[25]

The Sunna[26] and path of the Prophet constitute a proof of the necessity for establishing government. First, he himself established a government, as history testifies. He engaged in the implementation of laws, the establishment of the ordinances of Islam, and the administration of society. He sent out governors to different regions; both sat in judgment himself and appointed judges; dispatched emissaries to foreign states, tribal chieftains, and kings; concluded treaties and pacts; and took command in battle. In short, he fulfilled all the functions of government. Second, he designated a ruler to succeed him, in accordance with divine command. If God Almighty, through the Prophet, designated a man who was to rule over Muslim society after him, this is in itself an indication that government remains a necessity after the departure of the Prophet from this world. Again, since the Most Noble Messenger promulgated the divine command through his act of appointing a successor, he also implicitly stated the necessity for establishing a government.

It is self-evident that the necessity for enactment of the law, which necessitated the formation of a government by the Prophet (upon whom be peace), was not confined or restricted to his time, but continues after his departure from this world. According to one of the noble verses of the Qur'an, the ordinances of Islam are not limited with respect to time or place; they are permanent and must be enacted until the end of time. They were not revealed merely for the time of the Prophet, only to be abandoned thereafter, with retribution and the penal code of Islam no longer to be enacted, or the taxes prescribed by Islam no longer collected, and the defense of the lands and people of Islam suspended. The claim that the laws of Islam may remain in abeyance or are restricted to a particular time or place is contrary to the essential credal bases of Islam. Since the enactment of laws, then, is necessary after the departure of the Prophet from this world, and indeed, will remain so until the end of time, the formation of a government and the establishment of executive and administrative organs are also necessary. Without the formation of a government and the establishment of such organs to ensure that through enactment of the law, all activities of the individual take place in the framework of a just system, chaos and anarchy will prevail and social, intellectual, and moral corruption will arise. The only way to prevent the emergence of anarchy and disorder and to protect society from corruption is to form a government and thus impart order to all the affairs of the country.

Both reason and divine law, then, demonstrate the necessity in our time for what was necessary during the lifetime of the Prophet and the age of the Commander of the Faithful, 'Ali ibn Abi Talib (peace be upon them)—namely the formation of a government and the establishment of executive and administrative organs.

In order to clarify the matter further, let us pose the following questions: From the time of the Lesser Occultation[27] down to the present (a period of more than twelve centuries that may continue for hundreds of millenia if it is not appropriate for the Occulted Imam to manifest himself), is it proper that the laws of Islam be cast aside and remain unexecuted, so that everyone acts as he pleases and anarchy prevails? Were the laws that the Prophet of Islam labored so hard for twenty-three years to set forth, promulgate, and execute valid only for a limited period of time? Did God limit the validity of His laws to two hundred years? Was everything pertaining to Islam meant to be abandoned after the Lesser Occultation? Anyone who believes so, or voices such a belief, is worse situated than the person who believes and proclaims that Islam has been superseded or abrogated by another supposed revelation.[28]

No one can say it is no longer necessary to defend the frontiers and the territorial integrity of the Islamic homeland; that taxes such as the *jizya*, *kharaj*, *khums* and *zakat*[29] should no longer be collected; that the penal code of Islam, with its provisions for the payment of blood money and the exacting of requital, should be suspended. Any person who claims that the formation of an Islamic government is not necessary implicitly denies the necessity for the implementation of Islamic law, the universality and comprehensiveness of that law, and the eternal validity of the faith itself.

After the death of the Most Noble Messenger (peace and blessings be upon him), none of the Muslims doubted the necessity for government. No one said: "We no longer need a government." No one was heard to say anything of the kind. There was unanimous agreement concerning the necessity for government. There was disagreement only as to which person should assume responsibility for government and head the state. Government, therefore, was established after the Prophet (upon whom be peace and blessings), both in the time of the caliphs and in that of the Commander of the Faithful (peace be upon him); an apparatus of government came into existence with administrative and executive organs.

The nature and character of Islamic law and the divine ordinances of the *shari'a* furnish additional proof of the necessity for establishing government, for they indicate that the laws were laid down for the purpose of creating a state and administering the political, economic, and cultural affairs of society.

First, the laws of the *shari'a* embrace a diverse body of laws and regulations, which amounts to a complete social system. In this system of laws, all the needs of man have been met: his dealings with his neighbors, fellow citizens, and clan, as well as children and relatives; the concerns of private and marital life; regulations concerning war and peace and intercourse with other nations; penal and commercial law; and regulations pertaining to trade and agriculture. Islamic law contains provisions relating to the preliminaries of marriage and the form in which it should be contracted, and others relating to the development of the embryo in the womb and what food the parents should eat at the time of conception. It further stipulates the duties that are incumbent upon them while the infant is being suckled, and specifies how the child should be reared, and how the husband and the wife should relate to each other and to their children. Islam provides laws and instructions for all of these matters, aiming, as it does, to produce integrated and virtuous human beings who are walking embodiments of the law, or to put it differently, the law's voluntary and instinctive executors. It is obvious, then, how much care Islam devotes to government and the political and economic relations of society, with the goal of creating conditions conducive to the production of morally upright and virtuous human beings.

The Glorious Qur'an and the Sunna contain all the laws and ordinances man needs in order to attain happiness and the perfection of his state. The book *al-Kafi*[30] has a chapter entitled, "All the Needs of Men Are Set Out in the Book and the Sunna," the "Book" meaning the Qur'an, which is, in its own words, "an exposition of all things."[31] According to certain traditions, the Imam[32] also swears that the Book and the Sunna contain without a doubt all that men need.

Second, if we examine closely the nature and character of the provisions of the law, we realize that their execution and implementation depend upon the formation of a government, and that it is impossible to fulfill the duty of executing God's commands without there being established properly comprehensive administrative and executive organs. Let us now mention certain types of provision in order to illustrate this point; the others you can examine yourselves.

The taxes Islam levies and the form of budget it has established are not merely for the sake of providing subsistence to the poor or feeding the indigent among the descendants of the Prophet (peace and blessings be upon him); they are also intended to make possible the establishment of a great government and to assure its essential expenditures.

For example, *khums* is a huge source of income that accrues to the treasury and represents one item in the budget. According to our Shi'i school of thought, *khums* is to be levied in an equitable manner on all agricultural and commercial profits and all natural resources whether above or below the ground—in short, on all forms of wealth and income. It applies equally to the greengrocer with his stall outside this mosque and to the shipping or mining magnate. They must all pay one-fifth of their surplus income, after customary expenses are deducted, to the Islamic ruler so that it enters the treasury. It is obvious that such a huge income serves the purpose of administering the Islamic state and meeting all its financial needs. If we were to calculate one-fifth of the surplus income of all the Muslim countries (or of the whole world, should it enter the fold of Islam), it would become fully apparent that the purpose for the imposition of such a tax is not merely the upkeep of the *sayyids*[33] or the religious scholars, but on the contrary, something far more significant—namely, meeting the financial needs of the great organs and institutions of government. If an Islamic government is achieved, it will have to be administered on the basis of the taxes that Islam has established —*khums, zakat* (this, of course, would not represent an appreciable sum),[34] *jizya*, and *kharaj*.

How could the *sayyids* ever need so vast a budget? The *khums* of the bazaar of Baghdad would be enough for the needs of the *sayyids* and the upkeep of the religious teaching institution, as well as all the poor of the Islamic world, quite apart from the *khums* of the bazaars of Tehran, Istanbul, Cairo, and other cities. The provision of such a huge budget must obviously be for the purpose of forming a government and administering the Islamic lands. It was established with the aim of providing for the needs of the people, for public services relating to health, education, defense, and economic development. Further, in accordance with the procedures laid down by Islam for the collection, preservation, and expenditure of this income, all forms of usurpation and embezzlement of public wealth have been forbidden, so that the head of state and all those entrusted with responsibility for conducting public affairs (i.e., members of the government) have no privileges over the ordinary citizen in benefiting from the public income and wealth; all have an equal share.

Now, should we cast this huge treasury into the ocean, or bury it until the Imam returns, or just spend it on fifty *sayyids* a day until they have all eaten their fill? Let us suppose we give all this money to 500,000 *sayyids;* they would not know what to do with it. We all know that the *sayyids* and the poor have a claim on the public treasury only to the extent required for subsistence. The budget of the Islamic state is constructed in such a way that every source of income is allocated to specific types of expenditures.

Zakat, voluntary contributions and charitable donations, and *khums* are all levied and spent separately. There is a *hadith* to the effect that at the end of the year, *sayyids* must return any surplus from what they have received to the Islamic ruler, just as the ruler must aid them if they are in need.

The *jizya*, which is imposed on the *ahl adh-dhimma*,[35] and the *kharaj*, which is levied on agricultural land, represent two additional sources of considerable income. The establishment of these taxes also proves that the existence of a ruler and a government is necessary. It is the duty of a ruler or governor to assess the poll-tax to be levied on the *ahl adh-dhimma* in accordance with their income and financial capacity, and to fix appropriate taxes on their arable lands and livestock. He must also collect the *kharaj* on those broad lands that are the "property of God" and in the possession of the Islamic state. This task requires the existence of orderly institutions, rules and regulations, and administrative processes and policies; it cannot be fulfilled in the absence of order. It is the responsibility of those in charge of the Islamic state, first, to assess the taxes in due and appropriate measure and in accordance with the public good; then, to collect them; and finally, to spend them in a manner conducive to the welfare of the Muslims.

Thus, you see that the fiscal provisions of Islam also point to the necessity for establishing a government, for they cannot be fulfilled without the establishment of the appropriate Islamic institutions.

The ordinances pertaining to preservation of the Islamic order and defense of the territorial integrity and the independence of the Islamic *umma*[36] also demanded the formation of a government. An example is the command: "Prepare against them whatever force you can muster and horses tethered" (Qur'an, 8:60), which enjoins the preparation of as much armed defensive force as possible and orders the Muslims to be always on the alert and at the ready, even in time of peace.

If the Muslims had acted in accordance with this command and, after forming a government, made the necessary extensive preparations to be in a state of full readiness for war, a handful of Jews would never have dared to occupy our lands, and to burn and destroy the Masjid al-Aqsa[37] without the people's being capable

46

of making an immediate response. All this has resulted from the failure of the Muslims to fulfill their duty of executing God's law and setting up a righteous and respectable government. If the rulers of the Muslim countries truly represented the believers and enacted God's ordinances, they would set aside their petty differences, abandon their subversive and divisive activities, and join together like the fingers of one hand. Then a handful of wretched Jews (the agents of America, Britain, and other foreign powers) would never have been able to accomplish what they have, no matter how much support they enjoyed from America and Britain. All this has happened because of the incompetence of those who rule over the Muslims.

The verse: "Prepare against them whatever force you can muster" commands you to be as strong and well-prepared as possible, so that your enemies will be unable to oppress you and transgress against you. It is because we have been lacking in unity, strength, and preparedness that we suffer oppression and are at the mercy of foreign aggressors.

There are numerous provisions of the law that cannot be implemented without the establishment of a governmental apparatus; for example, blood money, which must be exacted and delivered to those deserving it, or the corporeal penalties imposed by the law, which must be carried out under the supervision of the Islamic ruler. All of these laws refer back to the institutions of government, for it is governmental power alone that is capable of fulfilling this function.

After the death of the Most Noble Messenger (peace and blessings be upon him), the obstinate enemies of the faith, the Umayyads[38] (God's curses be upon them) did not permit the Islamic state to attain stability with the rule of 'Ali ibn Abi Talib (upon whom be peace). They did not allow a form of government to exist that was pleasing to God, Exalted and Almighty, and to his Most Noble Messenger. They transformed the entire basis of government, and their policies were, for the most part, contradictory to Islam. The form of government of the Umayyads and the Abbasids,[39] and the political and administrative policies they pursued, were anti-Islamic. The form of government was thoroughly perverted by being transformed into a monarchy, like those of the

47

kings of Iran, the emperors of Rome, and the pharoahs of Egypt. For the most part, this non-Islamic form of government has persisted to the present day, as we can see.

Both law and reason require that we not permit governments to retain this non-Islamic or anti-Islamic character. The proofs are clear. First, the existence of a non-Islamic political order necessarily results in the non-implementation of the Islamic political order. Then, all non-Islamic systems of government are the systems of *kufr*,[40] since the ruler in each case is an instance of *taghut*,[41] and it is our duty to remove from the life of Muslim society all traces of *kufr* and destroy them. It is also our duty to create a favorable social environment for the education of believing and virtuous individuals, an environment that is in total contradiction with that produced by the rule of *taghut* and illegitimate power. The social environment created by *taghut* and *shirk*[42] invariably brings about corruption such as you can now observe in Iran, the corruption termed "corruption on earth."[43] This corruption must be swept away, and its instigators punished for their deeds. It is the same corruption that the Pharaoh generated in Egypt with his policies, so that the Qur'an says of him, "Truly he was among the corruptors" (28:4). A believing, pious, just individual cannot possibly exist in a socio-political environment of this nature and still maintain his faith and righteous conduct. He is faced with two choices: either he commits acts that amount to *kufr* and contradict righteousness, or in order not to commit such acts and not to submit to the orders and commands of the *taghut*, the just individual opposes him and struggles against him in order to destroy the environment of corruption. We have in reality, then, no choice but to destroy those systems of government that are corrupt in themselves and also entail the corruption of others, and to overthrow all treacherous, corrupt, oppressive, and criminal regimes.

This is a duty that all Muslims must fulfill, in every one of the Muslim countries, in order to achieve the triumphant political revolution of Islam.

We see, too, that together, the imperialists and the tyrannical self-seeking rulers have divided the Islamic homeland. They have separated the various segments of the Islamic *umma* from each

other and artificially created separate nations. There once existed
the great Ottoman State, and that, too, the imperialists divided.
Russia, Britain, Austria, and other imperialist powers united,
and through wars against the Ottomans, each came to occupy
or absorb into its sphere of influence part of the Ottoman realm.
It is true that most of the Ottoman rulers were incompetent, that
some of them were corrupt, and that they followed a monarchical
system. Nonetheless, the existence of the Ottoman State represented a threat to the imperialists. It was always possible that
righteous individuals might rise up among the people and, with
their assistance, seize control of the state, thus putting an end to
imperialism by mobilizing the unified resources of the nation.
Therefore, after numerous prior wars, the imperialists at the end
of World War I divided the Ottoman State, creating in its territories about ten or fifteen petty states.[44] Then each of these was
entrusted to one of their servants or a group of their servants, although certain countries were later able to escape the grasp of the
agents of imperialism.

In order to assure the unity of the Islamic *umma*, in order to
liberate the Islamic homeland from occupation and penetration
by the imperialists and their puppet governments, it is imperative
that we establish a government. In order to attain the unity and
freedom of the Muslim peoples, we must overthrow the oppressive
governments installed by the imperialists and bring into existence
an Islamic government of justice that will be in the service of the
people. The formation of such a government will serve to preserve the disciplined unity of the Muslims; just as Fatimat az-
Zahra[45] (upon whom be peace) said in her address: "The Imamate
exists for the sake of preserving order among the Muslims and
replacing their disunity with unity."

Through the political agents they have placed in power over
the people, the imperialists have also imposed on us an unjust
economic order, and thereby divided our people into two groups:
oppressors and oppressed. Hundreds of millions of Muslims are
hungry and deprived of all form of health care and education,
while minorities comprised of the wealthy and powerful live a
life of indulgence, licentiousness, and corruption. The hungry
and deprived have constantly struggled to free themselves from

the oppression of their plundering overlords, and their struggle continues to this day. But their way is blocked by the ruling minorities and the oppressive governmental structures they head. It is our duty to save the oppressed and deprived. It is our duty to be a helper to the oppressed and an enemy to the oppressor. This is nothing other than the duty that the Commander of the Faithful (upon whom be peace) entrusted to his two great offspring[46] in his celebrated testament: "Be an enemy to the oppressor and a helper to the oppressed."

The scholars of Islam have a duty to struggle against all attempts by the oppressors to establish a monopoly over the sources of wealth or to make illicit use of them. They must not allow the masses to remain hungry and deprived while plundering oppressors usurp the sources of wealth and live in opulence. The Commander of the Faithful (upon whom be peace) says: "I have accepted the task of government because God, Exalted and Almighty, has exacted from the scholars of Islam a pledge not to sit silent and idle in the face of the gluttony and plundering of the oppressors, on the one hand, and the hunger and deprivation of the oppressed, on the other." Here is the full text of the passage we refer to:

> "I swear by Him Who causes the seed to open and creates the souls of all living things that were it not for the presence of those who have come to swear allegiance to me, were it not for the obligation of rulership now imposed upon me by the availability of aid and support, and were it not for the pledge that God has taken from the scholars of Islam not to remain silent in the face of the gluttony and plundering of the oppressors, on the one hand, and the harrowing hunger and deprivation of the oppressed, on the other hand—were it not for all of this, then I would abandon the reins of government and in no way seek it. You would see that this world of yours, with all of its position and rank, is less in my eyes than the moisture that comes from the sneeze of a goat."[47]

How can we stay silent and idle today when we see that a band of traitors and usurpers, the agents of foreign powers, have appropriated the wealth and the fruits of labor of hundreds of millions of Muslims—thanks to the support of their masters and through the power of the bayonet—granting the Muslims not the least right to prosperity? It is the duty of Islamic scholars and all

Muslims to put an end to this system of oppression and, for the sake of the well-being of hundreds of millions of human beings, to overthrow these oppressive governments and form an Islamic government.

Reason, the law of Islam, the practice of the Prophet (upon whom be peace and blessings) and that of the Commander of the Faithful (upon whom be peace), the purport of various Qur'anic verses and Prophetic traditions—all indicate the necessity of forming a government. As an example of the traditions of the Imams, I now quote the following tradition of Imam Riza[48] (upon whom be peace):

'Abd al-Wahid ibn Muhammad ibn 'Abdus an-Nisaburi al-'Attar said, "I was told by Abu'l-Hasan 'Ali ibn Muhammad ibn Qutayba al-Naysaburi that he was told by Abu Muhammad al-Fadl ibn Shadhan al-Naysaburi this tradition. If someone asks, 'Why has God, the All-Wise, appointed the holders of authority and commanded us to obey them?' then we answer, 'For numerous reasons. One reason is this: Men are commanded to observe certain limits and not to transgress them in order to avoid the corruption that would result. This cannot be attained or established without there being appointed over them a trustee who will ensure that they remain within the limits of the licit and prevent them from casting themselves into the danger of transgression. Were it not for such a trustee, no one would abandon his own pleasure and benefit because of the corruption it might entail for another. Another reason is that we find no group or nation of men that ever existed without a ruler and leader, since it is required by both religion and worldly interest. It would not be compatible with divine wisdom to leave mankind to its own devices, for He, the All-Wise, knows that men need a ruler for their survival. It is through the leadership he provides that men make war against their enemies, divide among themselves the spoils of war, and preserve their communal solidarity, preventing the oppression of the oppressed by the oppressor.

" 'A further reason is this: were God not to appoint over men a solicitous, trustworthy, protecting, reliable leader, the community would decline, religion would depart, and the norms and ordinances that have been revealed would undergo change. Innovators would increase and deniers would erode religion, inducing doubt in the Muslims. For we see that men are needy and defective, judging by their differences of opinion and inclination and their diversity of state. Were a trustee, then, not appointed to preserve what has been revealed through the Prophet, corruption would ensue in the manner we have described. Revealed laws, norms, ordinances, and faith would be altogether changed, and therein would lie the corruption of all mankind.' "[49]

We have omitted the first part of the *hadith*, which pertains to prophethood, a topic not germane to our present discussion. What interests us at present is the second half, which I will now paraphrase for you.

If someone should ask you, "Why has God, the All-Wise, appointed holders of authority and commanded you to obey them?" you should answer him as follows: "He has done so for various causes and reasons. One is that men have been set upon a certain well-defined path and commanded not to stray from it, nor to transgress against the established limits and norms, for if they were to stray, they would fall prey to corruption. Now men would not be able to keep to their ordained path and to enact God's laws unless a trustworthy and protective individual (or power) were appointed over them with responsibility for this matter, to prevent them from stepping outside the sphere of the licit and transgressing against the rights of others. If no such restraining individual or power were appointed, nobody would voluntarily abandon any pleasure or interest of his own that might result in harm or corruption to others; everybody would engage in oppressing and harming others for the sake of their own pleasures and interests.

"Another reason and cause is this: we do not see a single group, nation, or religious community that has ever been able to exist without an individual entrusted with the maintenance of its laws and institutions—in short, a head or a leader; for such a person is essential for fulfilling the affairs of religion and the world. It is not permissible, therefore, according to divine wisdom, that God should leave men, His creatures, without a leader and guide, for He knows well that they depend on the existence of such a person for their own survival and perpetuation. It is under his leadership that they fight against their enemies, divide the public income among themselves, perform Friday and congregational prayer, and foreshorten the arms of the transgressors who would encroach on the rights of the oppressed.

"Another proof and cause is this: were God not to appoint an Imam over men to maintain law and order, to serve the people faithfully as a vigilant trustee, religion would fall victim to obsolescence and decay. Its rites and institutions would vanish; the customs and ordinances of Islam would be transformed or even deformed. Heretical innovators would add things to religion and atheists and unbelievers would subtract things from it, presenting it to the Muslims in an inaccurate manner. For we see that men are prey to defects; they are not perfect and must needs strive after perfection. Moreover, they disagree with each other, having varying inclinations and discordant states. If God, therefore, had not appointed over men one who would maintain order and law and protect the revelation brought by the Prophet, in the manner we have described, men would fall prey to corruption; the institutions, laws, customs, and ordinances of Islam would be transformed; and faith and its content would be completely changed, resulting in the corruption of all humanity."

As you can deduce from the words of the Imam (upon whom be peace), there are numerous proofs and causes that necessitate formation of a government and establishment of an authority. These proofs, causes, and arguments are not temporary in their validity or limited to a particular time, and the necessity for the formation of a government, therefore, is perpetual. For example, it will always happen that men overstep the limits laid down by Islam and transgress against the rights of others for the sake of their personal pleasure and benefit. It cannot be asserted that such was the case only in the time of the Commander of the Faithful (upon whom be peace) and that afterwards, men became angels. The wisdom of the Creator has decreed that men should live in accordance with justice and act within the limits set by divine law. This wisdom is eternal and immutable, and constitutes one of the norms of God Almighty. Today and always, therefore, the existence of a holder of authority, a ruler who acts as trustee and maintains the institutions and laws of Islam, is a necessity—a ruler who prevents cruelty, oppression, and violation of the rights of others; who is a trustworthy and vigilant guardian of God's creatures; who guides men to the teachings, doctrines, laws, and institutions of Islam; and who prevents the undesirable changes that atheists and the enemies of religion wish to introduce in the laws and institutions of Islam. Did not the caliphate of the Commander of the Faithful serve this purpose? The same factors of necessity that led him to become the Imam still exist; the only difference is that no single individual has been designated for the task.[50] The principle of the necessity of government has been made a general one, so that it will always remain in effect.

If the ordinances of Islam are to remain in effect, then, if encroachment by oppressive ruling classes on the rights of the weak is to be prevented, if ruling minorities are not to be permitted to plunder and corrupt the people for the sake of pleasure and material interest, if the Islamic order is to be preserved and all individuals are to pursue the just path of Islam without any deviation, if innovation and the approval of anti-Islamic laws by sham parliaments[51] are to be prevented, if the influence of foreign powers in the Islamic lands is to be destroyed—government is necessary. None of these aims can be achieved without government and the organs of the state. It is a righteous government, of course, that is needed, one presided over by a ruler who will be a trustworthy and righteous trustee. Those who presently govern us are of no use at all for they are tyrannical, corrupt, and highly incompetent.

In the past we did not act in concert and unanimity in order to establish proper government and overthrow treacherous and corrupt rulers. Some people were apathetic and reluctant even to discuss the theory of Islamic government, and some went so far as to praise oppressive rulers. It is for this reason that we find ourselves in the present state. The influence and sovereignty of Islam in society have declined; the nation of Islam has fallen victim to division and weakness; the laws of Islam have remained in abeyance and been subjected to change and modification; and the imperialists have propagated foreign laws and alien culture among the Muslims through their agents for the sake of their evil purposes, causing people to be infatuated with the West. It was our lack of a leader, a guardian, and our lack of institutions of leadership that made all this possible. We need righteous and proper organs of government; that much is self-evident.

3

THE FORM OF
ISLAMIC GOVERNMENT

ISLAMIC GOVERNMENT does not correspond to any of the existing forms of government. For example, it is not a tyranny, where the head of state can deal arbitrarily with the property and lives of the people, making use of them as he wills, putting to death anyone he wishes, and enriching anyone he wishes by granting landed estates and distributing the property and holdings of the people. The Most Noble Messenger (peace be upon him), the Commander of the Faithful (peace be upon him), and the other caliphs did not have such powers. Islamic government is neither tyrannical nor absolute, but constitutional. It is not constitutional in the current sense of the word, i.e., based on the approval of laws in accordance with the opinion of the majority. It is constitutional in the sense that the rulers are subject to a certain set of conditions in governing and administering the country, conditions that are set forth in the Noble Qur'an and the Sunna of the Most Noble Messenger. It is the laws and ordinances of Islam comprising this set of conditions that must be observed and practiced. Islamic government may therefore be defined as the rule of divine law over men.

The fundamental difference between Islamic government, on the one hand, and constitutional monarchies and republics, on the other, is this: whereas the representatives of the people or the monarch in such regimes engage in legislation, in Islam the legislative power and competence to establish laws belongs exclusively to God Almighty. The Sacred Legislator of Islam is the sole legislative power. No one has the right to legislate and no law may be executed except the law of the Divine Legislator. It is for this reason that in an Islamic government, a simple planning body takes the place of the legislative assembly that is one of the three branches of government. This body draws up programs for the different ministries in the light of the ordinances of Islam and thereby determines how public services are to be provided across the country.

The body of Islamic laws that exist in the Qur'an and the Sunna has been accepted by the Muslims and recognized by them as worthy of obedience. This consent and acceptance facilitates the task of government and makes it truly belong to the people. In contrast, in a republic or a constitutional monarchy, most of those claiming to be representatives of the majority of the people will approve anything they wish as law and then impose it on the entire population.

Islamic government is a government of law. In this form of government, sovereignty belongs to God alone and law is His decree and command. The law of Islam, divine command, has absolute authority over all individuals and the Islamic government. Everyone, including the Most Noble Messenger (peace be upon him) and his successors, is subject to law and will remain so for all eternity—the law that has been revealed by God, Almighty and Exalted, and expounded by the tongue of the Qur'an and the Most Noble Messenger. If the Prophet assumed the task of divine viceregency upon earth, it was in accordance with divine command. God, Almighty and Exalted, appointed him as His viceregent, "the viceregent of God upon earth"; he did not establish a government on his own initiative in order to be leader of the Muslims. Similarly, when it became apparent that disagreements would probably arise among the Muslims because their acquaintance with the faith was recent and limited, God Almighty charged the Prophet, by way of revelation, to clarify the question of succession immediately, there in the middle of the desert. Then the Most Noble Messenger (upon whom be peace) nominated the Commander of the Faithful (upon whom be peace) as his successor, in conformity and obedience to the law, not because he was his own son-in-law or had performed certain services, but because he was acting in obedience to God's law, as its executor.[52]

In Islam, then, government has the sense of adherence to law; it is law alone that rules over society. Even the limited powers given to the Most Noble Messenger (upon whom be peace) and those exercising rule after him have been conferred upon them by God. Whenever the Prophet expounded a certain matter or promulgated a certain injunction, he did so in obedience to divine law, a law that everyone without exception must obey and adhere to. Divine law obtains both for the leader and the led; the sole law that is valid and imperative to apply is the law of God. Obedience to the Prophet also takes place in accordance with divine decree, for God says: "And obey the Messenger" (Qur'an, 4:59). Obedience to those entrusted with authority is also on the basis of divine decree: "And obey the holders of authority from among you" (Qur'an, 4:59). Individual opinion, even if it be that of the Prophet himself, cannot intervene in matters of government or divine law; here, all are subject to the will of God.

Islamic government is not a form of monarchy, especially not an imperial system. In that type of government, the rulers are empowered over the property and persons of those they rule and may dispose of them entirely as they wish. Islam has not the slightest connection with this form and method of government. For this reason we find that in Islamic government, unlike monarchical and imperial regimes, there is not the slightest trace of vast palaces, opulent buildings, servants and retainers, private equerries, adjutants to the heir apparent, and all the other appurtenances of monarchy that consume as much as half of the national budget. You all know how the Prophet lived, the Prophet who was the head of the Islamic state and its ruler. The same mode of life was preserved by his successors until the beginning of the Umayyad period. The first two successors to the Prophet adhered to his example in the outer conduct of their personal lives, even though in other affairs they committed errors, which led to the grave deviations that appeared in the time of 'Uthman, the same deviations that have inflicted on us these misfortunes of the present day.[53] In the time of the Commander of the Faithful (peace be upon him), the system of government was corrected and a proper form and method of rule were followed. Even though that excellent man ruled over a vast realm that included Iran, Egypt, Hijaz,[54] and the Yemen among its provinces, he lived more frugally than the most impoverished of our students. According to tradition, he once bought two tunics, and finding one of them better than the other, he gave the better one to his servant Qanbar. The

57

other he kept for himself, and since its sleeves were too long for him, he tore off the extra portion. In this torn garment the ruler of a great, populous, and prosperous realm clothed himself.

If this mode of conduct had been preserved, and government had retained its Islamic form, there would have been no monarchy and no empire, no usurpation of the lives and property of the people, no oppression and plunder, no encroachment on the public treasury, no vice and abomination. Most forms of corruption originate with the ruling class, the tyrannical ruling family and the libertines that associate with them. It is these rulers who establish centers of vice and corruption, who build centers of vice and wine-drinking, and spend the income of the religious endowments constructing cinemas.[55]

If it were not for these profligate royal ceremonies,[56] this reckless spending, this constant embezzlement, there would never be any deficit in the national budget forcing us to bow in submission before America and Britain and request aid or a loan from them. Our country has become needy on account of this reckless spending, this endless embezzlement, for are we lacking in oil? Do we have no minerals, no natural resources? We have everything, but this parasitism, this embezzlement, this profligacy—all at the expense of the people and the public treasury—have reduced us to a wretched state. Otherwise he [the Shah] would not need to go all the way to America and bow down before that ruffian's desk, begging for help.

In addition, superfluous bureaucracies and the system of file-keeping and paper-shuffling that is enforced in them, all of which are totally alien to Islam, impose further expenditures on our national budget not less in quantity than the illicit expenditures of the first category. This administrative system has nothing to do with Islam. These superfluous formalities, which cause our people nothing but expense, trouble, and delay, have no place in Islam. For example, the method established by Islam for enforcing people's rights, adjudicating disputes, and executing judgments is at once simple, practical, and swift. When the juridical methods of Islam were applied, the *shari'a* judge in each town, assisted only by two bailiffs and with only a pen and an inkpot at his disposal, would swiftly resolve disputes among people and send them about their business. But now the bureaucratic organization of the Ministry of Justice has attained unimaginable proportions, and is, in addition, quite incapable of producing results.

It is things like these that make our country needy and produce nothing but expense and delay.

The qualifications essential for the ruler derive directly from the nature and form of Islamic government. In addition to general qualifications like intelligence and administrative ability, there are two other essential qualifications: knowledge of the law and justice.[57]

After the death of the Prophet (upon whom be peace), differences arose concerning the identity of the person who was to succeed him, but all the Muslims were in agreement that his successor should be someone knowledgeable and accomplished; there was disagreement only as to his identity.

Since Islamic government is a government of law, knowledge of the law is necessary for the ruler, as has been laid down in tradition. Indeed such knowledge is necessary not only for the ruler, but also for anyone holding a post or exercising some government function. The ruler, however, must surpass all others in knowledge. In laying claim to the Imamate, our Imams also argued that the ruler must be more learned than everyone else. The objections raised by the Shi'i *ulama* are also to the same effect. A certain person asked the caliph a point of law and he was unable to answer; he was therefore unfit for the position of leader and successor to the Prophet. Or again, a certain act he performed was contrary to the laws of Islam; hence he was unworthy of his high post.[58]

Knowledge of the law and justice, then, constitute fundamental qualifications in the view of the Muslims. Other matters have no importance or relevance in this connection. Knowledge of the nature of the angels, for example, or of the attributes of the Creator, Exalted and Almighty, is of no relevance to the question of leadership. In the same vein, one who knows all the natural sciences, uncovers all the secrets of nature, or has a good knowledge of music does not thereby qualify for leadership or acquire any priority in the matter of exercising government over those who know the laws of Islam and are just. The sole matters relevant to rule, those that were mentioned and discussed in the time of the Most Noble Messenger (upon whom be peace) and our Imams (upon whom be peace) and were, in addition, unanimously accepted by the Muslims, are: (1) the knowledgeability of the ruler or caliph, i.e., his knowledge of the provisions and ordinances of Islam; and (2) his justice, i.e., his excellence in belief and morals.

Reason also dictates the necessity for these qualities, because Islamic government is a government of law, not the arbitrary rule of an individual over the people or the domination of a group of individuals over the whole people. If the ruler is unacquainted with the contents of the law, he is not fit to rule; for if he follows the legal pronouncements of others, his power to govern will be impaired, but if, on the other hand, he does not follow such guidance, he will be unable to rule correctly and implement the laws of Islam. It is an established principle that "the *faqih* has authority over the ruler." If the ruler adheres to Islam, he must necessarily submit to the *faqih*, asking him about the laws and ordinances of Islam in order to implement them. This being the case, the true rulers are the *fuqaha*[59] themselves, and rulership ought officially to be theirs, to apply to them, not to those who are obliged to follow the guidance of the *fuqaha* on account of their own ignorance of the law.

Of course, it is not necessary for all officials, provincial governors, and administrators to know all the laws of Islam and be *fuqaha;* it is enough that they should know the laws pertaining to their functions and duties. Such was the case in the time of the Prophet and the Commander of the Faithful (peace be upon them). The highest authority must possess the two qualities mentioned—comprehensive knowledge and justice—but his assistants, officials, and those sent to the provinces need know only the laws relevant to their own tasks; on other matters they must consult the ruler.

The ruler must also possess excellence in morals and belief; he must be just and untainted by major sin. Anyone who wishes to enact the penalties provided by Islam (i.e., to implement the penal code), to supervise the public treasury and the income and expenditures of the state, and to have God assign to him the power to administer the affairs of His creatures must not be a sinner. God says in the Qur'an: "My covenant does not embrace the wrongdoer" (2:124);[60] therefore, He will not assign such functions to an oppressor or sinner.

If the ruler is not just in granting the Muslims their rights, he will not conduct himself equitably in levying taxes and spending them correctly and in implementing the penal code. It becomes possible then for his assistants, helpers, and confidants to impose their will on society, diverting the public treasury to personal and frivolous use.

Thus, the view of the Shi'a concerning government and the nature of the persons who should assume rule was clear from the time following the death of the Prophet (upon whom be peace and blessings) down to the beginning of the Occultation.[61] It specified that the ruler should be foremost in knowledge of the laws and ordinances of Islam and just in their implementation. Now that we are in the time of the Occultation of the Imam (upon whom be peace), it is still necessary that the ordinances of Islam relating to government be preserved and maintained, and that anarchy be prevented. Therefore, the establishment of government is still a necessity.

Reason also dictates that we establish a government in order to be able to ward off aggression and to defend the honor of the Muslims in case of attack. The *shari'a*, for its part, instructs us to be constantly ready to defend ourselves against those who wish to attack us. Government, with its judicial and executive organs, is also necessary to prevent individuals from encroaching on each other's rights. None of these purposes can be fulfilled by themselves; it is necessary for a government to be established. Since the establishment of a government and the administration of society necessitate, in turn, a budget and taxation, the Sacred Legislator has specified the nature of the budget and the taxes that are to be levied, such as *kharaj, khums, zakat,* and so forth.

Now that no particular individual has been appointed by God, Exalted and Almighty, to assume the function of government in the time of Occultation, what must be done? Are we to abandon Islam? Do we no longer need it? Was Islam valid for only two hundred years? Or is it that Islam has clarified our duties in other respects but not with respect to government?

Not to have an Islamic government means leaving our boundaries unguarded. Can we afford to sit nonchalantly on our hands while our enemies do whatever they want? Even if we do not put our signatures to what they do as an endorsement, still we are failing to make an effective response. Is that the way it should be? Or is it rather that government is necessary, and that the function of government that existed from the beginning of Islam down to the time of the Twelfth Imam (upon whom be peace) is still enjoined upon us by God after the Occultation even though He has appointed no particular individual to that function?

The two qualities of knowledge of the law and justice are present in countless *fuqaha* of the present age. If they would come together, they could establish a government of universal justice in the world.

If a worthy individual possessing these two qualities arises and establishes a government, he will possess the same authority as the Most Noble Messenger (upon whom be peace and blessings) in the administration of society, and it will be the duty of all people to obey him.

The idea that the governmental powers of the Most Noble Messenger (peace and blessings be upon him) were greater than those of the Commander of the Faithful (upon whom be peace), or that those of the Commander of the Faithful were greater than those of the *faqih*, is false and erroneous. Naturally, the virtues of the Most Noble Messenger were greater than those of the rest of mankind, and after him, the Commander of the Faithful was the most virtuous person in the world. But superiority with respect to spiritual virtues does not confer increased governmental powers. God has conferred upon government in the present age the same powers and authority that were held by the Most Noble Messenger and the Imams (peace be upon them) with respect to equipping and mobilizing armies, appointing governors and officials, and levying taxes and expending them for the welfare of the Muslims. Now, however, it is no longer a question of a particular person; government devolves instead upon one who possesses the qualities of knowledge and justice.

When we say that after the Occultation, the just *faqih* has the same authority that the Most Noble Messenger and the Imams had, do not imagine that the status of the *faqih* is identical to that of the Imams and the Prophet. For here we are not speaking of status, but rather of function. By "authority" we mean government, the administration of the country, and the implementation of the sacred laws of the *shari'a*. These constitute a serious, difficult duty but do not earn anyone extraordinary status or raise him above the level of common humanity. In other words, authority here has the meaning of government, administration, and execution of law; contrary to what many people believe, it is not a privilege but a grave responsibility. The governance of the *faqih* is a rational and extrinsic[62] matter; it exists only as a type of appointment, like the appointment of a guardian for a minor. With respect to duty and position, there is indeed no difference between the guardian of a nation and the guardian of a minor. It is as if the Imam were to appoint someone to the guardianship of a minor, to the governorship of a province, or to some other post. In cases like these, it is not reasonable that there would be a difference between the Prophet and the Imams, on the one hand, and the just *faqih*, on the other.

For example, one of the concerns that the *faqih* must attend to is the application of the penal provisions of Islam. Can there be any distinction in this respect between the Most Noble Messenger, the Imam, and the *faqih*? Will the *faqih* inflict fewer lashes because his rank is lower? Now the penalty for the fornicator is one hundred lashes. If the Prophet applies the penalty, is he to inflict one hundred fifty lashes, the Commander of the Faithful one hundred, and the *faqih* fifty? The ruler supervises the executive power and has the duty of implementing God's laws; it makes no difference if he is the Most Noble Messenger, the Commander of the Faithful or the representative or judge he appointed to Basra or Kufa, or a *faqih* in the present age.

Another of the concerns of the Most Noble Messenger and the Commander of the Faithful was the levying of taxes—*khums*, *zakat*, *jizya*, and *kharaj* on taxable lands. Now when the Prophet levied *zakat*, how much did he levy? One-tenth in one place and one-twentieth elsewhere? And how did the Commander of the Faithful proceed when he became ruler? And what now, if one of us becomes the foremost *faqih* of the age and is able to enforce his authority? In these matters, can there be any difference in the authority of the Most Noble Messenger, that of 'Ali, and that of the *faqih*? God Almighty appointed the Prophet in authority over all the Muslims; as long as he was alive, his authority extended over even 'Ali. Afterwards, the Imam had authority over all the Muslims, even his own successor as Imam; his commands relating to government were valid for everyone, and he could appoint and dismiss judges and governors.

The authority that the Prophet and the Imam had in establishing a government, executing laws, and administering affairs exists also for the *faqih*. But the *fuqaha* do not have absolute authority in the sense of having authority over all other *fuqaha* of their own time, being able to appoint or dismiss them. There is no hierarchy ranking one *faqih* higher than another or endowing one with more authority than another.

Now that this much has been demonstrated, it is necessary that the *fuqaha* proceed, collectively or individually, to establish a government in order to implement the laws of Islam and protect its territory. If this task falls within the capabilities of a single person, he has personally incumbent upon him the duty to fulfill it; otherwise, it is a duty that devolves upon the *fuqaha* as a whole. Even if it is impossible to fulfill the task, the authority vested in the *fuqaha* is not voided, because it has been vested in them by God. If they can, they must collect taxes, such as *zakat, khums,* and *kharaj,* spend them for the welfare of the Muslims, and also enact the penalties of the law. The fact that we are presently unable to establish a complete and comprehensive form of government does not mean that we should sit idle. Instead, we should perform, to whatever extent we can, the tasks that are needed by the Muslims and that pertain to the functions an Islamic government must assume.

To prove that government and authority belong to the Imam is not to imply that the Imam has no spiritual status. The Imam does indeed possess certain spiritual dimensions that are unconnected with his function as ruler. The spiritual status of the Imam is the universal divine viceregency that is sometimes mentioned by the Imams (peace be upon them). It is a viceregency pertaining to the whole of creation, by virtue of which all the atoms in the universe humble themselves before the holder of authority. It is one of the essential beliefs of our Shi'i school that no one can attain the spiritual status of the Imams, not even the cherubim or the prophets.[63] In fact, according to the traditions that have been handed down to us, the Most Noble Messenger and the Imams existed before the creation of the world in the form of lights situated beneath the divine throne; they were superior to other men even in the sperm from which they grew and in their physical composition.[64] Their exalted station is limited only by the divine will, as indicated by the saying of Jibra'il recorded in the traditions on the *mi'raj:* "Were I to draw closer by as much as the breadth of a finger, surely I would burn."[65] The Prophet himself said: "We have states with God that are beyond the reach of the cherubim and the prophets."[66] It is a part of our belief that the Imams too enjoy similar states, before the question of government even arises. For example, Fatima also possessed these states, even though she was not a ruler, a judge, or a governor.[67] These states are quite distinct from the function of government. So when we say that Fatima was neither a judge nor a ruler, this does not mean that she was like you and me, or that she has no spiritual superiority over us. Similarly, if someone says, in accordance with the Qur'an, that "The Prophet has higher claims on the believers than their own selves" (33:6), he has attributed to him something more exalted than his right to govern the believers. We will not examine these matters further here, for they belong to the area of another science.

To assume the function of government does not in itself carry any particular merit or status; rather it is a means for fulfilling the duty of implementing the law and establishing the Islamic order of justice. The Commander of the Faithful (upon whom be peace) said to Ibn 'Abbas, concerning the nature of government and command: "How much is this shoe worth?" Ibn 'Abbas replied: "Nothing." The Commander of the Faithful then said: "Command over you is worth still less in my eyes, except for this: by means of ruling and commanding you I may be able to establish the right"—i.e., the laws and institutions of Islam—"and destroy the wrong"[68]—i.e., all impermissible and oppressive laws and institutions.

Rule and command, then, are in themselves only a means, and if this means is not employed for the good and for attaining noble aims, it has no value in the eyes of the men of God. Thus the Commander of the Faithful says in his sermon in *Nahj al-Balagha:* "Were it not for the obligation imposed on me, forcing me to take up this task of government, I would abandon it."[69] It is evident, then, that to assume the function of government is to acquire a means and not a spiritual station, for if government were a spiritual station, nobody would be able to either usurp it or abandon it. Government and the exercise of command acquire value only when they become the means for implementing the law of Islam and establishing the just Islamic order; then the person in charge of government may also earn some additional virtue and merit.

Some people, whose eyes have been dazzled by the things of this world, imagine that leadership and government represented in themselves dignity and high station for the Imams, so that if others come to exercise power, the world will collapse. Now the Soviet ruler, the British Prime Minister, and the American President all exercise power, and they are all unbelievers. They are unbelievers, but they have political power and influence, which they use to execute anti-human laws and policies for the sake of their own interests.

It is the duty of the Imams and the just *fuqaha* to use government institutions to execute divine law, establish the just Islamic order, and serve mankind. Government in itself represents nothing but pain and trouble for them, but what are they to do? They have been given a duty, a mission to fulfill; the governance of the *faqih* is nothing but the performance of a duty.

When explaining why he assumed the tasks of government and rule, the Commander of the Faithful (upon whom be peace) declared that he did so for the sake of certain exalted aims, namely the establishment of justice and the abolition of injustice. He said, in effect: "O God, you know that it is not our purpose to acquire position and power, but rather to deliver the oppressed from the hands of the unjust. What impelled me to accept the task of command and rule over the people was this: God, Almighty and Exalted, has exacted a pledge from the scholars of religion and assigned to them the duty of not remaining silent in the face of the gluttony and self-indulgence of the unjust and the oppressor, on the one hand, and the wasting hunger of the oppressed, on the other." He also said: "O God! You know well that the struggle we have waged has not been for the sake of winning political power, nor for acquiring worldly goods and overflowing wealth." He went directly on to explain the goal for the sake of which he and his companions had been struggling and exerting themselves: "Rather it was our aim to restore and implement the luminous principles of Your religion and to reform the conduct of affairs in Your land, so that Your downtrodden servants might gain security and Your laws, which have remained unfulfilled and in abeyance, might be established and executed."[70]

The ruler who, by means of the organs of government and the power of command that are at his disposal, desires to attain the exalted aims of Islam, the same aims set forth by the Commander of the Faithful, must possess the essential qualities to which we have already referred; that is, he must know the law and be just. The Commander of the Faithful mentions next the qualities essential in a ruler immediately after he has specified the aims of government: "O God! I was the first person that turned toward You by accepting Your religion as soon as I heard Your Messenger (upon whom be peace) declare it. No one preceded me in prayer except the Messenger himself. And you, O people! You know well that it is not fitting that one who is greedy and parsimonious should attain rule and authority over the honor, lives, and income of the Muslims, and the laws and ordinances enforced among them, and also leadership of them.

"Furthermore, he should not be ignorant and unaware of the law, lest in his ignorance he mislead the people. He must not be unjust and harsh, causing the people to cease all traffic and dealing with him because of his oppressiveness. Nor must he fear states, so that he seeks the friendship of some and treats others with enmity. He must refrain from accepting bribes when he sits in judgment, so that the rights of men are trampled underfoot and the claimant does not receive his due. He must not leave the practice of the Prophet and law in abeyance, so that the community falls into misguidance and peril."[71]

Notice how this discourse revolves around two points, knowledge and justice, and how the Commander of the Faithful regards them as necessary qualities of the ruler. In the expression: "He should not be ignorant and unaware of the law, lest in his ignorance he mislead the people," the emphasis is upon knowledge, while in the remaining sentences the emphasis is upon justice, in its true sense. The true sense of justice is that the ruler should conduct himself like the Commander of the Faithful in his dealings with other states, in his relations and transactions with the people, in passing sentence and giving judgment, and in distributing the public income. To put it differently, the ruler should adhere to the program of rule that the Commander of the Faithful laid down for Malik Ashtar[72]—in reality, for all rulers and governors, for it is something like a circular addressed to all who exercise rule. If the *fuqaha* become rulers, they too should consider it their set of instructions.

Here is a tradition totally without ambiguity. The Commander of the Faithful (upon whom be peace) relates that the Most Noble Messenger (upon whom be blessings and peace) said: "O God! Have mercy on those that succeed me." He repeated this twice and was then asked: "O Messenger of God, who are those that succeed you?" He replied: "They are those that come after me, transmit my traditions and practice, and teach them to the people after me."

Shaykh Sadduq[73] (may God's mercy be upon him) has related this tradition with five chains of transmission (actually four, since two of them are similar in certain respects) in the following books: *Jami' al-Akhbar, 'Uyun Akhbar ar-Rida,* and *al-Majalis.*[74]

Among the cases where this tradition has been designated as *musnad,*[75] in one instance we find the words "and teach them," and in the other instances we find, "and teach them to the people." Wherever the tradition is designated as *mursal,*[76] we find only the beginning of the sentence, with the phrase "and teach them to the people after me" completely omitted.

We can make either of two assumptions with respect to this tradition. First, it is the only instance of the tradition, and the phrase beginning, "and teach them" either was later added to the end, or was indeed a part of the tradition, but was later omitted in certain versions. The second alternative is more probable. For if the phrase were added, we could not say that it was as the result of mistake or error, given that the tradition was handed down by several chains of transmission and the respective narrators lived at great distance from each other—one in Balkh, another in Nishapur, and still another elsewhere. Nor is it possible that this phrase was deliberately added; it is highly unlikely that it would have occurred to each of several people living far apart from each other to add such a sentence to the tradition. Therefore, if it is a single tradition, we can assert with certainty that either the phrase beginning, "and teach them" was omitted from one of the versions recorded by Shaykh Sadduq (or overlooked by the copyists who wrote down his work), or else Shaykh Sadduq himself failed to mention it for some other reason.

The second assumption would be that there are two separate traditions, one without the phrase "and teach them . . ." and the other with it. If the phrase is part of the tradition, it certainly does not apply to those whose task is simply the narration of tradition and who are not competent to express an independent juridical opinion or judgment. There are certain scholars of tradition who do not understand *hadith* at all; as implied in the saying: "Many a scholar of law falls short of being a *faqih*," they are merely a vehicle for the recording, collecting, and writing down of traditions and narrations and for placing them at the disposal of the people. It cannot be said of such scholars that they are the successors of the Prophet, teaching the sciences of Islam.[77] Their efforts on behalf of Islam and the Muslims are of course most valuable, and many scholars of tradition have indeed also been *fuqaha*, competent to express an independent opinion; e.g., Kulayni,[78] Shaykh Sadduq,[79] and his father (God's mercy on all of them). These three were *fuqaha*, and they taught the ordinances and sciences of Islam to the people. When we say that Shaykh Sadduq differed from Shaykh Mufid,[80] we do not mean that Shaykh Sadduq was unlearned in *fiqh*,[81] or that he was less learned than Shaykh Mufid. Shaykd Sadduq was, after all, the person who elucidated all the principles and schools of religion in a single sitting. He differed from Shaykh Mufid and others comparable to him in that they were *mujtahids* who brought their own reasoning to bear on traditions and narrations, while Shaykh Sadduq was a *faqih* who did not have recourse to his own reasoning, or did so only rarely.

The phrase we are discussing applies to those who expound the sciences of Islam, who expound the ordinances of Islam, and who educate the people in Islam, preparing them to instruct others in turn. In the same way, the Most Noble Messenger and the Imams (peace be upon them all) proclaimed and expounded the ordinances of Islam; they had teaching circles where they gave the benefit of their learning to several thousand people, whose duty it was, in turn, to teach others. That is the meaning implied in the phrase "and teach the people . . .": disseminating the knowledge of Islam among the people and conveying to them the ordinances of Islam. If we believe that Islam is for all people in the world, it becomes obvious to every rational mind that the Muslims, and particularly the scholars among them, have the duty of disseminating knowledge of Islam and its ordinances and acquainting the people of the world with them.

If we suppose that the phrase "and teach them to the people" does not belong at the end of the *hadith*, then we must see what the Prophet (peace and blessings be upon him) might have meant in his saying: "O God! Have mercy on those that succeed me: those that come after me and transmit my traditions and practice." The tradition, even in this form, still would not apply to those who merely relate traditions without being *fuqaha*. For the divine practices and norms constituting the totality of the ordinances of Islam are known as the practice of the Prophet by virtue of the fact that they were revealed to him. So anyone who wishes to disseminate the practices of the Most Noble Messenger must know all the ordinances of God; he must be able to distinguish the authentic from the false, those of absolute from those of limited application, and the general from the specific. Further, he must be able to discern rational categories, distinguish between traditions originating in circumstances of *taqiya*[82] and those originating otherwise, and be fully conversant with all the necessary criteria that have been specified. Traditionists who have not attained the level of *ijtihad*[83] and who merely transmit *hadith* know nothing about all this; hence they are incapable of discerning the true practice of the Messenger of God. Mere transmission could have no value in the eyes of the Messenger, and it was certainly not his desire that phrases like: "The Messenger of God said," or "It is related on the authority of the Messenger of God," should gain currency among the people, if the sentences prefaced by these phrases were counterfeited and not his. What he desired instead was that his true practice should be disseminated among the people and the real ordinances of Islam spread among them. The tradition: "Whoever preserves for my people forty traditions will be resurrected by God as a *faqih*"[84] and similar traditions praising the dissemination of *hadith* do not pertain to traditionists who have no concept of the nature of tradition. They pertain to those who are able to distinguish the true tradition of the Most Noble Messenger in accordance with the true ordinances of Islam. Such

70

persons are none other than the *mujtahids* and the *fuqaha;* they are the ones able to assess all different aspects and implications of a ruling, and to deduce the true ordinances of Islam on the basis of the criteria they have inherited from the Imams (upon whom be peace). They are the successors of the Most Noble Messenger, disseminating the divine ordinances and instructing men in the sciences of Islam. It is for them that the Prophet prayed when he said, "O God! Have mercy on my successors."

There is no doubt, therefore, that the tradition: "O God! Have mercy on my successors" does not relate to the transmitters of tradition who are mere scribes; a scribe cannot be a successor to the Prophet. The successors are the *fuqaha* of Islam. Dissemination of the ordinances of Islam, as well as the teaching and instruction of the people, is the duty of *fuqaha* who are just. For if they are not just, they will be like those who forged traditions harmful to Islam, like Samura ibn Jandab,[85] who forged traditions hostile to the Commander of the Faithful. And if they are not *fuqaha*, they cannot comprehend the nature of *fiqh* and the ordinances of Islam, and they may disseminate thousands of traditions in praise of kings that have been forged by the agents of the oppressors and pseudo-scholars attached to royal courts. It is easy to see what results they obtained on the basis of the two weak traditions that they set up against the Qur'an, with its insistent commands to rise up against kings and its injunctions to Moses to rebel against the Pharaoh.[86] Quite apart from the Glorious Qur'an, there are numerous traditions exhorting men to struggle against tyrants and those who pervert religion.[87] Lazy people among us have laid these aside and, relying on those two weak *hadiths* that may well have been forged by court preachers, tell us we must make peace with kings and give our allegiance to the court. If they were truly acquainted with tradition and knowledgeable about religion, they would act instead in accordance with the numerous traditions that denounce the oppressors. If it happens that they are acquainted with tradition, then we must conclude that they do not have the quality of justice. For, not being just and failing to eschew sin, they overlook the Qur'an and all the traditions that condemn the oppressor, and concentrate instead on those two weak *hadith*. It is the appetites of their stomachs that cause them to cling to them, not knowledge. Appetite and ambition make men subservient to royal courts; true tradition does not.

In any event, the dissemination of the sciences of Islam and the proclamation of its ordinances are the task of the just *fuqaha*—those who are able to distinguish the true ordinance from the false, and the traditions of the Imams (upon whom be peace) arising in conditions of *taqiya* from those originating otherwise. For we know that our Imams were sometimes subject to conditions that prevented them from pronouncing a true ordinance; they were exposed to tyrannical and oppressive rulers who imposed *taqiya* and fear upon them. Naturally, their fear was for religion not themselves, and if they had not observed *taqiya* in certain circumstances, oppressive rulers would have entirely rooted out true religion.

There cannot be the least doubt that the tradition we have been discussing refers to the governance of the *faqih*, for to be a successor means to succeed to all the functions of prophethood. In this respect what is implied by the sentence: "O God! Have mercy on my successors" is no less than what is implied by the sentence: " 'Ali is my successor," since the meaning of successorship is the same in both cases. The phrase "who come after me and transmit my traditions" serves to designate the successors, not to define succession, for succession was a well-known concept in the first age of Islam and did not require elucidation. Moreover, the person who asked the Prophet whom he meant by his successors was not enquiring after the meaning of successorship; he was requesting the Prophet to specify those whom he meant, as he indeed did in his reply. It is remarkable that nobody has taken the phrase: " 'Ali is my successor," or "the Imams are my successors," as referring to the simple task of issuing juridical opinions; instead, they derive the tasks of successorship and government from them, whereas they have hesitated to draw the same conclusion from the word "my successors" in the tradition under consideration. This is solely because they have imagined that succession to the position of the Most Noble Messenger has been limited or restricted to certain people, and that since each of the Imams was a successor, the religious scholars cannot act as successors, rulers, and governors. The result is that Islam must be without any leader to care for it, the ordinances of Islam must be in abeyance, the frontiers of Islam must be at the mercy of the enemies of religion, and various kinds of perversion that have nothing to do with Islam are gaining currency.

Muhammad ibn Yahya relates, on the authority of Ahmad ibn Ahmad, who heard it from Ibn Mahbub, who was informed of it by 'Ali ibn Abi Hamza, that the Imam Abu 'l-Hasan Musa, son of Ja'far,[88] (peace by upon them both) said: "Whenever a believer dies, the angels weep, together with the ground where he engaged in the worship of God and the gates of heaven that he entered by means of his good deeds. A crack will appear in the fortress of Islam, that naught can repair, for believers who are *fuqaha* are the fortresses of Islam, like the encircling walls that protect a city."[89]

In the same chapter of *al-Kafi*, there is another version of this tradition, which reads: "Whenever a believer who is a *faqih*. . ." instead of: "Whenever a believer. . . ." In contrast, at the beginning of the version we have cited, the expression "who is a *faqih*" is missing. Later in the seond version, however, when the cause for the angels' weeping is adduced, the expression "believers who are *fuqaha*" does occur. This makes it clear that the word *"faqih"* was omitted at the beginning of the tradition, particularly since the concept "fortress of Islam" is fully appropriate to the *faqih*.

The saying of the Imam that "believers who are *fuqaha* are the fortresses of Islam" actually ascribes to the *fuqaha* the duty of being guardians of the beliefs, ordinances, and institutions of Islam. It is clear that these words of the Imam are not an expression of ceremonial courtesy, like the words we sometimes exchange with each other (I call you "Support of the Shari'a," and you bestow the same title on me in return!). Nor do they have any similarity to the titles we use in addressing a letter to someone: "His Noble Excellency, the Proof of Islam."

If a *faqih* sits in the corner of his dwelling and does not intervene in any of the affairs of society, neither preserving the laws of Islam and disseminating its ordinances, nor in any way participating in the affairs of the Muslims or having any care for them, can he be called "the fortress of Islam" or the protector of Islam?

If the leader of a government tells an official or a commander, "Go guard such-and-such an area," will the duty of guarding that he has assumed permit him to go home and sleep, allowing the enemy to come and ravage that area? Or should he, on the contrary, strive to protect that area in whatever way he can?

Now if you say that we are preserving at least some of the ordinances of Islam, let me ask you this question. Are you implementing the penal law of Islam and the sanctions it provides? You will have to answer no.

So a crack has appeared in the protective wall surrounding Islam, despite your supposedly being its guardians.

Then I ask you: Are you guarding the frontiers of Islam and the territorial integrity of the Islamic homeland? To this your answer will be: "No, our task is only to pray!"

This means that a piece of the wall has collapsed.

Now I ask you: Are you taking from the rich what they owe the poor and passing it on to them? For that is your Islamic duty, to take from the rich and give to the poor. Your answer will be, in effect: "No, this is none of our concern! God willing, others will come and perform this task."

Then another part of the wall will have collapsed, and your situation will be like that of Shah Sultan Husayn waiting for the fall of Isfahan.[90]

What kind of fortress is this? Each of the corners is occupied by some "pillar of Islam," but all he can do is offer excuses when put to the test. Is that what we mean by "fortress"?

The meaning of the statement of the Imam that the *fuqaha* are the fortresses of Islam is that they have a duty to protect Islam and that they must do whatever is necessary to fulfill that duty. It is one of their most important duties and, moreover, an absolute duty, not a conditional one. It is an issue to which the *fuqaha* of Islam must pay particular attention. The religious teaching institution must give due thought to the matter and equip itself with the means and strength necessary to protect Islam in the fullest possible sense, just as the Most Noble Messenger and the Imams (peace be upon them) were the guardians of Islam, protecting its beliefs, laws, and institutions in the most comprehensive manner.

We have abandoned almost all aspects of our duty, restricting ourselves to passing on, from one generation to the next, certain parts of Islamic law and discussing them among ourselves. Many of the ordinances of Islam have virtually become part of the occult sciences, and Islam itself has become a stranger;[91] only its name has survived.

All the penal provisions of Islam, which represent the best penal code ever devised for humanity, have been completely forgotten; nothing but their name has survived. As for the Qur'anic verses stipulating penalties and sanctions, "Nothing remains of them but their recitation."[92] For example, we recite the verse: "Administer to the adulterer and the adultress a hundred lashes each" (24:2), but we do not know what to do when confronted with a case of adultery. We merely recite the verse in order to improve the quality of our recitation and to give each sound its full value. The actual situation prevailing in our society, the present state of the Islamic community, the prevalence of lewdness and corruption, the protection and support extended by our governments to adultery—none of this concerns us! It is enough that we understand what penalties have been provided for the adulterer and the adultress without attempting to secure their implementation or otherwise struggling against the existence of adultery in our society!

I ask you, is that the way the Most Noble Messenger (peace and blessings be upon him) conducted himself? Did he content himself with reciting the Qur'an, then lay it aside and neglect to ensure the implementation of its penal provisions? Was it the practice of the successors of the Prophet to entrust matters to the people and tell them, "We have no further concern with you"? Or, on the contrary, did they decree penalties for various classes of offender— whippings, stonings, perpetual imprisonment, banishment? Examine the sections of Islamic law relating to penal law and blood money: you will see that all of these matters are part of Islam and part of the reason for the coming of Islam. Islam came in order to establish order in society; leadership[93] and government are for the sake of ordering the affairs of society.

It is our duty to preserve Islam. This duty is one of the most important obligations incumbent upon us; it is more necessary even than prayer and fasting. It is for the sake of fulfilling this duty that blood must sometimes be shed. There is no blood more precious than that of Imam Husayn, yet it was shed for the sake of Islam, because of the precious nature of Islam. We must understand this matter well and convey it to others. You can be the true successors to the Prophet (peace and blessings be upon him) as the guardians of Islam only if you teach Islam to the people; do not say, "We will wait until the coming of the Imam of the Age." Would you consider postponing your prayer until the coming of the Imam? The preservation of Islam is even more important than prayer. Do not follow the logic of the governor of Khumayn[94] who used to say: "We must promote sin so that the Imam of the Age will come. If sin does not prevail, he will not manifest himself!"[95] Do not sit here simply debating among yourselves. Study all the ordinances of Islam, and propagate all aspects of the truth by writing and publishing books. It cannot fail to have an effect, as my own experience testifies.

'Ali relates, on the authority of his father, from an-Nawfali, who had it from as-Sukuni, who was told it by Abu 'Abdullah (upon whom be peace), that the Most Noble Messenger (peace and blessings be upon him) said: "The *fuqaha* are the trustees of the prophets, as long as they do not concern themselves with the illicit desires, pleasures, and wealth of this world." The Prophet was then asked: "O Messenger of God! How may we know if they do so concern themselves?" He replied: "By seeing whether they follow the ruling power. If they do that, fear for your religion and shun them."[96] Examination of the whole of this *hadith* would involve us in a lengthy discussion. We will speak only about the phrase: "The *fuqaha* are the trustees of the prophets," since it is what interests us here because of its relevance to the topic of the governance of the *faqih*.

First, we must see what duties, powers, and functions the prophets had in order to discover what the duties of the *fuqaha*, the trustees and successors of the prophets, are in turn.

In accordance with both reason and the essential nature of religion, the purpose for sending the prophets and the task of the prophets cannot be simply the delivering of judgments concerning a particular problem or the expounding of the ordinances of religion. These judgments and ordinances were not revealed to the Prophet (upon whom be peace and blessings) in order for him and the Imams to convey them truthfully to the people as a series of divinely appointed *muftis*,[97] and then pass this trust on in turn to the *fuqaha*, so that they might likewise convey them to the people without any distortion. The meaning of the expression:

"The *fuqaha* are the trustees of the prophets" is not that the *fuqaha* are trustees simply with respect to the giving of juridical opinions. For in fact the most important function of the prophets (peace be upon them all) is the establishment of a just social system through the implementation of laws and ordinances (which is naturally accompanied by the exposition and dissemination of the divine teachings and beliefs). This emerges clearly from the following Qur'anic verse: "Verily We have sent Our messengers with clear signs, and sent down with them the Book and the Balance, in order that men might live in equity" (57:25). The general purpose for the sending of prophets, then, is so that men's lives may be ordered and arranged on the basis of just social relations and true humanity may be established among men. This is possible only by establishing government and implementing laws, whether this is accomplished by the prophet himself, as was the case with the Most Noble Messenger (peace and blessings be upon him) or by the followers who come after him.

God Almighty says concerning the *khums:* "Know that of whatever booty you capture, a fifth belongs to God and His Messenger and to your kinsmen" (8:41). Concerning *zakat* He says: "Levy a tax on their property" (9:103). There are also other divine commands concerning other forms of taxation. Now the Most Noble Messenger had the duty not only of expounding these ordinances, but also of implementing them; just as he was to proclaim them to the people, he was also to put them into practice. He was to levy taxes, such as *khums, zakat,* and *kharaj,* and spend the resulting income for the benefit of the Muslims; establish justice among peoples and among the members of the community; implement the laws and protect the frontiers and independence of the country; and prevent anyone from misusing or embezzling the finances of the Islamic state.

Now God Almighty appointed the Most Noble Messenger (peace and blessings be upon him) head of the community and made it a duty for men to obey him: "Obey God and obey the Messenger and the holders of authority from among you" (4:59). The purpose for this was not so that we would accept and conform to whatever judgment the Prophet delivered. Conformity to the ordinances of religion is obedience to God; all activities that are conducted in accordance with divine ordinance, whether or not they

77

are ritual worship, are a form of obedience to God. Following the Most Noble Messenger, then, is not conforming to divine ordinances; it is something else. Of course, obeying the Most Noble Messenger is, in a certain sense, to obey God; we obey the Prophet because God has commanded us to do so. But if, for example, the Prophet, in his capacity as leader and guide of Islamic society, orders everyone to join the army of Usama,[98] so that no one has the right to hold back, it is the command of the Prophet, not the command of God. God has entrusted to him the task of government and command, and accordingly, in conformity with the interests of the Muslims, he arranges for the equipping and mobilization of the army, and appoints or dismisses governors and judges.

This being the case, the principle: "The *fuqaha* are the trustees of the prophets" means that all of the tasks entrusted to the prophets must also be fulfilled by the just *fuqaha* as a matter of duty. Justice, it is true, is a more comprehensive concept than trustworthiness, and it is possible that someone may be trustworthy with respect to financial affairs, but not just in a more general sense.[99] However, those designated in the principle: "The *fuqaha* are the trustees of the prophets" are those who do not fail to observe any ordinances of the law and who are pure and unsullied, as is implied by the conditional statement: "as long as they do not concern themselves with the illicit desires, pleasures, and wealth of this world"—that is, as long as they do not sink into the morass of worldly ambition. If a *faqih* has as his aim the accumulation of worldly wealth, he is no longer just and cannot be the trustee of the Most Noble Messenger (upon whom be peace and blessings) and the executor of the ordinances of Islam. It is only the just *fuqaha* who may correctly implement the ordinances of Islam and firmly establish its institutions, executing the penal provisions of Islamic law and preserving the boundaries and territorial integrity of the Islamic homeland. In short, implementation of all laws relating to government devolves upon the *fuqaha*: the collection of *khums, zakat, sadaqa, jizya*, and *kharaj* and the expenditure of the money thus collected in accordance with the public interest; the implementation of the penal provisions of the law and the enactment of retribution (which must take place under the direct supervision of the ruler, failing which the next-of-kin of the murdered person has no authority to act); the guarding of the frontiers; and the securing of public order.

Just as the Most Noble Messenger (peace and blessings be upon him) was entrusted with the implementation of divine ordinances and the establishment of the institutions of Islam, and just as God Almighty set him up over the Muslims as their leader and ruler, making obedience to him obligatory, so, too, the just *fuqaha* must be leaders and rulers, implementing divine ordinances and establishing the institutions of Islam.

Since Islamic government is a government of law, those acquainted with the law, or more precisely, with religion—i.e., the *fuqaha*—must supervise its functioning. It is they who supervise all executive and administrative affairs of the country, together with all planning.

The *fuqaha* are the trustees who implement the divine ordinances in levying taxes, guarding the frontiers, and executing the penal provisions of the law. They must not allow the laws of Islam to remain in abeyance, or their operation to be affected by either defect or excess. If a *faqih* wishes to punish an adulterer, he must give him one hundred lashes in the presence of the people, in the exact manner that has been specified. He does not have the right to inflict one additional lash, to curse the offender, to slap him, or to imprison him for a single day. Similarly, when it comes to the levying of taxes, he must act in accordance with the criteria and the laws of Islam; he does not have the right to levy even a *shahi*[100] in excess of what the law provides. He must not let disorder enter the affairs of the public treasury or even so much as a *shahi* be lost. If a *faqih* acts in contradiction to the criteria of Islam (God forbid!), then he will automatically be dismissed from his post, since he will have forfeited his quality of trustee.

Law is actually the ruler; the security of all is guaranteed by the law, and law is their refuge. Muslims and the people in general are free within the limits laid down by the law; when they are acting in accordance with the provisions of the law, no one has the right to tell them, "Sit here," or "Go there." An Islamic government does not resemble states where the people are deprived of all security and everyone sits at home trembling for fear of a sudden raid or attack by the agents of the state. It was that way under Mu'awiya[101] and similar rulers: the people had no security, and they were killed or banished, or imprisoned for lengthy periods, on the strength of an accusation or a mere suspicion, because the government was not Islamic. When an Islamic government is established, all will live with complete security under the protection of the law, and no ruler will have the right to take any step contrary to the provisions and laws of the immaculate *shari'a.*

The meaning of "trustee," then, is that the *fuqaha* execute as a trust all the affairs for which Islam has legislated—not that they simply offer legal judgments on given questions. Was that the function of the Imam? Did he merely expound the law? Was it the function of the prophets, from whom the *fuqaha* have inherited it as a trust? To offer judgment on a question of law or to expound the laws in general is, of course, one of the dimensions of *fiqh.* But Islam regards law as a tool, not as an end in itself. Law is a tool and an instrument for the establishment of justice in society, a means for man's intellectual and moral reform and his purification. Law exists to be implemented for the sake of establishing a just society that will morally and spiritually nourish refined human beings. The most significant duty of the prophets was the implementation of divine ordinances, and this necessarily involved supervision and rule.

There is a tradition of Imam Riza (upon whom be peace) in which he says approximately the following: "An upright, protecting, and trustworthy *imam* is necessary for the community in order to preserve it from decline," and then reasserts that the *fuqaha* are the trustees of the prophets. Combining the two halves of the tradition, we reach the conclusion that the *fuqaha* must be the leaders of the people in order to prevent Islam from falling into decline and its ordinances from falling into abeyance.

Indeed it is precisely because the just *fuqaha* have not had executive power in the lands inhabited by Muslims and their governance has not been established that Islam has declined and its ordinances have fallen into abeyance. The words of Imam Riza have fulfilled themselves; experience has demonstrated their truth.

Has Islam not declined? Have the laws of Islam not fallen into disuse in the Islamic countries? The penal provisions of the law are not implemented; the ordinances of Islam are not enforced; the institutions of Islam have disappeared; chaos, anarchy, and confusion prevail—does not all this mean that Islam has declined?

Is Islam simply something to be written down in books like *al-Kafi*[102] and then laid aside? If the ordinances of Islam are not applied and the penal provisions of the law are not implemented in the external world—so that the thief, the plunderer, the oppressor, and the embezzler all go unpunished, while we content ourselves with preserving the books of law, kissing them and laying them aside (even treating the Qur'an itself this way), and reciting *Ya-Sin* on Thursday nights[103]—can we say that Islam has been preserved?

Since many of us did not really believe that Islamic society must be administered and ordered by an Islamic government, matters have now reached such a state that in the Muslim countries, not only does the Islamic order not obtain, with corrupt and oppressive laws being implemented instead of the laws of Islam, but the provisions of Islam appear archaic even to the *'ulama*. So when the subject is raised, they say that the tradition: "The *fuqaha* are the trustees of the prophets" refers only to the issuing of juridical opinions. Ignoring the verses of the Qur'an, they distort in the same way all the numerous traditions that indicate that the scholars of Islam are to exercise rule during the Occultation. But can trusteeship be restricted in this manner? Is the trustee not obliged to prevent the ordinances of Islam from falling into abeyance and criminals from going unpunished? To prevent the revenue and income of the country from being squandered, embezzled, or misdirected?

It is obvious that all of these tasks require the existence of trustees, and that it is the duty of the *fuqaha* to assume the trust bequeathed to them, to fulfill it in a just and trustworthy manner.

The Commander of the Faithful (upon whom be peace) said to Shurayh[104]: "The seat [of judge] you are occupying is filled by someone who is a prophet, the legatee of a prophet, or else a sinful wretch."[105] Now since Shurayh was neither a prophet nor the legatee of a prophet, it follows that he was a sinful wretch occupying the position of judge. Shurayh was a person who occupied the position of judge in Kufa for about fifty or sixty years. Closely associated with the party of Mu'awiya, Shurayh spoke and issued *fatvas*[106] in a sense favorable to him, and he ended up rising in revolt against the Islamic state. The Commander of the Faithful was unable to dismiss Shurayh during his rule, because certain powerful figures protected him on the grounds that Abu Bakr and

'Umar had appointed him and that their action was not to be controverted. Shurayh was thus imposed upon the Commander of the Faithful, who did, however, succeed in ensuring that he abided by the law in his judgments.

It is clear from the foregoing tradition that the position of judge may be exercised only by a prophet or by the legatee of a prophet. No one would dispute the fact that the function of judge belongs to the just *fuqaha,* in accordance with their appointment by the Imams. This unanimity contrasts with the question of the governance of the *faqih:* some scholars, such as Naraqi,[107] or among more recent figures, Na'ini,[108] regard all of the extrinsic functions and tasks of the Imams as devolving upon the *faqih,* while other scholars do not. But there can be no doubt that the function of judging belongs to the just *fuqaha;* this is virtually self-evident.

Considering the fact that the *fuqaha* do not have the rank of prophethood, and they are indubitably not "wretched sinners," we conclude that, in the light of the tradition quoted above, they must be the legatees or successors of the Most Noble Messenger (peace and blessings be upon him). Since, however, the expression "legatee of a prophet" is generally assumed to refer to his immediate successors, this tradition and others similar to it are only rarely cited as evidence for the successorship of the *fuqaha.* The concept "legatee of a prophet" is a broad one, however, and includes the *fuqaha.* The immediate legatee of the Most Noble Messenger was of course the Commander of the Faithful (upon whom be peace), who was followed by the other Imams (peace be upon them), and the affairs of the people were entrusted to them. But no one should imagine that the function of governing or sitting in judgment was a form of privilege for the Imams. Rule was entrusted to them only because they were best able to establish a just government and implement social justice among the people. The spiritual stations of the Imams, which far transcend human comprehension, had no connection with their naming and appointing officials. If the Most Noble Messenger had not appointed the Commander of the Faithful to be his successor, he would still have possessed the same sublime spiritual qualities. It is not that the exercise and function of government bestow spiritual rank and privilege on a man; on the contrary, spiritual rank and privilege qualify a man for the assumption of government and social responsibilities.

In any event, we deduce from the tradition quoted above that the *fuqaha* are the legatees, at one remove, of the Most Noble Messenger (peace and blessings be upon him) and that all the tasks he entrusted to the Imams (peace be upon them) are also incumbent on the *fuqaha;* all the tasks that the Messenger performed, they too must perform, just as the Commander of the Faithful (peace be upon him) did.

There is another tradition that may serve as proof or support for our thesis, one that is, indeed, preferable with respect to both its chain of transmission and its meaning. One chain of transmission for it, that passing through Kulayni, is weak, but the other, mentioned by Sadduq and passing through Sulayman ibn Khalid, is authentic and reliable. This is the text of the tradition. Imam Ja'far as-Sadiq[109] said: "Refrain from judging, because judging is reserved for an *imam* who is knowledgeable of the law and legal procedure and who behaves justly toward all the Muslims; it is reserved for a prophet or the legatee of a prophet."

Notice that the person who wishes to sit in judgment must, first of all, be an *imam*. What is meant here by *imam* is the common lexical meaning of the word, "leader" or "guide," not its specific technical sense. In this context, the Prophet himself counts as an *imam*. If the technical meaning of *imam*[110] were intended, the specification of the attributes of justice and knowledge in the tradition would be superfluous. Second, the person who wishes to exercise the function of judge must possess the necessary knowledge. If he is an *imam* but unlearned in matters of law and juridical procedure, he does not have the right to be a judge. Third, he must be just. The position of judge, then, is reserved for those who possess these three qualifications—being a leader, and being knowledgeable and just. The tradition proceeds to clarify that these three qualifications can be found only in a prophet or the trustee of a prophet.

I stated earlier that the function of judge belongs exclusively to the just *faqih;* this is a fundamental aspect of *fiqh*, which is not a matter under dispute. Let us now see whether the threefold qualifications for exercising the function of judge are present in the *faqih.* Obviously we are concerned here only with the just *faqih*, not with any *faqih*. The *faqih* is, by definition, learned in matters pertaining to the function of judge, since the term *faqih* is applied to one who is learned not only in the laws and judicial procedure of Islam, but also in the doctrines, institutions, and ethics of the faith—the *faqih* is, in short, a religious expert in the full sense of the word. If, in addition, the *faqih* is just, he will be found to have two of the necessary qualifications. The third qualification is that he should be an *imam*, in the sense of leader. Now we have already stated that the just *faqih* occupies a position of guidance and leadership with respect to judging, in accordance with his appointment by the Imam (upon whom be peace). Further, the Imam has specified that the three necessary qualifications are not to be found in anyone except a prophet or the legatee of a prophet. Since the *fuqaha* are not prophets, they must be the legatees or successors of the prophets. Therefore, we come to the conclusion that the *faqih* is the legatee of the Most Noble Messenger (upon whom be peace and blessings), and in addition, during the Occultation of the Imam, he is the leader of the Muslims and the chief of the community. He alone may exercise the function of judge, and no one else has the right to occupy the position of judgeship.

The third tradition relates to a signed decree of the Imam from which certain conclusions may be deduced, as I propose to do.

It is related in the book *Ikmal ad-Din wa Itmam an-Ni'ma*[111] that Ishaq ibn Ya'qub wrote a letter to the Imam of the Age[112] (may God hasten his renewed manifestation) asking him for guidance in certain problems that had arisen, and Muhammad ibn 'Uthman al-'Umari,[113] the deputy of the Imam, conveyed the letter to him. A response was issued, written in the blessed hand of the Imam, saying: "In case of newly occuring social circumstances, you should turn for guidance to those who relate our traditions, for they are my proof to you, as I am God's proof."

What is meant here by the phrase "newly occurring social circumstances" (*havadis-i vaqi'a*) is not legal cases and ordinances. The writer of the letter did not wish to ask what was to be done in the case of legal issues that were without precedent. For the answer to that question would have been self-evident according to the Shi'i school, and unanimously accepted traditions specify that one should have recourse to the *fuqaha* in such cases.

Indeed people had recourse to the *fuqaha* and made enquiries of them even during the lifetime of the Imams (upon whom be peace). A person living in the time of the Lesser Occultation and in communication with the four deputies of the Imam, who wrote a letter to him and received an answer, must have known whom to refer to for the solution of legal cases. What is meant by *havadis-i vaqi'a* is rather the newly arising situations and problems that affect the people and the Muslims. The question Ishaq ibn Ya'qub was implicitly posing was this: "Now that we no longer have access to you, what should we do with respect to social problems? What is our duty?" Or he may have mentioned certain specific events and then asked: "To whom should we have recourse for guidance in these matters?" But it seems that his question was general in intent and that the Imam responded in correspondingly general fashion, saying, "With respect to such occurrences and problems, you should refer to those who narrate our traditions, i.e., the *fuqaha*. They are my proofs to you, and I am God's proof to you."

What is the meaning of "God's proof"?[114] What do you understand by this term? Can a single tradition count as a proof? If Zurara[115] related a tradition, would that make him a proof? Is the Imam of the Age comparable in authority to Zurara, whom we follow in the sense that we act upon a tradition of the Most Noble Messenger (peace and blessings be upon him) that Zurara has narrated? When it is said that the holder of authority is the proof of God, does it mean that he is a "proof" purely with respect to details of the law, with the duty of giving legal opinions? The Most Noble Messenger said: "I am now departing, and the Commander of the Faithful will be my proof to you." Do you deduce from this that after the Prophet departed, all tasks came to an end except delivering legal opinions, and that this was all that was left for the Commander of the Faithful (upon whom be peace)? Or on the contrary, does the term "proof of God" mean that just as the Most Noble Messenger was the proof and authoritative guide of all the people, just as God had appointed him to guide people in all matters, so too the *fuqaha* are responsible for all affairs and are the authoritative guides of the people?

A "proof of God" is one whom God has designated to conduct affairs; all his deeds, actions, and sayings constitute a proof for the

Muslims. If someone commits an offense, reference will be had to the "proof" for adducing evidence and formulating the charge. If the "proof" commands you to perform a certain act, to implement the penal provisions of the law in a certain way, or to spend the income derived from booty, *zakat,* and *sadaqa*[116] in a certain manner, and you fail to obey him in any of these respects, then God Almighty will advance a "proof" against you on the Day of Judgment. If, despite the existence of the "proof," you turn to oppressive authorities for the solution of your affairs, again God Almighty will refer to the "proof" as an argument against you on the Day of Judgment, saying: "I established a proof for you; why did you turn instead to the oppressors and the judicial system of the wrongdoers?" Similarly, God designates the Commander of the Faithful (upon whom be peace) as a "proof" against those who disobeyed him and followed false paths. Again, against those who assumed the caliphate, against Mu'awiya and the Umayyad caliphs, against the Abbasid caliphs, and those who acted in accordance with their desires, a proof and argument is established: "Why did you illicitly assume rule over the Muslims? Why did you usurp the caliphate and government, despite your unworthiness?"

God calls to account all oppressive rulers and all governments that act contrary to the criteria of Islam, asking them: "Why did you commit oppression? Why did you squander the property of the Muslims? Why did you organize millenary celebrations?[117] Why did you spend the wealth of the people on the coronation[118] and the abominable festivities that accompanied it?" If one of them should reply: "Given the circumstances of the day, I was unable to act justly, or to relinquish my pretentious, luxurious palaces; I had myself crowned to draw attention to my country and the degree of progress we had achieved," he will then be answered: "The Commander of the Faithful was also a ruler; he ruled over all the Muslims and the whole of the broad Islamic realm. Were you more zealous than he in promoting the glory of Islam, the Muslims, and the lands of Islam? Was your realm more extensive than his? The country over which you ruled was but a part of his realm; Iraq, Egypt, and the Hijaz all belonged to his realm, as well as Iran. Despite this, his seat of command was the mosque: the bench of the judge was situated in one corner of the mosque, while in another, the army would prepare to set out for battle. That army was composed of people who offered their prayers regularly, were firm believers in Islam; you know well how swiftly it advanced and what results it obtained!"

Today, the *fuqaha* of Islam are proofs to the people. Just as the Most Noble Messenger (upon whom be peace and blessings) was the proof of God—the conduct of all affairs being entrusted to him so that whoever disobeyed him had a proof advanced against him—so, too, the *fuqaha* are the proof of the Imam (upon whom be peace) to the people. All the affairs of the Muslims have been entrusted to them. God will advance a proof and argument against anyone who disobeys them in anything concerning government, the conduct of Muslim affairs, or the gathering and expenditure of public funds.

There can be no doubt concerning the meaning of the tradition we have quoted, although it is possible to have certain reservations about its chain of transmission. Nonetheless, even if one does not regard the tradition as being in its own right a proof of the thesis we have advanced, it serves to support the other proofs we have mentioned.

Another tradition that supports our thesis is the *maqbula*[119] of 'Umar ibn Hanzala. Since this tradition refers to a certain verse of the Qur'an, we must first discuss the verse in question as well as the verses that precede it in order to elucidate its meaning, before we go on to examine the tradition.

In the Name of God, the Compassionate, The Merciful.

Verily God commands you to return trusts to their owners, and to act with justice when you rule among men. Verily God counsels you thus, and God is all-hearing, all-seeing. O you who believe, obey God and obey the Messenger and the holders of authority from among you [i.e., those entrusted with leadership and government]. When you dispute with each other concerning a thing, refer it to God and His Messenger; if you believe in God and the Last Day, this will be best for you and the result, most beneficial. (4:58-59)

In these verses God commands us to return trusts to their owners. Some people believe that what is meant here by "trusts" is twofold: trusts pertaining to men (i.e., their property), and those pertaining to the Creator (i.e., the ordinances of the *shari'a*).[120] The sense of returning the divine trust would then be implementing the ordinances of Islam correctly and completely. Another group of exegetes believes instead that what is intended by "trust" is the imamate.[121] There is indeed a tradition that specifies: "We [the Imams, upon whom be peace] are those addressed in this verse," for God Almighty commands the Most Noble Messenger (peace and blessings be upon him) and the Imams to entrust governance and leadership to their rightful possessors. Thus the Most Noble Messenger entrusted governance to the Commander of the Faithful (peace be upon him), who entrusted it to his successor, and each of his successors among the Imams handed it on in turn.

The verse goes on to say: "and to act with justice when you rule among men." Those addressed here are the persons who hold the reins of affairs in their hands and conduct the business of government—not judges, for the judge exercises only a juridical function, not a governmental one. The judge is a ruler only in a limited sense; the decrees that he issues are exclusively judicial, not executive. Indeed, in forms of government that have emerged in recent centuries, the judges represent one of the three branches of power, the other two being the executive (consisting of the council of ministers) and the legislative or planning body (the assembly or parliament). More generally, the judiciary is one of the branches of government and it fulfills one of the tasks of government. We must therefore conclude that the phrase "when you rule among men" relates to all the affairs of government, and includes both judges and those belonging to the other branches of power.

Now it has been established that since all the concerns of religion constitute a divine trust, a trust that must be vested in its rightful possessors, a part of the trust must inevitably be government. Thus, in accordance with this verse, the conduct of all governmental affairs must be based on the criteria of justice, or to put it differently, on the law of Islam and the ordinances of the *shari'a*. The judge may not issue an incorrect verdict—i.e., one based on some illegitimate, non-Islamic code—nor may the judicial procedure he follows or the law on which he bases his verdict be non-Islamic and therefore invalid. For example, when those engaged in planning the affairs of the country draw up a fiscal program for the nation, they must not impose unjust taxes on peasants working publicly owned lands, reducing them to wretchedness and destroying the land and agriculture as a whole through the burden of excessive taxation. If the executive branch of government wishes to implement the juridical ordinances of the law and its penal provisions, they must not go beyond the limits of the law by inflicting extra lashes upon the offender or abusing him.

After the Commander of the Faithful (upon whom be peace) had cut off the hands of two thieves, he showed such love and concern in treating them and attending to their needs that they became his enthusiastic supporters. On another occasion, he heard that the plundering army of Mu'awiya had stolen an anklet from the foot of a *dhimmi*[122] woman. He became so distraught and his sensibilities were so offended that he said in a speech: "If a person were to die in circumstances such as mine, no one would reproach him." But despite all this sensitivity, the Commander of the Faithful was also a man who would draw his sword when it was necessary—to destroy the workers of corruption—with all the strength he could muster. This is the true meaning of justice.

The Most Noble Messenger (peace and blessings upon him) is the foremost example of the just ruler. When he gave orders for the conquest of a certain area, the burning of a certain place, or the destruction of a certain group whose existence was harmful for Islam, the Muslims, and mankind in general, his orders were just. If he had not given orders such as these, it would have been the opposite of justice, because it would have meant neglecting the welfare of Islam, the Muslims, and human society.

Anyone who rules over the Muslims, or over human society in general, must always take into consideration the public welfare and interest, and ignore personal feelings and interests. For this reason, Islam is prepared to subordinate individuals to the collective interest of society and has rooted out numerous groups that were a source of corruption and harm to human society.

Since the Jews of Bani Qurayza were a troublesome group, causing corruption in Muslim society and damaging Islam and the Islamic state, the Most Noble Messenger (peace and blessings be upon him) eliminated them.[123]

Indeed, there are two essential qualities in the believer: he executes justice whenever necessary, with the utmost force and decisiveness and without exhibiting the least trace of feeling;

and he displays the utmost love and solicitude whenever they are called for. In these two ways, the believer comes to serve as a refuge for society. Society, with both Muslim and non-Muslim members, will achieve security and tranquillity as the result of government exercised by believers, and everybody will live in ease and without fear. The fact that men in our age live in fear of their rulers is because existing governments are not based on law; they are a form of banditry. But in the case of a government headed by someone like the Commander of the Faithful (upon whom be peace), that is, in the case of an Islamic government, only the traitors and oppressors—those who transgress and encroach on the rights of their fellows—suffer fear; for the public at large, fear and anxiety are nonexistent.

In the second of the two verses we have quoted, God Almighty says: "O you who believe, obey God and obey the Messenger and the holders of authority among you" (4:59).

According to a certain tradition, the beginning of the first verse ("return trusts to their owners") is addressed to the Imams (upon whom be peace), the next part of that verse, concerning rule with justice, is addressed to those who exercise command, and the second verse ("O you who believe . . .") is addressed to the entire Muslim people. God commands them to obey Him by following His divine ordinances, and to obey His Most Noble Messenger (upon whom be peace and blessings) as well as the holders of authority (i.e., the Imams) by adhering to their teachings and following their governmental decrees.

I have already said that obedience to the commands of God Almighty is different from obedience to the Most Noble Messenger (peace and blessings be upon him). All the ordinances of divine law, whether or not they relate to worship, are the commands of God and to implement them is to obey God. The Most Noble Messenger did not issue any commands concerning prayer, and if he urged men to pray, it was by way of confirming and implementing God's command. When we pray, we too are obeying God; obeying the Messenger is different from obeying God.

The commands of the Most Noble Messenger (upon whom be peace and blessings) are those that he himself issued in the course of exercising his governmental function, as when, for example, he commanded the Muslims to follow the army of Usama,[124] to protect the frontiers of the Islamic state in a certain way, to levy taxes on certain categories of people, and in general to interact with people in certain prescribed ways. All of these were commands of the Prophet. God has laid upon us the duty of obeying the Messenger. It is also our duty to follow and obey the holders of authority, who, according to our beliefs, are the Imams (upon whom be peace). Of course, obedience to their governmental decrees is also a form of obedience to God. Since God Almighty has commanded us to follow the Messenger and the holders of authority, our obeying them is actually an expression of obedience to God.

The verse we have cited continues: "When you dispute with each other concerning a thing, refer it to God and His Messenger." Disputes that arise among people are of two kinds. First, there is the dispute arising between two groups or two individuals concerning a particular matter or claim. For example, someone may claim that there is a debt owed him, while the other party denies it; the truth of the matter must then be established, in accordance either with the *shari'a* or with customary law.[125] In such cases one must turn to judges, who will examine the matter and deliver an appropriate verdict. The first kind of dispute, then, is a civil one.

The second kind of dispute does not concern a disagreement of this type, but relates to oppression and crime. If a robber takes someone's property by force, for example, or makes illicit use of people's property, or if a burglar enters someone's house and carries off his property, the competent authority to whom one should have recourse is not the judge but the public prosecutor. In such matters as this, which relate to penal not civil law (apart from some cases, which are simultaneously civil and penal), it is primarily the public prosecutor who is the guardian of the law and its ordinances and the protector of society. He begins his task by issuing an indictment, and then the judge examines the matter and delivers his verdict. The verdicts issued, whether civil or penal in nature, are put into effect by another branch of power, the executive.

The Qur'an says, then, in effect: "Whenever a dispute arises among you concerning any matter, your point of reference must be God and His ordinances and the Messenger, the executor of those ordinances. The Messenger must receive the ordinances from God and implement them. If any dispute arises among you concerning a debt or a loan, the Messenger will intervene in his capacity as judge and deliver a verdict. If other disputes arise involving unlawful coercion or the usurpation of rights, again it is to the Prophet that you should have recourse. Since he is the head of the Islamic state, he is obliged to enact justice. He must dispatch an official whose duty it is to recover the usurped right and restore it to its owner. Further, in any matter where people had recourse to the Messenger, recourse must be had to the Imams, and obedience to the Imams is, in effect, obedience to the Most Noble Messenger."

In short, both of these verses, with all their components, embrace government in general as well as judgehood; they are not restricted in any way to the function of judging, quite aside from the consideration that certain verses of the Qur'an explicitly relate to government in the sense of the executive.

In the next verse, God says: "Have you not looked at those who claim to believe in what was revealed to you and what was revealed before you? They wish to seek justice from *taghut* [illegitimate powers], even though they have been commanded to disbelieve therein" (4:60). Even if we do not interpret *taghut* as oppressive governments and all illicit forms of power that have revolted against divine government in order to establish monarchy or some other form of rule, we must still interpret it as including both judges and rulers. For customarily, one has recourse to the judicial authorities to initiate legal proceedings and obtain redress and the punishment of the offender, but then, the juridical verdict that they reach must be implemented by the executive power, which usually forms a separate branch of the government. Tyrannical governments—including the judiciary, the executive, and all other components of the state—comprise what is meant by *taghut*, for they have rebelled against divine command by instituting evil laws, implementing them, and then making them the basis of judicial practice. God has commanded us to disbelieve in them; that is, to revolt against them and their commands and ordinances. All who wish to disbelieve, in this sense, in the *taghut* —that is, to rise up in disobedience against illegitimate ruling powers—have a formidable duty that they must strive to fulfill as far as they are able.

Now let us examine the tradition known as the *maqbula* of 'Umar ibn Hanzala to establish its meaning and intent. 'Umar ibn

Hanzala says: "I asked Imam Sadiq (upon whom be peace) whether it was permissible for two of the Shi'is who had a disagreement concerning a debt or a legacy to seek the verdict of the ruler or judge. He replied: 'Anyone who has recourse to the ruler or judge, whether his case be just or unjust, has in reality had recourse to *taghut* [i.e., the illegitimate ruling power]. Whatever he obtains as a result of their verdict, he will have obtained by forbidden means, even if he has a proven right to it, for he will have obtained it through the verdict and judgment of the *taghut*, that power which God Almighty has commanded him to disbelieve in.' " ("They wish to seek justice from illegitimate powers, even though they have been commanded to disbelieve therein" [4:60].)

'Umar ibn Hanzala then asked: "What should two Shi'is do then, under such circumstances?" Imam Sadiq answered: "They must seek out one of you who narrates our traditions, who is versed in what is permissible and what is forbidden, who is well acquainted with our laws and ordinances, and accept him as judge and arbiter, for I appoint him as judge over you."[126]

As both the beginning and the conclusion of this tradition make clear, and also the reference made by the Imam (peace be upon him) to the Qur'anic verse, the scope of the question put to the Imam was general, and the instructions he gave in response were also of general validity. I said earlier that for the adjudication of both civil and penal cases, one must have recourse to judges, as well as to the executive authorities or general governmental authorities. One has recourse to judges in order to establish the truth, reconcile enmities, or determine punishment; and to the executive authorities, in order to obtain compliance with the verdict given by the judge and the enactment of his verdict, whether the case is civil or penal in nature. It is for this reason that in the tradition under discussion the Imam was asked whether we may have recourse to the existing rulers and powers, together with their judicial apparatus.

In his answer the Imam forbids all recourse to illegitimate governments, including both their executive and their judicial branches. He forbids the Muslims to have recourse in any of their affairs to kings and tyrannical rulers, as well as to the judges who act as their agents, even if they have some well-established right that they wish to have enforced. Even if a Muslim's son has been

93

killed or his house has been ransacked, he does not have the right of recourse to oppressive rulers in order to obtain justice. Similarly, if a debt is owed to him and he has irrefutable evidence to that effect, again he may not have recourse to judges who are the servants and appointees of oppressors. If a Muslim does have recourse to them in such cases and obtains his undeniable rights by means of those illegitimate powers and authorities, the result he obtains will be *haram*,[127] and he will have no right to make use of it. Certain *fuqaha* have even gone so far as to say that in cases where property is restored, the same rule applies. For example, if your cloak is stolen from you, and you regain it through the intervention of an illegitimate authority, you have no right to wear it. This particular ruling is open to discussion, but there is no doubt in more general cases. For example, if someone has a debt owed to him and, in order to obtain it, has recourse to a body or authority other than that specified by God, and he subsequently receives his due, he may not legitimately put it to use. The fundamental criteria of the *shari'a* make this necessary.

So this is the political ruling of Islam. It is a ruling that makes Muslims refrain from having recourse to illegitimate powers and their appointed judges, so that non-Islamic and oppressive regimes may fall and the top-heavy judicial systems that produce nothing for the people but trouble may be abolished. This, in turn, would open the way for having recourse to the Imams (upon whom be peace) and those to whom they have assigned the right to govern and judge. The Imams wanted to prevent kings and the judges appointed by them from attaining any form of authority, for God Himself had commanded men to disbelieve in kings and unjust rulers (i.e., to rebel against them),[128] and to have recourse to them would conflict with this duty. If you disbelieve in them and regard them as oppressors who are unfit to rule, you must not have recourse to them.

What, then, is the duty of the Islamic community in this respect? What are they to do when new problems occur and dispute arises among them? To what authority should they have recourse? In the tradition previously quoted, the Imam (upon whom be peace) said: "They must seek out one of you who narrates our traditions, who is versed in what is permissible and what is forbidden"—that is, whenever disputes arise among them, they

94

should seek to have them resolved by those who narrate our *hadith*, are acquainted with what God has made permissible and forbidden, and comprehend our ordinances in accordance with the criteria of reason and the *shari'a*. The Imam did not leave any room for ambiguity lest someone say, "So, scholars of tradition are also to act as authorities and judges." The Imam mentioned all the necessary qualifications and specified that the person to whom we have recourse must be able to give an opinion concerning what is permissible and forbidden in accordance with the well-known rules, must be acquainted with the ordinances of Islam, and must be aware of the criteria needed to identify the traditions originating in *taqiya* or similar circumstances (which are not to be taken as valid). It is obvious that such knowledge of the ordinances of Islam and expertise in the science of tradition is different from mere ability to narrate tradition.

In the same tradition the Imam goes on to say: "I appoint him as ruler over you"—that is, "I appoint as ruler over you one who possesses such qualifications; I appoint anyone who possesses them to conduct the governmental and judicial affairs of the Muslims, and the Muslims do not have the right to have recourse to anyone other than him." Therefore, if a robber steals your property, you should bring your complaint to the authorities appointed by the Imam. If you have a dispute with someone concerning a debt or a loan and you need the truth of the matter to be established, again you should refer the matter to the judge appointed by the Imam, and not to anyone else. This is the universal duty of all Muslims, not simply of 'Umar ibn Hanzala, who, when confronted by a particular problem, obtained the ruling.

This decree issued by the Imam, then, is general and universal in scope. For just as the Commander of the Faithful (upon whom be peace), while he exercised rule, appointed governors and judges whom all Muslims were bound to obey, so, too, Imam Sadiq (upon whom be peace), holding absolute authority and empowered to rule over all the *'ulama*, the *fuqaha*, and the people at large, was able to appoint rulers and judges not only for his own lifetime, but also for subsequent ages. This indeed he did, naming the *fuqaha* as "rulers," so that no one might presume that their function was restricted to judicial affairs and divorced from the other concerns of government.

We may also deduce from the beginning and end of this tradition, as well as from the Qur'anic verse to which it refers, that the Imam was not concerned simply with the appointing of judges and did not leave other duties of the Muslims unclarified, for otherwise, one of the two questions posed to him—that concerned with seeking justice from illicit executive authorities—would have remained unanswered.

This tradition is perfectly clear; there are no doubts surrounding its chain of transmission or its meaning. No one can doubt that the Imam (peace be upon him) designated the *fuqaha* to exercise the functions of both government and judgeship. It is the duty of all Muslims to obey this decree of the Imam.

In order to clarify the matter still further, I will adduce additional traditions, beginning with that of Abu Khadija.

Abu Khadija, one of the trusted companions of Imam Sadiq (upon whom be peace), relates: "I was commanded by the Imam to convey the following message to our friends [i.e., the Shi'a]: 'When enmity and dispute arise among you, or you disagree concerning the receipt or payment of a sum of money, be sure not to refer the matter to one of these malefactors for judgment. Designate as judge and arbiter someone among you who is acquainted with our injunctions concerning what is permitted and prohibited, for I appoint such a man as judge over you. Let none of you take your complaint against another of you to the tyrannical ruling power.' "[129]

The meaning of the phrase "dispute concerning a thing" relates to civil disputes, so that the first part of the Imam's decree means that we are not to have recourse to the malefactors. By "malefactors" are meant those judges whom the rulers of the day and illegitimate governments have allowed to occupy the position of judge. The Imam goes on to say, "Let none of you take your complaint against another of you to the tyrannical ruling power." That is to say, "Whatever personal disputes arise among you, do not have recourse to tyrannical authorities and illegitimate powers; do not seek their aid in matters relating to the executive." The expression "tyrannical ruler" refers, in general, to all illegitimate powers and authorities (that is, all non-Islamic rulers) and embraces all three branches of government—judicial, legislative, and executive. Considering that earlier in the tradition, recourse to tyrannical judges is prohibited, however, it appears that this second prohibition relates to the executive branch. The final sentence is not a repetition of the preceding statement. First, the Imam prohibits having recourse to impious judges in the various matters that are their concern (interrogation, the establishment of proof, and so on), designates those who may act as judge, and clarifies the duties of his followers. Then he declares that they must refrain from having recourse to illegitimate rulers. This makes it plain that the question of judges is separate from that of having recourse to illegitimate authority; they are two different subjects. Both are mentioned in the tradition of 'Umar ibn Hanzala; there, the seeking of justice from both illegitimate authorities and judges is forbidden. In the tradition of Abu Khadija, the Imam has appointed only judges, but in that reported by 'Umar ibn Hanzala, the Imam has designated both those who are to act as ruler and executive and those who are to act as judge.

In accordance with the tradition narrated by Abu Khadija, then, the Imam designated the *fuqaha* as judges in his own life-time, and according to that narrated by 'Umar ibn Hanzala, he assigned them both governmental and judicial authority. We must now examine whether the *fuqaha* automatically forfeited those functions when the Imam left this world. Were all the judges and rulers appointed by the Imams somehow dismissed from their functions when the Imams left?

The governance of the Imams differs, of course, from that of all others; according to the Shi'i school, all the commands and instructions of the Imams must be obeyed, both during their life-time and after their death. But, aside from this consideration, let us see what becomes of the functions and duties they have assigned in this world to the *fuqaha*.

In all existing forms of government, whether monarchical, republican, or following some other model, if the head of state dies or circumstances change so that there is a change in administration, military ranks and appointments are not affected. For example, a general will not automatically be deprived of his rank, an ambassador will not be dismissed from his post, and a minister of finance or a provincial or local governor will not be removed.

The new administration or successor administration may, of course, dismiss or transfer them from their posts, but their functions are not automatically withdrawn from them.

Obviously, certain powers do automatically terminate with the death of the person who conferred them. Such is the case with *ijaza-yi hasbiya*, the authority given someone by a *faqih* to fulfill certain tasks on his behalf in a given town; when the *faqih* dies, this authority expires. But, in another case, if a *faqih* appoints a guardian for a minor or a trustee for an endowment, the appointments he makes are not annulled by his death but continue in force.

The judicial and governmental functions assigned by the Imams to the *fuqaha* of Islam are retained permanently. The Imam (upon whom be peace) was certainly aware of all aspects of the matter, and there can be no possibility of carelessness on his part. He must have known that in all governments of the world the position and authority of individual officeholders is not affected by the death or departure of the head of state. If he had intended that the right to govern and judge should be withdrawn after his death from the *fuqaha* whom he had designated, he would have specified that to be the case, saying: "The *fuqaha* are to exercise these functions as long as I live."

According to this tradition, then, the *'ulama* of Islam have been appointed by the Imam (upon whom be peace) to the positions of ruler and judge, and these positions belong to them in perpetuity. The possibility that the next Imam would have annulled this ruling and dismissed the *fuqaha* from these twin functions is extremely small. For the Imam forbade the Muslims to have recourse to kings and their appointed judges for the purpose of obtaining their rights, and designated recourse to them as equivalent to recourse to the *taghut;* then, referring to the verse that ordains disbelief in *taghut*,[130] he appointed legitimate judges and rulers for the people. If his successor as Imam were not to have assigned the same functions to the *fuqaha*, what should the Muslims have done, and how would they have resolved their differences and disputes? Should they have had recourse to sinners and oppressors, which would have been equivalent to recourse to the *taghut* and thus a violation of divine command? Or should they have had recourse to no one at all, depriving themselves of all authority and refuge, which would have allowed anarchy to take over, with people freely usurping each other's property, transgressing against each other's rights, and being completely unrestrained in all they did?

We are certain that if Imam Sadiq (upon whom be peace) assigned these functions to the *fuqaha*, neither his son Musa nor any of the succeeding Imams abrogated them. Indeed, it is not possible for them to have abrogated these functions and said: "Henceforth, do not have recourse to the just *fuqaha* for the settlement of your affairs; instead, turn to kings, or do nothing at all and allow your rights to be trampled underfoot."

Naturally, if an Imam appoints a judge to a certain city, his successor may dismiss that judge and appoint another in his place, but the positions and functions that have been established cannot themselves be abolished. That is self-evident.

The tradition that I shall now quote supports the thesis I have been advancing. If the only proof I had were one of the traditions I have been citing, I would be unable to substantiate my claim. Its essence, however, has been proved by the traditions already cited; what follows now is by way of supplementary evidence. Imam Sadiq (upon whom be peace) relates that the Prophet (upon whom and whose family be peace and blessings) said: "For whoever travels a path in search of knowledge, God opens up a path to paradise, and the angels lower their wings before him as a sign of their being well pleased [or God's being well pleased]. All that is in the heavens and on earth, even the fish in the ocean, seeks forgiveness for him. The superiority of the learned man over the mere worshipper is like that of the full moon over the stars. Truly the scholars are the heirs of the prophets; the prophets bequeathed not a single dinar or dirham; instead they bequeathed knowledge, and whoever acquires it has indeed acquired a generous portion of their legacy."[131]

The links in the chain of transmission of this tradition are all trustworthy; in fact, Ibrahim ibn Hashim, father of 'Ali ibn Ibrahim, is not moderately trustworthy but outstandingly so. The same tradition has been narrated with a slightly different text by another chain of transmission, one that is sound as far as Abu 'l-Bukhturi, although Abu 'l-Bukhturi himself is of questionable reliability. Here is the second version of the tradition: "Muhammad ibn Yahya relates, on the authority of Ahmad ibn Muhammad ibn 'Isa, who was told it by Muhammad ibn Khalid, to whom it was narrated by Abu 'l-Bukhturi, that Imam Ja'far as-Sadiq (upon whom be peace) said: 'The scholars are the heirs of the prophets, for although the prophets bequeathed not a single dinar or dirham, they bequeathed their sayings and traditions. Whoever, then, acquires a portion of their traditions has indeed acquired a generous portion of their legacy. Therefore, see from whom you may acquire this knowledge, for among us, the Family of the Prophet, there are in each generation just and honest people who will repel those who distort and exaggerate, those who initiate false practices, and those who offer foolish interpretations [that is, they will purify and protect religion from the influence of such biased and ignorant people and others like them].' "[132]

Our purpose in citing this tradition (which has also been referred to by the late Naraqi) is that it clarifies the meaning of the expression: "The scholars are the heirs of the prophets." There are several matters that must be explained at this point.

First, who are "the scholars"? Is it intended to mean the scholars of the Muslim community or the Imams (upon whom be peace)? Some people are of the opinion that probably the Imams are intended. But it would appear that, on the contrary, the scholars of the community—the 'ulama—are intended. The tradition itself indicates this, for the virtues and qualities of the Imams that have been mentioned elsewhere are quite different from what this tradition contains. The statement that the prophets have bequeathed traditions and whoever learns those traditions acquires a generous portion of their legacy cannot serve as a definition of the Imams. It must therefore refer to the scholars of the community. In addition, in the version narrated by Abu 'l-Bukhturi, after the phrase: "The scholars are the heirs of the prophets," we read: "Therefore, see from whom you may acquire this knowledge." It seems that what is intended here is that, indeed, the scholars are the heirs of the prophets, but one must be careful in the choice of a person from whom to acquire the knowledge the prophets have bequeathed. It would contradict the obvious meaning of the tradition, therefore, to maintain that the Imams are intended by the expression "heirs of the prophets" and that it is

from them that people must acquire knowledge. Anyone acquainted with the traditions that relate to the status of the Imams
and the rank accorded them by the Most Noble Messenger (peace
and blessings be upon him and his family) will immediately realize that it is not the Imams but the scholars of the community who
are intended in this tradition. Similar qualities and epithets have
been used for the scholars in numerous other traditions; e.g., "The
scholars of my community are like all the prophets preceding me,"
and "The scholars of my community are like the prophets of the
Children of Israel."

To conclude, then, it is obvious that the *'ulama*—the scholars—are intended here.

There is a second objection that might be raised here, which
calls for clarification. It might be said that the expression: "The
scholars are the heirs of the prophets" cannot be used as a proof of
our thesis—the governance of the *faqih*—since the prophets
(*anbiya*) have only one dimension of prophethood, which is that
they derive knowledge from an exalted source by means of revelation, inspiration, or some other method, and this does not imply
or require rule over the people or the believers. If God Almighty
has not bestowed leadership and rule on the prophets, they can
in no wise possess it; they are only prophets in the narrow sense of
the word. If they have been ordained to communicate the knowledge they have received, then it will be their duty at most to communicate it to the people. For in our traditions, a distinction is
made betwen the prophet (*nabi*) and the messenger (*rasul*): the
latter has the mission of communicating the knowledge he has received, while the former merely receives it. In addition, the state
of prophethood (*nubuvvat*) is different from that of governance
(*vilayat*), and it is this titular designation of "prophet" (*nabi*) that
has been used in this tradition. The scholars have been made the
successors of the prophets with respect to this titular designation,
and since this designation does not imply or necessitate governance (*vilayat*), we cannot deduce from the tradition that the scholars are to possess governance. If the Imam had said that the scholars
hold the rank of Moses or Jesus, we would naturally infer that
the scholars possess all of the aspects and qualities of Moses or
Jesus, including governance, but since he did not say this and did

101

not assign to the scholars the rank of any particular person among the prophets, we cannot draw that particular conclusion from the tradition in question.

In answer to this objection, it must first be stated that the criterion for the understanding of traditions and their wording must be common usage and current understanding, not precise technical analysis, and we, too, follow this criterion. Once a *faqih* tries to introduce subtle technical points into the understanding of traditions, many matters become obscured. So if we examine the expression: "The scholars are the heirs of the prophets" in the light of common usage, will it occur to us that only the titular designation of "prophet" is intended in the tradition, and that the scholars are heirs only to what is implied in that designation? Or on the contrary, does this expression provide a general principle that can be applied to individual prophets? To put it differently: if we were to ask someone who is aware only of the common usage of words, "Is such-and-such a *faqih* a successor of Moses and Jesus?" he would answer—in the light of the tradition under discussion—"Yes, because Moses and Jesus are prophets." Again, if we were to ask, "Is the *faqih* an heir to the Most Noble Messenger (peace and blessings be upon him and his family)?" he would answer, "Yes, because the Most Noble Messenger is one of the prophets."

We cannot, therefore, take the word "prophets" as a titular designation, particularly since it is in the plural. If the singular "prophet" were used in the tradition, then it might be possible that only the titular designation were intended, but since the plural is used, it means "every one of the prophets," not "every one of the prophets with respect to that by virtue of which they are prophets." This latter sense would indeed indicate that the titular designation exclusively was intended, as distinct from all other designations, so that the expression would come to mean, "The *faqih* enjoys the stature of the prophet (*nabi*), but not that of the messenger (*rasul*) nor that of the ruler (*vali*)." Analyses and interpretations like these, however, go against both common usage and reason.

For a third objection, let us suppose that the scholars are given the stature of the prophets with respect to their titular designation, with respect to that by virtue of which they are prophets.

We must then regard the scholars as possessing all the attributes that God Almighty has designated the prophets as possessing, in accordance with this same equation of the scholars with the prophets. If, for example, someone says that so-and-so enjoys the same rank as the just and says next that we must honor the just, we infer from the two statements taken together that we must honor the person in question. This being the case, we can infer from the Qur'anic verse: "The prophet has higher claims on the believers than their own selves" (33:6) that the *'ulama* possess the function of governance just as the prophet does. For what is implicit in having "higher claims" is precisely governance and command. In commenting upon the verse in question, the work *Majma' al-Bahrayn*[133] cites a tradition of Imam Baqir (upon whom be peace): "This verse was revealed concerning governance and command." The prophet, then, is empowered to rule and govern over the believers, and the same rule and governance that has been established for the Most Noble Messenger (peace and blessings be upon him and his family) is also established for the scholars, for both in the verse quoted and in the tradition under discussion the titular designation "prophet" has been used.

We can, moreover, refer to a number of verses that designate the prophet as possessing various qualities and attributes, as, for example: "Obey God and obey the Messenger and the holders of authority from among you" (Qur'an, 4:59). Although a distinction is made in certain traditions between "prophet" and "messenger" with respect to the mode of revelation, rationally and in common usage the two words denote the same meaning. According to common usage, the "prophet" is one who receives tidings from God, and the "messenger" is one who conveys to mankind what he has received from God.

A fourth objection might also be raised. The ordinances that the Most Noble Messenger (peace and blessings be upon him and his family) left are a form of legacy, even though they are not designated technically as such, and those who take up those ordinances are his heirs. But what proof is there that the function of governance that the Prophet exercised could be bequeathed or inherited? It might be that what could be bequeathed and inherited consisted only of his ordinances and his traditions, for the tradition states that the prophets bequeathed knowledge, or, in the version narrated by Abu 'l-Bukhturi, that they bequeathed "a legacy of their sayings and traditions." It is apparent, then, that they bequeathed their traditions, but governance cannot be bequeathed or inherited.

This objection is also unjustified. For governance and command are extrinsic and rational matters; concerning these matters we must have recourse to rational persons. We might ask them whether they regard the transfer of governance and rule from one person to another by way of bequest as possible. For example, if a rational person is asked, "Who is heir to the rule in such-and-such a country?" will he answer that the position of ruler cannot be inherited, or say instead that such-and-such a person is the heir to the crown and the throne? "Heir to the throne" is a well-known current expression. There can be no doubt that, rationally speaking, governance can be transferred from one person to another just like property that is inherited. If one considers first the verse: "The prophet has higher claims on the believers than their own selves," and then the tradition: "The scholars are the heirs of the prophets," he will realize that both refer to the same thing: extrinsic matters that are rationally capable of being transferred from one person to another.

If the phrase: "The scholars are the heirs of the prophets" referred to the Imams (upon whom be peace)—as does the tradition to the effect that the Imams are the heirs of the Prophet (peace and blessings be upon him and his family) in all things—we would not hesitate to say that the Imams are indeed the heirs of the Prophet in all things, and no one could say that the legacy intended here refers only to knowledge and legal questions. So if we had before us only the sentence: "The scholars are the heirs of the prophets" and could disregard the beginning and end of the tradition, it would appear that all functions of the Most Noble Messenger that were capable of being transmitted—including rule over people—and that devolved on the Imams after him, pertain also to the fuqaha, with the exception of those functions that must be excluded for other reasons and which we too exclude wherever there is reason to do so.

The major problem still remaining is that the sentence: "The scholars are heirs of the prophets" occurs in a context suggesting that the traditions of the prophets constitute their legacy. The authentic tradition narrated by Qaddah reads: "The prophets bequeathed not a single dinar or dirham; instead they bequeathed knowledge." That related by Abu 'l-Bukhturi reads: "Although the prophets did not bequeath a single dinar or dirham, they bequeathed their sayings and traditions." These statements provide a context suggesting that the legacy of the prophets is their traditions, and that nothing else has survived of them that might be inherited, particularly since the particle *"innama"* occurs in the text of the tradition, indicating exclusivity.

But even this objection is faulty. For if the meaning were indeed that the Most Noble Messenger (peace and blessings be upon him and his family) had left nothing of himself that might be inherited except his traditions, this would contradict the very bases of our Shi'i school. The Prophet did indeed leave things that could be inherited, and there is no doubt that among them was his exercise of rule over the community, which was transmitted by him to the Commander of the Faithful (upon whom be peace), and then to each of the other Imams (peace be upon them all) in succession. The particle *"innama"* does not always indicate exclusivity, and indeed there are doubts that it ever does; in addition, *"innama"* does not occur in the text narrated by Qaddah, but only in that related by Abu 'l-Bukhturi, whose chain of transmission is weak, as I have already said.

Now let us examine in turn each of the sentences in the text narrated by Qaddah in order to see whether the context does, in fact, indicate that the legacy of the prophets consists exclusively of their traditions.

"For whoever travels a path in search of knowledge, God opens up a path to paradise." This is a sentence in praise of scholars, but not in praise of *any* scholar, so that we imagine the sentence to be uniformly praising all types of scholar. Look up the traditions in *al-Kafi* concerning the attributes and duties of scholars, and you will see that in order to become a scholar and an heir of the prophets, it is not enough to study a few lines. The scholar also has duties he must perform, and therein lies the real difficulty of his calling.

"The angels lower their wings before him as a sign of their being well pleased with him." The meaning of "lower their wings" is obvious to those who concern themselves with these matters. It is an act signifying humility and respect.

"All that is in the heavens and on earth, even the fish in the ocean, seeks forgiveness for him." This sentence does not require detailed explanation because it is not relevant to our present theme.

"The superiority of the learned man over the mere worshipper is like that of the full moon over the stars." The meaning of this sentence is clear.

"Truly the scholars are the heirs of the prophets." The entire tradition, from its beginning down to and including this sentence, is in praise of the scholars and in exposition of their virtues and qualities, one of these qualities being that they are the heirs of the prophets. Being the heirs of the prophets becomes a virtue for the scholars when they exercise governance and rule over the people, like the prophets, and obedience to them is a duty.

The meaning of the next expression in the tradition, "The prophets bequeathed not a single dinar or dirham," is not that they bequeathed nothing but learning and traditions. Rather it is an indication that although the prophets exercised authority and ruled over people, they were men of God, not materialistic creatures trying to accumulate worldly wealth. It also implies that the form of government exercised by the prophets was different from monarchies and other current forms of government, which have served as means for the enrichment and gratification of the rulers.

The way of life of the Most Noble Messenger (peace and blessings be upon him) was extremely simple. He did not use his authority and position to enrich his material life in the hope of leaving a legacy. What he did leave behind was knowledge, the most noble of all things, and in particular, knowledge derived from God Almighty. Indeed, the singling out of knowledge for mention in this tradition may have been precisely because of its nobility.

It cannot be said that since the qualities of the scholars are mentioned in this verse together with their being heirs to knowledge and not heirs to property, therefore, the scholars are heirs *only* to knowledge and traditions.

In certain cases, the phrase: "What we leave behind is charity" has been added to the tradition, but it does not truly belong there. Found only in Sunni versions of the tradition, it has been added for political reasons.[134]

The most we can say with respect to the context these sentences provide for the statement: "The scholars are heirs to the prophets" is that the statement cannot be taken in an absolute sense, which would mean that everything that pertains to the prophets also pertains to the scholars. Nor can the statement, because of its context, be taken in the restricted sense that the scholars are heirs *only* to the knowledge of the prophets. If that were the sense, the tradition would contradict the other traditions we quoted earlier in connection with our theme and tend to negate them. A restricted sense cannot be derived from this.

For the sake of argument, if it were true that this tradition means that the Most Noble Messenger (peace and blessings be upon him and his family) left no legacy but knowledge, and that rulership and governance can be neither bequeathed nor inherited, and if, too, we did not infer from the Prophet's saying: "'Ali is my heir" that the Commander of the Faithful (peace be upon him) was indeed his successor, then we would be obliged to have recourse to *nass*[135] with respect to the successorship of the Commander of the Faithful and the remaining Imams (peace be upon them). We would then follow the same method with respect to the exercise of governance by the *faqih*, for according to the tradition cited above, the *fuqaha* have been appointed to the functions of successorship and rule. Thus we have reconciled this tradition with those that indicate appointment.

In his *'Awa'id*,[136] Naraqi quotes the following tradition from the *Fiqh-i Rizavi*[137]: "The rank of the *faqih* in the present age is like that of the prophets of the Children of Israel." Naturally, we cannot claim that the *Fiqh-i Rizavi* was actually composed by Imam Riza, but it is permissible to quote it as a further support for our thesis.

It must be understood that what is meant by "the prophets of the Children of Israel" are indeed prophets, not *fuqaha* who lived in the time of Moses and may have been called prophets for some reason or other. The *fuqaha* who lived in the time of Moses were all subject to his authority and exercised their functions in obedience to him. It may be that when he dispatched them somewhere to convey a message, he would also appoint them as "holders of authority"—naturally, we are not precisely informed about these matters—but it is obvious that Moses himself was one of the prophets of the Children of Israel, and that all of the functions that existed for the Most Noble Messenger (peace and blessings be upon him and his family) also existed for Moses, with a difference, of course, in rank, station, and degree. We deduce from the general scope of the word "rank" in this tradition, therefore, that the same function of rulership and governance that Moses exercised exists also for the *fuqaha*.

The *Jami' al-Akhbar*[138] contains the following tradition of the Most Noble Messenger (peace and blessings be upon him and his family): "On the Day of Judgment I will take pride in the scholars of my community, for the scholars of my community are like the prophets preceding me." This tradition also serves to support my thesis.

In the *Mustadrak*,[139] a tradition is quoted from the *Ghurar*[140] to the following effect: "The scholars are rulers over the people." One version reads *"hukama"* ("wise men") instead of *"hukkam"* ("rulers"), but this appears to be incorrect. According to the *Ghurar*, the form *"hukkam"* is correct. The meaning of this tradition is self-evident, and if its chain of transmission is valid, it may also serve to support my thesis.

There are still additional traditions that may be quoted. One of them is quoted in *Tuhaf al-'Uqul*[141] under the heading: "The Conduct of Affairs and the Enforcement of Ordinances by the Scholars." The tradition consists of two parts. The first is a tradition transmitted by the Lord of the Martyrs (peace be upon him) from the Commander of the Faithful, 'Ali (peace be upon him), and concerns the enjoining of the good and the prohibition of the evil. The second part is the speech of the Lord of the Martyrs concerning the governance of the *faqih* and the duties that are incumbent upon the *fuqaha*, such as the struggle against oppressors and tyrannical governments in order to establish an Islamic government and implement the ordinances of Islam. In the course of this celebrated speech, which he delivered at Mina,[142] he set forth the reasons for his own *jihad* against the tyrannical Umayyad state. Two important themes may be deduced from this tradition. The first is the principle of the governance of the *faqih,* and the second is that the *fuqaha*, by means of *jihad* and enjoining the good and forbidding the evil, must expose and overthrow tyrannical rulers and rouse the people so that the universal movement of all alert Muslims can establish Islamic government in place of tyrannical regimes.

This is the tradition.[143] The Lord of the Martyrs (upon whom be peace) said: "O people, take heed of the counsel God gave His friends when He rebuked the rabbis by saying, 'Why do their scholars and rabbis not forbid their sinful talk and consumption of what is forbidden [that is, such talk and consumption on the part of the Jews]? Truly what they have done is evil' (Qur'an, 5:63). Again God says: 'Cursed by the tongue of David and Jesus, son of Mary, are those among the Children of Israel who have failed to believe on account of their rebellion and transgression. They did not prevent each other from committing vile and corrupt acts; what they did was abominable!' (Qur'an, 5:78). God blamed and reproached them because they saw with their own eyes the oppressors committing vile and corrupt acts, but did not stop them, out of love for the income they received from them as well as fear of persecution and injury. However, God orders us to fear Him, not men, and He says: 'The believing men and women are friends and protectors to each other; they enjoin the good and forbid the evil' (Qur'an, 9:71).

"We see that in this verse, in the course of enumerating the attributes of the believers, the attributes that indicate mutual affection, solicitude, and the desire to guide each other, God begins with enjoining the good and forbidding the evil, considering this the prime duty. For He knows that if this duty is performed and is established within society, performance of all other duties will follow, from the easiest to the most difficult. The reason for this is that enjoining the good and forbidding the evil means summoning people to Islam, which is a struggle to establish correct belief in the face of external opposition, while at the same time vindicating the rights of the oppressed; opposing and struggling against oppressors within the community; and endeavoring to ensure that public wealth and the income derived from war are distributed in accordance with the just laws of Islam, and that taxes [zakat and all other forms of fiscal income, whether compulsory or voluntary] are collected, levied, and expended in due and proper form.

"O scholars, you who are celebrated and enjoy good repute on account of your learning! You have achieved fame in society because of your devotion, the good counsel you impart, and the guidance you dispense. It is on account of God that men venerate and stand in awe of you, so that even the powerful fear you and feel compelled to rise respectfully before you, and men who are not subject to you and over whom you hold no authority willingly regard themselves as your subordinates and grant you favors they deny themselves. When the people do not receive their due from the public treasury, you intervene and act with the awesomeness and imperiousness of monarchs and the stature of the great. Have you not earned all these forms of respect and prestige because of men's hopes that you will implement God's laws, even though in most instances you have failed to do so?

"You have failed to enforce most of the rights you were entrusted to preserve. You have neglected the rights of the oppressed and the lowly, squandered the rights of the weak and the powerless, but pursued assiduously what you regard as your personal rights. You have not spent your money or risked your lives for the sake of the One Who gave you life, nor have you fought against any group or tribe for the sake of God. You desire, and regard it as your due, that He should grant you paradise, the company of the Prophet, and security from hellfire in the hereafter. You who have such expectations of God, I fear that the full weight of His wrath will descend upon you, for although it is by His might and glory that you have achieved high rank, you show no respect to those who truly know God and wish to disseminate their knowledge, while you yourselves enjoy respect among God's bondsmen on His account.

"I am also afraid for you for another reason: you see the covenants enacted with God* being violated and trampled underfoot, yet you show no anxiety. When it comes to the covenants enacted with your fathers, you become greatly disturbed and anxious if they are only violated in part, but the pledges you have given to the Most Noble Messenger** are a matter of complete indifference

---

* I.e., the social contracts that establish the institutions of society and determine social relations in Islam. (Kh.)

** I.e., Islamic relationships based upon the oath of loyalty sworn to the Prophet and the similar pledge to obey and follow his successors, 'Ali and his descendants, given to the Prophet at the pool of Khum. (Kh.)

to you. The blind, the dumb, and the poverty-stricken cultivators of the land everywhere lack protectors and no mercy is shown them. You do not behave in accordance with your function and rank, nor do you support or pay any regard to those who do so behave and who strive to promote the standing of the religious scholars. You purchase your safety from the oppressive ruling powers with flattery, cajolery, and compromise.

"All these activities have been forbidden you by God, and He has, moreover, commanded you to forbid each other to engage in them, but you pay no attention. The disaster that has befallen you is greater than what has befallen others, for the true rank and degree of 'ulama has been taken away from you. The administration of the country, the issuing of judicial decrees, and the approving of legislative programs should actually be entrusted to religious scholars who are guardians of the rights of God and knowledgeable about God's ordinances concerning what is permitted and what is forbidden. But your position has been usurped from you, for no other reason than that you have abandoned the pivot of truth—the law of Islam and God's decree—and have disagreed about the nature of the Sunna, despite the existence of clear proofs.

"If you were true men, strong in the face of torture and suffering and prepared to endure hardship for God's sake, then all proposed regulations would be brought to you for your approval and for you to issue; authority would lie in your hands. But you allowed the oppressors to take away your functions and permitted government, which is supposed to be regulated by the provisions of the *shari'a,* to fall into their hands, so that they administer it on the shaky basis of their own conjectures and suppositions and make arbitrariness and the satisfaction of lust their consistent practice. What enabled them to gain control of government was your fleeing in panic from being killed, your attachment to the transitory life of this world. With that mentality and the conduct it inspires, you have delivered the powerless masses into the clutches of the oppressors. While some cringe like slaves under the blows of the oppressors, and others search in misery and desperation for bread and water, the rulers are entirely absorbed in the pleasures of kingship, earning shame and disgrace for themselves with their licentiousness, following evil counselors, and showing impudence toward God. One of their appointed spokesmen mounts the *minbar*[144] in each city. The soil of the homeland is defenseless before them, and they grab freely whatever they want of it. The people are their slaves and are powerless to defend themselves. One ruler is a dictator by nature, malevolent and rancorous; another represses his wretched subjects ruthlessly, plundering by imposing on them all kinds of burdens; and still another refuses in his absolutism to recognize either God or the Day of Judgment! Is it not strange—how can one not think it strange—that society is in the clutches of a cunning oppressor whose tax collectors are oppressors and whose governors feel no compassion or mercy toward the believers under their rule?

"It is God Who will judge concerning what is at dispute among us and deliver a decisive verdict concerning all that occurs among us.

"O God! You know that everything we did [that is, the struggle in which they had recently engaged against the Umayyads] was not prompted by rivalry for political power, nor by a search for wealth and abundance; rather it was done in order to demonstrate to men the shining principles and values of Your religion, to reform the affairs of Your land, to protect and secure the indisputable rights of Your oppressed servants, and to act in accordance with the duties You have established and the norms, laws, and ordinances You have decreed.

"So, O scholars of religion! You are to help us reach this goal, win back our rights from those powers who have considered it acceptable to wrong you and who have attempted to put out the light kindled by your Prophet. God the One suffices us—upon Him do we rely, to Him do we turn, in His hands lies our fate, and to Him shall we return."

When the Lord of the Martyrs said at the beginning of this sermon: "O people, take heed of the counsel God gave His friends when He rebuked the rabbis," his address was not restricted to a particular group of people—those present in the assembly, the inhabitants of a certain city, town, or country, or even all people alive in the world at the time. Rather it embraces all who hear the summons at whatever time, for it begins with the expression "O people" (*ya ayyuha 'n-nas*), which occurs in the Qur'an with the same universal meaning.[145] When God rebukes the rabbis—the Jewish scholars—and condemns their behavior, He is at the same time addressing His friends (*awliya*) and advising them. The word *"awliya"* means here those who have set their faces toward God and hold responsible positions in society, not the Twelve Imams.[146]

God says in the verse we are examining: "Why do their scholars and rabbis not forbid their sinful talk and consumption of what is forbidden? Truly what they have done is evil." Thus He reproaches the rabbis and Jewish religious scholars for failing to prevent the oppressors' sinful talk—a term that includes lying, slander, distorting the truth, and so forth—and consumption of what is forbidden. It is obvious that this reproach and upbraiding is not confined to the scholars of the Jews, nor for that matter to those of the Christians; it applies also to the religious scholars in Islamic society, or indeed, any other society. If the religious scholars of Islamic society are silent, therefore, in the face of the policies of the oppressors, they too are reproached and condemned by God; and here there is no distinction between scholars of the past, present, and future—they are equal in this regard. The Lord of the Martyrs (upon whom be peace) made reference to this verse of the Qur'an so that the religious scholars of Islamic society would take heed, awaken, and no longer neglect their duty of enjoining the good and forbidding the evil or stay silent in the face of the oppressive and deviant ruling classes.

There are two points to which he draws attention by citing this verse. First, the religious scholars' neglect of their duties is more harmful than the failure of others to perform their normal duties. If a bazaar merchant, for example, does something wrong, it is only he who suffers the harm that results. But if the religious scholars fail in fulfilling their duties, by keeping silent, let us say, in the face of tyranny, Islam itself suffers as a result. But if, on the contrary, they act in accordance with their duty and speak out when they should, eschewing silence, then Islam itself will benefit.

Secondly, although all things contrary to the *shari'a* must be forbidden, emphasis has been placed on sinful talk and consumption of what is forbidden, implying that these two evils are more dangerous than all others and must therefore be more diligently combatted. Sometimes the statements and propaganda put forth by oppressive regimes are more harmful to Islam and the Muslims than their actions and policy, endangering the whole repute of

Islam and the Muslims. God reproaches the religious scholars, therefore, for failing to prevent the oppressors from uttering dishonest words and spreading sinful propaganda. He says in effect: "Why did they not denounce the man who falsely claimed to be God's viceregent on earth and the instrument of His will, who claimed to be enforcing God's laws in the right way and to have a correct understanding and practice of Islamic justice, even though he was incapable of comprehending what justice is? Claims like these are a form of sinful talk that is extremely harmful to society. Why did the religious scholars not prevent them from being made? The tyrants who uttered this nonsense committed treason and brought evil innovations[147] into Islam; why did the religious scholars not stand in their way and make them desist from these sins?"

If someone interprets God's ordinances in a way displeasing to Him, thus introducing an evil innovation in Islam, or executes laws that are anti-Islamic, claiming to be acting in accordance with the requirements of Islamic justice, it is the duty of the religious scholars to proclaim their opposition. If they fail to do so, they will be cursed by God, as is apparent both from the verse under discussion and from this tradition: "When evil innovations appear, it is the duty of the scholar to bring forth his knowledge [by condemning them]; otherwise, God's curse will be upon him."

In such cases, the expression of opposition and the expounding of God's teachings and ordinances that stand in contradiction to innovation, oppression, and sin are also useful in themselves, for they make the masses aware of the corruption of society and the wrongdoing of the treacherous, sinful, and irreligious rulers. The people will then rise up in revolt and refuse to collaborate any longer with the tyrants or to obey corrupt and treacherous ruling powers. The expression of opposition by religious scholars is a form of "forbidding the evil" on the part of the religious leadership, which creates in its wake a wave of broad opposition and "forbidding the evil" on the part of all religiously inclined and honorable people. If the oppressive and deviant rulers do not bow to the wishes of such an oppositional movement by returning to the straight path of Islam and obedience to God's laws, but attempt to silence it by force of arms, they will, in effect, have engaged in armed aggression against the Muslims and acquired the status of a rebellious group (*fi'a baghiya*). It will then be the duty of the Muslims to engage in an armed *jihad* against that ruling group in order to make the policies ruling society and the norms of government conform to the principles and ordinances of Islam.

It is true that at present, you do not have the power to prevent the innovative practices of the rulers or to halt the corruption in which they are engaged. But at least do not stay silent. If they strike you on the head, cry out in protest! Do not submit to oppression; such submission is worse than oppression itself. In order to counteract their press and propaganda apparatus, we must create our own apparatus to refute whatever lies they issue and to proclaim that Islamic justice is not what they claim it is, but on the contrary, has a complete and coherent program for ordering the affairs of the family and all Muslim society. All these matters must be made clear so that people can come to know the truth and coming generations will not take the silence of the religious leaders as proof that the deeds and policies of the oppressors conform to the *shari'a*, and that the perspicuous religion of Islam allows them to "consume what is forbidden," or in other words, to plunder the wealth of the people.

Since the range of thought of some people is confined to the mosque we are now sitting in and is incapable of extending any further, when they hear the expression "consumption of what is forbidden," they can only think of some corner grocer who is (God forbid) selling his customers short. They never think of the whole range of more important forms of "consuming what is forbidden," of plunder. Huge amounts of capital are being swallowed up; our public funds are being embezzled; our oil is being plundered; and our country is being turned into a market for expensive, unnecessary goods by the representatives of foreign companies, which makes it possible for foreign capitalists and their local agents to pocket the people's money. A number of foreign states carry off our oil after drawing it out of the ground, and the negligible sum they pay to the regime they have installed returns to their pockets by other routes. As for the small amount that goes into the treasury, God only knows what it is spent on. All of this is a form of "consumption of what is forbidden" that takes place on an enormous scale, in fact on an international scale. It is not merely an evil, but a hideous and most dangerous evil. Examine carefully the conditions of society and the actions of the government and its component organs, and then you will understand what hideous "consumption of what is forbidden" is taking place now. If an earthquake occurs in some corner of the country, it too becomes a means for the ruling profiteers to increase their illegal income: they fill their pockets with the money that is supposed to go to the victims of the earthquake. Whenever our oppressive, anti-national rulers enter into agreements with foreign states or companies, they pocket huge amounts of our people's money and lavish additional huge sums on their foreign masters. It is a veritable flood of forbidden consumption that sweeps past us, right before our eyes. All this misappropriation of wealth goes on and on: in our foreign trade and in the contracts made for the exploitation of our mineral wealth, the utilization of our forests and other natural resources, construction work, road building, and the purchase of arms from the imperialists, both Western and communist.

We must end all this plundering and usurpation of wealth. The people as a whole have a responsibility in this respect, but the responsibility of the religious scholars is graver and more critical. We must take the lead over other Muslims in embarking on this sacred *jihad*, this heavy undertaking; because of our rank and position, we must be in the forefront. If we do not have the power today to prevent these misdeeds from happening and to punish these embezzlers and traitors, these powerful thieves that rule over us, then we must work to gain that power. At the same time, to fulfill our minimum obligation, we must not fail to expound the truth and expose the thievery and mendacity of our rulers. When we come to power, we will not only put the country's political life, economy, and administration in order, we will also whip and chastise the thieves and the liars.

They set fire to the Masjid al-Aqsa.[148] We cry out: "Leave the Masjid al-Aqsa half-burned to the ground; do not erase all traces of the crime!" But the Shah's regime opens an account, sets up a fund, and starts collecting money from the people supposedly to rebuild the Masjid al-Aqsa, but really to fill the pockets of our rulers while also covering up the the crime committed by Israel.

These are the disasters that are afflicting the nation of Islam and that have brought us to our present state. Is it not the duty of the scholars of Islam to speak out about all this? "Why do their rabbis not forbid their consumption of what is forbidden?" Why do our Muslim scholars not protest? Why do they say nothing about all this plundering?

To return to the sermon of the Lord of the Martyrs (upon whom be peace), he continues with a reference to the verse: "Cursed are those among the Children of Israel who have failed to believe" (5:78). This is not relevant to our present discussion. Then he says: "God reproached and blamed them [the rabbis] because they saw with their own eyes the oppressors committing vile and corrupt acts but did not stop them." According to the Lord of the Martyrs, their silence was due to two factors: greed and baseness. Either they were covetous persons who profited materially from the oppressors, accepting payment to keep quiet, or they were faint-hearted cowards who were afraid of them.

Consult the traditions referring to enjoining the good and forbidding the evil. There the conduct of those who constantly invent excuses in order to escape from doing their duty is condemned and their silence is considered shameful. "God says: 'Do not fear men, but fear me' (2:150). This verse means roughly: 'Why do you fear men? Our friends (awliya) have given up their lives for the sake of Islam; you should be prepared to do the same.'

"Elsewhere in the Qur'an God also says: 'The believers, men and women, are friends and protectors to each other; they enjoin the good and forbid the evil; . . . they establish the prayer, pay the zakat, and obey God and His Messenger' (9:71). In this verse, God mentions the duty of enjoining the good and forbidding the evil first because He knows that if this duty is correctly performed, all other duties, whether easy or difficult, will fall into place. For enjoining the good and forbidding the evil means summoning men to Islam while at the same time remedying oppression, opposing the oppressor, making just distribution of the spoils of war, and levying and spending taxes in just and due form."

If the duty of enjoining the good and forbidding the evil is properly performed, all other duties will automatically fall into place. If the good is enjoined and the evil forbidden, the oppressors and their agents will be unable to usurp the people's property and dispose of it according to their own whims; they will be unable to squander the taxes taken from the people. For he who enjoins the good and forbids the evil actively calls men to Islam by remedying injustice and opposing the oppressor.

Enjoining the good and forbidding the evil has been made a duty primarily for the sake of accomplishing these high aims. We have restricted it, however, to a narrow category of affairs where harm is suffered chiefly by the individual who is guilty of a sin by deed or by omission. We have the idea firmly in our heads that the instances of evil we are called upon to combat (*munkarat*) are only the things we encounter or hear about in everyday life. For example, if someone plays music while we are riding on the bus,[149] or the owner of a coffee house does something wrong, or someone eats in the middle of the bazaar during Ramadan,[150] we regard all these things as instances of evil we must denounce. Meanwhile, we remain totally oblivious to far greater evils. Those who are destroying the welfare of Islam and trampling on the rights of the weak—it is they whom we must force to desist from evil.

If a collective protest were made against the oppressors who commit an improper act or crime, if several thousand telegrams were sent to them from all the Islamic countries telling them to desist, to relinquish their errors, they certainly would desist. If every time a step were taken or a speech given against the interests of Islam and the welfare of the people, those responsible were condemned throughout the country, in every single village and hamlet, they would be obliged to retreat. Could they possibly do otherwise? Never! I know them; I know what kind of people they are. They are very cowardly and would retreat very quickly. But if they see that we are more gutless than they are, they will give themselves airs and do whatever they want.

When the 'ulama of Qum met and banded together on one occasion, and the provinces supported them by sending delegations and delivering speeches to show their solidarity, the regime retreated and canceled the measure we were objecting to.[151] Afterwards they were able to cool our enthusiasm and weaken us; they divided us up and invented a separate "religious duty" for each of us. As a result of the differing opinions that appeared among us, they grew bold again, and now they do whatever they want with the Muslims and this Islamic country of ours.

The Lord of the Martyrs (upon whom be peace) speaks of "summoning men to Islam while at the same time remedying oppression and opposing the oppressors"; it is for the sake of these great aims that enjoining the good and forbidding the evil has been made a duty. If some poor grocer does something wrong, he has not harmed Islam, but only himself. In performing our duty of enjoining the good and forbidding the evil, we must pay closest attention to those who harm Islam and those who, under various pretexts, plunder the people's means of livelihood.

On occasion we read in the paper—sometimes it is stated humorously, sometimes seriously—that many of the items collected for the victims of floods or earthquakes are picked up by our rulers for their own use. One of the 'ulama of Malayer told me that the people had wanted to send a truckload of shrouds for the victims of some disaster, but the police refused to let them through and even tried to confiscate the load! "Enjoining the good and forbidding the evil" is most imperative in such cases.

Now let me ask you, were the subjects mentioned by the Lord of the Martyrs in his sermon addressed only to his companions who were gathered around him listening to his words? Does not the phrase "O people, take heed" address us too? Are we not included in "people"? Should we not profit from this address of the Lord of the Martyrs?

As I stated at the beginning of this discussion, the subjects contained in the sermon of the Lord of the Martyrs were not intended for a single group or class. His address was more in the nature of a circular directed to all commanders, ministers, rulers, *fuqaha*— in short, to the whole world, particularly those who are alive and fully conscious. The circulars he issued belong together with the Qur'an in the sense that they demand our obedience until the Day of Resurrection. The verse referred to in the address speaks only of the Jewish scholars and rabbis, but its purport is universal. The Jewish scholars and rabbis were condemned by God because fear or covetousness made them keep silent in the face of the misdeeds of the oppressors, whereas if they had spoken or cried out in protest, they could have prevented oppression from occurring. If the 'ulama of Islam likewise fail to rise up against the oppressors and remain silent instead, they too will be condemned.

After addressing the people in general, the Lord of the Martyrs then turns to a particular group, the 'ulama of Islam, and tells them: "You enjoy prestige and standing in society; the nation of

Islam respects and venerates you. You are held in awe and have high standing in society because you are expected to rise up against the oppressors in defense of the truth and to compel the oppressor to enforce the rights of the oppressed. Men have placed their hopes in you for the establishment of justice and the prevention of transgression by the oppressors.

"Thus you have reached a certain station and rank. But you have failed to perform the duties of your station. If some harm were to befall the father of one of you, or if—God forbid—someone were to insult him, you would be greatly distressed and would cry out in protest. But now that God's covenants are being violated before your very eyes and Islam is being dishonored, you keep silent and are not distressed even in your hearts, for if you were distressed, you would be bound to raise your voices in protest. The blind, the dumb, and the poverty-stricken cultivators of the land are being destroyed and nobody shows any concern; no one is concerned for the wretched, barefooted people."

Do you imagine all that bombastic propaganda being broadcast on the radio is true? Go see for yourself at first hand what state our people are living in. Not even one out of every two hundred villages has a clinic. No one is concerned about the poor and the hungry, and they do not allow the measures Islam has devised for the sake of the poor to be implemented. Islam has solved the problem of poverty and inscribed it at the very top of its program: "*Sadaqat* is for the poor."[152] Islam is aware that first, the conditions of the poor must be remedied, the conditions of the deprived must be remedied. But *they* do not allow the plans of Islam to be implemented.

Our wretched people subsist in conditions of poverty and hunger, while the taxes that the ruling class extorts from them are squandered. They buy Phantom jets so that pilots from Israel and its agents can come and train in them in our country.[153] So extensive is the influence of Israel in our country—Israel, which is in a state of war with the Muslims, so that those who support it are likewise in a state of war with the Muslims—and so great is the support the regime gives it, that Israeli soldiers come to our country for training! Our country has become a base for them! The markets of our country are also in their hands. If matters go on this way, and the Muslims continue to be apathetic, the Muslims will lose all say in the commercial life of the country.

To return to the address of the Lord of the Martyrs (upon whom be peace): "You have not made proper use of your station. Not only do you do nothing yourselves; you fail to support the person who does want to do his duty. The only source of concern and satisfaction for you is that you have the support and respect of the oppressor, that he addresses you as 'Noble Shaikh'! What the nation suffers at the hands of the government is of no concern to you. The disaster that has befallen you is greater than what has befallen others for the true rank and degree of 'ulama have been taken away from you. The administration of affairs and the implementation of law ought to be undertaken by those who are knowledgeable concerning God and are trustees of God's ordinances concerning what is permitted and what is forbidden. But that rank has been taken away from you."

The Imam (upon whom be peace) could have said at this point: "What is my right has been taken away from me, but you do not come to my aid," or, "The rights of the Imams have been taken away, but you have kept silent." Instead, he spoke of those "knowledgeable concerning God" (al-'ulama bi-'llah), meaning the religious scholars (rabbaniyun) or leaders. Here he is not referring to the philosophers or mystics, for the person knowledgeable concerning God is the one who is learned in God's ordinances. It is such a person who is designated a religious scholar (ruhani or rabbani), naturally on condition that spirituality (ruhaniyat) and orientation to God Almighty be fully apparent in him.

The Imam went on: "But your position has been usurped from you, for no other reason but that you have abandoned the pivot of truth and have disagreed about the nature of the Sunna, despite the existence of clear proofs. But if you were to show strength in the face of hardship and suffering for God's sake, then the conduct of affairs, as willed by God, would be restored to you; command and authority would be yours."

If you were to act correctly and perform your duty, you would see that the conduct of affairs would be bound over to you. If the form of government willed by Islam were to come into being, none of the governments now existing in the world would be able to resist it; they would all capitulate. But unfortunately, we have failed to establish such a government. Even in the earliest age of Islam, its opponents hindered its establishment and prevented government from being entrusted to the person chosen by God and His Messenger precisely in order to prevent what has happened.

"You allowed the oppressors to take away your functions." When you failed to perform your duties and abandoned the task of government, it became possible for the oppressors to take over the position that was legitimately yours. "You allowed the affairs of God to fall into their hands, so they came to conduct them on the basis of their suppositions and arbitrary desires. What enabled them to win this control was your panic-stricken flight from being killed, and your attachment to the life of this world. You have delivered the powerless into their clutches, so that some of the people are now subjugated like slaves and others are deprived of even their livelihood." All of this applies to the age we live in; in fact, it applies more fully to the present than to the time of the Imam (upon whom be peace). "The rulers are entirely absorbed in the pleasures of kingship, earning shame and disgrace for themselves with their licentiousness, following evil counselors, and showing impudence toward God. One of their appointed spokesmen mounts the *minbar* in each city to tell lies." In those days, preachers would praise the oppressors from the *minbar*. Today, radio stations fill the air with propaganda on their behalf and maliciously misrepresent the ordinances of Islam.

"The earth is defenseless against them." Now, too, the oppressors can freely exploit the earth, without any obstruction; there is no one to stand in their way. "They grab freely whatever they want [of the earth]. The people are their slaves and are powerless to defend themselves. One ruler is an obstinate tyrant, while another represses his wretched subjects ruthlessly, and still another refuses in his absolutism to recognize God as the beginning and end of all things. Is it not strange—how could one not think it strange—that the world is in the clutches of cunning tyrants, oppressive tax collectors, and governors who have no compassion for the believers under their rule?

"It is God Who will judge concerning what is at dispute among us, and deliver a decisive verdict concerning all that occurs among us.

"O God! You know that everything we did was not prompted by rivalry for political power, nor by desire for the chattels of this world. Rather it was done in order to demonstrate the signs of Your religion, to reform the affairs of Your land, to protect the oppressed among Your servants, and to act in accordance with the duties, norms, and ordinances You have established.

"So, O scholars of religion! Help us reach our goal and obtain our rights. The oppressors will wax strong in their efforts against you and will attempt to put out the light kindled by your Beloved [the Prophet]. But God suffices us; upon Him do we rely, to Him do we turn, and to Him is our journeying."

As we said, the entire address from beginning to end is addressed to the *'ulama*. There is no indication that the persons intended by the expression "those knowledgeable about God" are the Imams (upon whom be peace). They are the scholars of Islam, the *rabbaniyun*. The designation *rabbani* refers to one who believes in God, fulfills God's ordinances, and is knowledgeable concerning those ordinances, as a trustee of God's decrees concerning what is permitted and what is forbidden.

When the Imam (upon whom be peace) said that the conduct of affairs belongs to the *'ulama*, he did not mean to restrict this function to a period of ten or twenty years, or simply to the city and people of Medina. It is apparent from the whole speech that his meaning was more universal, that he had in mind a vast community that would undertake the establishment of justice.

If the *'ulama*, who are the trustees of God's decrees concerning what is permitted and what is forbidden and who possess the two characteristics of knowledge and justice as set forth above—if they were to implement God's ordinances, to execute the penal provisions of the law, and generally to conduct and administer the affairs of the Muslims, the people would no longer be hungry and wretched and the laws of Islam would no longer be in abeyance.

The tradition containing this noble speech, then, is part of the evidence supporting our thesis, the governance of the *faqih*. Were its chain of transmission not weak, we could cite it as a direct proof. Even as it stands, we might say that the content of the tradition, being veracious, bears witness that it was uttered by one of the *ma'sumin*.[154]

We have now completed our discussion of the governance of the *faqih;* we have nothing further to say on the subject. There is no need to go into details such as the manner in which *zakat* is to be collected or spent, or how the penal provisions of the law are to be implemented. We have set forth the main principles of the subject and shown that the same governance that was exercised by the Most Noble Messenger (upon whom and whose family be peace and blessings), and by the Imams (upon whom be peace), is also the prerogative of the *fuqaha*. There can be no doubt about this. If there is any evidence, however, that in certain specific cases the *faqih* does not possess the same right of governance, we naturally exclude such cases from the operation of the general rule.

As I stated previously, the subject of the governance of the *faqih* is not something new that I have invented; since the very beginning, it has been mentioned continually.

The ruling given by the late Mirza Hasan Shirazi[155] prohibiting the use of tobacco was in effect a governmental ruling; hence all other *fuqaha* were obliged to follow it, and indeed the great *'ulama* of Iran did follow it, with only a few exceptions. It was not a judicial ruling on a matter being disputed by a few individuals, based purely on his own determination. It was instead a governmental ruling, based on the interests of Islam and the Muslims and his determination of a secondary consideration (*'unvan-i sanavi*).[156] As long as this secondary consideration obtained, the ruling retained its validity, and when the consideration no longer applied, the ruling also ceased to apply.

Again, when Mirza Muhammad Taqi Shirazi[157] gave orders for *jihad*—or "defense," they called it—all the *'ulama* obeyed, because his order was a governmental ruling.

It is related that the late Kashif al-Ghita[158] also used to expound much of what I have said. Among other modern scholars, the late Naraqi also was of the opinion that the *fuqaha* are entitled to exercise all the worldly functions of the Most Noble Messenger (upon whom and whose family be peace and blessings). The late

Na'ini also believed that the doctrine of the governance of the *faqih* may be deduced from the *maqbula* of 'Umar ibn Hanzala.[159]

In any case, this subject is by no means new. I have simply examined it at greater length, with reference to the different branches of government, to give the subject greater clarity for my listeners. In accordance with the commands of God Almighty, as expressed in His Book and by the tongue of His Most Noble Messenger (upon whom and whose family be peace and blessings), I have also set forth certain matters of importance to the present age.

We have stressed the main principles of the subject. Now it is up to the present and future generations to discuss it further and reflect upon it, and to find a way to translate it into reality, eschewing all forms of apathy, weakness, and despair. God Almighty willing, by means of mutual consultation and the exchange of views, they will develop a method for establishing an Islamic government with all its various branches and departments. They will entrust the affairs of government to persons who are honest, intelligent, believing, and competent and remove traitors from control of the government, the homeland, and the treasury of the Muslims. Let them be assured that God Almighty is with them.

4

PROGRAM FOR THE ESTABLISHMENT OF AN ISLAMIC GOVERNMENT

IT IS OUR DUTY TO WORK toward the establishment of an Islamic government. The first activity we must undertake in this respect is the propagation of our cause; that is how we must begin.

It has always been that way, all over the world: a group of people came together, deliberated, made decisions, and then began to propagate their aims. Gradually the number of like-minded people would increase, until finally they became powerful enough to influence a great state or even to confront and overthrow it, as was the case with the downfall of Muhammad 'Ali Mirza and the supplanting of his absolute monarchy with constitutional government.[160] Such movements began with no troops or armed power at their disposal; they always had to resort to propagating the aims of their movement first. The thievery and tyranny practiced by the regime would be condemned and the people awakened and made to understand that the thievery inflicted on them was wrong. Gradually the scope of this activity would be expanded until it came to embrace all groups of society, and the people, awakened and active, would attain their goal.

You have neither a country nor an army now, but propagating activity is possible for you, because the enemy has been unable to deprive you of all the requisite means.

You must teach the people matters relating to worship, of course, but more important are the political, economic, and legal aspects of Islam. These are, or should be, the focus of our concern. It is our duty to begin exerting ourselves now in order to establish a truly Islamic government. We must propagate our cause to the people, instruct them in it, and convince them of its validity. We must generate a wave of intellectual awakening, to emerge as a current throughout society, and gradually, to take shape as an organized Islamic movement made up of the awakened, committed, and religious masses who will rise up and establish an Islamic government.

Propagation and instruction, then, are our two fundamental and most important activities. It is the duty of the *fuqaha* to promulgate religion and instruct the people in the creed, ordinances, and institutions of Islam, in order to pave the way in society for the implementation of Islamic law and the establishment of Islamic institutions. In one of the traditions we have cited, you will have noticed that the successors of the Most Noble Messenger (upon whom be peace and blessings) are described as "teaching the people"—that is, instructing them in religion.

This duty is particularly important under the present circumstances, for the imperialists, the oppressive and treacherous rulers, the Jews, Christians, and materialists are all attempting to distort the truths of Islam and lead the Muslims astray. Our responsibilities of propagation and instruction are greater than ever before. We see today that the Jews (may God curse them) have meddled with the text of the Qur'an and have made certain changes in the Qur'ans they have had printed in the occupied territories.[161] It is our duty to prevent this treacherous interference with the text of the Qur'an. We must protest and make the people aware that the Jews and their foreign backers are opposed to the very foundations of Islam and wish to establish Jewish domination throughout the world. Since they are a cunning and resourceful group of people, I fear that—God forbid!—they may one day achieve their goal, and that the apathy shown by some of us may allow a Jew to rule over us one day. May God never let us see such a day!

At the same time, a number of orientalists serving as propaganda agents for the imperialist institution are also active in endeavors to distort and misrepresent the truths of Islam. The agents of imperialism are busy in every corner of the Islamic world drawing our youth away from us with their evil propaganda. They are not converting them into Jews and Christians; they are corrupting them, making them irreligious and indifferent, which is sufficient for their purposes. In our own city of Tehran now there are centers of evil propaganda run by the churches, the Zionists, and the Baha'is in order to lead our people astray and make them abandon the ordinances and teachings of Islam. Do we not have a duty to destroy these centers that are damaging to Islam? Is it enough for us simply to possess Najaf? (Actually, we do not even have Najaf!)[162] Should we be content to sit lamenting in Qum, or should we come to life and be active?

You, the younger generation in the religious institution, must come fully to life and keep the cause of God alive. Develop and refine your thinking, and lay aside your concern with the minutiae and subtleties of the religious sciences, because that kind of concentration on petty detail has kept many of us from performing our more important duties. Come to the aid of Islam; save Islam! They are destroying Islam! Invoking the laws of Islam and the name of the Most Noble Messenger (upon whom be peace and blessings), they are destroying Islam! Agents—both foreigners sent by the imperialists and natives employed by them—have spread out into every village and region of Iran and are leading our children and young people astray, who might otherwise be of service to Islam one day. Help save our young people from this danger!

It is your duty to disseminate among the people the religious knowledge you have acquired and to acquaint them with the subjects you have learned. The scholar or the *faqih* is accorded praise and glorified in the traditions because he is the one who makes the ordinances, doctrines, and institutions of Islam known to the people and instructs them in the Sunna of the Most Noble Messenger (upon whom be peace and blessings). You now must devote your energies to the tasks of propagation and instruction in order to present Islam more fully to the people.

It is our duty to dispel the doubts about Islam that have been created; until we have erased these doubts from people's minds, we will not be able to accomplish anything. We must impress upon ourselves and upon the next generation—and even the generation after that—the necessity for dispelling these doubts about Islam that have arisen in the minds of many people, even the educated among us, as the result of centuries of false propaganda. You must acquaint the people with the world-view, social institutions, and form of government proposed by Islam, so that they may come to know what Islam is and what its laws are.

It is the duty of the teaching institution today in Qum, Mashhad, and elsewhere to propagate Islam, to expound this faith and school of thought. In addition to Islam, you must make yourselves known to the people of the world and also authentic models of Islamic leadership and government. You must address yourselves to the university people in particular, the educated class. The students have had their eyes opened. I assure you that if you present Islam and Islamic government to the universities accurately, the students will welcome it and accept it. The students are opposed to tyranny; they are opposed to the puppet regimes imperialism imposes; they are opposed to thievery and the plundering of public wealth; they are opposed to this consumption of what is forbidden and this deceitful propaganda. But no student could be opposed to Islam, whose form of government and teachings are beneficial to society. The students are looking to Najaf, appealing for help. Should we sit idle, waiting for them to enjoin the good upon us and call us to our duties?[163] Our young people studying in Europe are enjoining the good upon us; they say to us: "We have organized Islamic associations; now help us!"[164]

It is our duty to bring all these matters to the attention of the people. We must explain what the form of government is in Islam and how rule was conducted in the earliest days of Islamic history. We must tell them how the center of command and the seat of the judiciary under it were both located in part of the mosque, at a time when the Islamic state embraced the farthest reaches of Iran, Egypt, the Hijaz, and the Yemen. Unfortunately, when government passed into the hands of the next generations, it was converted into a monarchy, or even worse than a monarchy.

The people must be instructed in these matters and helped to mature, intellectually and politically. We must tell them what kind of government we want, what kinds of people would assume responsibility for affairs in the government we propose, and what policies and programs they would follow. The ruler in Islamic society is a person who treats his brother 'Aqil[165] in such a way that he would never request extra support from the public treasury (lest there be economic discrimination among the Muslims), and who requires his daughter to account for the guaranteed loan she

129

has obtained from the public treasury, telling her, "If you do not pay back this loan, you will be the first woman of the Bani Hashim[166] to have her hand cut off." That is the kind of ruler and leader we want, a leader who will put the law into practice instead of his personal desires and inclinations; who will treat all members of the community as equals before the law; who will refuse to countenance privilege or discrimination in any form; who will place his own family on an equal footing with the rest of the people; who will cut off the hand of his own son if he commits a theft; who will execute his own brother and sister if they sell heroin (not execute people for possession of ten grams of heroin when his own relatives operate gangs that bring into the country heroin by the hundred-weight).[167]

Many of the ordinances of Islam that refer to worship also pertain to social and political functions. The forms of worship practiced in Islam are usually linked to politics and the gestation of society. For example, congregational prayer, the gathering on the occasion of the *hajj*, and Friday prayer, for all their spirituality, exert a political as well as moral and doctrinal influence. Islam has provided for such gatherings so that religious use might be made of them; so that feelings of brotherhood and cooperation may be strengthened, intellectual maturity fostered, solutions found for political and social problems, with *jihad* and collective effort as the natural outcome.

In non-Islamic countries, or Islamic countries ruled by non-Islamic governments, whenever they want the people to assemble like this, millions must be spent out of the national treasury or budget, and even then the result is unsatisfactory; such meetings lack spontaneity and spirit and are of no real consequence. In Islam, however, anyone who wishes to perform the *hajj* departs of his own will and goes on the *hajj*. Also people go eagerly to take part in congregational prayer. We must take advantage of these assemblies to propagate and teach religion and to develop the ideological and political movement of Islam.

Some people are completely unaware of all this; they are only concerned about the correct pronunciation of *"wa la'd-dallin."*[168] When they go on the *hajj*, instead of exchanging ideas with their Muslim brothers, propagating the beliefs and ordinances of Islam, and seeking solutions to the universal problems and afflictions of the Muslims (for example, rallying to liberate Palestine, which is part of the Islamic homeland)—instead of doing all this, they exacerbate the differences that exist among Muslims. The first Muslims, on the other hand, used to accomplish important business on the occasion of the *hajj* or at their Friday gatherings. The Friday sermon was more than a *sura* from the Qur'an and a prayer followed by a few brief words. Entire armies used to be mobilized by the Friday sermon and proceed directly from the mosque to the battlefield—and a man who sets out from the mosque to go into battle will fear only God, not poverty or hardship, and his army will be victorious and triumphant. When you look at the Friday sermons given in that age and the sermons of the Commander of the Faithful (upon whom be peace), you see that their purpose was to set people in motion, to arouse them to fight and sacrifice themselves for Islam, to resolve the sufferings of the people of this world.

If the Muslims before us had gathered every Friday and reminded themselves of their common problems, and solved them or resolved to solve them, we would not be in the position we find ourselves in today. Today we must start organizing these assemblies in earnest and make use of them for the sake of propagation and instruction. The ideological and political movement of Islam will thus develop and advance toward its climax.

Make Islam known to the people, then, and in so doing, create something akin to 'Ashura.[169] Just as we have steadfastly preserved the awareness of 'Ashura (peace be upon its founder) and not let it be lost, so that people still gather during Muharram and beat their breasts, we should now take measures to create a wave of protest against the state of the government; let the people gather, and the preachers and *rauzakhwans*[170] firmly fix the issue of government in their minds.

If you present Islam accurately and acquaint people with its world-view, doctrines, principles, ordinances, and social system, they will welcome it ardently (God knows, many people want it). I have witnessed that myself. A single word was enough once to cause a wave of enthusiasm among the people, because then, like now, they were all dissatisfied and unhappy with the state of affairs. They are living now in the shadow of the bayonet, and repression will let them say nothing. They want someone to stand up fearlessly and speak out. So, courageous sons of Islam, stand up! Address the people bravely; tell the truth about our situation to the masses in simple language; arouse them to enthusiastic activity, and turn the people in the street and the bazaar, our simple-hearted workers and peasants, and our alert students into dedicated *mujahids*.[171] The entire population will become *mujahids*. All segments of society are ready to struggle for the sake of freedom, independence, and the happiness of the nation, and their struggle needs religion. Give the people Islam, then, for Islam is the school of *jihad,* the religion of struggle; let them amend their characters and beliefs in accordance with Islam and transform themselves into a powerful force, so that they may overthrow the tyrannical regime imperialism has imposed on us and set up an Islamic government.

Only those *fuqaha* who make the people acquainted with the beliefs and institutions of Islam, and who defend and protect them, are truly "citadels of Islam."[172] They must deliver rousing, impassioned speeches and lead the people in order to fulfill this function. Only then, if they live to be, say, 120, will the people feel that Islam has suffered a misfortune with their passing and that a gap has appeared in the Muslim community, or as the tradition puts it, "A crack will appear in the fortress of Islam." Will some irremediable deficiency occur in Islamic society now if one of us dies after spending his life at home reading books? What loss could our death mean? But when Islam lost Imam Husayn (upon whom be peace), then indeed the loss was irreparable. A loss occurs with the death of people who have preserved the doctrines, laws, and social institutions of Islam, like Khwaja Nasir ad-Din Tusi[173] or 'Allama Hilli.[174] But what have you or I done for Islam that our passing should remind men of that tradition? If a thousand of us were to die, nothing would happen. The only explanation for this is that either we are not true *fuqaha* or we are not true believers.

No reasonable person expects our activities of propagation and instruction to lead quickly to the formation of an Islamic government. In order to succeed in establishing an Islamic government, we must have several kinds of continuous activities. Ours is a goal that will take time to achieve. Sensible people in this world lay one stone in position on the ground in the hope that someone two hundred years later will come to finish a building mounted upon it so that the goal will finally be reached. Once the caliph said to an old man who was planting a walnut tree: "Old man! Why plant this walnut tree, which will not bear fruit until fifty years from now, by which time you will be dead?" The man replied: "Others planted so that we might eat. We are planting so that others may eat."

We must persevere in our efforts even though they may not yield their result until the next generation, for our service is devoted to Islam and the cause of human happiness. If it were for a personal cause, we might say: "Why trouble ourselves! Our efforts cannot benefit us, but only those who come later." If the Lord of the Martyrs (upon whom be peace), who risked and indeed sacrificed all his material interests, had thought that way, acting only for himself and his personal benefit, he would have compromised with Yazid[175] at the very beginning and settled the whole affair— the Umayyad rulers were only too anxious for him to swear allegiance to them and accept them as rulers. What could have been better for them than to have the grandson of the Prophet (upon whom be peace and blessings), the Imam of the Age, call them "Commander of the Faithful" and recognize their rule? But his concern was the future of Islam and the Muslims. So that Islam might be propagated among men in the future, and its political and social order established in society, he opposed the Umayyads, fought against them, and ultimately sacrificed himself.

Examine carefully one of the traditions I have cited above. You will see that Imam Sadiq (upon whom be peace) was subjected to pressure by oppressive rulers and therefore chose *taqiya*. He had no executive power, and most of the time he was confined under surveillance. Nevertheless, he kept informing the Muslims of their duties and appointing judges for them. What was the reason for this, and what benefit was there in appointing and dismissing judges?

Great men, with broad horizons of thought, never despair or pay attention to the circumstances in which they find themselves —imprisonment or captivity, for example, which may continue indefinitely; instead, they continue making plans for the advancement of their cause. Either they will carry out their plans themselves, or if they are not granted the opportunity, others will follow their plans, even if it is two or three hundred years later. The foundations of many great movements in history were laid in this way. Sukarno, the former president of Indonesia, conceived and drew up his plans in prison and later put them into practice.

Imam Sadiq (upon whom be peace) not only laid down plans; he also made appointments to certain posts. If his appointments had been intended for that time, naturally they would have been pointless, but in reality, he was thinking of the future. He was not like us, thinking only of ourselves and concerned with our personal predicaments; he was concerned with the *umma*, with humanity as a whole, and he wished to reform mankind by implementing the laws of justice. Thus, more than a thousand years ago, he had to lay down a pattern of government and make his appointments, so that on the day when the nations awoke and the Muslims came to their senses, there would be no confusion and the form of Islamic government and its leadership would be known.

Generally speaking, Islam, the Shi'i school of thought, and indeed, all religions and schools of thought have advanced and progressed in this fashion: they all started with nothing but a plan, which came to fruition later because of the fortitude and dedication of the respective leaders and prophets.

Moses was a mere shepherd, and for years he followed that calling. When he was summoned to do battle with the pharaoh, he had no supporter or helper. But as a result of his innate ability and his steadfastness, he overthrew the rule of the pharaoh with a staff. Now imagine that staff in the hands of you or me; would we have been able to achieve the same result? It takes the determination, seriousness, and resourcefulness of a Moses to make that staff capable of overthrowing a pharaoh; not everyone can perform such a feat.

When the Most Noble Messenger (upon whom be peace and blessings) was given his prophetic mission and began to propagate his message, an eight-year old child (the Commander of the Faithful, upon whom be peace) and a forty-year old woman (his wife Khadija) were the only people who believed in him; he had no one else. Everyone knows of the vexations that plagued the Prophet, the obstacles that were placed in his way, the opposition that he faced. Yet he never despaired or said, "I am all alone." He persisted and, with his spiritual power and firm resolve, was able to advance his cause from nothing to the point it has reached today, where seven hundred million people are gathered under his banner.

The Shi'i school of thought also began from zero. On the day that the Most Noble Messenger (upon whom be peace and blessings) laid its foundations, he was greeted with mockery. He invited people to his house and told them, "The man who possesses such-and-such qualities is to be my minister," meaning the Commander of the Faithful (upon whom be peace). At the time, the Commander of the Faithful had not yet reached adulthood, although he always possessed a great spirit, the greatest in the world. But no one rose to pay him respect, and someone even turned to Abu Talib[176] and said to him in jest, "You are to march under the banner of your son now!"

Also on the day of the Prophet's announcement to the people that the Commander of the Faithful (upon whom be peace) was to succeed him and govern, some expressed apparent admiration and satisfaction, but the opposition to him began on that very day and continued down to the end. If the Most Noble Messenger (upon whom be peace and blessings) had appointed him only as an authority to be consulted on legal problems, there would have been no opposition to him. Since he assigned him the rank of successor, however, and said that he was to rule over the Muslims and be entrusted with the destiny of the Islamic nation, various sorts of discontent and opposition arose. If you, too, were to sit at home today and not intervene in the affairs of the country, no one would disturb you. They trouble you only when you try to intervene in the destiny of the nation. It was because they intervened in the affairs of government and the country that the Commander of the Faithful and his followers were harrassed and persecuted. But they did not abandon their activity and their struggle, with the result that today, thanks to their labors, there are about two hundred million Shi'is in the world.

To present Islam properly to the people, the religious teaching institution must be reformed. The syllabus and methods of propagation and instruction must be improved; apathy, laziness, despair, and lack of self-confidence must be replaced by diligence, endeavor, hope, and self-confidence; the effects left on the minds of some people by foreigners' insinuating propaganda must be erased; the attitudes of the pseudo-saintly, who, despite their position within the teaching institution, make it difficult for people to gain a true appreciation of Islam and the necessity for social reforms, must be changed; and the court-affiliated *akhunds*,[177] who have sold their religion for worldly gain, must be divested of their garb and expelled from the religious institution.

The agents of imperialism, together with the educational, propaganda, and political apparatuses of the anti-national puppet governments they have installed, have been spreading poison for centuries and corrupting the minds and morals of the people. Those who have entered the religious institution have naturally brought with them traces of this corruption, for the religious institution makes up part of society and part of the people. We must therefore strive to reform, intellectually and morally, the members of the religious institution, and to remove the traces left on their minds and spirits by the insinuating propaganda of the foreigners and the policies of corrupt and treacherous governments.

One can easily observe the effects of which I speak. For example, sometimes I see people who sit in the centers of the religious institution saying to each other, "These matters are beyond us; what business are they of ours? All we are supposed to do is offer our prayers and give our opinions on questions of religious law." Ideas like these are the result of several centuries of malicious propaganda on the part of the imperialists, penetrating deep into the very heart of Najaf, Qum, Mashhad, and the other religious centers; causing apathy, depression, and laziness to appear; and preventing people from maturing, so that they constantly make excuses for themselves and say, "These matters are beyond us!"

These ideas are wrong. What are the qualifications of those who now rule the Muslim countries? What gives them the ability to rule that we allegedly lack? Who among them has any more ability than the average man? Many of them have never studied anything! Where did the ruler of the Hijaz ever go to study? As for Riza Khan, he was totally illiterate, an illiterate soldier, no more! It has been the same throughout history: many arbitrary and tyrannical rulers have been totally lacking in any capacity to govern society or administer the nation, and devoid of learning and accomplishment. What did Harun ar-Rashid[178] ever study, or any other man who ruled over realms as vast as his? Study—the acquisition of knowledge and expertise in various sciences—is necessary for making plans for a country and for exercising executive and administrative functions; we too will make use of people with those qualifications. But as for the supervision and supreme administration of the country, the dispensing of justice, and the establishment of equitable relations among the people—these are precisely the subjects that the *faqih* has studied. Whatever is needed to preserve national independence and liberty is, again, precisely what the *faqih* has to offer. For it is the *faqih* who refuses to submit to others or fall under the influence of foreigners, and who defends the rights of the nation and the freedom, independence, and territorial integrity of the Islamic homeland, even at the cost of his life. It is the *faqih* who does not deviate either to the left or to the right.

Rid yourselves of your depression and apathy. Improve your methods and program of propagation, try diligently to present Islam accurately, and resolve to establish an Islamic government. Assume the lead and join hands with the militant and freedom-loving people. An Islamic government will definitely be established; have confidence in yourselves. You have the power, courage, and sense of strategy it takes to struggle for national liberty and independence, you who succeeded in waking the people and inspiring them to struggle, causing imperialism and tyranny to tremble. Day by day, you are accumulating more experience and your ability to deal with the affairs of society is increasing. Once you have succeeded in overthrowing the tyrannical regime, you will certainly be capable of administering the state and guiding the masses.

The entire system of government and administration, together with the necessary laws, lies ready for you. If the administration of the country calls for taxes, Islam has made the necessary provision; and if laws are needed, Islam has established them all. There is no need for you, after establishing a government, to sit down and draw up laws, or, like rulers who worship foreigners and are infatuated with the West, run after others to borrow their laws. Everything is ready and waiting. All that remains is to draw up ministerial programs, and that can be accomplished with the help and cooperation of consultants and advisers who are experts in different fields, gathered together in a consultative assembly.

Fortunately, the Muslim peoples are ready to follow you and are your allies. What we are lacking are the necessary resolve and armed power, and these, too, we shall acquire, God willing. We need the staff of Moses and the resolve of Moses; we need people who are able to wield the staff of Moses and the sword of the Commander of the Faithful (peace be upon him).

But the gutless people who now sit in the religious centers are certainly not capable of establishing and maintaining a government, for they are so gutless that they cannot wield even a pen or undertake any activity at all. The foreigners and their agents have filled our ears with their propaganda so often that we have begun to believe we are incapable of anything: "Go mind your own business! Attend to your schools, your classes, your studies. What business of yours are these matters? They're beyond your capacity!" I cannot disabuse some people of these notions and make them understand that they must become leaders of humanity, that they are at least the equals of others and are capable of administering the country. What qualifications do others have that they lack? All one can say is that some of the others went abroad to enjoy themselves, and maybe studied a little while they were there. (We do not say they should not study. We are not opposed to study or learning. Let them go to the moon, found an atomic industry; we will not stand in their way. However, we have duties as well.)

Give them Islam, proclaim to the world the program of Islamic government; maybe the kings and presidents of the Muslim countries will understand the truth of what we say and accept it. We would not want to take anything away from them; we will leave anyone in his place who faithfully follows Islam.

Today we have 700 million Muslims in the world, 170 million or more of whom are Shi'is. They are all ready to follow us, but we are so lacking in resolve that we are unable to lead them. We must establish a government that will enjoy the trust of the people, one in which the people have confidence and to which they will be able to entrust their destiny. We need trustworthy rulers who will guard the trust the people have placed with them, so that protected by them and the law, the people will be able to live their lives and go about their tasks in tranquillity.

These are the things to which you should be devoting your thought. Do not despair, do not imagine that this task is impossible. God knows that your capacity and courage are not less than those of others—unless, of course, the meaning of courage is oppressing and slaughtering the people; that kind of courage we certainly don't have.

Once that man came to see me while I was in prison[179] along with Aqa-yi Qummi[180] (may God preserve him), who is under arrest again now. He said: "Politics is all dirt, lying, and viciousness; why don't you leave it to us?"

What he said was true in a sense; if that is what politics really consists of, it belongs exclusively to them. But the politics of Islam, of the Muslims, of the guiding Imams who lead God's servants by means of politics, is quite different from the politics he was speaking of.

Afterwards, he told the newspapers: "An agreement has been reached to the effect that the religious leaders will not interfere in politics." As soon as I was released, I denied his statement from the *minbar*. I said: "He is lying; if Khomeini or anyone else gives such a pledge, he will be expelled from the religious institution!"[181]

At the outset they plant in your minds the suggestion that politics means lying and the like, so that you lose all interest in national affairs and they can proceed with their business undisturbed, doing whatever they like and indulging all their vices. Meanwhile, you are to sit here offering prayers for their welfare: "May God perpetuate their rule!" They, of course, do not have the intelligence to elaborate such a plan themselves (thank God!); it is their masters and the experts who advise them that devised this plan. The British imperialists penetrated the countries of the East more than three hundred years ago. Being knowledgeable about all aspects of these countries, they drew up elaborate plans for assuming control of them. Then came the new imperialists, the Americans and others. They allied themselves with the British and took part in the execution of their plans.

Once when I was in Hamadan, a former student of the religious sciences, a man who had foresaken the religious garb but preserved his Islamic ethics, came to see me and showed me a map on which certain places had been marked in red. He told me that those red symbols indicated all the mineral resources existing in Iran that had been located by foreign experts.

Foreign experts have studied our country and have discovered all our mineral reserves—gold, copper, petroleum, and so on. They have also made an assessment of our people's intelligence and come to the conclusion that the only barriers blocking their way are Islam and the religious leadership.

They have known the power of Islam themselves for it once ruled part of Europe, and they know that true Islam is opposed to their activities. They have also realized they cannot make the true religious scholars submit to their influence, nor can they affect their thinking. From the very outset, therefore, they have sought to remove this obstacle from their path by disparaging Islam and besmirching the religious leaders. They have resorted to malicious propaganda so that today, we imagine that Islam simply consists of a handful of legal topics. They have also tried to destroy the reputation of the *fuqaha* and the *'ulama,* who stand at the head of Islamic society, by slanderous accusations and other means. For example, that shameless agent of imperialism wrote in his book[182]: "Six hundred of the *'ulama* of Najaf and Iran were on the payroll of the British. Shaykh Murtaza[183] took the money for only two years before he realized where it was coming from. The proof may be found in documents preserved in the India Office archives." Imperialism tells him to insult the *'ulama* so that it may reap the benefits. Imperialism dearly wants to present all the *'ulama* as being on its payroll so that they will lose the respect of the people and the people will turn away from them. At the same time, they have tried with their propaganda and insinuations to present Islam as a petty, limited affair, and to restrict the functions of the *fuqaha* and *'ulama* to insignificant matters. They have constantly tried to persuade us that the only duty of the *fuqaha* is to give their opinion on legal problems.

Some people, lacking in correct understanding, have believed them and gone astray. They have failed to realize that all this is part of a plan designed to destroy our independence and establish control over all aspects of life in the Islamic countries. Unwittingly, they have assisted the propaganda organs of imperialism in carrying out its policies and reaching its goals. The propaganda institutions of imperialism have sought to persuade us that religion must be separate from politics, that the religious leaders must not interfere in social matters, and that the *fuqaha* do not have the duty of overseeing the destiny of the Islamic nation. Unfortunately, some people have believed them and fallen under their influence, with the result that we see. This result is what the imperialists have always desired, desire now, and will desire in the future.

Look at the religious teaching centers and you will see the effects of this imperialist campaign of persuasion and propaganda. You will see negligent, lazy, idle, and apathetic people who do nothing but discuss points of law and offer their prayers, and are incapable of anything else. You will also encounter ideas and habits that are born of the same imperialist propaganda—for example, the idea that to speak is incompatible with the dignity of the *akhund;* the *akhund* and the *mujtahid* should not be able to speak, or if they are, they should not say anything except, *"La ilaha illa 'Llah,"* or maybe one word more! But that is wrong, and contrary to the Sunna of God's Messenger (upon whom be peace and blessings). God has praised speech and expression, as well as writing and the use of the pen. For example, He says in *Surat ar-Rahman:* He taught him [man] expression" (55:4), counting the instruction in speech that He gave man as a great blessing and a source of nobility. Speech and expression are necessary for promulgating the ordinances of God and the teachings and doctrines of Islam; it is by means of them that we can instruct the people in their religion and fulfill the duty indicated in the phrase: "They instruct the people."[184] The Most Noble Messenger and the Commander of the Faithful both delivered speeches and sermons; they were men of eloquence.

These foolish ideas that exist in the minds of some people help the imperialists and the oppressive governments in their attempts to keep the Muslim countries in their present state and to block the progress of the Islamic movement. Such ideas are characteristic of those who are known as saintly but in reality are pseudo-saints, not true ones. We must change the way they think and make clear our attitudes toward them, for they are blocking our movement and the reforms we want to carry out, and are keeping our hands tied.

The late Burujirdi,[185] the late Hujjat,[186] the late Sadr,[187] and the last Khwansari[188] (may God be pleased with all of them) had gathered in our house one day to discuss some political matter. I said to them: "Before anything else, you must decide what to do with these pseudo-saints. As long as they are there, our situation is like that of a person who is attacked by an enemy while someone else keeps his hands bound behind him. These persons who are known as saints but are pseudo-saints, not real ones, are totally unaware of the state of society, and if you want to do something—take over a government, assume control of the Majlis, stop the spread of corruption—they will destroy your standing in society. Before everything else, you must decide what to do with them."

The state of Muslim society today is such that these false saints prevent Islam from exerting its proper influence; acting in the name of Islam, they are inflicting damage upon Islam. The roots of this group that exists in our society are to be found in the centers of the religious institution. In the centers at Najaf, Qum, Mashhad, and elsewhere, there are individuals who have this pseudo-saintly mentality, and from their base within the religious institution, they infect the rest of society with their evil ideas and attitudes. It is they who will oppose anyone who tells the people: "Come now, awaken! Let us not live under the banner of others! Let us not be subject to the impositions of Britain and America! Let us not allow Israel to paralyze the Muslims!"

First, we must advise these pseudo-saints and try to awaken them. We must say to them: "Can you not see the danger? Do you not see that the Israelis are attacking, killing, and destroying and the British and Americans are helping them? You sit there watching, but you must wake up; you must try to find a remedy for the ills of the people. Mere discussion is not enough. Simply pronouncing opinions on points of law is of no use by itself. Do not keep silent at a time when Islam is being destroyed, Islam is being wiped out, like the Christians who sat discussing the Holy Ghost and the Trinity until they were destroyed.[189] Wake up! Pay some attention to reality and the questions of the day. Do not let yourselves be so negligent. Are you waiting for the angels to come and carry you on their wings? Is it the function of the angels to pamper the idle? The angels spread their wings beneath the feet of the Commander of the Faithful (upon whom be peace) because he was of benefit to Islam: he made Islam great, secured the expansion of Islam in the world and promoted its interests. Under his leadership, a free, vital, virtuous society came into being and won fame; everyone had to bow before its might, even the enemy. But why should anyone bow before you, whose only activity is offering opinions on points of law?"

If our pseudo-saints do not wake up and begin to assume their responsibilities after repeated admonition and advice, it will be obvious that the cause of their failure is not ignorance, but something else. Then, of course, we will adopt a different attitude toward them.

The centers of the religious institution are places for teaching, instruction, propagation, and leadership. They belong to the just *fuqaha*, learned scholars, teachers, and students. They belong to those who are the trustees and successors of the prophets. They represent a trust, and it is obvious that a divine trust cannot be placed in the hands of anyone. Whoever wishes to assume such a weighty responsibility, to administer the affairs of the Muslims and to act as the deputy of the Commander of the Faithful (upon whom be peace), to settle matters concerning the honor, property, and lives of the people, as well as the booty taken in war and the penal provisions of the law—such a person must be totally disinterested in the world and devoid of worldly ambition. Anyone whose efforts are oriented to this world—even in matters that are inherently legitimate—cannot be the trustee of God and is not worthy of our trust. Any *faqih* who joins the state apparatus of the oppressors and becomes a hanger-on of the court is not a trustee and cannot exercise God's trust. God knows what misfortunes Islam has suffered from its inception down to the present at the hands of these evil *'ulama!* Abu Hurayra[190] was one of the *fuqaha*, but God knows what judgments he falsified for Mu'awiya and others like him, and what damage he inflicted upon Islam. When an ordinary person enters the service of an oppressive government, he is to be accounted a sinner, but no greater harm will come of it.

But when a *faqih* like Abu Huraya or a judge like Shurayh joins such a government, he improves its standing while besmirching the reputation of Islam. When a *faqih* enters the service of an oppressive government, it is as if the whole *'ulama* entered it along with him; it is no longer a question of a single individual. It is for this reason that the Imams (upon whom be peace) strictly forbade their followers to join government service, and told them that the situation they found themselves in had come about because some of them had done so.

The obligations that are incumbent on the *fuqaha* do not apply to others; on account of their position and function, the *fuqaha* must avoid and relinquish even things that are otherwise licit. In cases where others are permitted to resort to *taqiya*, the *fuqaha* may not. The purpose of *taqiya* is the preservation of Islam and the Shi'i school; if people had not resorted to it, our school of thought would have been destroyed. *Taqiya* relates to the branches *(furu')* of religion—for example, performing ablution in different ways. But when the chief principles of Islam and its welfare are endangered, there can be no question of silence or *taqiya*. If they try to force a *faqih* to mount the *minbar* and speak in a way contrary to God's command, can he obey them, telling himself, "*Taqiya* is my religion and the religion of my forefathers"?[191] The question of *taqiya* does not even arise here. If a *faqih* anticipates that by his entering the service of an oppressive government, oppression will be furthered and the reputation of Islam soiled, he must not enter its service, even if he is killed as a result. There is no acceptable excuse he can offer, unless his entry into the service of the state has some rational basis, as was the case with 'Ali ibn Yaqtin,[192] whose motives in joining state service are well known, and with Khwaja Nasir Tusi[193] (may God be pleased with him), whose action resulted in benefits also well-known.

The true *fuqaha* of Islam are, of course, free of all guilt in this respect. From the beginning of Islam down to the present, their example is clear and shines before us like a light; they are untouched by guilt. The *akhunds* who joined the service of governments in past ages did not belong to our school. Not only did our *fuqaha* oppose the rulers, they also suffered imprisonment and torture on account of their disobedience.[194] Let no one imagine that the *'ulama* of Islam have ever entered the service of the state

144

or do so now. Upon occasion, of course, they have entered it in order to bring the state under their control or transform it; were such a thing possible now, it would be our duty to do so. But that is not what I am speaking of. Our problem is the people who wear turbans on their heads, have read a few books somewhere or other (or not read them, as the case may be), and have joined the service of the government in order to fill their stomachs or increase the scope of their authority. What are we to do with them?

Those persons are not Muslim *fuqaha;* they are people whom SAVAK has issued a turban and told to pray. If SAVAK cannot force the congregational imams to be present on the occasion of government-sponsored festivities and other ceremonies, it will have its own people on hand ready to say: "Greater be his glory!" (Yes, they have recently begun to say, "Greater be his glory!" when they mention the name of the Shah.) These persons are not *fuqaha;* the people have recognized them for what they are. A certain tradition warns us to guard our religion against these people, lest they destroy it. They must be exposed and disgraced so that they may come to lose whatever standing they enjoy among the people. If their standing in society is not destroyed, they will destroy the standing of the Imam of the Age and the standing of Islam itself.

Our youths must strip them of their turbans. The turbans of these *akhunds,* who cause corruption in Muslim society while claiming to be *fuqaha* and *'ulama,* must be removed. I do not know if our young people in Iran have died; where are they? Why do they not strip these people of their turbans? I am not saying they should be killed; they do not deserve to be killed. But take off their turbans! Our people in Iran, particularly the zealous youths, have a duty not to permit these *akhunds,* these reciters of "Greater be his glory!" to appear in society and move among the people wearing turbans. They do not need to be beaten much; just take off their turbans, and do not permit them to appear in public wearing turbans. The turban is a noble garment; not everyone is fit to wear it.

As I have said, the true *'ulama* of Islam are free of all guilt in this respect; they have never joined the service of the government. Those who are affiliated with the government are parasites trying to grow fat on religion and the *'ulama,* but they have nothing to do with the *'ulama,* and the people recognize them for what they are.

We too have difficult tasks facing us. We must improve our-selves spiritually and improve our way of life. We must become more ascetic than before and completely shun the goods of this world. All of you must equip yourselves to protect the divine trust that has been vested in you. Become worthy trustees, and hold the world in less esteem. Naturally, you cannot be like the Comman-der of the Faithful (upon whom be peace), who said that the world was no more to him than the snot of a goat; but turn away from the desire for worldly gain, purify your souls, turn toward God Al-mighty, cultivate piety. If your purpose in studying is—God for-bid—to secure your future livelihood, you will never become *fuqaha* or trustees of Islam. Prepare yourselves to be of use to Is-lam; act as the army for the Imam of the Age, in order to be able to serve him in spreading the rule of justice. The mere existence of righteous people has a beneficial effect on society—as I myself have observed, one becomes purified by walking with them and keeping company with them. Act so that your deeds, conduct, character, and aversion to worldly ambition will have an uplift-ing effect on the people. They will imitate your example, and you will become models for them and soldiers of God. Only thus can you make Islam and Islamic government known to the people.

I am not telling you to abandon your studies. Indeed you must study, become *fuqaha*, devote yourselves to *fiqh*, and not permit *fiqh* to decline in the centers of the religious institution. Unless you are *fuqaha*, you will not be able to serve Islam. But while you study, be concerned, too, with representing Islam accurately to the people. Islam is now a stranger; no one knows Islam properly. You must convey Islam and its ordinances to the people so that they understand what Islam is, what Islamic government is, what prophethood and imamate mean, and in the broadest terms, why Islam was revealed and what its goals are. Thus Islam will gradu-ally become known, and, God willing, an Islamic government will one day be established.

Let us overthrow tyrannical governments by: (1) severing all relations with governmental institutions; (2) refusing to cooperate with them; (3) refraining from any action that might be construed as aiding them; and (4) creating new judicial, financial, economic, cultural, and political institutions.

It is the duty of all of us to overthrow the *taghut;* i.e., the illegitimate political powers that now rule the entire Islamic world. The governmental apparatus of tyrannical and anti-popular regimes must be replaced by institutions serving the public good and administered according to Islamic law. In this way, an Islamic government will gradually come into existence. In the Qur'an, God Almighty has forbidden men to obey the *taghut*—illegitimate regimes—and encouraged them to rise up against kings, just as He commanded Moses to rebel. There are a number of traditions encouraging people to fight against oppressors and those who wish to pervert religion. The Imams (upon whom be peace), joined by their followers, the Shi'a, have always fought against tyrannical governments and illegitimate regimes, as one can easily see by examining their biographies and way of life. Most of the time they were subject to the pressures of tyrannical and oppressive rulers, and were compelled to observe *taqiya* out of extreme fear—not fear for themselves, of course, but fear for their religion, as is evident from an examination of the relevant traditions. Tyrannical rulers, for their part, stood in terror of the Imams. They were aware that if they gave the Imams the slightest opportunity, they would rebel and deprive them of their life, which was synonymous with pleasure-seeking and licentiousness. This is the reason we see Harun arresting Imam Musa ibn Ja'far[195] (upon whom be peace) and imprisoning him for several years, and after him, Ma'mun[196] transporting Imam Riza (upon whom be peace) to Marv[197] and confining him there for many years before finally poisoning him. Harun and Ma'mun acted as they did not because the Imams were *sayyids*—i.e., descendants of the Prophet—and the rulers were opposed to the Prophet; indeed, both Harun and Ma'mun were Shi'is.[198] They were motivated entirely by considerations of state: they knew that the descendants of 'Ali laid claim to the caliphate and that their earnest desire was to establish an Islamic government, considering this to be their duty. One day, it was suggested to Imam Musa that he delineate the boundaries of Fadak[199] so that it might be returned to him. According to a certain tradition, he drew a map of the entire Islamic realm and said, "Everything within these boundaries is our legitimate right. We should rule over it, and you are usurpers." The tyrannical rulers thus saw that if Imam Musa ibn Ja'far were free, he would make life impossible for them and might lay the groundwork for a rebellion and the overthrow of their rule. So they did not give him the slightest opportunity. Have no doubt that if he had had the chance, he would indeed have rebelled and overthrown the ruling usurpers.

Ma'mun similarly kept Imam Riza under surveillance, cunningly and hypocritically addressing him as "Cousin" and "Descendant of God's Messenger" out of fear that one day he might rise and destroy the foundations of his rule. Since he was indeed a descendant and a legatee of the Prophet (upon whom be peace and blessings), he could not be allowed to go free in Medina. The tyrannical rulers desired rule and were ready to sacrifice everything for its sake; they had no personal enmity with anyone. If—God forbid—the Imam (upon whom be peace) had frequented their court, he would have been shown the utmost veneration and respect; they would even have kissed his hand. According to tradition, when Imam Riza came into the presence of Harun, the ruler ordered that the Imam be carried on horseback all the way to his throne and showed him all possible veneration. But when it was time to distribute the shares that were to be given from the treasury and it was the turn of the Bani Hashim to receive their share, Harun awarded them only a very small amount. His son Ma'mun who was present was surprised at the contrast between the veneration he had just witnessed and the allotment he now saw being made. Harun told him: "You do not understand. The Bani Hashim must remain in this state. They must always be poor, imprisoned, banished, afflicted, even poisoned or killed; otherwise, they will rise up against us in revolt and ruin our lives."

The Imams (upon whom be peace) not only fought against tyrannical rulers, oppressive governments, and corrupt courts themselves; they also summoned the Muslims to wage *jihad* against those enemies. There are more than fifty traditions in *Wasa'il ash-Shi'a*,[200] the *Mustadrak*,[201] and other books calling on the Muslims to shun tyrannical rulers and governments and to fill with earth the mouths of those who praise them, and threatening anyone who does so much as lend their panegyrists a pen or fill their inkwells. In short, the Imams have given orders that all relations with such rulers be severed and that no one collaborate with them in any way. In contrast to these traditions are others that praise the learned

148

scholar and the just *faqih,* and emphasize their superiority over other men. Taken together, these two classes of traditions form a program for the establishment of Islamic government. First, the people are induced to turn away from the tyrannical government of the oppressors and destroy their house of oppression; then the houses of the *fuqaha* are to open their doors to the people: *fuqaha* who are just and ascetic and who fight in God's way to implement the laws of Islam and establish its social system.

The Muslims will be able to live in security and tranquillity and preserve their faith and morals only when they enjoy the protection of a government based on justice and law, a government whose form, administrative system, and laws have been laid down by Islam. It is our duty now to implement and put into practice the plan of government established by Islam. I hope that by presenting the system of government and the political and social principles of Islam to broad segments of humanity, we will create a strong new current of thought and a powerful popular movement that will result in the establishment of an Islamic government.

O God, foreshorten the arms of the oppressors that are stretched out against the lands of the Muslims and root out all traitors to Islam and the Islamic countries. Awaken the heads of the Muslim states from their deep sleep so that they may exert themselves on behalf of their people's interests and renounce divisiveness and the quest for personal gain. Grant that the younger generation studying in the religious colleges and the universities may struggle to reach the sacred aims of Islam and strive together, with ranks united, first, to deliver the Islamic countries from the clutches of imperialism and its vile agents, and then to defend them. Grant that the *fuqaha* and the scholars may strive to guide and enlighten the minds of the people, to convey the sacred aims of Islam to all Muslims, particularly the younger generation, and to struggle for the establishment of an Islamic government. From You is success, and there is neither recourse nor strength except in God, the Exalted, the Sublime.

Notes

1. *Faqih:* one learned in the principles and ordinances of Islamic law, or more generally, in all aspects of the faith. For a full discussion of the term, see p. 84.

2. This is an allusion to the celebrated saying of the Prophet: "Islam will again become a stranger among men, as it was in the beginning, but blessed is the state of the stranger."

3. *Hadith:* a tradition setting forth a saying or deed of the Prophet, or in Shiʻi usage, of one of the Twelve Imams.

4. *Mujtahid:* an authority on divine law who practices *ijtihad*, that is, "the search for a correct opinion . . . in the deducing of the specific provisions of the law from its principles and ordinances" (Muhammad Sanglaji, *Qaza dar Islam* [Tehran, 1338 Sh./1959], p. 14).

5. *Akhund:* a word of uncertain etymology that originally denoted a scholar of unusual attainment, but was later applied to lesser-ranking scholars, and then acquired a pejorative connotation, particularly in secularist usage.

6. *ʻUlama:* the scholars of Islam.

7. Concerning the influence of Belgian constitutional law on the six-man committee that drafted the Supplementary Constitutional Laws of 1907, see A.K.S. Lambton, "Dustur, iv: Iran," *Encyclopaedia of Islam* new ed., II, 653-654, and Mustafa Rahimi, *Qanun-i Asasi-yi Iran* (Tehran, 1347 Sh./1968), p. 94.

8. Articles 35 through 57 of the Supplementary Constitutional Laws approved on October 7, 1906 relate to "the rights of the throne." See E.G. Browne, *The Persian Revolution of 1905-1909* (Cambridge, 1911), pp. 337-379.

9. In the seventh year of the Islamic era, the Prophet Muhammad wrote not only to Heraclius and the ruler of Iran (probably Parviz), but also to the rulers of Egypt and Abyssinia, inviting them all to embrace Islam

and abandon unjust rule. See Muhammad Hamidullah, *Le Prophete de l'Islam* (Paris, 1959), I, 196-197, 212, 230, 241.

10. The Lord of the Martyrs: Imam Husayn, grandson of the Prophet.

11. In 60/680, Imam Husayn refused to swear allegiance to Yazid, son of Mu'awiya and second caliph of the Umayyad dynasty, since Yazid did not possess legitimate authority and had succeeded to the caliphate by hereditary succession. The ensuing death of the Imam in battle at Karbala has always been commemorated by Shi'i Muslims as the supreme example of martyrdom in the face of tyranny. It served as an important point of both ideological and emotive reference throughout the Islamic Revolution in Iran.

12. No detailed study has yet been made of the British role in the early part of the constitutional movement. Some of the relevant documents, however, are to be found in *General Report on Persia for the Year 1906* (file F.O. 416/30, Public Records Office, London).

13. *Shari'a:* the all-embracing law of Islam derived from the Qur'an, the normative practice and authoritative pronouncements of the Prophet, and a number of secondary sources.

14. A law promulgated in July 1969 provided the death penalty for anyone in possession of more than two kilograms of opium or ten grams of heroin, morphine, or cocaine. The first ten executions were carried out in December 1969 and by 1974, 236 people had been executed on charges under this law. See Ulrich Gehrke, *Iran: Natur, Bevolkerung, Geschichte, Kultur, Staat, Wirschaft* (Tubingen and Basel, 1976), p. 281. It is probable that the law was also used to provide a cover for the execution of political prisoners who had no involvement with narcotics. Concerning the royal family's own involvement in the drug trade, see p. 163, n. 167.

15. We have not been able to determine whether this is an allusion to a particular school established by foreigners. Before the Islamic Revolution, there were a number of foreign-run schools in Iran—secular and missionary—that in effect alienated their students from Islamic culture and society.

16. *Taqiya:* prudential dissimulation of one's true beliefs under conditions of acute danger, a practice based on Qur'an, 3:28. For a fuller discussion of *taqiya*, see 'Allamah Tabataba'i, *Shi'ite Islam* (Albany, N.Y., 1975), pp. 223-225, and also p. 144 of the present work.

17. This is a reference to an earlier and briefer series of talks given by Imam Khomeini on the subject of Islamic government. The Iranian

embassy in Baghdad had sought to prevent the published text of those talks from being distributed.

18. The Commander of the Faithful: 'Ali ibn Abi Talib, cousin and son-in-law of the Prophet, and first of the Twelve Imams of Shi'i belief. He exercised rule from 35/656 until his martyrdom in 40/661.

19. Imam Hasan: son of Imam 'Ali and second of the Imams. He died in 50/670 after spending most of his life in seclusion in Medina.

20. Imam Baqir: the fifth Imam. He was born in 57/675 and spent most of his life in Medina, dying there in 114/732.

21. The "quality of justice" that is demanded of a religious scholar includes not only the practice of equity in all social dealings, but also complete abstention from major sins, the consistent performance of all devotional duties, and the avoidance of conduct incompatible with decorum.

22. "O Messenger! Proclaim what has been revealed to you by your Lord, for if you do not, you will not have fulfilled the mission He has entrusted to you" (5:70).

23. Xenomaniacs: those infatuated with foreign and especially Western models of culture. This is a translation of a Persian term, *gharbzadaha*, popularized by Jalal Al-i Ahmad (d. 1969) in his book *Gharbzadagi* ("Xenomania"). He was a writer of great influence and Imam Khomeini was acquainted with his work. See the commemorative supplement on Jalal Al-i Ahmad in the Tehran daily newspaper *Jumhuri-yi Islami*, Shahrivar 20, 1359/October 12, 1980, p. 10.

24. *Azan:* the call to prayer.

25. *Vali amr:* "the one who holds authority," a term derived from Qur'an, 4:59: "O you who believe! Obey God, and obey the Messenger and the holders of authority (*uli 'l-amr*) from among you."

26. Sunna: the practice of the Prophet, accepted by Muslims as the norm and ideal for all human behavior.

27. Lesser Occultation: *ghaybat-i sughra*, the period of about 70 years (260/872-329/939) when, according to Shi'i belief, Muhammad al-Mahdi, the Twelfth Imam, absented himself from the physical plane but remained in communication with his followers through a succession of four appointed deputies. At the death of the fourth deputy no successor was named, and the Greater Occultation (*ghaybat-i kubra*) began, and continues to this day.

28. The allusion is probably to the Baha'is, who claim to have received a succession of post-Qur'anic revelations.

29. *Jizya:* a tax levied on non-Muslim citizens of the Muslim state in exchange for the protection they receive and in lieu of the taxes, such as *zakat,* that only Muslims pay. *Kharaj:* a tax levied on certain categories of land. *Khums:* a tax consisting of one-fifth of agricultural and commercial profits (see p. 44). *Zakat:* the tax levied on various categories of wealth and spent on the purposes specified in Qur'an, 9:60.

30. *al-Kafi:* one of the most important collections of Shi'i *hadith,* compiled by Shaykh Abu Ja'far al-Kulayni (d. 329/941). Two fascicules of this work have recently been translated into English by Sayyid Muhammad Hasan Rizvi and published in Tehran.

31. Qur'an, 16:89.

32. The reference is probably to Imam Ja'far as-Sadiq, whose sayings on this subject are quoted by 'Allama Tabataba'i in *al-Mizan fi Tafsir al-Qur'an* (Beirut, 1390/1979), XII, 327-328.

33. *Sayyids:* the descendants of the Prophet through his daughter Fatima and son-in-law 'Ali, the first of the Twelve Imams.

34. *Zakat* would not represent an appreciable sum presumably because it is levied on surplus wealth, the accumulation of which is inhibited by the economic system of Islam.

35. *Ahl adh-dhimma:* non-Muslim citizens of the Muslim state, whose rights and obligations are contractually determined.

36. *Umma:* the entire Islamic community, without territorial or ethnic distinction.

37. Masjid al-Aqsa: the site in Jerusalem where the Prophet ascended to heaven in the eleventh year of his mission (Qur'an, 17:1); also the complex of mosques and buildings erected on the site. The chief of these was extensively damaged by arson in 1969, two years after the Zionist usurpation of Jerusalem.

38. Umayyads: members of the dynasty that ruled at Damascus from 41/632 until 132/750 and transformed the caliphate into a hereditary institution. Mu'awiya, frequently mentioned in these pages, was the first of the Umayyad line.

39. Abbasids: the dynasty that replaced the Umayyads and established a new caliphal capital in Baghdad. With the rise of various local rulers, generally of military origin, the power of the Abbasids began to decline from the fourth/tenth century and it was brought to an end by the Mongol conquest in 656/1258.

40. *Kufr:* the rejection of divine guidance; the antithesis of Islam.

41. *Taghut:* one who surpasses all bounds in his despotism and tyranny and claims the prerogatives of divinity for himself, whether explicitly or implicitly. See also p. 92.

42. *Shirk:* the assignment of partners to God, either by believing in a multiplicity of gods, or by assigning divine attributes and prerogatives to other-than-God.

43. "Corruption on earth": a broad term including not only moral corruption, but also subversion of the public good, embezzlement and usurpation of public wealth, conspiring with the enemies of the community against its security, and working in general for the overthrow of the Islamic order. See the commentary on Qur'an, 5:33 in Tabataba'i, *al-Mizan,* V, 330-332.

44. It may be apposite to quote here the following passage from a secret report drawn up in January 1916 by T.E. Lawrence, the British organizer of the so-called Arab revolt led by Sharif Husayn of Mecca: "Husayn's activity seems beneficial to us, because it marches with our immediate aims, the breakup of the Islamic bloc and the defeat and disruption of the Ottoman Empire. . . . The Arabs are even less stable than the Turks. If properly handled they would remain in a state of political mosaic, a tissue of small jealous principalities incapable of political cohesion." See Philip Knightley and Colin Simpson, *The Secret Lives of Lawrence of Arabia* (New York, 1971), p. 55.

45. Fatimat az-Zahra: Fatima, the daughter of the Prophet and wife of Imam 'Ali.

46. I.e., Hasan and Husayn.

47. See *Nahj al-Balagha,* ed. Subhi as-Salih (Beirut, 1397/1967).

48. Imam Riza: eighth of the Twelve Imams, born in 148/765 and died in 203/817 in Tus (Mashhad). According to Shi'i belief, he was poisoned by the Abbasid caliph Ma'mun, who had appointed him as his successor at first, but then grew fearful of the wide following he commanded (see p. 148). His shrine in Mashhad is one of the principal centers of pilgrimage and religious learning in Iran.

49. The text of this tradition is to be found in Shaykh Sadduq, *'Ilal ash-Shara'i'* (Qum, 1378/1958), I, 183.

50. That is, in the absence of the Imam or an individual deputy named by him (as was the case during the Lesser Occultation), the task devolves upon the *fuqaha* as a class. See argument on pp. 62-125.

51. Here the allusion may be in particular to the so-called Family Protection Law of 1967, which Imam Khomeini denounced as contrary to

Islam in an important ruling. See Imam Khomeini, *Tauzih al-Masa'il*, n.p., n.d., pp. 462-463, par. 2836, and p. 441.

52. It is the belief of Shi'i Muslims that the Prophet appointed Imam 'Ali as his successor at a gathering near the pool of Khumm during his return to Medina from Mecca, after having performed the last pilgrimage in his life.

53. The attribution of errors to Abu Bakr and 'Umar and deviations to 'Uthman is a part of Shi'i belief and is entirely to be expected in this context. Worthy of note, however, is the statement here that Abu Bakr and 'Umar adhered to the example of the Prophet in their personal lives. It would be difficult to find such a positive evaluation in the utterances of a leading Shi'i scholar before Imam Khomeini. See also the statement on p. 55.

54. Hijaz: the region in Western Arabia that includes Mecca and Medina.

55. After the Revolution, extensive evidence came to light of misappropriation of the religious endowments. Land was being given to cabaret singers and members of the royal family by the state-controlled administration of the endowments. See the article on this subject in the Tehran daily *Kayhan*, Isfand 27, 1357/March 18, 1979. Concerning attempts by the regime to build a cinema in Qum, see S.H.R., *Barrasi va Tahlili az Nihzat-i Imam Khumayni* (Najaf? 1356 Sh./1977), pp. 103-104.

56. A reference to the coronation ceremonies of 1967.

57. Concerning the precise meaning of "justice," see n. 21 above.

58. The reference here is to certain shortcomings Shi'is have traditionally perceived in the exercise of rule by Abu Bakr.

59. *Fuqaha:* the plural of *faqih* (see n. 1 above).

60. The words are God's since they are Qur'anic, but in the context in which they appear, the speaker is Abraham. After asking God that prophethood be vested in his progeny, Abraham excludes any of his descendants who might be wrongdoers from exercising the prophetic function.

61. Occultation: see n. 27 above.

62. The "governance" (*vilayat*) of the *faqih* is extrinsic (*i'tibari*) to his person; he exercises it only by virtue of the acquired attribute of just *faqih*.

63. The "governance" (*vilayat*) of the Imams is intrinsic to their persons, unlike that of the *fuqaha;* moreover, its scope is not limited to men but embraces the whole of creation. They therefore exercise "cosmic

governance" (*vilayat-i takvini*), in part through the performance of miracles. This form of *vilayat* is common to the Imams and to the foremost of the prophets, who exercised a governmental function while also propagating a divine message. The statement here that "no one can attain the spiritual status of the Imams, not even the cherubim or the prophets" thus carries the strict sense that the Imams are superior to those prophets whose mission lacked the dimension of governmental leadership. Concerning the different types of *vilayat*, see Murtaza Mutahhari, *Valiha va Vilayatha* (Qum, 1355 Sh./1975).

64. Concerning these attributes of the Imams, see Henri Corbin, *Histoire de la philosophie islamique* (Paris, 1964), pp. 74 ff.

65. The archangel Jibra'il (Gabriel) accompanied the Most Noble Messenger on his *mi'raj* (ascension to the divine presence), but being of lowlier station than the Messenger, he was unable to endure the splendor of the divine presence.

66. A well-known tradition relating to the *mi'raj*.

67. Fatima, the daughter of the Prophet, shared in the exalted states of the Prophet and the Twelve Imams in that she possessed the same quality of *'ismat* (divinely bestowed freedom from error and sin) that they did. As daughter of the Prophet and wife of the first Imam, she served, moreover, as a link between the Prophet and his successors.

68. *Nahj al-Balagha*, p. 76.

69. *Nahj al-Balagha*, p. 50.

70. *Nahj al-Balagha*, p. 188-189.

71. See p. 50.

72. Malik Ashtar: the governor appointed to Egypt by Imam 'Ali. For the text of the Imam's instructions to him, see *Nahj al-Balagha*, pp. 426-445. A complete translation is contained in William C. Chittick, *A Shi'ite Anthology* (Albany, N.Y., 1980), pp. 68-82.

73. Shaykh Sadduq: also known as Ibn Babuyah, one of the most important of the early Shi'i scholars. He died in 381/991.

74. *Jami' al-Akhbar:* a collection of Shi'i traditions. *'Uyun Akhbar ar-Rida:* a collection of traditions relating to Imam Riza, compiled by Shaykh Sadduq for Sahib ibn 'Abbad, celebrated minister of the Buwayhid dynasty and patron of learning. *al-Majalis:* also known as *al-Amali,* the record of a series of discourses given by Shaykh Sadduq concerning all aspects of Shi'i Islam.

75. *Musnad:* a *hadith* that goes back to the Prophet by an unbroken chain of transmission.

76. *Mursal:* a *hadith* whose chain of transmission goes only as far back as a "follower" (member of the second generation of Islam) who does not mention the name of the companion of the Prophet from whom he heard it.

77. That is, there is a functional distinction between the scholar of *hadith* and the *faqih,* although it is possible for a single individual to embody the two functions.

78. Kulayni: see n. 30 above.

79. Shaykh Sadduq: see n. 73 above.

80. Shaykh Mufid: the common designation of Muhammad al-Harithi, a Shi'i scholar who died in 413/1022.

81. *Fiqh:* jurisprudence; the discipline devoted to the study of the principles and ordinances of Islamic law.

82. *Taqiya:* see n. 16 above.

83. *Ijtihad:* see n. 4 above.

84. A well-known tradition that has led to the compilation of anthologies of forty *hadith* intended for memorization by those who wish to attain the promised reward.

85. Samura ibn Jandab: more fully, Abu Sa'id Samura ibn Jandab al-Qazari, a companion of the Prophet who accompanied him in numerous battles. He later settled in Basra, where he temporarily acted as governor on a number of occasions during the rule of Mu'awiya, first Umayyad caliph.

86. One of the two weak traditions referred to here is probably: "The sultan is the shadow of God upon earth; whoever respects him, respects God, and whoever affronts him, affronts God." For a critique of this alleged tradition, see Nasir ad-Din al-Albani, *Silsilat al-Ahadith ad-Da'ifa wa'l-Maudu'a* (Damascus, 1384/1964), I, i, 98. The other weak tradition may be that cited on p. 220.

87. For example, there is a tradition that says: "A word of truth spoken in the presence of an unjust ruler is a meritorious form of *jihad,*" and two others close with the phrase "there is no obeying the one who disobeys God." For these and similar traditions, see Abdullah Fahd an-Nafisi, *'Indama yahkum al-Islam* (London, n.d.), pp. 142-146.

88. Imam Abu 'l-Hasan Musa, son of Ja'far: seventh of the Twelve Imams, and generally known as Imam Musa al-Kazim. He was born in Medina in 128/744 and died in prison in Baghdad in 183/799.

89. See Shaykh Abu Ja'far al-Kulayni, *al-Kafi,* Eng. trans. Sayyid Muhammad Hasan Rizvi (Tehran, 1398/1978), I, ii, 94-95.

90. Shah Sultan Husayn was the last monarch of the Safavid dynasty, which ruled over Iran from the beginning of the sixteenth century until the second decade of the eighteenth. Among the least competent of the Safavid rulers, he devoted his energies to debauchery and failed to organize the defense of his capital city, Isfahan, against Afghan invaders, to whom it fell in 1722 after a six-month siege. See L. Lockhart, *The Fall of the Safavi Dynasty* (Cambridge, 1958), pp. 144-170.

91. See n. 2 above.

92. Part of a long *hadith* concerning a dream in which the Messenger foresaw the misdeeds of the Umayyads.

93. The expression translated here as "leadership" is *imamat-i i'tibari;* see n. 62 above.

94. Khumayn: the native town of Imam Khomeini.

95. Since the Imam of the Age—i.e., the Twelfth Imam—will emerge from his occultation at a time when injustice fills the earth, it has sometimes been thought that all positive action to remedy injustice must be postponed until his coming.

96. See Kulayni, *al-Kafi*, I, ii, 118-119.

97. *Mufti:* a scholar who pronounces an authoritative opinion (*fatva*) on a point of law.

98. Usama: that is, Usama ibn Zayd, a beloved companion of the Prophet who was placed in charge of a military expedition when he was only eighteen. He died in 59/679.

99. See n. 21 above.

100. *Shahi:* now obsolete, formerly the smallest unit of Iranian currency, worth one-twentieth of a rial.

101. Mu'awiya: first of the Umayyad caliphs and an adversary of Imam 'Ali. He ruled from 41/661 to 60/680.

102. See n. 30 above.

103. *Ya-Sin* is the thirty-sixth chapter of the Qur'an. Its recitation is recommended as particularly meritorious on certain occasions, among them Thursday night, because it leads into Friday, the best of all days.

104. Shurayh: more fully, Shurayh ibn al-Harith al-Kindi, judge of Kufa appointed by 'Umar. He retained this position under 'Uthman, 'Ali, and the Umayyads and died a centenarian in 87/706.

105. From *Wasa'il ash-Shi'a*, a collection of Shi'i traditions by Muhammad Hasan al-Hurr al-'Amuli (d. 1104/1693).

106. *Fatvas:* the plural of *fatva* (an authoritative opinion on a point of law).

107. Naraqi: that is, Hajj Mulla Ahmad Naraqi, a scholar of importance in the early nineteenth century, d. 1244/1829. He not only was a prolific author, but also clashed repeatedly with the monarch of his day, Fath ' Ali Shah. See Hamid Algar, *Religion and State in Iran, 1785-1906* (Berkeley, 1969), pp. 57, 89.

108. Na'ini: that is, Mirza Muhammad Husayn Na'ini, an important scholar of the early twentieth century, 1277/1860-1354/1936. Concerning his book on Shi'i political theory, *Tanbih al-Umma va Tanzih al-Milla,* see Abdul-Hadi Ha'iri, *Shi'ism and Constitutionalism in Iran* (Leiden, Netherlands, 1977), pp. 165-220.

109. Imam Ja'far as-Sadiq: sixth of the Twelve Imams, 83/702-140/757. Also referred to as Imam Sadiq, he was particularly important for his role in developing the religious sciences.

110. The technical sense of the word *imam* is that which it acquires when applied to the Twelve Imams, who were not only successors to the Prophet but also endowed with lofty spiritual virtues.

111. *Ikmal ad-Din wa Itmam an-Ni'ma:* a work by Shaykh Sadduq on the occultation of the Imam.

112. Imam of the Age: the Twelfth Imam. See n. 95 above.

113. Muhammad ibn 'Uthman al-'Umari: the second deputy of the Imam during the Lesser Occultation. See n. 27 above.

114. The designation *hujjat* ("proof") given to the Imams has a two-fold sense. First, through the qualities they manifest, they are proofs of the existence of God and of the veracity of the religion He has revealed. Second, they constitute proofs to be advanced on the Day of Judgment against those who claim they were uninformed of God's law. See Abdulaziz Abdulhussein Sachedina, *Islamic Messianism* (Albany, N.Y., 1980), pp. 66-67.

115. Zurara: more fully, 'Abd Rabbih Zurara ibn A'yan, an authority on the traditions of the fourth, fifth, and sixth Imams, d. 150/767.

116. *Sadaqa:* voluntary payments collected by the Muslim state to be spent for purposes of charity.

117. The Shah organized his vulgar and criminally extravagant celebration of two-and-a-half millenia of monarchical rule in October 1971, some two years after these lectures were given in Najaf. Preparations for the event, however, were begun in the late 1960's. See also pp. 200-208.

118. In 1967 the Shah had himself and his wife crowned.

119. *Maqbula:* a *hadith* to which one may make acceptable reference.

120. See, for example, Isma'il Haqqi al-Burusawi, *Ruh al-Bayan* (Istanbul, 1390/1970), II, 227-228.

121. See, for example, Tabataba'i, *al-Mizan*, IV, 385.

122. *Dhimmi:* one of the *ahl adh-dhimma*, concerning whom see n. 35 above.

123. The Bani Qurayza were a Jewish tribe inhabiting Medina. During the Battle of the Ditch in the fifth year of Islam, they collaborated with a Meccan force that came to attack the city. The menfolk of the tribe were put to death for their treachery.

124. Usama: see n. 98 above.

125. The reference to customary law (*'urf*) is not intended to sanction, but merely to clarify, existing juridical practice.

126. This tradition is contained in al-'Amuli, *Wasa'il ash-Shi'a*, XVII, 98.

127. *Haram:* categorically forbidden by religious law.

128. See Qur'an, 2:256.

129. See al-'Amuli, *Wasa'il ash-Shi'a*, XVIII, 100.

130. Here, "disbelief" implies disobedience. See p. 92.

131. This tradition is quoted in Kulayni, *al-Kafi*, I, ii, 85-86.

132. Kulayni, *al-Kafi*, I, 78-79.

133. There are a number of works by this title. The reference here may be to the Qur'an commentary written in the eleventh/seventeenth century by Ziya ad-Din Yusuf Qazvini. See Agha Buzurg Tihrani, *adh-Dhari'a ila Tasanif ash-Shi'a* (Tehran, 1390/1970), XX, 23.

134. After the death of the Prophet, his daughter Fatima asked for the arable lands near Fadak (a small town near Medina) to be assigned to her as a legacy from her father, since in his lifetime the Prophet had used the produce of the land for the upkeep of his wives. Abu Bakr refused, citing the words of the Prophet: "We prophets bequeath no legacies; what we leave behind is charity (*sadaqa*)." See al-Baladhuri, *al-Futuh*, ed. de Goeje (Leiden, Netherlands, 1886), pp. 29-33. For Shi'i tradition, Fadak became a symbol of unjust denial.

135. *Nass:* a clear and authoritative text, unequivocal in its meaning.

136. Naraqi (n. 107 above) wrote a comprehensive book on the principles of *fiqh* entitled *'Awa'id al-Ayyam min Qawa'id al-Fuqaha al-A'lam.*

137. *Fiqh-i Rizavi:* a work purporting to contain the legal pronouncements of Imam Riza, of disputed authenticity. See Tihrani, *adh-Dhari'a,* XVI, 292-293.

138. See n. 74 above.

139. *Mustadrak:* that is, *Mustadrak al-Wasa'il,* a supplement to *Wasa'il ash-Shi'a* (see n. 105) composed by Mirza Husayn Nuri (d. 1320/1902).

140. Possibly *Ghurar al-Fara'id wa Durar al-Qala'id,* a work on the principles of *fiqh* by Muhsin ibn Hasan al-A'raji (d. 1227/1812). See Tihrani, *adh-Dhari'a,* XVI, 41-42.

141. *Tuhaf al-'Uqul:* a collection of sermons and aphorisms of the Imams compiled by Shaykh Abu Muhammad al-Halabi, a contemporary of Shaykh Sadduq and teacher of Shaykh Mufid.

142. Mina: a small town near Mecca.

143. Imam Khomeini quotes the Arabic text of the tradition before giving his own translation in Persian. We have rendered into English only the Persian translation, which is slightly fuller in parts than the Arabic original.

144. *Minbar:* the pulpit in the mosque.

145. See, for example, 2:168, 4:170, 7:150, 10:57, and many other verses.

146. The word *awliya*—like the cognate *vilayat*—has numerous different meanings. It is used here in the general sense that can be deduced from Qur'an, 10:62-63: "Verily the friends *(awliya)* of God—those who believe and guard against evil—shall suffer no fear nor shall they grieve."

147. Evil innovation: *bid'at,* a belief or practice not compatible with either the Qur'an or the Sunna.

148. Masjid al-Aqsa: see n. 37 above.

149. Among the different schools of Islamic law, the Shi'i school manifests the greatest disapproval of music. Music in a public place is doubly reprehensible since it is an imposition on the unwilling listener.

150. There are certain circumstances that may dispense one from fasting during Ramadan, notably illness, but out of respect for the sanctity of the month and the fasting of others, one must refrain from eating in public.

151. A reference to the agitation against the new laws on the election of local councils promulgated by the Shah's regime on October 6, 1962. These laws no longer specified that candidates were to be Muslim, and they were seen as a prelude to increased participation in public life by the Baha'is and eventual abolition of the Constitution of 1906. After a

prolonged campaign against the laws, in which Imam Khomeini took a prominent part, they were annulled by the government on November 28, 1962. See S.H.R., *Barrasi va Tahlili,* pp. 142-187.

152. Qur'an, 9:60.

153. One indication of the close ties existing with Israel was the regular contacts that took place between Iranian generals and high-ranking members of the Zionist armed forces. For example, General Palizban met in Occupied Palestine with Moshe Dayan and Arik Sharon, most probably in 1974. Photographs of the meeting, showing all participants with cordial smiles, were discovered after the Revolution and published in the newspaper *Jumhuri-yi Islami* on Shahrivar 26, 1359/September 17, 1980.

154. *Ma'sumin:* those possessing the quality of *'ismat* (see n. 67 above); i.e., the Prophet, Fatima, and the Twelve Imams.

155. Mirza Hasan Shirazi: a *mujtahid,* d. 1312/1894. After the production and marketing of tobacco in Iran had been made the monopoly of a British company, he declared in December 1891 that "the use of tobacco is tantamount to war against the Imam of the Age." In obedience to his declaration, all of Iran boycotted tobacco, forcing the cancellation of the concession in early 1892. See Algar, *Religion and State,* pp. 205-215.

156. "Secondary consideration": *'unvan-i sanavi,* a contingent circumstance of legal significance. Tobacco as a substance was religiously unobjectionable; it was the circumstance of the British monopoly that furnished the legal grounds for its prohibition.

157. Mirza Muhammad Taqi Shirazi: a pupil of Mirza Hasan and an important Shi'i scholar, d. 1338/1921. He was a leading force in the resistance by the Shi'i *'ulama* opposed to the imposition of British rule on Iraq at the end of World War I. See Muhammad Hirz ad-Din, *Ma'arif ar-Rijal* (Najaf, 1384/1964), II, 215-218.

158. Kashif al-Ghita: more fully, Muhammad Husayn Kashif al-Ghita, a leading Shi'i scholar of Iraq, 1295/1876-1373/1954. He was active politically as well as academically throughout his life. See the biographical introduction to his *Asl ash-Shi'a wa Usuluha,* 7th ed. (Beirut, 1377/1957), pp. 7-21.

159. See p. 93.

160. On June 23, 1908, Muhammad 'Ali Shah carried out with Russian aid a military coup against the first Iranian Majlis. He was overthrown and constitutional rule restored on July 16, 1909, as a result of popular resistance, largely directed by the most important religious scholars of the day in Najaf. See Browne, *The Persian Revolution of 1905-1909,* chs. 7-10.

161. Soon after the Six-Day War, it was reported that copies of the Qur'an were circulating in the territories seized by the Zionists, as well as in African countries, from which all verses critical of the Jews had been excised.

162. Najaf is the main center of learning in the Shi'i world. The lament here that "we do not even have Najaf" refers to the restrictions and pressure placed on the Shi'i scholars of Najaf by the Baathist regime of Baghdad. The Baathist persecution of Najaf reached a highpoint in May 1969 —ten months before these lectures were given—when a number of *'ulama* were arrested and tortured and religious endowments were confiscated. See anon., *Hayat-e-Hakeem*, in Eng. (Karachi, 1973), pp. 73-84.

163. Insofar as the "enjoining of the good" is the particular duty of the religious scholars, it would be shaming for them to need a reminder from students.

164. Throughout his exile in Najaf, Imam Khomeini gave special attention to the Islamic associations of Iranian students in Europe and the United States, sending them guidance and encouragement. For an example of his messages to the Iranian Muslim students in North America, see pp. 209-211.

165. 'Aqil ibn Abi Talib: brother of Imam 'Ali. After Imam 'Ali assumed the caliphate, 'Aqil is related to have asked him to withdraw 40,000 dirhams from the public treasury to enable him to settle a debt. When his request was denied, 'Aqil abandoned his brother and joined the camp of Mu'awiya in Damascus.

166. Bani Hashim: the Meccan clan to which the Prophet and his descendants belonged.

167. An allusion to the activities of Ashraf, the Shah's twin sister, who was reported in 1960 to have been detained by the Swiss police after large quantities of heroin were found in her possession. See Bahman Nirumand, *Persien, Modell eines Entwicklungslandes* (Hamburg, 1967), pp. 133-134.

168. *Wa la 'd-dallin:* "not those who go astray," a phrase occurring in the seventh verse of the opening chapter of the Qur'an that is recited in every prayer. The letter *d* in *'d-dallin* represents an Arabic sound that does not exist in Persian and it is generally pronounced by Persian speakers as a *z*. Nonetheless, there are those—in Iran and elsewhere—who devote excessive energy to the task of giving the letter its Arabic value when reciting the verse in prayer.

169. 'Ashura: the tenth day of Muharram; the day on which Imam Husayn was martyred in Karbala. See n. 11 above.

170. *Rauzakhwans:* those who specialize in reciting narrations, often versified, of the martyrdom of the Imams. The first part of the designation, *rauza*, is taken from the title of one such narrative, *Rauzat ash-Shuhada*, by Husayn Va'iz Kashifi (d. 910/1504).

171. *Mujahids:* those who engage in *jihad*, who struggle for the attainment of God's purposes on earth.

172. "Citadels of Islam": see the tradition cited on p. 73.

173. Khwaja Nasir ad-Din Tusi: one of the most outstanding of all Shi'i scholars, 597/1201-672/1274. He wrote voluminously not only on the religious sciences, but also on philosophy, mathematics, and astronomy. He joined the entourage of the Mongol conqueror Hulagu when he was passing through Iran on his way to Baghdad, a circumstance that has led many to accuse him of complicity in the conquest. Concerning his associations with the Mongols, see A.H. Hairi, "Nasir ad-Din Tusi: His Alleged Role in the Fall of Baghdad," *Actes du Ve Congres international d'Arabisants et d'Islamisants* (Brussels, 1971), pp. 255-266.

174. 'Allama Hilli: more fully, 'Allama ibn al-Mutahhar al-Hilli, another important Shi'i scholar who lived in the period of Mongol domination of Iran, 648/1250-716/1325. Concerning his scholarly and political activities, see Michel Mazzaoui, *The Rise of the Safawids* (Wiesbaden, 1972), pp. 27-34.

175. Yazid: second Umayyad caliph and adversary of Imam Husayn. He ruled from 60/680 to 64/683.

176. Abu Talib: father of Imam 'Ali. According to Shi'i belief, he embraced Islam; but according to Sunni belief, he did not.

177. *Akhund:* see n. 5 above.

178. Harun ar-Rashid: Abbasid caliph who reigned from 180/186-193/809 and was the contemporary of the seventh and eighth Imams, Musa al-Kazim and Riza.

179. "That man" was Hasan Pakravan, head of SAVAK between 1961 and 1965, executed after the triumph of the Islamic Revolution. This visit occurred on July 2, 1963 when Imam Khomeini was being detained at the 'Ishratabad garrison in Tehran. See S.H.R., *Barrasi va Tahlili*, p. 575.

180. Aqa-yi Qummi: that is, Ayatullah Hasan Tabataba'i Qummi, a religious leader of Mashhad who actively cooperated with Imam Khomeini in the movement of Khurdad 15.

181. For the text of this speech, given at the Masjid-i A'zam in Qum on March 6, 1964, see anon., *Biyugrafi-yi Pishva*, n.p., n.d., II, 109-138.

182. The reference may be to a passage in Mahmud Mahmud, *Tarikh-i Ravabit-i Siyasi-yi Iran va Inglis* (Tehran, 1332 Sh./1953), VI, 1743. Sultan Ghazi ad-Din Haydar of Oudh established an endowment of a hundred lakhs of rupees for the support of the needy in Najaf and Karbala. After his principality was absorbed into British India, the administration of the endowment passed into British hands. Concerning the Oudh bequest and its recipients, see Algar, *Religion and State*, pp. 237-238.

183. Shaykh Murtaza: that is, Shaykh Murtaza Ansari, first *mujtahid* to become the sole source of guidance (*marja'-i taqlid*) of the Shi'i world, 1216/1801-1281/1865. He was the author of *al-Makasib*, a major work on Shi'i jurisprudence. See Algar, *Religion and State*, pp. 162-164.

184. See p. 68.

185. Burujirdi: that is, Ayatullah Husayn Burujirdi, concerning whom, see p. 15.

186. Hujjat: that is, Ayatullah Muhammad Hujjat, a teacher for many years and an associate of Ayatullah Ha'iri, 1310/1862-1372/1953. He was responsible for the building of Hujjatiya Madrasa. See Muhammad Sharif Razi, *Ganjina-yi Danishmandan* (Tehran, 1352 Sh./1973), I, 305-335.

187. Sadr: that is, Ayatullah Sadr ad-Din, 1299/1882-1373/1953, another of the chief associates of Ha'iri in Qum. See Razi, *Ganjina-yi Danishmandan*, I, 326-335.

188. Khwansari: that is, Ayatullah Muhammad Taqi Khwansari, a religious scholar who combined militancy with learning, 1305/1888-1371/1952. He fought against the British occupiers of Iraq under the leadership of Mirza Muhammad Taqi Shirazi (see n. 157) before joining the circle of Ha'iri in Qum. See Razi, *Ganjina-ya Danishmandan*, I, 322-326.

189. Possibly a reference to the Christological disputes of Byzantium.

190. Abu Hurayra: a companion of the Prophet, d. 59/679. He is reported to have narrated 5,374 of the Prophet's traditions, more than any other companion. He was named governor of Bahrayn by 'Umar, judge of Medina by 'Uthman, and governor of Medina by Mu'awiya. Shi'i scholars have regarded him as unreliable and even dishonest. For a defense of his probity, see 'Abd al-Mun'im al-'Ali, *Difa' 'an Abi Hurayra* (Baghdad and Beirut, 1393/1974).

191. A celebrated saying of Imam Ja'far as-Sadiq.

192. 'Ali ibn Yaqtin: an early Shi'i traditionist, 124/742-182/798. He associated with Mansur, the first Abbasid caliph, and is said to have assisted him in planning Baghdad.

193. See n. 173 above.

194. Although a pattern of alliance between Sunni *fuqaha* and rulers can be discerned in Islamic history, it is worth noting that there have been numerous important exceptions, e.g., Abu Hanifa (80/669-152/769), founder of the most widespread Sunni law school, who was imprisoned by the Abbasid caliph Mansur.

195. See n. 88 above.

196. Ma'mun: Abbasid caliph from 198/813 to 218/833, and persecutor of Imam Riza (see n. 48 above).

197. Marv: a city in Transoxiana.

198. Ma'mun and his father Harun were Shi'is in the sense that they implicitly recognized the authority of Imam Riza in their dealings with him.

199. Fadak: see n. 134 above.

200. *Wasa'il ash-Shi'a:* see n. 105.

201. *Mustadrak:* see n. 139 above.

II

Speeches and Declarations

1943

A Warning to the Nation

Neither a speech nor, strictly speaking, a declaration, this is an extract from Kashf al-Asrar, *a book published by Imam Khomeini in 1943, soon after the forced abdication of Riza Shah. The book was written at the behest of Ayatullah Burujirdi in systematic refutation of an anti-religious tract that had appeared a few years earlier. Given its wide-ranging contents and those of the book it was designed to refute, as well as the currency of anti-religious literature in the period of Riza Shah,* Kashf al-Asrar *is largely political in nature and, in fact, constitutes his first public political statement. The extract given here is a fitting introduction to this section of our anthology because of the warning note on which it ends.* Source: Kashf al-Asrar *(n.p., 1943), pp. 221-224.*

WHEN A GOVERNMENT DOES NOT perform its duty, it becomes oppressive. If it does perform its duty, not only is it not oppressive, it is cherished and honored by God. The duty of government, therefore, must be clarified in order for us to establish whether the present government is oppressive or not.

Reason and experience alike tell us that the governments now existing in the world were established at bayonet-point, by force. None of the monarchies or governments that we see in the world are based on justice or a correct foundation that is acceptable to reason. Their foundations are all rotten, being nothing but coercion and force. Reason can never accept that a man who is no different from others in outward or inward accomplishments, unless maybe he is inferior to them, should have his dictates considered proper and just and his government legitimate, merely because he has succeeded in gathering around himself a gang to plunder the country and murder its people.

Do you know what justice is? If you do not know, ask your reason, for reason acts like an eye for man. You have justice when everyone is permitted freely to dispose of the property he has acquired by legitimate means, and injustice when someone is permitted to transgress against the property and rights of others. This is unjust and evil, whoever the transgressor may be and however powerful, no matter how obscure and powerless the person is who is condemned to suffer his oppression. This Hitlerite mentality you idiotically praise from afar, which says, "I will occupy Poland by tank and bayonet, even though a hundred thousand families may perish," is one of the most poisonous and heinous products of the human mind.[1] Every lover of justice must oppose it, and those wise men who are concerned for the future of the world must root out such thoughts as these in order for the world to attain tranquillity.

The only government that reason accepts as legitimate and welcomes freely and happily is the government of God, Whose every act is just and Whose right it is to rule over the whole world and all the particles of existence. Whatever He makes use of is His own property, and whatever He takes, from whomever He takes, is again His own property. No men can deny this except the mentally disturbed.

It is in contrast with the government of God that the nature of all existing governments becomes clear, as well as the sole legitimacy of Islamic government. The duty of our government, which is among the smaller states in the world, is to conform to this legitimate government by making the laws passed by the Majlis a kind of commentary on the divine law. It will thus become apparent that the law of Islam is the most advanced law in the world, and that its implementation will lead to the establishment of the Virtuous City.[2]

We do not say that government must be in the hands of the *faqih;* rather we say that government must be run in accordance with God's law, for the welfare of the country and the people demands this, and it is not feasible except with the supervision of the religious leaders. In fact, this principle has been approved and ratified in the Constitution[3] and in no way conflicts with public order, the stability of the government, or the interests of the country. If it were implemented, everyone in the country, with no exception, from the religious leaders to the tradesmen, soldiers, and hawkers in the street, would cooperate with the government and strive earnestly to attain the independence and greatness of the nation.

Look at the present state of the various components of the government. Notice first the deplorable state of the court, and then consider the various ministries, examining one by one the officials who are content to sit behind their desks in utter idleness. Then proceed to inspect the army, and see what mentality motivates the troops and their commanders. Descending the scale, take a look at the civil and military administration in all the provinces. Finally, step over to the Consultative Assembly and watch the legislature at work! Wherever you go and whomever you encounter, from the streetsweeper to the highest official, you will see nothing but disordered thoughts, confused ideas, contradictory opinions, self-interest, lechery, immodesty, criminality, treachery, and thousands of associated vices. Then you will understand how our country's income is obtained, and on what it is spent.

Given such circumstances, the details of which I must not disclose, it should not be expected that the government would be regarded as just and legitimate in religious circles. Nor should the wretched masses of the people, before whose eyes all these criminal and treacherous acts are committed and who are each subjected to some injustice by an official every hour, be expected to cooperate with the government, or to regard treachery against this treacherous government as forbidden. If just one article of the Constitution were to be implemented, that specifying that all laws contrary to the *shari'a* are invalid,[4] everyone in the country would join together in harmony, and the country would move forward with the speed of lightning. All the deplorable institutions mentioned above would be transformed into new and rational institutions, and through the joint efforts of all the people, the educated and the masses alike, the country would attain a state unparalleled in the world.

We know that all this is unpalatable to those who have grown up with lechery, treachery, music and dancing, and a thousand other varieties of corruption. Of course, they regard the civilization and advancement of the country as dependent upon women's going naked in the streets, or to quote their own idiotic words, turning half the population into workers by unveiling them (we

171

know only too well what kind of work is involved here). They will not agree to the country's being administered rationally and in accordance with God's law. We have nothing to say to those whose powers of perception are so limited that they regard the wearing of European hats, the cast-offs of the wild beasts of Europe, as a sign of national progress. We do not expect them to accept a few words of sense from us; the foreigners have stolen their reason, intelligence, and all other senses. They have forfeited their faculties so completely to the foreigners that they even imitate them in matters of time; what is left for us to say to them? As you all know, noon is now officially reckoned in Tehran twenty minutes before the sun has reached the meridian, in imitation of Europe. So far, no one has stood up to ask, "What nightmare is this into which we are being plunged?"

The day everyone was forced to wear the Pahlavi cap,[5] it was said, "We need to have a national symbol. Independence in matters of dress is proof and guarantee of the independence of a nation." Then a few years later, everyone was forced to put on European hats, and suddenly the justification changed: "We have dealings with foreigners and must dress the same way they do in order to enjoy greatness in the world." If a country's greatness depended on its hat, it would be a thing very easily lost![6]

While all this was going on, the foreigners, who wished to implement their plans and rob you of one hat while putting another on your head, watched you in amusement from afar and laughed at your infantile games. With a European hat on your head, you would parade around the streets enjoying the naked girls, taking pride in this "achievement," totally heedless of the fact that meanwhile, the historic patrimony of the country was being plundered from one end to the other, all its sources of wealth were being carried off, and you yourselves were being reduced to a pitiful state by the TransIranian Railroad.[7]

You all cursed and condemned the agreement concluded by Vusuq ad-Daula with the British,[8] and you were right to do so. But then they fastened the same plans around your neck, in a worse form than before,[9] and you declared them to be a sign of the progress achieved by the country during the Pahlavi period (although there were people among you who were secretly grieving and who would not so much as breathe for fear of the bayonet). There is much to be said, much that is weighing on my mind, but where are the ears to listen to me, where is the perception to understand me? In short, these idiotic and treacherous rulers, these officials — high and low — these reprobates and smugglers must change in order for the country to change. Otherwise, you will experience worse times than these, times so bad that the present will seem like paradise by comparison.

April 3, 1963

In Commemoration of the Martyrs at Qum

This declaration was given from Qum on the occasion of the fortieth day after the assault on Fayziya Madrasa that took place on March 22, 1963. Source: *Khomeini va Junbish* (a collection of speeches and declarations) (n.p., 1394/1974), pp. 1-3.

FORTY DAYS HAVE NOW PASSED since the beating, wounding and killing of our dear ones; those the victims of the slaughter at Fayziya Madrasa left behind have now been plunged into mourning for forty days. Yesterday the father of Sayyid Yunus Rudbari (may God have mercy upon him) came to see me, with his back bent and his face deeply marked by the great tragedy he has suffered. What words are there to console those mothers who have lost their children, those bereaved fathers?

Indeed, we must offer our condolences to the Prophet of Islam (peace and blessings be upon him and his family) and the Imam of the Age (may God hasten his renewed manifestation), for it is for the sake of those great ones that we have endured these blows and lost our young men. Our crime was defending the laws of Islam and the independence of Iran. It is because of our defense of Islam that we have been humiliated and brought to expect imprisonment, torture, and execution. Let this tyrannical regime perform whatever inhuman deed it wishes—let it break the arms and legs of our young men, let it chase our wounded from the hospitals, let it threaten us with death and the violation of our honor, let it destroy the institutions of religious learning, let it expel the doves of this Islamic sanctuary from their nests!

During these past forty days, we have been unable to obtain a precise count of the dead, the wounded, and those whose property has been plundered. We do not know how many people have been buried, how many are languishing in dungeons, how many have gone into hiding. In fact, all these years after the event, we still do not know the exact number of people killed at the mosque of Gauhar Shad, when the bodies were carried away loaded on trucks.[10]

The problem we confront is that whatever authority you address will tell you: "Whatever was done, was on the orders of His Imperial Majesty; we had no choice in the matter." Everyone, from the Prime Minister down to the police chief and the governor of Qum, tell us in effect: "We received orders from His Imperial Majesty. The crimes at Fayziya Madrasa were committed on his orders. The wounded were expelled from the hospitals on his orders, and it was he who commanded us to attack your homes with commandos and whores and to plunder your homes if you attempted to do anything in response to Ayatullah Hakim.[11] It is also His Imperial Majesty's command that we seize and forcibly draft the *tullab*,[12] without the slightest legal justification. Furthermore, it is the command of His Imperial Majesty that we attack the university and assault the students."

Government officials attribute all these violations of the law to the Shah. If this attribution is justified, we must recite funeral prayers for Islam, Iran, and legality. If it is not, and they are lying in attributing all these crimes, violations of the law, and inhuman acts to the Shah, then why does he not defend himself, so that the people may know how they should treat the government and punish it for its deeds at the appropriate time?

I have repeatedly pointed out that the government has evil intentions and is opposed to the ordinances of Islam. One by one, the proofs of its enmity are becoming clear. The Ministry of Justice has made clear its opposition to the ordinances of Islam by various measures like the abolition of the requirement that judges be Muslim and male; henceforth, Jews, Christians, and the enemies of Islam and the Muslims are to decide on affairs concerning the honor and person of the Muslims. The strategy of this government and certain of its members is to bring about the total efface-ment of the ordinances of Islam. As long as this usurpatory and rebellious government is in power, the Muslims can have no hope for any good.

I don't know whether all these uncivilized and criminal acts have been committed for the sake of the oil in Qum, whether the religious teaching institution is to be sacrificed for the sake of oil.[13] Or is all this being done for the sake of Israel, since we are considered an obstacle to the conclusion of a treaty with Israel directed against the Islamic states?[14] In any event, we are to be destroyed. The tyrannical regime imagines that through these inhuman acts and this repression it can deflect us from our aim, which is none other than the great aim of Islam—to prevent oppression, arbitrary rule, and the violation of the law; to preserve the rights of Islam and the nation; and to establish social justice.

But it causes us not the least concern that the sons of Islam should be drafted into the army. Let our young men enter the barracks, educate our troops, and raise their level of thinking; let a few enlightened and freedom-loving people appear among our troops so that, by the grace of God Almighty, Iran may attain its dignity and freedom. We know that the commanders of the great Iranian army, its respectable officers, and its noble members share our aims and are ready to sacrifice themselves for the sake of the dignity of Iran. I know that no officer with a conscience approves of these crimes and acts of brutality, and I am aware of (and deplore) the pressures to which they are subject. I extend a fraternal hand to them in the hope of obtaining the salvation of Islam and Iran. I know that their hearts are troubled by this subordination to Israel, and that they do not wish Iran to be trampled by the boots of the Jews.

I declare to the heads of the Muslim states, whether Arab or non-Arab: The 'ulama of Islam, the religious leaders and pious people of Iran, together with its noble army, are the brothers of the Muslim states and share their interests. They abhor and are disgusted with the treaty with Israel, the enemy of Islam and Iran. I say this quite clearly; if they wish, let the agents of Israel come put an end to my life!

It is fitting that the Muslim nation, whether in Iran or abroad, should commemorate the great tragedy suffered by Islam and the disasters inflicted on the religious teaching institution on the fortieth day after their occurrence. If they are not prevented by the agents of the government, they should hold ceremonies of mourning and curse those responsible for these atrocities.

The Afternoon of 'Ashura

This speech, delivered at Fayziya Madrasa in Qum, is particularly notable for its fearless words of reproach addressed to the Shah. Source: *Khomeini va Junbish,* pp. 4-7.

IT IS NOW THE AFTERNOON of 'Ashura. Sometimes when I recall the events of 'Ashura, a question occurs to me: If the Umayyads[15] and the regime of Yazid ibn Mu'awiya[16] wished to make war against Husayn, why did they commit such savage and inhuman crimes against the defenseless women and innocent children? What was the offense of the women and children? What had Husayn's six month-old infant done?[17] It seems to me that the Umayyads had a far more basic aim: they were opposed to the very existence of the family of the Prophet. They did not wish the Bani Hashim[18] to exist and their goal was to root out this "goodly tree."[19]

A similar question occurs to me now. If the tyrannical regime of Iran simply wished to wage war on the *maraji'*,[20] to oppose the *'ulama,* what business did it have tearing the Qur'an to shreds on the day it attacked Fayziya Madrasa? Indeed, what business did it have with the madrasa or with its students, like the eighteen year-old *sayyid* who was killed? What had he done against the Shah, against the government, against the tyrannical regime? We come to the conclusion that this regime also has a more basic aim: they are fundamentally opposed to Islam itself and the existence of the religious class. They do not wish this institution to exist; they do not wish any of us to exist, the great and the small alike.

Israel does not wish the Qur'an to exist in this country. Israel does not wish the *'ulama* to exist in this country. Israel does not wish a single learned man to exist in this country. It was Israel that assaulted Fayziya Madrasa by means of its sinister agents. It is still assaulting us, and assaulting you, the nation; it wishes to seize your economy, to destroy your trade and agriculture, to appropriate your wealth. Israel wishes to remove by means of its agents anything it regards as blocking its path. The Qur'an is blocking its path; it must be removed. The religious scholars are blocking its path; they must be eliminated. Fayziya Madrasa and other centers of knowledge and learning are blocking its path; they must be destroyed. The *tullab* might later come to block their path; they must be killed, pushed off the roof, have their heads and arms broken. In order for Israel to attain its objectives, the government of Iran has continually affronted us in acccordance with goals and plans conceived in Israel.

Respected people of Qum! On the day that mendacious, that scandalous referendum took place—that referendum contrary to all the interests of the Iranian nation and conducted at bayonet-point[21]—you witnessed a gang of hooligans and ruffians prowling around Qum, on foot and riding in cars, going down the streets and thoroughfares of this center of religious learning that stands next to the shrine of Fatima, the Immaculate One[22] (peace be upon her)! They were shouting: "Your days of parasitism are at an end! Your days of eating *pulao* are over!"

Now, these students of the religious sciences who spend the best and most active part of their lives in these narrow cells, and whose monthly income is somewhere between 40 and 100 tumans —are they parasites? And those to whom one source of income alone brings hundreds of millions of tumans are not parasites? Are the *'ulama* parasites—people like the late Hajj Shaykh 'Abd al-Karim,[23] whose sons had nothing to eat on the night that he died; or the late Burujirdi,[24] who was 600,000 tumans in debt when he departed from this world? And those who have filled foreign banks with the wealth produced by the toil of our poverty-stricken people, who have erected towering palaces but still will not leave the people in peace, wishing to fill their own pockets and those of Israel with our resources—they are not parasites? Let the world judge, let the nation judge who the parasites are!

Let me give you some advice, Mr. Shah! Dear Mr. Shah, I advise you to desist in this policy and acts like this. I don't want the people to offer up thanks if your masters should decide one day that you must leave. I don't want you to become like your father.[25]

Iranian nation! Those among you who are thirty or forty years of age or more will remember how three foreign countries attacked us during World War II. The Soviet Union, Britain, and America invaded Iran and occupied our country. The property of the people was exposed to danger and their honor was imperilled. But God knows, everyone was happy because the Pahlavi had gone!

Shah, I don't wish the same to happen to you; I don't want you to become like your father. Listen to my advice, listen to the *'ulama* of Islam. They desire the welfare of the nation, the welfare of the country. Don't listen to Israel; Israel can't do anything for you. You miserable wretch, forty-five years of your life have passed; isn't it time for you to think and reflect a little, to ponder about where all this is leading you, to learn a lesson from the experience of your father? If what they say is true, that you are opposed to Islam and the religious scholars, your ideas are quite wrong. If they are dictating these things to you and then giving them to you to read, you should think about it a little. Why do you speak without thinking? Are the religious scholars really some form of impure animal? If they are impure animals, why do the people kiss their hands? Why do they regard the very water they drink as blessed? Are we really impure animals? I hope to God that you did not have in mind the *'ulama* and the religious scholars when you said, "The reactionaries are like an impure animal," because if you did, it will be difficult for us to tolerate you much longer, and you will find yourself in a predicament. You won't be able to go on living; the nation will not allow you to continue this way. The religious scholars and Islam are Black Reaction! And you have carried out your White Revolution in the midst of all this Black Reaction! What do you mean, a White Revolution? Why do you try to deceive the people so? Why do you threaten the people so?[26]

I was informed today that a number of preachers and speakers in Tehran were taken to the offices of SAVAK and were threatened with punishment if they speak on three subjects. They were not to say anything bad about the Shah, not to attack Israel, and not to say that Islam is endangered. Otherwise, they can say what they like! But all of our problems and all our differences with the government comprise exactly these three! If we overlook these three subjects, we have no dispute with the government. Even if we do not say that Islam is endangered, will that mean that Islam is not endangered? Or if we do not say, "The Shah is such-and-such," will that mean that he is not in fact such-and-such? And

179

what is this tie, this link, between the Shah and Israel that makes SAVAK consider the Shah an Israeli? Does SAVAK consider the Shah a Jew?

Mr. Shah! Maybe those people want to present you as a Jew so that I will denounce you as an unbeliever and they can expel you from Iran and put an end to you! Don't you know that if one day, some uproar occurs and the tables are turned, none of those people around you will be your friends? They are friends of the dollar; they have no religion, no loyalty. They are hanging responsibility for everything around your miserable neck!

You know that vile individual—I'll mention his name at the appropriate time—who came to Fayziya Madrasa and whistled to signal for the commandos to gather, then ordered them to attack, to assault, to plunder all the rooms in the madrasa and destroy everything. When he is asked, "Why did you commit these crimes?" he replies, "The Shah told us to do it. It was his royal command that we destroy Fayziya Madrasa and slaughter these people."

There is much to be said, far more than you can even imagine. Certain things are happening that endanger our country and our Islam. The things that are happening to this nation and those that are about to happen fill me with anxiety and sorrow. I feel anxiety and sorrow at the state of Iran, at the state of our ruined country, at the state of this cabinet, at the state of those running our government.

I pray to God Almighty that He remedy our affairs.

October 27, 1964

The Granting of Capitulatory Rights to the U.S.

Imam Khomeini delivered this speech in front of his residence in Qum. Together with the declaration he issued on the same subject, it was the immediate cause for his forced exile from Iran on November 4, 1964. Source: S.H.R., *Barrasi va Tahlili az Nihzat-i Imam Khomeini* (Najaf? n.d.), pp. 716-726.

I CANNOT EXPRESS THE SORROW I feel in my heart. My heart is constricted. Since the day I heard of the latest developments affecting Iran, I have barely slept; I am profoundly disturbed, and my heart is constricted. With sorrowful heart, I count the days until death shall come and deliver me.

Iran no longer has any festival to celebrate; they have turned our festival into mourning.[27] They have turned it into mourning and lit up the city; they have turned it into mourning and are dancing together with joy. They have sold us, they have sold our independence; but still they light up the city and dance.

If I were in their place, I would forbid all these lights; I would give orders that black flags be raised over the bazaars and houses, that black awnings be hung! Our dignity has been trampled underfoot; the dignity of Iran has been destroyed. The dignity of the Iranian army has been trampled underfoot!

A law has been put before the Majlis according to which we are to accede to the Vienna Convention,[28] and a provision has been added to it that all American military advisers, together with their families, technical and administrative officials, and servants— in short, anyone in any way connected to them—are to enjoy legal immunity with respect to any crime they may commit in Iran.

If some American's servant, some American's cook, assassinates your *marja'*[29] in the middle of the bazaar, or runs over him, the Iranian police do not have the right to apprehend him! Iranian courts do not have the right to judge him! The dossier must be

181

sent to America, so that our masters there can decide what is to be done!

First, the previous government approved this measure without telling anyone, and now the present government just recently introduced a bill in the Senate and settled the whole matter in a single session without breathing a word to anyone. A few days ago, the bill was taken to the lower house of the Majlis and there were discussions, with a few deputies voicing their opposition, but the bill was passed anyhow. They passed it without any shame, and the government shamelessly defended this scandalous measure. They have reduced the Iranian people to a level lower than that of an American dog. If someone runs over a dog belonging to an American, he will be prosecuted. Even if the Shah himself were to run over a dog belonging to an American, he would be prosecuted. But if an American cook runs over the Shah, the head of state, no one will have the right to interfere with him.

Why? Because they wanted a loan and America demanded this in return. A few days after this measure was approved, they requested a $200 million loan from America and America agreed to the request. It was stipulated that the sum of $200 million would be paid to the Iranian government over a period of five years, and that $300 million would be paid back to America over a period of ten years. So in return for this loan, America is to receive $100 million—or 800 million tumans—in interest. But in addition to this, Iran has sold itself to obtain these dollars. The government has sold our independence, reduced us to the level of a colony, and made the Muslim nation of Iran appear more backward than savages in the eyes of the world!

What are we to do in the face of this disaster? What are our religious scholars to do? To what country should they present their appeal?

Other people imagine that it is the Iranian nation that has abased itself in this way. They do not know that it is the Iranian government, the Iranian Majlis—the Majlis that has nothing to do with the people. What can a Majlis that is elected at bayonet-point have to do with the people? The Iranian nation did not elect these deputies. Many of the high-ranking *ulama* and *maraji'* ordered a boycott of the elections, and the people obeyed them and did not vote. But then came the power of the bayonet, and these deputies were seated in the Majlis.

They have seen that the influence of the religious leaders prevents them from doing whatever they want, so now they wish to destroy that influence!

According to a history textbook printed this year and taught to our schoolchildren now, one containing all kinds of lies and inaccurate statements, "It has now become clear that it is to the benefit of the nation for the influence of the religious leaders to be rooted out."

They have come to understand well that:

If the religious leaders have influence, they will not permit this nation to be the slaves of Britain one day, and America the next.

If the religious leaders have influence, they will not permit Israel to take over the Iranian economy; they will not permit Israeli goods to be sold in Iran—in fact, to be sold duty-free!

If the religious leaders have influence, they will not permit the government to impose arbitrarily such a heavy loan on the Iranian nation.

If the religious leaders have influence, they will not permit such misuse to be made of the public treasury.

If the religious leaders have influence, they will not permit the Majlis to come to a miserable state like this; they will not permit the Majlis to be formed at bayonet-point, with the scandalous results that we see.

If the religious leaders have influence, they will not permit girls and boys to wrestle together, as recently happened in Shiraz.

If the religious leaders have influence, they will not permit people's innocent daughters to be under young men at school; they will not permit women to teach at boys' schools and men to teach at girls' schools, with all the resulting corruption.

If the religious leaders have influence, they will strike this government in the mouth, they will strike this Majlis in the mouth and chase these deputies out of both its houses!

If the religious leaders have influence, they will not permit a handful of individuals to be imposed on the nation as deputies and participate in determining the destiny of the country.

If the religious leaders have influence, they will not permit some agent of America to carry out these scandalous deeds; they will throw him out of Iran.

So the influence of the religious leaders is harmful to the nation? No, it is harmful to you, harmful to you traitors, not to the nation! You know that as long as the religious leaders have influence, you cannot do everything you want to do, commit all the crimes you want, so you wish to destroy their influence. You thought you could cause dissension among the religious leaders with your intrigues, but you will be dead before your dream can come true. You will never be able to do it. The religious leaders are united.[30]

I esteem all the religious leaders. Once again, I kiss the hand of all the religious leaders. If I kissed the hands of the *maraji'* in the past, today I kiss the hands of the *tullab.* I kiss the hands of the simple grocer.

Gentlemen, I warn you of danger!

Iranian army, I warn you of danger!

Iranian politicians, I warn you of danger!

Iranian merchants, I warn you of danger!

'Ulama of Iran, *maraji'* of Islam, I warn you of danger!

Scholars, students! Centers of religious learning! Najaf, Qum, Mashhad, Tehran, Shiraz! I warn you of danger!

The danger is coming to light now, but there are other things that are being kept hidden from us. In the Majlis they said, "Keep these matters secret!" Evidently they are dreaming up further plans for us. What greater evil are they about to inflict upon us? Tell me, what could be worse than slavery? What could be worse than abasement? What else do they want to do? What are they planning?

What disasters this loan has brought down upon the head of the nation already! This impoverished nation must now pay $100 million in interest to America over the next ten years. And as if that were not enough, we have been sold for the sake of this loan!

What use to you are the American soldiers and military advisers? If this country is occupied by America, then what is all this noise you make about progress? If these advisers are to be your servants, then why do you treat them like something superior to masters? If they are servants, why not treat them as such? If they are your employees, then why not treat them as any other government treats its employees? If our country is now occupied by the U.S., then tell us outright and throw us out of this country!

What do they intend to do? What does this government have to say to us? What is this Majlis doing? This illegal, illicit Majlis; this Majlis that the *maraji'* have had boycotted with their *fatvas* and decrees; this Majlis that makes empty noises about independence and revolution, that says: "We have undergone a White Revolution"!

I don't know where this White Revolution is that they are making so much fuss about. God knows that I am aware of (and my awareness causes me pain) the remote villages and provincial towns, not to mention our own backward city of Qum. I am aware of the hunger of our people and the disordered state of our agrarian economy. Why not try to do something for this country, for this population, instead of piling up debts and enslaving yourselves? Of course, taking the dollars means that someone has to become a slave; you take the dollars and use them, and we become slaves! If an American runs over me with his car, no one will have the right to say anything to him!

Those gentlemen who say we must hold our tongues and not utter a sound—do they still say the same thing on this occasion? Are we to keep silent again and not say a word? Are we to keep silent while they are selling us? Are we to keep silent while they sell our independence?

By God, whoever does not cry out in protest is a sinner! By God, whoever does not express his outrage commits a major sin!

Leaders of Islam, come to the aid of Islam!

'Ulama of Najaf, come to the aid of Islam!

'Ulama of Qum, come to the aid of Islam! Islam is destroyed!

Muslim peoples! Leaders of the Muslim peoples! Presidents and kings of the Muslim peoples! Come to our aid! Shah of Iran, save yourself!

Are we to be trampled underfoot by the boots of America simply because we are a weak nation and have no dollars? America is worse than Britain; Britain is worse than America. The Soviet Union is worse than both of them. They are all worse and more unclean than each other! But today it is America that we are concerned with.

185

Let the American President know that in the eyes of the Iranian people, he is the most repulsive member of the human race today because of the injustice he has imposed on our Muslim nation. Today the Qur'an has become his enemy, the Iranian nation has become his enemy. Let the American government know that its name has been ruined and disgraced in Iran.

Those wretched deputies in the Majlis begged the government to ask "our friends" the Americans not to make such impositions on us, not to insist that we sell ourselves, not to turn Iran into a colony. But did anyone listen?

There is one article in the Vienna Convention they did not mention at all—Article 32. I don't know what article that is; in fact, the chairman of the Majlis himself doesn't know. The deputies also don't know what that article is; nonetheless, they went ahead and approved and signed the bill. They passed it, even though some people said, "We don't know what is in Article 32." Maybe those who objected did not sign the bill. They are not quite so bad as the others, those who certainly did sign. They are a herd of illiterates.

One after another, our statesmen and leading politicians have been set aside. Our patriotic statesmen are given nothing to do. The army should know that it will also be treated the same way: its leaders will be set aside, one by one. What self-respect will remain for the army when an American errand boy or cook has priority over one of our generals? If I were in the army, I would resign. If I were a deputy in the Majlis, I would resign. I would not agree to be disgraced.

American cooks, mechanics, technical and administrative officials, together with their families, are to enjoy legal immunity, but the 'ulama of Islam, the preachers and servants of Islam, are to live banished or imprisoned. The partisans of Islam are to live in Bandar 'Abbas[31] or in prison, because they are religious leaders or supporters of the religious leaders.

The government clearly documents its crimes by putting out a history textbook that says, "It is to the benefit of the nation to root out the influence of the religious leaders." This means that it is for the benefit of the nation that the Messenger of God should play no role in its affairs. For the religious leaders of themselves have nothing; whatever they have, they have from the Messenger of God. So the government wants the Messenger of God to play no role in our affairs, so that Israel can do whatever it likes, and America likewise.

All of our troubles today are caused by America and Israel. Israel itself derives from America; these deputies and ministers that have been imposed upon us derive from America—they are all agents of America, for if they were not, they would rise up in protest.

I am now thoroughly agitated, and my memory is not working so well. I cannot remember precisely when, but in one of the earlier Majlises, where Sayyid Hasan Mudarris[32] was a deputy, the government of Russia gave Iran an ultimatum—I can't remember its exact content—to the effect that "Unless you accept our demand, we will advance on Tehran by way of Qazvin and occupy it!" The government of the day put pressure on the Majlis to accept the Russian demand.

According to an American historian, a religious leader with stick in hand (the late Mudarris) came up to the tribune and said: "Now that we are to be destroyed, why should we sign the warrant for our own destruction?" The Majlis took courage from his act of opposition, rejected the ultimatum, and Russia was unable to do anything!

That is the conduct of a true religious leader; a thin, emaciated man, a mere heap of bones, rejects the ultimatum and demand of a powerful state like Russia. If there were a single religious leader in the Majlis today, he would not permit these things to happen. It is for this reason that they wish to destroy the influence of the religious leaders, in order to attain their aims and desires!

There is so much to be said, there are so many instances of corruption in this country, that I am unable in my state at the moment to present to you even what I know. It is your duty, however, to communicate these matters to your colleagues. The 'ulama must enlighten the people, and they in turn must raise their voices in protest to the Majlis and the government and say, "Why did you do this? Why have you sold us? We did not elect you to be our representatives, and even if we had done so, you would forfeit your posts now on account of this act of treachery."

This is high treason! O God, they have committed treason against this country. O God, this government has committed treason against the Qur'an. All the members of both houses who gave their agreement to this affair are traitors. Those old men in the Senate are traitors, and all those in the lower house who voted in favor of this affair are traitors. They are not our representatives. The whole world must know that they are not the representatives of Iran. Or, suppose they are; now I dismiss them. They are dismissed from their posts and all the bills they have passed up until now are invalid.

According to the very text of the law, according to Article 2 of the Supplementary Constitutional Law, no law is valid unless the *mujtahids* exercise a supervisory role in the Majlis. From the beginning of the constitutional period down to the present, has any *mujtahid* ever exercised supervision? If there were five *mujtahids* in this Majlis, or even one single religious leader of lesser rank, they would get a punch in the mouth; he would not allow this bill to be enacted, he would make the Majlis collapse.

As for those deputies who apparently opposed this affair, I wish to ask them in protest: If you were genuinely opposed, why did you not pour soil on your heads? Why did you not rise up and seize that wretch[33] by the collar? Does "opposition" mean simply to sit there and say, "We are not in agreement," and then continue your flattery as usual? You must create an uproar, right there in the Majlis. You must not permit there to be such a Majlis. Is it enough to say simply, "I am opposed," when the bill passes nevertheless?

We do not regard as law what they claim to have passed. We do not regard this Majlis as a Majlis. We do not regard this government as a government. They are traitors, guilty of high treason!

O God, remedy the affairs of the Muslims! O God, bestow dignity on this sacred religion of Islam! O God, destroy those individuals who are traitors to this land, who are traitors to Islam, who are traitors to the Qur'an.

And peace be upon you, and also God's mercy.

April 16, 1967

Open Letter to Prime Minister Hoveyda

Written in Najaf, this missive from an exiled and apparently powerless figure may have escaped Hoveyda's notice at the time, but he had cause to remember it after the triumph of the Islamic Revolution.[34] *Source: Khomeini va Junbish, pp. 32-35.*

Mr. Hoveyda:

It is necessary for me to offer you some advice and to remind you of certain things that need to be said, whether or not you are free to accept them.

Throughout this long period that I have been away from my homeland because of the crime of opposing the legal immunity of the Americans—a shattering blow to the foundations of our national independence—and have been compelled to live in exile, contrary to the law of the land, the *shari'a,* and the Constitution, I have been observing the misfortunes that have been descending on our oppressed and defenseless people. I have been kept informed of the oppression inflicted on our noble people by the tyrannical regime, and I have suffered correspondingly.

It is greatly to be regretted that the reforms proclaimed by yourself and the rest of them have not gone beyond the stage of loud propaganda proclaimed over the radio, in the unfree press of our country, and in a few books filled with all kinds of bombast. The poverty and wretchedness of our people increase every day, as does the bankruptcy of the bazaar and its respected merchants. The only result of all this hullaballoo and bombastic propaganda has been to create a black market for the foreigners and to keep the people in a state of poverty and backwardness while you make claims of progress. In compliance with the wishes of those who want to keep the peoples of the East in a state of backwardness, you and your predecessor have run a police regime, a medieval regime, a regime of the bayonet, of torture and imprisonment, a regime of repression and denied liberty, a regime of terror and thievery.

While invoking constitutionalism, you have created the worst form of tyrannical and arbitrary government. While speaking of Islam, you have tried to inflict grievous blows on the Noble Qur'an and its heavenly injunctions. While mentioning the exalted teachings of Islam, you have trampled the ordinances of Islam underfoot one by one, and if (God forbid) you are given the opportunity, you will continue to do so.

Yes, with your empty claims of progress and advancement, you have kept the country in a state of backwardness.

All these are bitter truths that I must report to the world, and I must point an accusing finger at those responsible for them, so that those who are unaware (or pretend to be unaware) come to recognize their duty and are no longer taken in by your hypocrisy and deceit. The anti-national festivals organized several times each year for the benefit of a certain person[35] are one form of this hypocrisy and deceit that, on each occasion, bring disaster to Islam, the Muslims, and the poverty-stricken, barefoot people of Iran. The huge expenditures that are required are extorted from the people at bayonet-point. It is said that one of these festivals, which one can only call licentiousness and an affront to the sensibilities of the nation, cost 4000 million rials,[36] half of it taken from the national treasury and the other half extorted directly from the bazaar merchants and others by force and intimidation. They bleed the hearts of the poor for money to satisfy arrogance and selfish ambition. As long as our nation is in this state, and is unaware of its duties and its rights, every day is a festival and a cause of rejoicing for you, and misfortune and misery for the nation. The honor of Islam and the Muslims is violated in conjunction with these festivals in ways that the pen is ashamed of recording.

Sitting in your opulent palaces, which you change once every few years, you spend millions of tumans with an extravagance our people cannot even imagine and steal it all from the purse of our wretched nation. You witness complacently the hunger and poverty of our people, the bankruptcy of the bazaar, the unemployment of our educated youth, the sorry state of our agriculture and industry, the domination of the country's economy by Israel, and even, according to some reports, Israel's interference in our educational system. You see that most of the villages near the capital, let alone those in remote regions, lack the basic necessities of life—clean drinking water, bathhouses, and medical care. You see the diffusion of moral corruption, dishonesty, and irreligion in the depth of the countryside. You see funds set up that are supposedly cooperatives, but in fact are a means for government officials to rob and plunder the peasants, who come ruefully to understand that they have been cheated. Finally you see all the illegal imprisonment, terror, and threats that are inflicted on the people, while you are immersed in your pleasures, enjoyments, and shameful games and recite the funeral prayers over this cemetery called Iran.

How does your conscience permit you to fawn so much before the foreigners for the sake of this fleeting power, to surrender the resources of the nation to them for nothing or for a small price, to inflict such cruelty and oppression on your subjects—this ill-fated nation? How does your conscience permit you to represent your government, your nation, this Islamic land, as backward in the eyes of the world? For violation of the Constitution is a sign of backwardness; the illegal and fradulent referendum is a sign of backwardness; the refusal to let the people freely choose their representatives, and the appointment instead of disreputable individuals, on orders from above and without the participation of the people—this, too is a sign of weakness and backwardness. You and your like know that if the nation were to determine its own destiny, you would not last a minute and would be pushed completely aside.

Give speakers and writers their freedom for ten days, and they will reveal all of your crimes. You are not strong enough to grant freedom, for "The traitor is a coward." Yes, the denial of freedom of the press and the authority of the so-called security organization to dictate the contents of the press are a sign of backwardness.

The periodic celebrations for things that are completely unknown in other countries and the imposition of backbreaking expenditures on the people are a sign of backwardness.

Submission to the demands of the pseudo-state of Israel and endangering the economy of this country are a sign of weakness, servility, and treachery to Islam and the Muslims.

The granting of legal immunity to foreigners is a great proof of backwardness, of lack of self-respect and unconditional submission. You know well what treason to Islam and this country you committed by approving that bill, and what a blow you inflicted on our national independence. (Naturally, anyone who opposes that bill must be a traitor and deserving of exile.)

Mr. Hoveyda, your regrettable speeches, which have unfortunately been published, contain certain confessions that harm the very foundations of our national independence, and I am ashamed to have to remind you of them. Why don't you stop those books from being printed and distributed?

Are you deliberately mocking our country's self-esteem, or are your brains so defective that you are unable to perceive what you are doing? What sin have the 'ulama committed, apart from offering advice—the 'ulama, who are the guardians of the independence and integrity of the Muslim countries? What sin have the institutions of religious learning committed, apart from serving Islam, the Muslims, and the Muslim countries?

Regarding the 'ulama as an obstacle in their path, the foreigners have decided to destroy them, and you and your like carry out their orders because you are ruled by the dollar. The assault on the religious teaching institution, the armed attack on Fayziya Madrasa and the courtyard of the shrine in Qum, the massacres on Khurdad 15—what can all this be called except blind service to the lords of the dollar? Subjecting the maraji', the 'ulama, and the students of the religious sciences to pressure and mounting assaults on the university—what was the result of this except service to the foreigners? They do not want the Muslim peoples to be ruled by the Noble Qur'an and its ordinances, for that would prevent them from plundering the peoples' resources. They do not want anyone to be free to speak, while they demand legal immunity for themselves, and they do not want us to live freely among the people. You are nothing more than an official charged with executing their orders. You are blind and deaf, and have no right to pose questions.

The religious teaching institutions were—and still are—veritable armies of learning, morality, and honesty in a true and authentic sense, not as bombastic propaganda. If you are really friends of learning, why do you so savagely attack centers of learning? Why do you cause bloodshed at Fayziya Madrasa and the university? Why do you treat our students this way, both at home and abroad?

Mr. Hoveyda! It is my duty to offer advice to you and your like. You are all part of this nation, and it is in this land that you have been brought up and have come to attain your present titles. Do not mock the self-esteem of this nation. Instead of all this boasting and noise, perform some service for the barefoot masses of this country. At the very least, stop vexing them under so many pretexts. Do not extort so much from the impoverished tradesmen; do not bring such pressure to bear on the *'ulama* and the students at the religious institution and the university, simply in order to satisfy the lusts of others. Do not conclude a treaty of brotherhood with Israel, the enemy of Islam and the Muslims, which has turned more than a million defenseless Muslims into refugees. Do not offend the sensibilities of the Muslims. Do not permit Israel and its treacherous agents to penetrate further the bazaar of the Muslims; do not endanger the economy of the country for the sake of Israel and its agents.

Do not sacrifice our culture to your whims; fear God, the Great. Do not deceive our girls and carry them off to the barracks; do not betray the honor of the Muslims. You used to deny this bitter truth and regard anyone who pointed it out as deserving punishment; now that you have carried out your intention, do you still deny it?[37] Do you deny the abominations and uncivilized acts you have committed in preparing for the twenty-five hundredth anniversary celebrations?

Fear the wrath of God! Fear the wrath of the people! Do not mock God's ordinances while speaking of "progressive" religion; do not violate the commands of Islam while invoking the Qur'an. Do not behave in this barbaric manner toward the servants of our culture and our nation, the students at our religious institutions, by forcing them to perform useless military service. Finally, do not compel the *'ulama* of the nation to change their treatment of you and your like.

All of this was a mere fraction of the atrocious offenses you and your like have committed against both the religious and the worldly interests of our people. There are many things to be said; I have said only a few in the hope that you will pay heed and come to your senses. It may be, too, that our dear *maraji'*, *'ulama*, and preachers will realize where their duty lies, and that the young, the intellectuals, and the different classes of society will also awaken to their duties. Perhaps humanitarian groups, those who claim to be the friends of humanity, will also bestir themselves, and the United Nations and similar organizations will no longer consent for weak nations to be downtrodden for the sake of the great powers. Perhaps, finally, the ruling class and tyrannical regime of Iran will come to their senses before it is too late.

"Verily your Lord is watchful, and He encompasses the unbelievers in ways they know not" (Qur'an, 89:14).

And peace be upon him who follows right guidance.

Message to the Pilgrims

This was the first of Imam Khomeini's messages to the Muslims of the world gathered together on the occasion of the pilgrimage to Mecca. Several Iranians who distributed this message from Najaf among the pilgrims in Mecca were arrested by the Saudi authorities and kept in leg-irons for more than two years until they were set free through the intercession of the Saudi ambassador in Tehran. Source: *Khomeini va Junbish*, pp. 56-57.

NOW THAT, BECAUSE OF THE APATHY and negligence of the Muslim peoples, the foul claws of imperialism have clutched at the heart of the lands of the people of the Qur'an, with our national wealth and resources being devoured by imperialism despite our supposed ownership of them, with the poisonous culture of imperialism penetrating to the depths of towns and villages throughout the Muslim world, displacing the culture of the Qur'an, recruiting our youth en masse to the service of foreigners and imperialists, and corrupting them day by day with some new tune, some new deceptive formula—now that these disasters have descended upon us, it is incumbent upon you, O beloved Muslims, who have gathered here in the land of revelation to perform the rites of pilgrimage, to make use of this opportunity to find a solution to these problems that beset us.

You must take part in an exchange of views for this purpose, and remember that this great meeting, which takes place every year in this sacred land by the order of God, imposes on you the duty to strive for the realization of the sacred ideals of Islam, the lofty goals of the sacred law of Islam, the progress and advancement of the Muslims, and the unity of the Muslim community. Unite and cooperate for the sake of independence and the elimination of the cancer of imperialism. Listen to the people of each Muslim land explain their problems, and then neglect no measure necessary for the solution of those problems. Consider the poor and needy in the Islamic lands. Turn your attention to the liberation of the Islamic land of Palestine from the grasp of Zionism, the enemy of Islam and humanity. Do not hesitate to assist and cooperate with those heroic men who are struggling to liberate Palestine.

It is the particular duty of the scholars and the learned men who are assembled here, from whatever country they may be, to consult among each other and then issue well-argued and substantiated declarations and have them distributed both here, among the Muslim community in the land of revelation, and in their homelands upon their return. In these declarations they should demand that the heads of Muslim states make the goals of Islam the focus of their policies, that they put aside their disputes and work out a plan for liberating their peoples from the grasp of imperialism.

If the heads of Muslim states were to abandon their mutual disputes in order to acquaint themselves with the lofty goals of Islam and to orient their policies in accordance with Islam, they would no longer be the abject captives of imperialism. It is those disputes between the heads of Muslim states that have allowed the problem of Palestine to arise and that do not permit it to be solved. If the 700 million Muslims, with the vast countries that they inhabit, had the political maturity to unite and organize themselves in a single front, it would not be possible for the big imperialist powers to penetrate their countries, let alone a handful of Jews who are the servants of imperialism.

At this great pilgrimage gathering, an occasion that should serve to benefit Islam and the Muslims, we see that certain poison pens in the service of imperialism have for several years been seeking to sow dissension in the ranks of the Muslims, here in the very land that witnessed revelation, and in a manner entirely contrary to the aims of the Prophet (upon whom be peace). Pamphlets like *al-Khutut al-'Arida*[38] are being published and distributed here in order to serve the imperialists, who hope to use lies and slander to separate a group of 170 million people from the ranks of the Muslims. It is surprising that the authorities in the Hijaz would permit such misleading material to be distributed in the land of revelation. The Muslim peoples must shun such divisive and imperialist-inspired books and publications, and reject those opponents of Islamic unity.

At this sacred pilgrimage gathering, the Muslims must exchange their views concerning the basic problems of Islam and the special problems of each Muslim country. The people of each country should, in effect, present a report concerning their own state to the Muslims of the world, and thus all will come to know what their Muslim brothers are suffering at the hands of imperialism and its agents.

In accordance with this duty, then, I will now set forth some of the problems that beset the oppressed people of Iran, so that the Muslims of the world may know what is happening to the defenseless people of that country.

The sinister influence of imperialism is especially evident in Iran. Israel, the universally recognized enemy of Islam and the Muslims, at war with the Muslim peoples for years, has, with the assistance of the despicable government of Iran, penetrated all the economic, military, and political affairs of the country; it must be said that Iran has become a military base for Israel, which means, by extension, for America. Foreigners enjoy complete immunity in Iran, but religious scholars, men of learning and education, and all other classes as well are exposed to all kinds of oppression. Respectable merchants, one after another, are reduced to bankruptcy. The pitiless tyranny of the regime has the people by the throat; the stifling of expression, feudal imprisonment, and torture are the order of the day. Under various deceptive names, such as the Literacy Corps and the Health Corps, the sinister designs of imperialism are being advanced in the towns and villages of the country, and immorality spreads until it is becoming universal.

The campaign against knowledge and education continues at full spate, since it is desired to keep our people backward at the behest of the imperialists. Invoking Islam and pretending to be Muslims, they strive to annihilate Islam, and they abolish and obliterate the sacred commands of the Qur'an one after the other. The religious scholars and students writhe beneath the pressure of the agents of imperialism. They intend to appropriate schools, mosques, and other religious institutions, and a program to that effect has already begun to be implemented. Upon empty pretexts, universities are attacked and students are dragged off from universities to prisons and barracks. We have been greatly disturbed by recent events at Iranian universities, by the savage and pitiless attacks of the tyrannical regime on students. This inhuman behavior is yet another example of the plans drawn up by the imperialists to suppress students and universities in Iran. We strongly

197

condemn these barbaric, medieval attacks, and we express our confidence that the honorable and patriotic students of Iran will never retreat or surrender.

The shameful, bloody so-called White Revolution, which in a single day caused fifteen thousand Muslims to be killed by tanks and machine guns, has made the fate of our people still bleaker and darker and worsened the life of the enslaved peasantry. In many of our cities and most villages, clinics, doctors, and medicines are not to be found. There is no trace of schools, bathhouses, or clean drinking water. As some newspapers admit, the poor children are so hungry that they go to graze in the fields. Yet the tyrannical regime spends hundreds of millions of tumans of the country's wealth on various shameful "festivals": the birthday of this or that person, the twenty-fifth anniversary of the accession to the throne, the coronation, and worst and most catastropic of all, the vile festival of the twenty-five hundredth anniversary of the monarchy.

God knows what disasters and misfortunes this festival will bring down upon the people, and how the agents of imperialism will use it as a means of extortion and plunder. If the huge and staggering budget that is to be wasted on this absurdity were spent feeding the hungry and securing them a means of livelihood, our afflictions would be reduced. But their selfishness and greed for profit do not permit them to give any thought to the people. Using the Muslims' money, the tyrannical regime proposes to celebrate a festival and light up our cities for the sake of kings who in every age crushed the people beneath the boots of their soldiers, who always opposed true religion, who were the bitter enemies of Islam, and who tore up the blessed letter of the Prophet (may God's peace be upon him). And we all know who the representative of this line in the present age is. Let the world know that these festivals and celebrations have nothing to do with the noble Muslim people of Iran, and that all who organize and participate in these festivals are traitors to Islam and the people of Iran.

I extend my hand to all the people of Islam and to all who struggle throughout the world against imperialism and the imperialists to obtain the independence of the Muslim countries and to break the chains of captivity. I pray that God Almighty may drive away from us the evil of tyrannical regimes and the filthy agents of imperialism, and that He may accept from all of us this performance of the rites of pilgrimage.

May peace, the compassion of God, and His blessings be upon you.

The Incompatibility of Monarchy With Islam

This declaration was issued from Najaf in condemnation of the Shah's plans to impose on the nation the celebration of two-and-a-half millenia of monarchy. Source: Khomeini va Junbish, *pp. 36-53.*

I FEEL IT IS MY DUTY on certain occasions to draw attention to some aspects of the problems facing the people of Islam, and it may be that you will consider it your duty also to attempt to aid your Muslim brothers, even if only by way of declarations, telegrams, and letters.

The greatest disaster that befell Islam was the usurpation of rule by Mu'awiya from 'Ali (upon whom be peace), which caused the system of rule to lose its Islamic character entirely and to be replaced by a monarchical regime. This disaster was even worse than the tragedy of Karbala and the misfortunes that befell the Lord of the Martyrs (upon whom be peace), and indeed it led to the tragedy of Karbala. The disaster that did not permit Islam to be correctly presented to the world was the greatest disaster of all.

The people of Islam should mourn the usurpation of rule from 'Ali (upon whom be peace) and commemorate those few years when he was the blessed embodiment of Islamic rule. They should commemorate his justice, the fact that he was a part of his people, that his standard of living was lower than that of others while his spirit rose ever higher above the horizons. One should commemorate a ruler who, when he hears that an anklet has been stolen from a non-Muslim woman living under the protection of Islam, wishes to die of shame; who, when he thinks that someone may be going hungry in his realm, suffers hunger voluntarily himself. One should commemorate a rule that uses the sword to protect its people and protect them from fear. But as for a regime founded on oppression and thievery whose only aim is to satisfy its own lustful desires—only when it is overthrown can the people celebrate and rejoice.

"As for those who disbelieve, they engage in pleasure and in eating as the beasts eat, and the fire shall be their abode" (Qur'an, 47:12). One who eats and takes his pleasure with no concern for what is permitted or forbidden, for the manner in which he has acquired his property, who pays no attention to the condition of the people or to the ordinances of the law—such a man lives like an animal. A ruler who fits this description and wishes to rule over the people and the nation in accordance with his carnal and bestial desires will produce nothing but disaster. The people must mourn the existence of such a government and weep over their misfortunes; to celebrate in such circumstances would be totally senseless.

Now, according to numerous letters and reports I have received, one of the unfortunate aspects of the present situation in Iran is that a large number of people have died of hunger. While these tragic circumstances and conditions prevail, millions of tumans are to be spent celebrating in honor of the monarchy. According to reports, 80 million tumans are to be spent on decorating and lighting up Tehran alone. Experts have been invited from Israel to take care of the arrangements—from Israel, that stubborn enemy of Islam and the Qur'an, which a few years ago attempted to corrupt the text of the Qur'an,[39] and now imputes to the Qur'an unworthy statements, which our students abroad vigorously refute and deny (may God strengthen them). Israel, which is at war with the Muslims and plans to occupy all the lands of Islam up to Iraq and (God forbid) to destroy the noble shrines of Islam! Israel, which set fire to the Masjid al-Aqsa,[40] a crime that the Iranian regime tried to cover up with all sorts of propagandistic proposals to rebuild the mosque! Israel, which has turned more than a million Muslims into refugees and occupied the lands of the Muslims! That state is now to arrange the celebrations for the Iranian monarchy, and that state is supplied with Iranian oil by tankers. Ought the people of Iran to celebrate the rule of a traitor to Islam and the interests of the Muslims who gives oil to Israel? Who was responsible for the events of Khurdad 15; who killed, according to one of the *'ulama,* four hundred people in Qum alone; who had fifteen thousand people massacred throughout Iran; who sent his agents to Fayziya Madrasa to insult the Qur'an and Imam Ja'far[41] (upon whom be peace)? They set fire to the students' turbans, threw some of them off the roof of the building, and behaved scandalously, filling the prisons with our patriots. Many of these best sons of our people were tortured to death in prison by his agents. Are we now to honor the rule of such a monarch with a celebration?

What benefit have our people ever derived from such rulers that we should now celebrate and light up our cities? Are we to commemorate Agha Muhammad Qajar,[42] that bloodthirsty savage? Or the monarch who massacred people in the mosque of Gauhar Shad[43] in such numbers that the walls were stained with blood and the gates of the mosque had to be closed so that none might see the spectacle?

God only knows what disasters the Iranian monarchy has given rise to since its very beginning and what crimes it has committed. The crimes of the kings of Iran have blackened the pages of history. It is the kings of Iran that have constantly ordered massacres of their own people and had pyramids built with their skulls.[44] Even those that were reputed to be "good" were vile and cruel. It is related that one such "good" monarch,[45] for whose soul prayers are said, once on the way to Shah 'Abd al-'Azim ordered a group of soldiers that had assembled about his coach to ask for bread to be strangled with a rope, and the order was carried out in part before the intervention of some respected person caused the rest to be spared. This was one of the "good" monarchs; the deeds of the evil monarchs one can scarcely comprehend.

Tradition relates that the Prophet (upon whom be peace) said that the title of King of Kings, which is borne by the monarchs of Iran, is the most hated of all titles in the sight of God. Islam is fundamentally opposed to the whole notion of monarchy. Anyone who studies the manner in which the Prophet established the government of Islam will realize that Islam came in order to destroy these palaces of tyranny. Monarchy is one of the most shameful and disgraceful reactionary manifestations.

Are millions of tumans of the people's wealth to be spent on these frivolous and absurd celebrations? Are the people of Iran to have a festival for those whose behavior has been a scandal throughout history and who are a cause of crime and oppression, of abomination and corruption, in the present age?

Only recently, because of a slogan uttered in the university that ran counter to his lowly inclinations, he sent his bandits to the university and had them beat the students atrociously. According to reports that reached here, some female students needed surgery as a result of the blows and wounds they received. Their only crime was opposing the twenty-five hundredth anniversary celebrations and saying, "We have no need of this festival. Put an end to the hunger of our people; do not celebrate over the corpses of our people."

This crime happened just recently, but here in Najaf no one is aware of it! Why is Najaf so sound asleep? Why is it not trying to help the wretched and oppressed people of Iran? Is our only duty to sit here studying the principles and details of religious law? Should we pay no attention to the disasters that afflict the Muslims? Should we do nothing to help them? Do we not feel any duty and responsibility in the face of God and the nation? We who depend on Islam for our living—are we not to lift a finger for the sake of Islam and the Muslims? Are we not to protest that the toil of the people is to be spent on this shameful festival and that the nation is to be driven to famine and bankruptcy? Why is money being extorted by pressure and force from merchants, craftsmen, and workers for this useless occasion? Why is no attention paid instead to the state of the nation, to the elementary needs of the people in the villages and the provinces?

People address themselves to us constantly from all over Iran, asking permission to use the charitable taxes demanded by Islam for the building of bathhouses, for they are without baths. What has happened to all those gilded promises, those pretentious claims that Iran is progressing on the same level as the more developed countries of the world, that the people are prosperous and content? Are the people prosperous when they sell their children because of hunger?[46]

Are we not to protest that the oil belonging to Iran and Islam is sold to a state at war with the Muslims? Why is Israel able to gain influence in the affairs of a Muslim country? Of course, the answer will be, "We are given orders, and we have no choice but to obey. These are our orders, and we have to carry them out." The Shah himself in one of his speeches, which was later reproduced in a book, stated, "The allies, after occupying Iran, thought it fitting that I should be in control of affairs, and they agreed to my accession to the throne." May God curse them for thinking it fitting and casting us into disaster! Naturally, someone who is a puppet has to serve his masters; he cannot do otherwise. And they follow their desires and appetites ("They eat as the beasts eat"); they care not where their nourishment comes from nor how it is obtained. As long as their needs and requirements are met, the world may drown in blood and fire, and entire peoples may be destroyed.

Are we not to speak out about these chronic ailments that afflict us? Not to say a single word about all these disasters? Is it incompatible with our position as religious scholars to speak out? Were not the Prophet and the Commander of the Faithful, 'Ali (peace be upon both of them) religious scholars, and did they not preach long sermons? In the Shaqshaqiya sermon[47] about a certain person who made illicit use of the money belonging to the community, far harsher and more uncompromising expressions occur than those we have used. How is it that now, when it is the turn of the present generation of religious scholars to speak out, we invent excuses and say that it is "incompatible" with our status to speak out?

How often we have been told we must not interfere in affairs of state! It seems that we have in fact come to believe that it is not our duty to concern ourselves with the affairs of the country and the government, that we have no duty of any kind, and that we should not struggle for justice. In reality, since the very beginning of history, the prophets and scholars of religion have always had the duty of resisting and struggling against monarchs and tyrannical governments. Did they think that interference in political affairs was not part of their spiritual duty? When Moses was entrusted by God Almighty with the task of destroying the emperor of his day, was he unaware that one must not struggle against kings? When the Prophet and the Immaculate Imams (upon all of whom be peace) rose up against kings and tyrannical governments, not giving up the struggle even under conditions of extreme difficulty, was it that they were mistaken?

The Lord of the Martyrs (upon whom be peace) summoned the people to rise in revolt by means of sermon, preaching, and correspondence and caused them to rebel against a monarch. Imam Hasan (upon whom be peace) struggled against the king of his day, Mu'awiya, as far as he was able, and when he was betrayed by a group of self-seeking, opportunistic followers and left without support, the very peace treaty that he signed with

Mu'awiya disgraced that monarch, just as Imam Husayn's bloody revolt later disgraced Yazid. This struggle and confrontation has continued without respite, and the great scholars of Islam have always fought against the tyrannical bandits who enslaved their peoples for the sake of their passions and squandered their country's wealth on trivial amusements. Whenever a vital and alert nation gave them support, they were successful in their struggle. If we too are vital and alert now, we will be successful. But unfortunately, instead of there being unity and harmony among us, each one persists in his own individual opinion, and naturally, if 100 million people have 100 million different opinions, they will be unable to accomplish anything, for "The hand of God is with the group." Solidarity and unity are essential, and isolated individuals can achieve nothing.

If the 'ulama of Qum, Mashhad, Tabriz, Isfahan, Shiraz, and the other cities in Iran were to protest collectively today against this scandalous festival, to condemn these extravangances that are destroying the people and the nation, be assured that results would be forthcoming. There are more than 150,000 students and scholars of the religious sciences in Iran. If all these scholars, authorities, proofs of Islam, and ayatullahs were to break the seal of silence and make a collective protest to remove the endorsements of their silence from the list of crimes committed by the regime, would they not achieve their aims? Would the authorities arrest them all, imprison and banish them, destroy them? If they were able to, they would destroy me before anyone else, but their interests do not permit them to do so.

Would that they did destroy me, so that I might no longer be tormented by the tragic state of our country. The tyrannical regime imagines that I am very happy and satisfied with my life, and so they think they can threaten me. But what life is this that I lead? Death as soon as possible would be better than this life; then I might join the presence of the Most Noble One in the hereafter and be delivered from this life of misfortune. What life is it that I lead, constantly hearing the cries and moans of our oppressed and tyrannized people? The crimes committed by this tyrannical regime and the acts of treachery against Islam and the Muslims have robbed me of all peace. News constantly arrives to the effect that the prisons are full of patriots, that innocent people are

205

dying from the effects of pitiless torture, that bandits and ruffians are attacking the university to kill and wound the students, and that girls are being tortured by having boiling water poured on their heads. It is just like the time of Ibn Ziyad[48] and Hajjaj,[49] when if it was thought that someone might be a follower of the Shi'a, he was seized and destroyed. So, too, they attack and arrest and torture now on the strength of mere suspicion. Nobody's life is safe. If someone offers religious advice or utters a word from the pulpit, he is immediately carried off to prison. If someone distributes a few copies of a critical pamphlet, they arrest him and take him off to some unknown destination.

This is the situation in our ruined homeland. Does not all this need to be said? Must not these atrocities be exposed? I consider it my duty to cry out with all the strength at my command and to write and publish with whatever power my pen may have. Let my colleagues do the same—if they consider it proper, if they regard themselves as belonging to the nation of Islam, if they consider themselves to be Shi'a—let them give some thought to what needs to be done. And if they do not consider it proper, they must decide for themselves, and may God Almighty forgive them. What are we to do in the face of all these problems? Under these circumstances, when the foundations of Islam are being destroyed and every last possession of the deprived and poverty-stricken people of Iran is being plundered for the sake of this abominable festival, is there really no path of action open to us? Should we just sit here talking about the principles of ethics? Speaking about moral refinement? If our ethics and our morals were truly in order, we would not be in the situation we are in today.

Come to your senses; awaken Najaf! Let the voice of the oppressed people of Iran be heard throughout the world. Protest to the government of Iran by letter and telegraph. It costs nothing to write a letter; for God's sake, write to the Iranian government. Tell them to abandon this abominable festival, these scandalous extravagances. If these latest excesses are not prevented, still worse misfortunes will descend upon us and we will be confronted with even more distasteful events. Every day new events are created, new disasters for the wretched people of Iran. They even have a special expert for dreaming up these events, these idiotic spectacles. If matters continue on their present course, we will be faced with events in the near future that none of us can even imagine.

Demand of the learned scholars and authorities of Najaf that they give some advice to the Iranian government—I do not even say they must protest. Rather, by way of advice and counsel, let them ask that this plundering and squandering be brought to an end, that they cease behaving toward our people in this way, that the huge budget of the government be spent on our wretched and hungry people. Let them request that the hungry be fed. If one hundred telegrams were sent to Iran by the religious scholars and students of Najaf, in a polite form and even using the title "Highness," it would probably have some effect. But unfortunately, such an idea occurs to no one, and I should be grateful that no one complains to me about my criticisms of the Iranian government!

I tell you plainly that a dark, dangerous future lies ahead and that it is your duty to resist and to serve Islam and the Muslim peoples. Protest against the pressure exerted upon our oppressed people every day. Purge yourselves of your apathy and selfishness; stop seeking excuses and inventing pretexts for evading your responsibility. You have more forces at your disposal than the Lord of the Martyrs (upon whom be peace) did, who resisted and struggled with his limited forces until he was killed. If (God forbid) he had been a weak, apathetic, and selfish person, he could have come up with some excuse for himself and remained silent. His enemies would have been only too happy for him to remain silent so that they could attain their vile goals, and they were afraid of his rebelling. But he dispatched Muslim[50] to procure the people's allegiance to him so that he might overthrow that corrupt government and set up an Islamic government. If he had sat in some corner in Medina and had nothing to do with anyone, everyone would have respected him and come to kiss his hand. And if you sit silently by, you too will be respected, but it will be the kind of respect that is give a dead saint. A dead saint is respected by everyone, but a living saint or Imam has his head cut off.

I proclaim to the governments and heads of state that mean to take part in this abominable festival that it has no connection with the people of Iran, and that to participate in it is to participate in the murder of the oppressed people of Iran. Let all Muslim heads of state take note in particular that this festival is *anti-Islamic* and that it is being arranged by Israeli experts and engineers; they should therefore shun all partipation in it.

It is the duty of the Muslim people of Iran to refrain from participation in this illegitimate festival, to engage in passive struggle against it, to remain indoors during the days of the festival, and to express by any means possible their disgust and aversion for anyone who contributes to the organization or celebration of the festival. Let the festival organizers know that they are despised by the Islamic community and by all alert peoples throughout the world, that they are hated by all lovers of freedom, and that Islam and the Muslims are repelled by the very notion of monarchy.

It is also your duty to make your opposition to this festival known by any means at your disposal and to pray for your fellow Muslims—those wretched, starved, and hungry people in Iran—for those who suffer imprisonment, torture, and banishment; for those innocent girls who have severe wounds inflicted on them. Pray for them and for all victims of the Iranian regime, and ask God Almighty to grant them His aid.

And peace be upon you.

July 10, 1972

Message to the Muslim Students
in North America

Written in Najaf, this is an example of the numerous letters sent by Imam Khomeini to Iranian Muslim students in North America, Europe, and elsewhere encouraging them in their religious and political activities.
Source: *Khomeini va Junbish*, pp. 98-99.

WE HAVE RECEIVED YOUR ESTEEMED LETTERS. Your efforts, enlightened Muslim youths, and untiring struggles for the correct comprehension of Islam and to make known the truth of the Noble Qur'an are a source of hope and satisfaction to all conscious Muslims. I express my appreciation of your Islamic spirit and your search for the truth, noble youths. At the same time I consider it necessary to remind you that while advancing on this sacred path, you will encounter numerous difficulties and dangers, and from every side the hidden hands of the enemies of Islam will attempt to prevent you from reaching your sacred goal.

The agents and servants of imperialism know that if the peoples of the world, particularly the young and educated generation, become acquainted with the sacred principles of Islam, the downfall and annihilation of the imperialists will be inevitable, and also the liberation of the resources of exploited nations and peoples from their control. Therefore, they engage in sabotage and try to prevent the resplendent visage of Islam from showing itself by poisoning and polluting the minds and thoughts of the young, and try to pervert them with all kinds of alluring schools of thought and deceptive slogans. It is your duty, Muslim youths, when you examine the truths of Islam with respect to politics, economics, society, and the like, to keep in mind the purity and originality of Islam and not to forget the superiority that separates Islam from all other schools of thought. Never confuse the Noble Qur'an and the salvation-bestowing path of Islam with erroneous and delusive schools of thought that are the product of the human mind. You must be aware that as long as the people of Islam are subjected to these imperialist schools, as long as they compare divine laws with those of other schools and put them together on

209

the same level, tranquillity and freedom will be denied to the Muslims. These different schools offered to the Muslims from the left and the right are only for the purpose of leading them astray; the desire is to keep the Muslims abject, humiliated, backward, and enslaved forever, and to keep them away from the liberating teachings of the Noble Qur'an.

Imperialism of the left and imperialism of the right have joined hands in their efforts to annihilate the Muslim peoples and their countries; they have come together in order to enslave the Muslim peoples and plunder their abundant capital and natural resources. Israel was born out of the collusion and agreement of the imperialist states of East and West. It was created in order to suppress and exploit the Muslim peoples, and it is being supported today by all the imperialists. Britain and the U.S., by strengthening Israel militarily and politically and supplying it with lethal weapons, are encouraging Israel to undertake repeated aggression against the Arabs and the Muslims and to continue the occupation of Palestine and other Islamic lands. The Soviet Union, by preventing the Muslims from arming themselves adequately, by its deceit, treachery, and conciliatory policy, is guaranteeing the existence of Israel.

If the Muslim states and peoples had relied on Islam instead of relying on the Eastern or Western bloc—had placed before their eyes the luminous and liberating teachings of the Noble Qur'an, and then practiced those teachings—they would not be enslaved today by the Zionist aggressors, terrorized by American Phantoms, and at the mercy of the satanic cunning of the Soviet Union. It is the gulf between the Muslim states and the Noble Qur'an that has plunged our people into this dark and catastrophic situation and placed the destiny of the Muslim peoples and countries in the hands of the treacherous policies of imperialism of the right and the left.

It is your duty, respected youths of Islam, you who are the source of hope for the Muslims, to awaken people, to expose the sinister and destructive designs of imperialism. Strive harder for the propagation of Islam. Learn and apply the sacred teachings of the Qur'an. With utter devotion, exert yourselves to diffuse and propagate Islam among non-Muslims and to advance the great aims of Islam. Devote greater attention to planning the foundations of an Islamic state and studying the problems involved. Be well prepared, organize and unite, press your ranks close together. Have unity of thought and cultivate a readiness to sacrifice. Do your utmost to expose the plans of the tyrannical regime of Iran against Islam and the Muslims. Convey to the world the voices of your tortured Muslim brothers in Iran and demonstrate solidarity with them. Protest against the savagery, the murder, the disregard for the law, and all the other crimes that are constantly being committed in Iran. With God's aid, it may then be possible to create the foundation for the independence and freedom of Iran and to put an end to the oppression of the tyrannical regime and the servants of imperialism, so that the dangers threatening Islam and the Muslims today will be removed.

Convey my greetings to all those who are working for the sake of Islam.

And peace be upon you, as well as God's mercy.

February 19, 1978

In Commemoration of the First Martyrs of the Revolution

Imam Khomeini delivered this speech at the mosque of Shaykh Ansari in Najaf forty days after the massacre of demonstrators that took place in Qum on January 8, 1978. The demonstrators were protesting the publication of defamatory articles about him in the government-controlled Iranian press. Source: *Sukhanrani-yi Imam Khomeini dama zilluh* (Najaf: Ruhaniyun-i Mubariz [Kharij az Kishvar], 1398/1978), pp. 15-50.

AS WE ARE GATHERED HERE, according to the information reaching us, all the major cities of Iran are closed down: Tehran, Tabriz, Mashhad, Qum. Some cities are completely closed, such as Qum, while in others, the bazaar and other centers of activity are closed. We have been informed that the Tehran bazaar is completely closed, except for a few merchants who may have some connection with the regime.

These closings represent a form of active protest against the person of the Shah. The people have identified the true criminal. It was obvious before, it is true, but some people didn't recognize him as such or didn't dare speak out. Thanks be to God, this barrier of fear has collapsed and the people have discovered the true criminal and come to understand who is responsible for the misery of our nation.

The center for religious learning in Qum has proven its vitality; the people of Qum and the respected students of the religious sciences have fought the government and the agents of the Shah with their bare hands, with a courage rarely equalled in history, and yielded their martyrs. When the agents of the regime spilled into the streets and alleyways of Qum and attacked the people—according to the reports we have received—the people resisted them to the utmost degree possible, both before and after the massacre, thus proving how alive they are. They proved that they were alive, not dead! The great *maraji'* of Islam in Qum have expressed themselves courageously both in their speeches and in their declarations, including the one they issued two or three days ago on the occasion of the fortieth day after the massacre and the general strike ordained for that day, and they have stated who is responsible for the crime—not explicitly, it is true, but by implication, which is more effective. May God keep them steadfast.

The students of the religious sciences live in a place that is subject to attack by those bandits, but yesterday they organized an impressive mourning ceremony, which was attended by a large number of people, and some youths told the truth fearlessly at the meeting.

As we sit here in Najaf, a great meeting is taking place at the Masjid-i A'zam in Qum, according to reliable information. I don't know what the government intends to do about this meeting. Are its agents going to attack again, to kill and to plunder? We are anxious for the people of all the major cities in Iran, like Mashhad, where the government shows a particular sensitivity; Tabriz, which the government is watching carefully; and Qum, the center of all our struggles.

In accordance with the prediction of the Prophet's family (peace be upon them) that Qum would be a center of learning whence knowledge would be disseminated to all lands,[51] we now see that it is not knowledge alone that is disseminated from Qum, but knowledge and action together.

Qum is the center of Islamic activity; Qum is the center of the Islamic movement. The movement starts out from Qum, from the city itself, from the *tullab*, from the *'ulama*, from the teachers (may God support all of them), from the masses of its people who are the faithful soldiers of Islam, and spreads to all parts of Iran. Let us see whether it spreads to us here in Najaf.

All the miseries that we have suffered, still suffer, and are about to suffer soon are caused by the heads of those countries that have signed the Declaration of Human Rights, but that at all times have denied man his freedom. Freedom of the individual is the most important part of the Declaration of Human Rights. Individual human beings must all be equal before the law, and they must be free. They must be free in their choice of residence and occupation. But we see the Iranian nation, together with many others, suffering at the hands of those states that have signed and ratified the Declaration.

The U.S. is one of the signatories to this document. It has agreed that the rights of man must be protected and that man must be free. But see what crimes America has committed against man. As long as I can remember—and I can remember back further than many of you, for you are younger than I—America has created disasters for mankind. It has appointed its agents in both Muslim and non-Muslim countries to deprive everyone who lives under their domination of his freedom. The imperialists proclaim that man is free only in order to deceive the masses. But people can no longer be deceived. All these declarations they make, supposedly in favor of human rights, have no reality; they are designed to deceive. They draw up some pleasant-looking, high-sounding declaration with thirty articles relating to human rights and then neglect to enact a single one of them! The Declaration of Human Rights exists only to deceive the nations; it is the opium of the masses. What we have said is true not only of America but also of Britain, another power that signed and ratified the Declaration of Human Rights—Britain, whose civilization and democracy everybody praises so much without realizing that they are repeating the propaganda slogans Britain is cunningly feeding people; Britain, which is meant to practice true constitutionalism! But have we not seen, despite all this propaganda, what crimes Britain has committed in India, Pakistan, and its other colonies?

The imperialist states, like America and Britain, brought Israel into existence, and we have seen what misery they have inflicted on the Muslim peoples by means of Israel, and what crimes they are now committing against the Muslims, particularly the Shi'a.[52] In Lebanon they install one agent[53] and reduce the country to its present miserable state, and in Egypt they install another, by the name of Sadat, whose every act is devoted to serving imperialism. A short time ago, he went to Israel and gave Israel official recognition and approved all that the Israelis had to say. The Shah of Iran also says it is necessary to make peace with Israel. In fact, this wretch recognized Israel twenty years ago. We were in Qum at the time. He gave his recognition to a government of unbelievers—of Jews, at that—thereby affronting Islam, the Qur'an, the Muslim governments, and all the Muslim people. The name of Israel was not openly mentioned at first, but later it was.

Also for as long as I can remember, during the past fifty years
—throughout these fifty years of national mourning in Iran, these
fifty years of disaster inflicted on our nation by this scandalous
family—it was Britain, another signatory to the Declaration of
Human Rights, that kept the Iranian people repressed and afflicted.
In fact, it was Britain that brought Riza Shah to power, according
to its own admission, broadcast over Radio Delhi at the time.[54]
For almost twenty years, we, the religious scholars, were subject
to intense pressure; Riza Shah wished to expunge every trace of
the *shari'a*, although naturally he didn't succeed. He forbade
every form of Islamic propagation and deprived the people of all
their liberties. The meetings that take place now were not held
then, because the people had not been enlightened. The Shah
himself wrote in his book (although it was deleted from later edi-
tions): "When the allies came to Iran, they thought it fitting that
I should be placed on the throne, and that the throne should remain in my family." Curses be upon them for what they thought
fit!

As for America, a signatory to the Declaration of Human
Rights, it imposed this Shah upon us, a worthy successor to his
father. During the period he has ruled, this creature has transformed Iran into an official colony of the U.S. What crimes he has
committed in service to his masters!

What crimes that father and this son have committed against
the Iranian nation since their appointment by the signatories to
the Declaration of Human Rights. All they have to offer humanity
is repression; we have witnessed part of it, and we have heard of
part of it. But hearing is not enough truly to understand. You may
have heard what happened to the people in the time of Riza Khan,
but you cannot perceive what the people themselves actually
went through. You cannot yourselves experience what this man
is doing now. You can understand what has happened to the
Iranian people during the last few days as a result of recent events,
but you cannot actually experience it.

It is not at all unlikely that at this very moment a battle is
taking place in Iran, a battle between the people and the agents of
the Shah; we do not have precise information. According to reports just received, agents of the regime have attacked the fore-

court of the Masjid-i Shah in Tehran and forced a few shops there to open their shutters, but the Tehran bazaar as a whole has not surrendered.

The government has sent a circular to all the bazaars in Iran forbidding anyone to close his shop and threatening severe punishment for disobedience. Nevertheless, not a single bazaar in Iran has paid any attention to those threats; not even the Tehran bazaar, which lies within close range of the regime. The rest of the people also pay no heed to those empty noises. Whereas they were able to intimidate the people in the past and their propaganda had some effect, now people are willing to be killed; they will not surrender, and their struggle continues.

Today, forty days have passed since the death of the students of the religious sciences, the 'ulama, and the pious people of Qum. How the people have wept and mourned during the last forty days for the youths who were killed!

Yes, today is the fortieth day after the death of people of learning, and of young and pious people in Qum, killed at the hands of the Shah's agents!

The people of Iran have proven how fully alive they are and established it for all eternity; may God keep them in this state. The religious center in Qum has also established for all eternity how fully alive it is. Right now, as we are sitting here, the *tullab*, together with all the noble people of Iran, are in a state of intense activity. You do not know what is happening now in Mashhad; everything is closed down in Mashhad. The same is true in Azerbayjan; we don't know what is happening there either. According to reports we have received, everything is closed down in Qum; not a single grocer's shop is open. Even Tehran is ninety-percent closed, and it is no easy thing to close down Tehran. The closing down of Tehran is a good punch in the mouth for those babblers, those people who once said, "Six million of the Iranian people are in agreement with us and have voted in favor of our White Revolution."[55]

They were talking nonsense when they made that claim. I was in Iran at the time, and I sent some people to Tehran to find out what this referendum was that they wanted to stage. When they returned, they told me that not more than two thousand people had gone to cast their votes, and even those two thousand were government employees.

Yes, they once said, "Six million of the Iranian people are with us, and since the rest of the people are elderly, or women, or else infants, and hence unable to vote, the six-point program has been given unanimous approval." The Shah, too, would repeatedly claim in his speeches that "The people are with me. There are only a handful of people who say something against me every now and then and they are Islamic Marxists." With this kind of hullabaloo they try to pretend that they have the support of the people. But this general strike is itself a living answer to them.

Now you will see what an uproar they'll make after this general closing down of the bazaars all across the country, just as they did before after the week-long closing of the bazaar in Qum, the eight-day closing in Isfahan, the two or three days of partial closing and the one day of complete closing in Tehran, as well as other closings in the provinces. They got hold of some unsuspecting wretches and loaded them on buses, sent circulars to the government offices and schools, then gathered up some of their own people, and organized a demonstration!

Is that freedom? Most government offices paid no attention to the circulars they received, and as for those wretches who had been loaded on the buses and falsely told they were being taken on a pilgrimage to Qum, they found out halfway there what was happening. Those who could, fled; those who could not, who were compelled to take part in the ceremonies, had the air of participating in a funeral. However much they were told to say, "May the Shah live forever," they remained silent. According to my informant, they were as silent as if they were attending a funeral. Yes, it was the funeral of the Shah, but those people ruling us cannot understand; they are incapable of human behavior. We can't turn them into decent human beings. If they would compromise a little with the people, if they would pay some heed to the people's demands, if they would perform their true duties and move in the direction of Islam and the laws of Islam, the people would not be so bitterly opposed to them. But the people see that His Imperial Majesty is against whatever they attach value to. He is against the Islamic calendar.[56] To be against the Islamic

217

calendar is to be against Islam itself; in fact the worst thing that this man has done during his reign is to change the calendar. Changing the calendar is even worse than the massacres; it is an affront to the Most Noble Messenger himself (peace and blessings be upon him). But they will never be successful.

Yes, with one hand they change the calendar, and with the other they attack the madrasas. They have raided and plundered our madrasas several times now. Before, it was Fayziya Madrasa that they attacked and made the scene of their crimes; now they attack Hujjatiya Madrasa, Khan Madrasa, and Haqqani Madrasa[57] —in fact any madrasa with open gates where people congregate. According to the reports that reached us, all the doors and windows at Khan Madrasa have been knocked in and broken by rifle butts, and a student of the religious sciences was shot and killed at the gate of Hujjatiya Madrasa. One of the *'ulama* from here who went there told me when he came back that there was a stream of blood from the place where the student had been shot to the edge of the pool in the madrasa courtyard.

Do you think it is the police chief of Qum who does these things? Don't say it is the police who do these things; it is the Shah! The Shah personally gives the orders and tells them to kill; they won't kill anyone unless he tells them to. Is it a small matter to open fire on a whole nation with rifles and machine guns? The people are devoted to the religious center in Qum and greatly respect it. So can it be a small thing to open fire on it with machine guns? Can the police chief of Tehran, the police chief of Qum, the SAVAK chief of Tehran, the SAVAK chief of Qum, or even the Prime Minister give orders for such a thing to be done? It is the Shah who determines everything; he is the real criminal. And it is the signatories to the Declaration of Human Rights who have imposed him on us.

The religious center in Qum has brought Iran back to life; it has performed a service to Islam that will endure for centuries. This service must not be underestimated; pray for the religious center in Qum and pray that we will come to resemble it. The name of the religious center in Qum will remain inscribed in history for all time. By comparison with Qum, we here in Najaf are dead and buried; it is Qum that has brought Islam back to life. It is the center in Qum and the preaching of its *maraji'* and *'ulama* that have awakened the universities, those same places where we religious scholars used to be accused of being the opium of the people and the agents of the British and other imperialists. No, all that was the propaganda of Britain, Germany, the Soviet Union, and others, designed to misrepresent us and make the *'ulama* and their institutions appear to be the opium of the people.

The imperialists know full well how active the religious scholars are, and what an activist and militant religion Islam is. So they drew up a plan to bring the religious scholars into disrepute, and for several centuries propagated the notion that religion must be separated from politics. Some of our *akhunds* came to believe it and began asking, "What business do we have with politics?" The posing of this question means the abandonment of Islam; it means burying Islam in our cells in the *madrasa!* It means burying Islam in our books! The imperialists dearly wish that religion could be separated from politics, and our politicians, in turn, have filled people's mouths with these words, so that some of us have come to believe them and ask, "What business do we have with politics? Leave politics to those whose business it is, and if they slap us in the face, let us turn the other cheek!"

This idea of turning the other cheek has been wrongly attributed to Jesus (peace be upon him); it is those barbaric imperialists that have attributed it to him. Jesus was a prophet, and no prophet can be so illogical.[58]

Look at the history of the prophets. You will see that Jesus (upon whom be peace) did not remain among his people very long before he was taken up to heaven. But you all know well that Abraham (upon whom be peace), who in one sense stood at the beginning of the line of prophets, took up his axe to shatter all the idols; he was not afraid of being cast into the fire and burned. If he had been afraid, he would not have been a prophet. This man who stood alone in the face of such great forces and who was then cast into the fire—he could not follow a logic that required him, if slapped on one cheek, to turn the other cheek for it to be slapped, too. That is the logic of the indolent, the logic of those who do not know God and who have not studied the Qur'an.

Then look at Moses (upon whom be peace). He was a simple shepherd; he stood alone with his staff against the Pharaoh who was claiming divinity. These people, too—the Shah and his gang

—would like to claim divinity for themselves, but they realize there would be no takers for their claim. But if we were to relax our vigilance, he too would say, "I am your lord, the most high." There have always been people who made these absurd claims, and there always will be.

And then there is the Most Noble Messenger (peace and blessings be upon him). He began his mission alone, prepared himself for thirteen years, and then fought for a decade. He did not ask himself, "What business do I have with politics?" Instead, he administered the entire Islamic realm. The same was true of the Commander of the Faithful (upon whom be peace): he ruled, engaged in politics, and fought wars, never saying, "Let me sit at home and devote myself to prayer and devotional reading; what business do I have with politics?"

But now we find one of the *'ulama* (may God grant him mercy) expressing himself as follows: "If the Imam of the Age (peace be upon him) thinks it necessary, he will come. I cannot claim to be more concerned for Islam than he is; so if the Imam sees what is happening, let him come himself to remedy our affairs! Why should I do anything?"

That is the logic of people who want to avoid responsibility. After a diligent search, they come up with a couple of traditions telling us, for example, to make our peace with kings or to pray for them. But such traditions are contrary to the Qur'an. They have not read the Qur'an. Even if they can find a hundred such traditions, they will still be beating their heads against the wall, because such traditions are contrary to the custom of the prophets. Islam does not recognize or accept such traditions. There is a tradition that says: "Whoever wishes long life for a king will be resurrected together with him." Could a Muslim possibly wish long life for a king, so that he might commit more injustice? Could anyone wish to maintain relations with someone who slaughters people, who slaughters *'ulama?*

Do you know how many of our great *'ulama*, our valued teachers, are now living in prison or banishment? The same *'ulama* and religious scholars who until recently were living in banishment, as soon as they were released and returned to their home towns, clenched their fists and began to speak against the government and against the Shah. They were re-arrested. The same noble young man who delivered a speech at the commemorative gathering yesterday afternoon had previously endured imprisonment and banishment; it is quite likely that he has been arrested again now, or that he will be tomorrow. This is the true son of Islam, the true Muslim: when he comes out of prison, he clenches his fist and resumes his struggle. If a Muslim shows no concern for the affairs of his fellow Muslims, he is not a Muslim—the Prophet (upon whom be peace) stated this in a tradition—even if he constantly says, *"La ilaha illa 'Llah."* The Muslim is the person who works to benefit Islam and his fellow Muslims.

They kill our young men, and we shouldn't care? They kill our *'ulama,* and we shouldn't care? They kill the believers and the Muslims, and we shouldn't care? We are supposed to agree to all this, or do something that suggests our agreement? Then we must become different human beings!

In Iran, our young men were imprisoned and banished, and now they are subject to the same measures again. But when these courageous youths come back from prison or banishment, they begin their struggle again, returning to the themes of their earlier preaching. Again, they are banished. But if they are banished and released ten times over, they will still be the same persons that they were in the beginning. For it is Islam that has trained them. If the Commander of the Faithful (upon whom be peace) had been killed and then brought back to life a hundred times, he would still be the same Commander of the Faithful. But take some apathetic person and kill him; when you bring him back to life, he will be as apathetic as before.

We have suffered, and continue to suffer, all these misfortunes at the hands of governments who have signed the Declaration of Human Rights and who loudly proclaim men's right to freedom. Before, it was the British that brought us misfortune; now it is the Soviets on the one hand, and the Americans on the other. All our miseries are caused by those imperialists; if they would stop protecting the Iranian government, the people would skin them alive. The Iranian government granted absolute immunity to the American advisers and got a few dollars in exchange. How many American officers there are in Iran now, and what huge salaries they receive! That is our problem—everything in our treasury has to be emptied into the pockets of America, and if there is any slight remainder, it has to go to the Shah and his gang. They buy themselves villas abroad and stuff their bank accounts with the people's money, while the nation subsists in poverty. At the same time, they say constantly, "Iran is one of the most advanced countries in the world. It is now on a par with America, or at least Japan (maybe a bit more advanced than Japan)." But the absurdity of these words and the corrupt frame of mind that underlies them have become apparent to everyone. Even the corner grocer will tell you, "The Shah is talking nonsense." But he's quite unashamed and goes right on talking. We can't do anything about it.

After these events, this general strike and shutdown, you will see in tomorrow's newspapers that they're back to their old bombastic claims: "All the people are with us; the few individuals who oppose us are all deviants." Yes, the *ulama* and the great *maraji'* of Qum who have proclaimed a general shutdown are all reactionaries. You and I, and people like us, are all obscurantists and reactionaries in their view; they are the progressives, and they tell you our country is a progressive country. And everybody is Muslim; everybody is learned in Islam! The religious scholars are enlightened and in agreement with them! The "true" religious scholars—that's what they call them—are all in agreement with them!

The only problem is that you won't find these true religious scholars anywhere outside the newspapers, where it says, "The true religious scholars are in agreement with us." Which "true" religious scholars? Can any Muslim agree with you? What Muslim can consent to the killing of an innocent person? Yes, it may happen that sometimes a Muslim or a scholar is afraid and says nothing, whereas at other times he is not afraid and speaks out; sometimes a student of the religious sciences is afraid and does not leave his home, whereas at other times he is not afraid and cries out in protest! But *agreement!* That is the wrong word; what scholar could possibly agree with you? Could someone be a religious scholar and agree with a massacre? Is it at all possible? Can someone believe in Islam and agree with abolishing the Islamic calendar in favor of the calendar of the unbelievers? Could any Muslim agree with this scandalous uncovering of women? The women of Iran have risen up against the Shah themselves and given a punch in the mouth to him with the cry, "We don't want to be forced into immorality! We want to be free!" His answer is, "But you are free! The only thing is that you cannot go to school wearing a chador or headcovering!"

I don't know what this state of affairs is in Iran. What kind of misbegotten monsters are this Shah and his government?

We are faced with so many difficulties; I cannot possibly tell you all of them. God knows, the problems that are referred to me by the people! They tell me, for example, "We want to build a water-storage tank at such-and-such a place, because there the people have no water." Now if people don't have water, do they have electricity? Do they have paved roads? They have nothing!

Ignore the northern sections of Tehran where they have put things in order; go take a look at the south of the city—go look at those pits, those holes in the ground where people live, dwellings you reach by going down about a hundred steps into the ground; homes people have built out of rush matting or clay so their poor children can have somewhere to live. I am talking about Tehran, not some distant village or town; that is the way Tehran is. When you enter Tehran, you see all the cars and that deceptive exterior, but you haven't gone to the other side of Tehran to see what state that is in. They don't have any drinking water. They have to take their pitchers and climb up those hundred steps until they come to a water faucet, then fill their pitchers, and climb down again. Picture some poor woman in the middle of the biting winter climbing up and down those steps to fetch water for her children. A reliable informant told me that some poor woman who was living in one of those holes brought her children and sat down right in the middle of Paminar Avenue, until finally people gathered around and helped her find a place to live. That is our highly advanced country with its capital city, Tehran.

In one of their own newspapers they wrote that in some part of the country—I can't remember exactly where; I think it was somewhere in the region of Shushtar—when the people wake up in the morning, they wash the trachoma-infected eyes of their children with urine so they can open their eyes. That is the state of our country, our advanced and progressive country!

What happens to all that money? Is our country poor? Our country has an ocean of oil. It has iron; it has precious metals. Iran is a rich country. But those so-called friends of humanity have appointed their agent to rule this country in order to prevent the poor from benefiting from its riches. Everything must go into his masters' pockets and be spent on their enjoyment. If some small bit of the country's resources is left, the Shah and his gang grab it; there is enough left for them to have a villa, a palace, an estate awaiting them wherever they travel, in addition to all their money in the bank.

This Carter fooled people for a time, and they said he would do all kinds of things if he came to power. Later he said clearly— after all, liars have short memories—"There can be no question of human rights in countries where we have military bases; human rights must not even be mentioned." For after all, freedom is part of human rights. First he says human rights are inalienable, and then he says, "I don't want to hear about human rights." Of course, he's right from his own point of view; he uses the logic of bandits. The head of a government that has signed the Declaration of Human Rights says, "We have military bases in Iran; we can't talk about human rights there. Respect for human rights is feasible only in countries where we have no military bases." What miseries America, for all its boasting about human rights, has inflicted on the peoples of Latin America, in its own hemisphere!

The logic of bandits cannot be other than banditry, expressed with machine guns and rifles, by the gunning down of religious scholars, by the destruction of Fayziya Madrasa and the subsequent closing and sequestration of that center of Ja'fari Shi'ism. Fayziya Madrasa has been closed for several years now. They plundered the Madrasa and robbed its students; they burned the turbans of the *tullab* and even burned their books! They insulted the Qur'an itself! That is the logic of bandits. As you know, the students in Qum then made their headquarters in Hujjatiya and Khan Madrasas, and there, too, they have been attacked and beaten. But if they are beaten and expelled from their madrasa a hundred times, they will establish their base in yet another madrasa, for they have come to life, they have awakened!

As we sit here, I don't know what is happening to our brothers in Iran. But I am certain of this much, that an impressive ceremony was organized yesterday afternoon in memory of those who were killed in Qum. And today, too, the Masjid-i A'zam in Qum is full of people; the bazaars and streets of Qum are all closed down. The bazaars in other towns have also been closed, as far as I know. There is no news yet from Shiraz and Isfahan, but I'm sure the bazaars are closed there, too; they can't possibly be open.

This is a bewildering situation. Their logic is the logic of the machine gun, and the logic of all too many of us is silence. They say we must keep silent, nothing can be done. Their logic is to slap us, and our logic is to be slapped! They claim Jesus (peace be upon him) recommended turning the other check, but that is the logic of the apathetic!

Jesus (peace be upon him) was a great prophet; he began his struggle in the cradle when he said, "I shall now call to prayer." According to the Qur'an, he was a prophet while still in the cradle;[59] is it possible that such a person could utter such apathetic, cowardly words? This recommendation to turn the other cheek was invented by those who claim some affiliation to Jesus (we cannot call them Christians); they deceived the Christians and other simpletons and made them completely passive toward their governments.

There are people among us who tell us we must swallow whatever poison the "holders of authority" wish to force down our throats, simply because they are the "authorities." We musn't say a word against them, these tyrannical "authorities."

A certain *akhund* wrote to me a few years ago to ask me, "Why do you oppose the government? Do you not know that 'God gives rule to whomever He wishes'?" I didn't even answer him; he wasn't worth answering. But his question involved a clear denial of the Qur'an. In a certain sense, God gave kingship to the Pharaoh, but did not Moses oppose him? Nimrod's kingship was also a divine gift in the sense that everything is from God, but did not Abraham move against him and oppose him? Mu'awiya also represented the "holders of authority," so why did, first, the Commander of the Faithful and later, Imam Hasan (peace be upon them) oppose him? And then Imam Husayn (peace be upon him) gathered up his family and fifty or sixty followers and rose up in revolt against another "holder of authority," Yazid. Why did he do that? What nonsense some people speak!

Those "holders of authority" who are mentioned right after God and the Messenger in the Qur'anic verse "Obey God and obey the Messenger and the holders of authority from among you"

225

(4:59) must also be close to God and the Messenger in their practice. They must be the shadow of God and the Messenger. Yes, the Islamic ruler is the shadow of God, but what is meant by shadow is something that has no motion of itself. Your shadow does not move by itself; it moves only when you move. Islam recognizes a person as the "shadow of God" who abandons all individual volition in the sense that he acts only in accordance with the ordinances of Islam, so that his motion is dependent, not independent. The Messenger of God (peace and blessings be upon him) was indeed a true shadow of God; but is this vile Shah a shadow of God? Yes, a few thoughtless people among us say so, but that would mean that Yazid was also a "holder of authority" and anyone who rebelled against him deserved to be killed! In fact, in the time of Yazid, the Umayyad judges delivered a verdict that Imam Husayn, the Lord of the Martyrs, was deserving of death!

We have not read the Qur'an properly and have not understood the logic of the Qur'an. Above all else, we must study the Qur'an; the Qur'an has given instructions for everything and made clear what our duties are. It has told us how we are to treat kings. Why does the Qur'an repeat the story of Moses (peace be upon him) so frequently? Is it just meant to be an entertaining story? If the Qur'an wanted to tell us a story, once would be enough. So what is the purpose behind the Qur'an's insistence on repeating the story of Moses and his opposition to the Pharaoh? To make us understand!

The Qur'an constantly discusses warfare against the unbelievers, and mentions the question of the hypocrites; is this purely for the purpose of telling us a story? Is the Qur'an a book of stories? The Qur'an is a book designed to produce true human beings; it is a book intended to create active human beings; it is a book that deals with everything in this world, from beginning to end, and all the stages in man's development. It is a book that regulates man's spiritual life and orders his government. Everything is there, in the Qur'an, in the Sunna of the Most Noble Messenger (peace and blessings be upon him and his family), and in the traditions of the Immaculate Imams (peace be upon them), but careful study of all these is needed in order for us to understand what we must do. We constantly read in the Qur'an that the Pharaoh acted in a certain way and Moses in another way, but we don't think about why the Qur'an tells us all this. It tells us this so that we may act like Moses toward the Pharaoh of our age; let us pick up our staffs and oppose this vile Shah. At the very least, let no one support this regime.

May God Almighty grant all of you success. May God Almighty remove this evil from rule over the Muslims. May God, Exalted and Almighty, preserve our people in the midst of their tribulation. May God, Exalted and Almighty, grant the Muslims a favorable result in this, their struggle.

And peace be upon you, and the mercy and blessings of God.

February 27, 1978

Message to the People of Azerbayjan

This is a declaration issued from Najaf on the occasion of the popular uprising in Tabriz. Source: *Sukhanrani-yi Imam Khomeini dama zilluh,* pp. 57-63.

GREETINGS TO THE COURAGEOUS and Godfearing people of beloved Azerbayjan! Salutations to the upright men and honorable youths of Tabriz and to all those who have risen up against this dangerous Pahlavi family and nullified all its empty boasts with their cries of "Death to the Shah!"

Long life to the beloved struggling people of Tabriz, who with their great uprising have given a painful punch in the mouth to those babblers! With their raucous propaganda, they designated the bloody revolution of imperialism (something opposed, one hundred percent, by the noble people of Iran) the "White Revolution of the Shah and the People," and they call this slavish servant of the foreigners and imperialists the "savior of the country." This wretch, who has surrendered the great sources of wealth of this oppressed population to the foreigners with both hands, and who gives them back the paltry sums he receives in payment in order to buy pieces of scrap metal that are of no use whatsoever to the nation, is supposed to be the "savior of the country." The country's so-called savior has squandered its self-respect and reduced Iran to the status of a backward colony by granting legal immunity to foreigners. He is supposedly a "guardian of freedom," but he does not allow anyone, anywhere in the country, to utter a word of criticism. The shadow of his abominable police force hovers over the country. He is a "justice-loving" ruler, but he sees fit every now and then to plunge the country into mourning with a massacre.

I do not know what words I can use to console the respected people of Tabriz, its bereaved mothers and distressed fathers, or what I can say in condemnation of these successive, incessant massacres. I do not know the exact extent of the crimes that have been committed, nor the number of those killed and wounded. But it appears from the blaring propaganda of the regime that the extent of its crimes surpasses the imagination, and yet despite this, the Shah wishes to put on trial those members of the police who did not enact a slaughter of the proportions he desired.

We were still grieving over the painful memories of Qum when this hideous atrocity occurred in Tabriz, saddening every Muslim and redoubling our grief. Noble people of Azerbayjan, I give you glad tidings of ultimate victory! It was you, proud Azerbayjanis, who devotedly arose during the Constitutional Revolution in order to crush despotism and end the arbitrary and tyrannical rule of kings.[60] The tyranny of those kings appears as nothing when compared to the tyranny of Muhammad Riza Khan Pahlavi and his disgraceful father. The whole of Iranian history does not record a series of bloodthirsty massacres like those enacted by this ferocious bandit. Nor, in the history of constitutional government in Iran, do we find a Majlis like this one, where the respected and pious people of Azerbayjan are supposed to be represented by a handful of irreligious ruffians. More than this, however, we should not expect from a Majlis imposed on the people by the Shah.

Now, after the criminal massacres and bloodshed that have taken place in Tabriz, a few SAVAK agents have been sent into the streets in different parts of the country, accompanied by workers driven at bayonet-point, to shout and demonstrate on behalf of this criminal and treacherous regime, and thereby to wash away the traces of shame from the face of the tyrannical, bloodthirsty Shah. They are unaware that those traces cannot be washed away even by the waters of Zamzam and Kauthar,[61] for history has recorded the sufferings endured by the people at the hands of this criminal father and son and the record will soon be revealed.

Now, as I compose this letter of sorrow, I do not know what is befalling my dear brothers in Tabriz. Has the Shah desisted from his crimes, even if only temporarily? Or does he now wish so to terrorize the survivors of the massacre that they dare not even breathe? In any event, he must realize it is too late; the people of Iran have chosen their path and they will not rest until they have overthrown these criminals and avenged themselves and their fathers on this bloodthirsty family.

God, the Invincible, has willed that the voices of the people should now be raised against the Shah and his regime throughout the country, and these voices will be raised ever louder. The religious leaders will hoist the banner of Islam to exact vengeance on this Zuhhak[62] of the age, and the nation of Islam, with their hearts in unison and obeying the life-giving teachings of the Qur'an, will expunge every trace of this anti-Islamic regime that wishes to revive Zoroastrianism.[63] "Verily the dawn is near" (Qur'an, 11:81).

Let the noble, cherished, and beloved people of Azerbayjan (may God support them) know that they are not alone in their struggle for justice, independence, and freedom and their efforts to defend the Qur'an. Great cities like Shiraz, Isfahan, Ahvaz, and especially Qum, the center of the religious institution and the stronghold of Imam Sadiq (God's peace be upon him), and the great city of Tehran, have added their voices to theirs, and are united with them in their disgust at this foul Pahlavi family.

The slogan heard in every street and alley of every city and village is: "Death to the Shah." However much his vile agents try to divert responsibility for these crimes away from their main source—the Shah—to the government and its officials, no one believes them. Remarkably enough, a government delegation is reported to have gone to Azerbayjan to tell the people that the Shah was unaware of the crimes being committed. But who gives any credence to this claim, apart from the members of SAVAK and the Majlis? And even they know in their hearts that it is false.

I ask of God Almighty that He remedy the affairs of the Muslims, remove the evil of the oppressors, and eliminate all traces of this family.

And may peace be upon you, and also the mercy of God.

Message to the People of Abadan

Imam Khomeini issued this declaration from Najaf on the occasion of the government-ordered immolation of more than four hundred people in the Cinema Rex, Abadan. Source: copy of the declaration circulated in North America by the Muslim Students' Association (Persian-Speaking Group).

I HAVE BEEN GREATLY SORROWED by the appalling news of the immolation of several hundred of our countrymen in that calculated manner.

I do not think any Muslim could perpetrate such a deed, or indeed, any human being, except those who have accustomed themselves to committing similar acts and whose savagery and barbarity have placed them beyond the pale of humanity. I have not yet been informed of all the details, but what is certain is that this inhuman act, contrary to all the laws of Islam, cannot have been committed by the opponents of the Shah, who have risked their lives for the sake of the interests of Islam and Iran and the lives and property of the people and are devoting themselves to the defense of their fellow countrymen.

The evidence points to the criminal hand of the tyrannical regime, which wishes to distort the image of the humane Islamic movement of our people. Lighting a ring of fire around the cinema and then having its doors locked by the cinema staff was something only the authorities had the power to do. The speech of the Shah to the effect that his opponents are promising the people a "great terror"[64] and the repetition of this claim shortly after the incident, pointing to the fire as the "great terror" that had been promised, furnish another indication of the conspiracy behind this abominable tragedy; for, after all, the Shah has no powers of foretelling the future! The Shah also gave an interview in which he said he would destroy the whole nation of Iran, which provides still further evidence. As for the expressions of regret broadcast over the propaganda loudspeakers of the regime by persons whose arms are plunged up to the elbow daily in the blood of our compatriots, these, too, are a great proof of the satanic plan of the Shah and his gang, the same people who have enacted terrible massacres in most of the cities of Iran.

These oppressed people who are being slaughtered daily by those same criminals and put to death in appalling ways—are they not our fellow-countrymen? All indications are that the heart-rending incident in Abadan has the same origin as the massacres that have taken place in other Iranian cities. Who benefits from these crimes other than the Shah and his accomplices? Who is there—other than the Shah—that has ever enacted savage slaughters of the people every now and then, and presented us with such barbaric scenes as this? This heart-rending tragedy is intended by the Shah to be his masterpiece, to provide material to be exploited to the utmost by his extensive domestic and foreign propaganda apparatus.[65] He will no doubt have ordered the press and media that are under his control at home, as well as the organs of the oil-hungry foreigners abroad, to publish the news of this event as widely as possible and to attribute it to the deprived and oppressed people of Iran, so that the Iranian nation in its search for justice will be presented as a group of savages who do not believe in any humane or Islamic criteria.

I warn the great Iranian nation that the regime may commit similar savage acts in other cities of Iran in the hope of defiling the pure demonstrations of our courageous people, who have watered the roots of the tree of Islam with their blood. All our speakers and preachers should make clear to the people the dangers that threaten the continuation of the liberating Islamic Revolution.

I offer my condolences for this great tragedy to the Muslim people of Iran, and especially to the oppressed people of Abadan and the families that have suffered bereavement.

I ask God Almighty to grant victory to Islam and the Muslims and to foreshorten the arms of the foreigners and their agents.

Declaration on the Occasion of 'Id al-Fitr

The prayers of 'Id al-Fitr, coming at the end of the month of Ramadan, were accompanied by mass demonstrations on a scale unequalled in Iranian history, demanding the ouster of the Shah and the installation of an Islamic government. This message of Imam Khomeini from Najaf was designed to maintain the momentum of the revolutionary movement. Source: copy of the declaration circulated in North America by the Muslim Students' Association (Persian-Speaking Group).

I OFFER MY CONGRATULATIONS to the courageous Muslim people of Iran on the occasion of this great and happy Islamic festival.

This past month witnessed your endurance of the bloodshed inflicted on you by the tyrant as you sought to gain the path of salvation and nobly struggled for your lofty human aims. It was a month of sacrifice for the sake of God, a month of clear opposition between truth and falsehood, and "Verily falsehood is bound to vanish" (Qur'an, 17:81).

This year's 'Id al-Fitr has been an epic celebration of heroism for all segments of our population. It was a day that demonstrated to the whole world the intellectual and practical maturity of our people, and declared with the utmost clarity that the wish of the entire nation is for the Shah to leave, and for his regime of oppression and exploitation of our Muslim people to be abolished. After performing the 'Id prayer, the Muslim people of Iran performed another valuable act of worship by uttering thundering cries of protest against this tyrannical bandit regime and demanding a government of divine justice. To struggle for the sake of these goals is one of the greatest forms of worship, and to make sacrifices for them is in conformity with the customs of the prophets, particularly the Most Noble Messenger of Islam and his great successor, the Commander of the Faithful.

I thank the Iranian nation for the sacrifices it has made, and I beseech God Almighty to grant it further greatness and strength with the aid of the Qur'an and the ordinances of Islam.

A momentous duty now confronts all the Muslims, particularly the religious and political leaders, as well as others in a position of influence. Our nation has now come to a fork in the road. In one direction lies victory and the expulsion of the Shah, and in the other, eternal humiliation beneath the boots of his executioners. We must choose between dignity and honor in the sight of God and man, and (God forbid) perpetual abasement and indignity. I know the Muslim nation of Iran will never submit to abasement.

Noble people of Iran! Press forward with your movement and do not slacken for a minute, as I know full well you will not! Be certain that, God willing, victory and triumph are near.

Let no one imagine that after the blessed month of Ramadan, his God-given duties have changed. These demonstrations that break down tyranny and advance the goals of Islam are a form of worship that is not confined to only certain months or days, for the aim is to save the nation, to enact Islamic justice, and to establish a divine government on the firm basis of justice.

At every available opportunity and on every occasion, organize meetings in mosques and public places on an even wider scale than before, and defend the Qur'an and Islamic justice. Any diversionary voice that is raised, by no matter whom, is satanic; it benefits the oppressive rulers and harms Islam and the nation.[66] Pay no attention to the deceptive words of the Shah, his government, and its supporters, for their only aim is to gain another reprieve for their satanic selves. In order to deceive the people, they mouth empty speeches about freedom at a time when their jails still overflow with religious leaders and university students, with merchants and politicians, with workers and peasants. Religious and political leaders have been banished to remote parts of the country for the crime of speaking the truth and demanding freedom. How can one speak of freedom when the press is still subject to censorship, when the discussion of fundamental matters vital to the country is forbidden, and a semi-military government is in force all across Iran?

The Iranian people will never surrender to the Shah's police; instead, they will continue their public protests. The Iranian people will no longer be deceived by the tricks of the regime.

Proof indicates, and the bereaved people declare, that the cinema in Abadan was set on fire by the criminal Shah and his government. Four hundred people were burned to death in order to fulfill the promise of a "great terror" that was a theme in his propaganda against our sacred movement. This strategem has not worked, but you will see someone or some few brought forward sooner or later to "confess" that they were involved in the affair.[67] They will be either government stooges, or else persons chosen from among the best and most religious, whom the Shah will seize the opportunity to kill.

The Shah and his government are in a state of armed rebellion against the justice-seeking people of Iran, against the Constitution, and against the liberating decrees of Islam. They are therefore traitors, and to obey them is to obey the *taghut*.[68] Do not give them the slightest respite, and inform the whole world of their barbarous deeds with your strikes and protest demonstrations.

Our struggling brothers should establish as much contact as possible with foreign newsmen and make them understand that it is the Shah himself and his government that are responsible for the continuing repression and violation of the Constitution. They should make the world understand that the former Shah had the provision establishing the Pahlavi dynasty inserted in the Constitution by force,[69] and that no Iranian accepts this provision. Furthermore, they should expose the false propaganda directed against our Islamic movement from abroad, and not allow the movement to be condemned by those ignorant of its true nature. Let those militant persons who are now outside the country try to enlighten public opinion wherever they are, and in general increase to the fullest their activity connected with the situation in Iran.

I thank the Iranian army for not opening fire on the huge marches that took place in Tehran and the provinces—marches of patriotic people enraged by fifty years of oppressive rule by the Pahlavi dynasty—and thereby defiling their hands with a great crime of the kind our rulers are always committing. At this critical juncture, when our country stands on the edge of a precipice and is confronted with the choice of either total collapse or genuine independence, I extend my hand to all those in the army, air force, and navy who are faithful to Islam and the homeland and ask them to assist us in preserving our independence and emerging from the yoke of slavery and humiliation.

Proud soldiers who are ready to sacrifice yourself for your country and homeland, arise! Suffer slavery and humiliation no longer! Renew your bonds with the beloved people and refuse to go on slaughtering your children and brothers for the sake of the whims of this family of bandits! Speakers and writers should do their utmost to explain the thoughts that are agitating our brothers in the army, and the Iranian people must respect them, for they are our brothers.

Is it not in the interest of the government itself that it should step aside, instead of disgracing itself further in the eyes of the public? Is it not time for the Shah to step aside so that the people can decide their own destiny in peace, and determine who the traitors are that deserve punishment? Is it proper that hundreds of thousands of the sons and daughters of this oppressed nation should be slaughtered in order to let the Shah continue his cruelty a few days longer? Is it possible to take a single step toward the salvation of Iran as long as these traitors to Islam and the nation—headed by the Shah—are still there? It is our hope that in the near future the arms of the traitors will be foreshortened so that the final solution to our problems can be put forward.

Most importantly, it must be stated that after this tyrannical regime has been abolished, we will announce our fundamental program, which will be inspired by the progressive ideas of Islam. Then it will be seen that all the claims made by the traitors concerning Islam—concerning the rights of women and the religious minorities, as well as other matters—are nothing but cheap lies and poisonous propaganda trumpeted over the Shah's propaganda loudspeakers at home and abroad in order to confuse people and in the hope of arresting or defeating our movement. It is to be hoped that all that we propose will become clear very soon, once the tyrannical regime has been swept away.

God Almighty, grant that our movement may continue to blossom and the liberating demonstrations of our people continue to expand until the foundations of tyranny and oppression have been destroyed.

Message to the Pilgrims

This was written in Najaf shortly before Imam Khomeini left Iraq for France. It is an appeal to the Muslims of the world for solidarity with the Iranian people. Although some of the persons distributing the message were arrested by the Saudi authorities, it was widely circulated among the pilgrims and later turned up in the Islamic press of many countries. Source: a pamphlet prepared by the Muslim Students' Association (Persian-Speaking Group), containing the text of the message in Persian, Arabic, Turkish, Urdu, Malay-Indonesian, French, and English.

NOW THAT IT IS THE SEASON OF PILGRIMAGE to the sacred House of God and Muslims have come from all over the world to visit God's House, it is necessary that they pay attention to one of the most important aspects of this great gathering while they are performing the noble rites of the hajj, and examine the social and political circumstances of the Islamic countries. They must inform themselves of the hardships that their brothers in faith are suffering and strive to relieve those hardships, in accordance with their Islamic and moral duty. To concern oneself with the affairs of the Muslims is one of the significant duties of Islam.

Now, O visitors to the sacred House of God, I present you with a report on the problems afflicting the Muslim people of Iran, and I request aid from Muslims in every part of the world. For fifty years, Iran, which has about thirty million Muslims, has been in the grip of the Pahlavi dynasty, a self-proclaimed servant of foreign powers. During those fifty dark years, the great people of Iran have been writhing under police repression, suffocation, and spiritual torture.

The Shah has given foreigners all the subterranean wealth and vital interests belonging to the people. He has given oil to America; gas to the Soviet Union; pastureland, forests, and part of the oil to England and other countries. The people have been deprived of all the necessities of life and kept in a state of backwardness. The imperialist system has taken control of the army, the education, and the economy of our country, and has taken away from our people all opportunity for development.

Now that our people in recent years have awakened, risen up to gain their rights, and cried out against oppression, they have been answered with machine guns, tanks, and cannons. The massacres that have occurred in the cities of Iran in recent months are a cause of shame to history. With the support of America and with all the infernal means at his disposal, the Shah has fallen on our oppressed people, turning Iran into one vast graveyard. General strikes engulf the country, and the Shah wishes to avenge himself on his oppressed people during his last moments. Martial law has cast its sinister shadow over the people, and his mercenaries and commandos are busy killing young and old, men and women.

I have not been permitted to continue my activity in any Islamic country, my activity that consists of conveying to the world the cry of my oppressed people. Because I must at all events fulfill my religious and ethical duty, I have been obliged to leave the Islamic world in the hope of alerting human society to the suffering of the oppressed people of Iran. I shall continue to live abroad until I have the opportunity to continue my work in one of the Muslim countries.

Now, O Muslims of the world, show concern for the problem of Iran, and convey to the world the cry of thirty million oppressed Muslims. The Most Noble Messenger (peace and blessings be upon him) is reported to have said: "He who arises in the morning and gives no thought to the affairs of the Muslims is not a Muslim."

O God, I have conveyed the message, and peace be upon those who follow true guidance.

October 11, 1978

In Commemoration of the Martyrs of Tehran

This declaration was issued from Neauphle-le-Chateau forty days after the massacre of "Bloody Friday," September 9, 1978, urging steadfastness and persistence. Source: copy of the declaration circulated in North America by the Muslim Students' Association (Persian-Speaking Group).

NOW THAT FORTY DAYS HAVE PASSED since the death of our beloved martyrs in Tehran, after so many similar days of commemoration following massacres, and now that government by the bayonet has been officially established, we must anticipate still more such days. Now that the sinister specter of military government has added its dark shadow to the darkness of monarchy and inflicted further misery on our deprived people; now that the hands of the oppressive superpowers can be seen emerging from the sleeves of the Shah's butchers and slaughtering the dear Muslims—the superpowers that plunder our abundant resources despite the firm resolve of our people to prevent them; now that the "guardians of human rights" are peddling the wares of the "great civilization" over the heaped-up corpses of our young;[70] now that, thanks to Carter, our people have attained the freedom and independence the Shah feels they deserve—now that all of this has happened, our country sits mourning without any protector. I am mourning here in the West, and you are mourning in the East.

As long as the criminal hands of the oil-hungry superpowers are at work in our country, the gates of happiness and freedom will remain closed to us.

My beloved ones, summon up all your strength and break open the chains of slavery! One after the other, remove the treacherous pawns of the Shah from the scene and cut off the greedy hands of those that manipulate them and their like in the Islamic countries. The way to happiness, freedom, and independence is barred by those pawns and those who manipulate them, so scatter their ranks and save the country!

According to the way Carter thinks, all the crimes, savagery, and repression the Shah practices represent efforts to establish democracy and find progressive solutions for social problems. He accuses the Iranian people of being opposed to the freedom the Shah wishes to give them[71]—as if all the strikes and protest movements taking place all over Iran were an attempt to evade freedom! But he should realize that this kind of nonsense no longer has any effect and people have come to recognize the Shah for what he is.

Great people of Iran! The history of Iran, even world history, has never witnessed a movement like yours; it has never experienced a universal uprising like yours, noble people!

Today primary school children of seven or eight stand ready to sacrifice themselves and shed their blood for the sake of Islam and the nation; when has anything like that been seen? Our lion-hearted women snatch up their infants and go to confront the machine guns and tanks of the regime; where in history has such valiant and heroic behavior by women been recorded? Today the thunderous cry of "Death to the Shah!" arises from the heart of the primary school child and the infirm old man alike, and it has blackened the days of this vile Pahlavi regime and so shattered the nerves of the Shah that he seeks to calm himself with the blood of our children and young people.

Beloved sisters and brothers! Be steadfast; do not weaken or slacken your efforts. Your path is the path of God and His elect. Your blood is being shed for the same cause as the blood of the prophets and the Imams and the righteous. You will join them, and you have no cause to grieve, therefore, but every reason for joy.

Make firm your ranks, strengthen your resolve, preserve your unity of purpose, and join together with all Muslim elements, particularly those in the army. Convey my greetings to them, and tell them that those people their machine guns are killing are their brothers and sisters. Tell them not to disgrace themselves before God and man any longer in order to satisfy the passions of the Shah, but instead to accept the welcoming embrace of the people.

My dear ones! Avoid all disagreement, for disagreement is the work of the devil. Continue your sacred movement in unison for the sake of the ultimate goal, which is the overthrow of the corrupt Pahlavi regime and the liberation of the destiny and resources of our country from foreign control. Fear nothing in your pursuit of these Islamic goals, for no power can halt this great movement. You are in the right; the hand of God Almighty is with you, and it is His will that those who have been oppressed should assume leadership and become heirs to their own destiny and resources.[72]

At the earliest opportunity, I will go to an Islamic country where I will be able to continue my activities, and God Almighty willing, I will spend the rest of my life in the path of God, which means serving you. Until now, none of the Muslim governments have issued me an invitation, but as soon as I am assured freedom of speech and expression in some Muslim country, I shall go there. For the time being, I shall remain here.

When one is in the service of Islam, the question of inconvenience—the inconvenience that may arise from being in some particular location—does not arise. What is important is duty and the voice of one's conscience. Whatever I may be able to do and whatever ultimately happens to me, I am embarrassed in front of you who are shedding your blood for the sake of freedom and Islam. What gladdens my heart in this painful place is the opportunity to serve you. I share the sorrow of those families throughout the country who, in the midst of their bereavement, are the pride of Iran, and my heart is pained by the memory of those primary school children who were recently killed by the tyrant Shah.[73]

I declare the fortieth day after the massacre in Tehran to be a day of public mourning, and I too will be in mourning.

I ask of God Almighty that our movement may continue.

And peace be upon you, and the mercy and blessings of God.

Muharram: The Triumph of Blood
Over the Sword

Imam Khomeini issued this declaration from Neauphle-le-Chateau one week before the beginning of Muharram, the month in which the Iranian people, emulating Imam Husayn (whose martyrdom took place on the tenth day of the month) advanced their confrontation with the Shah's regime to a point of no return. After Muharram, it was clear that the regime could not survive. Source: copy of the declaration circulated in North America by the Muslim Students' Association (Persian-Speaking Group).

WITH THE APPROACH OF MUHARRAM, we are about to begin the month of epic heroism and self-sacrifice—the month in which blood triumphed over the sword, the month in which truth condemned falsehood for all eternity and branded the mark of disgrace upon the forehead of all oppressors and satanic governments; the month that has taught successive generations throughout history the path of victory over the bayonet; the month that proves the superpowers may be defeated by the word of truth; the month in which the leader of the Muslims taught us how to struggle against all the tyrants of history, showed us how the clenched fists of those who seek freedom, desire independence, and proclaim the truth may triumph over tanks, machine guns, and the armies of Satan, how the word of truth may obliterate falsehood.

The leader of the Muslims taught us that if a tyrant rules despotically over the Muslims in any age, we must rise up against him and denounce him, however unequal our forces may be, and that if we see the very existence of Islam in danger, we must sacrifice ourselves and be prepared to shed our blood.

Now the regime of the Shah is ruling tyrannically over our oppressed people today. He continues to rule in defiance of the law and the wishes of the people, who have risen up against him throughout Iran, and he threatens the higher interests of the Muslims and the dictates of Islam with imminent destruction for the sake of his own satanic rule and his parasitic masters. It is the duty of the entire nation that has now risen in revolt to pursue and broaden its struggle against the Shah with all its strength and to bring down his harmful, disastrous regime.

The military government is usurpatory and contrary to both the law of the land and the *shari'a*. It is the duty of everyone to oppose it, to refrain from aiding it in any way, to refuse to pay taxes or render any other assistance to this oppressive regime of transgressors, and it is the duty of all oil company officials and workers to prevent the export of oil, this vital resource.

Do those workers and officials know that the bullets that pierce the breasts of our precious youths, that drown our men, our women, our infants in blood, are paid for with the money earned by the oil that their exhausting labor produces? Do they know that the major part of the oil used by Israel, that obstinate enemy of Islam and usurper of the rights of Muslims, is provided by the Shah? If the usurpatory government wishes to continue this act of treason by bringing pressure to bear on the workers, the question of oil may be settled once and for all.

It is the duty of those well informed about the state of the country to draw up lists of the ministers serving in this usurpatory government, or the traitors and officers who are ordering crimes and massacres throughout the country, so that the people will know what to do with them at the appropriate time.

Let the government and senior army commanders know that if they do not cease supporting the criminal Shah, that traitor to Islam and our Islamic land, they will be requited for their deeds in the near future.

Now, with the month of Muharram here like a divine sword in the hands of the soldiers of Islam, our great religious leaders and respected preachers, and all the followers of the Lord of the Martyrs (peace and blessings be upon him), they must make the maximum use of it. Trusting in the power of God, they must tear out the remaining roots of this tree of oppression and treachery, for the month of Muharram is the month in which the forces of Yazid and the stratagems of Satan are defeated.

Let assemblies for the commemoration of the Lord of the Oppressed, the Leader of the Free—assemblies in which intelligence triumphs over ignorance, justice over injustice, loyalty over treachery, and Islamic government over government of the *taghut*—let these assemblies be organized as magnificently and

243

as frequently as possible. Let the bloodstained banners of 'Ashura be raised wherever possible, as a sign of the coming day when the oppressed shall avenge himself on his oppressor.

Respected preachers, dear speakers! Attend even more than before to your duty of exposing the crimes of the regime, so that you may hold your heads high in the presence of God Almighty and the Lord of the Age (may God hasten his renewed manifestation). The students and scholars at the religious teaching institutions who are leaving these days for the villages and provincial towns in order to enlighten their inhabitants must inform the deprived peasantry of the atrocities committed by the Shah and his slaughters of defenseless people. They must point out to them that contrary to the poisonous propaganda of the Shah and his hangers-on, an Islamic state is not the protector of the capitalists and big landlords. Those meaningless words are intended only to divert them from the path of the truth. Let them be assured that Islam stands on the side of the weak, the peasants, and the needy. Assure them that in a government based on truth, they will be protected in the best way possible.

Dear young people at the centers of religious learning, the universities, the schools and teachers' training colleges! Respected journalists! Deprived workers and peasants! Militant and enlightened bazaar merchants and tradesmen! And all other classes of the population, from the proud nomadic tribes to the deprived dwellers in slums and tents! Advance together, with a single voice and a single purpose, to the sacred aim of Islam—the abolition of the cruel Pahlavi dynasty, the destruction of the abominable monarchical regime, and the establishment of an Islamic republic based on the progressive dictates of Islam! Victory is yours, nation arisen in revolt!

There is no need to remind you that mourning assemblies must be fully independent, and not depend on permission by the police or that subversive body called the security organization. Dear people, organize your gatherings without referring to the authorities, and if you are prevented from holding them, gather in public squares, in thoroughfares and streets, and proclaim the sufferings endured by Islam and the Muslims and the treacherous acts of the Shah's regime.

The history of Iran is witnessing today the most sensitive days that Islam and our dear Muslims have experienced. Today, great nation, you have come to a fork in the road: one way leads to eternal dignity and splendor, and the other (God forbid), to perpetual humiliation and degradation.

There is no excuse for any class of people in the nation to remain inactive today; silence and apathy mean suicide, or even aid to the tyrannical regime. To abandon the straightforward path of the nation and Islam would be treason to Islam and the nation, and support for the enemies of Islam and the nation. The traitors who imagine that they can defeat this Islamic movement and save the Shah by keeping silent, or in some cases even moving to support his tyrannical regime, are mistaken. For now it is too late, and the Shah is on his way out; no one can save the Shah by selling himself. Even if he were to be saved, he would not remain loyal to those who saved him, as we can all see.

I extend a hand of affection and devotion to the noble people of Iran, who, with power they derive from Islam, have given a heavy punch in the mouth to the Shah and his supporters. The martyrs Iran has offered, for the sake of justice and divine aims, I regard as an eternal source of pride. I offer my congratulations to the mothers and fathers of those youths who have given their lives for the cause of Islam and freedom. I envy those dear, noble youths who have sacrificed themselves for the sake of the Friend.

The echo of the great Iranian Revolution is reverberating throughout the Islamic world as well as other countries, and it is a source of pride to them, too. Noble nation, you have alerted the noble young people of other Islamic nations, and we may hope that your powerful hand will raise up the proud banner of Islam in all regions. This is my petition to God, the Exalted.

May peace be upon you, and also the mercy and blessings of God.

Formation of the Council of
the Islamic Revolution

This declaration, issued at Neauphle-le-Chateau, sets forth the political framework for the establishment of the revolutionary political order and warns against the possibility of a military coup d'etat. Source: copy of the declaration circulated in North America by the Muslim Students' Association (Persian-Speaking Group).

PEACE AND GREETINGS to the heroic and noble people of Iran! Peace be upon the martyrs who have fallen in God's path.

Now that the day of victory is nigh for our courageous people, now that the pure blood of those dear and innocent ones slaughtered by the Shah's bloodthirsty executioners in the struggle to defend justice and truth is about to bear fruit in Iranian soil, I consider it necessary to bring several points to the attention of the Iranian nation and the people of the world.

1. In accordance with the rights conferred by the law of Islam and on the basis of the vote of confidence given me by the overwhelming majority of the Iranian people,[74] for the sake of attaining the Islamic goals of the people, a temporary council has been appointed, to be known as the Council of the Islamic Revolution. It is to be composed of competent, committed, and trustworthy Muslims and to begin functioning soon. The composition of this Council will be disclosed at the first appropriate occasion. Well-defined, specific tasks have been assigned to this Council. It has been entrusted with the task of examining and studying conditions for the establishment of a transitional government and making all the necessary preliminary arrangements. The composition of the transitional government will also be disclosed at the first opportune and appropriate moment, and it too will begin functioning. The new government will be entrusted with the following tasks:

a. the formation of a Constituent Assembly composed
of the elected representatives of the people in order

to discuss for approval the new Constitution of the
Islamic Republic;

b. the implementation of elections based on the principles approved by the Constituent Assembly and the
new Constitution; and

c. the transfer of power to the representatives chosen in
in those elections.

2. The present government, having been appointed by the
deposed Shah and the two houses of the existing Iranian Parliament, is illegal and will never be accepted by the people. Collaboration with this usurpatory government in any manner or form
is forbidden by religion and a crime under the law. In the same way
that the respectable and courageous officials of some ministries
and government offices have already done, everybody must refuse
obedience to these usurpatory ministers and deny them access to
their ministries whenever possible. The demands of the oppressed
people of Iran are not restricted to the departure of the Shah and
the abolition of the monarchy. Their struggle will continue until
the establishment of an Islamic Republic that guarantees the freedom of the people, the independence of the country, and the attainment of social justice. It is only through the departure of the
Shah and the transfer of power to the people that tranquillity will
return to our beloved country, and it is only through the establishment of a government of Islamic justice, confirmed and supported by the people and functioning with their full and active
participation, that the vast cultural, economic, and agricultural
damage inflicted by the corrupt regime of the Shah can be repaired
and the reconstruction of the country for the benefit of the working
and oppressed classes can begin.

3. There is a possibility that the treacherous Shah, now about
to depart, will commit a further crime—a military coup d'etat;
I have frequently warned that this is probable. It would be his
last blow. The courageous people of Iran know that there are
only a few slavish and bloodthirsty individuals in the army, who
apparently occupy important positions and whose identities are
known to me, and that the honorable elements in the army will

never permit these slaves of the Shah to commit such a crime against their nation and religion. In accordance with my God-given and national duty, I alert the Iranian army to this danger and I demand that all commanders and officers resolutely prevent the enactment of any such conspiracy and not permit a few blood-thirsty individuals to plunge the noble people of Iran into a blood-bath. Iranian army, this is your God-given duty. If you obey these congenital traitors, you will be accountable to God, Exalted and Almighty, condemned by all humanitarians, and cursed by future generations. The courageous people of Iran must prepare them-selves with all possible means to confront such a conspiracy and, with their trust placed in God Almighty, they need not fear those whose only goal is personal profit. Indeed, the ardent struggle of the Iranian people has already shown that they are not afraid, and they know that the present traitors have lost all sense of direction, just like the traitors who have already chosen to flee (taking with them the stolen wealth of the people). The Iranian people must treat the honorable officers and commanders of the army with respect. They must recognize that a few treacherous members of the army cannot sully the army as a whole. The record and respon-sibility of the few bloodthirsty individuals is something separate from those of the army as a whole. The army belongs to the people, and the people belong to the army. The army will not suffer any harm as a result of the departure of the Shah.

4. The honorable people of Iran must not cease their ardent struggle until they finally attain their aims, and indeed, they show no sign of ceasing it. They must continue their strikes and demon-strations, and if club-wielding thugs and other trouble-makers attack them, they can defend themselves, even if it results in the death of their attackers.[76]

I pray God Almighty that He grant victory to Islam and the Muslims and destroy the enemies of the noble people of Iran.

May the peace and mercy of God be upon you.

The Fortieth Day After 'Ashura

In this declaration issued at Neauphle-le-Chateau, Imam Khomeini calls for continued demonstrations and gives miscellaneous instructions reflecting the gradual transfer of authority already taking place. Source: copy of the declaration circulated in North America by the Muslim Students' Association (Persian-Speaking Group).

THE FORTIETH DAY AFTER THE ANNIVERSARY of the martyrdom of the leader of the oppressed and the Lord of the Martyrs, Imam Husayn (peace and blessings be upon him), has now arrived. The upright and conscious people of Iran have observed many such days of mourning. What disasters and inhuman crimes we have witnessed this year, following on fifty years of usurpatory rule by the Pahlavi dynasty! All fifty years have been bitter and painful, but most bitter and painful of all have been the past twelve months and more in which our courageous people have risen up against tyranny and imperialism. This year, the commemoration of the fortieth day after the anniversary of the Imam's martyrdom has come in the midst of a whole series of fortieth-day commemorations of the martyrdom of the followers of that great Islamic figure. It is as if the blood of our martyrs were the continuation of the blood of the martyrs of Karbala, and as if the commemoration of our brothers were the echo of the commemoration of those brave ones who fell at Karbala. Just as their pure blood brought to an end the tyrannical rule of Yazid, the blood of our martyrs has shattered the tyrannical monarchy of the Pahlavis.

The fortieth-day commemoration of Imam Husayn has an exceptional and ideal meaning this year. It is our religious and national duty to organize great marches and demonstrations on this day. With marches and demonstrations all across the country, our great people must bury once and for all this stinking carrion of monarchy. They must proclaim their opposition to the illegal Regency Council and declare, once again, their support for the Islamic Republic.

It is necessary for me to draw the attention of the courageous people of Iran to a number of matters.

1. According to information we have been given, at night, officials of the Shah's government are taking away grain stored in granaries and silos in order to create an artificial famine. It is the absolute duty of the people of Tehran and the provincial cities firmly to prevent this from happening. They must appoint a number of trustworthy individuals to oversee this matter in order to neutralize this inhuman plan of the government. Inattention to this matter will constitute punishable neglect of God's law.

2. According to other information given us, the American government is preparing either to steal or to blow up the weapons and equipment whose purchase it imposed on the Iranian people in exchange for oil. Indeed, according to the disclosures made by some news agencies, it may already have removed some weapons or equipment from Iran. It is the duty of the commanders and officers of the army and the other armed forces to prevent this from taking place, and it is the duty of the people to cooperate with the army in fulfilling this important task. Further destruction and plundering of the national wealth must be prevented. Let respectable officers in the army know that any laxity in this matter will count as treason to the country and to Islam.

3. Let the peasants pay particular attention to the sowing of crops, particularly crops that do not require irrigation. It is possible that the agents of corruption may attempt to create an artificial famine and expose the country to hardship.

4. Islamic banks should give interest-free loans to the peasants so that they may continue agricultural activity. Let all Muslims participate with the banks in this vital matter so that the diabolical conspiracy for creating famine may be defeated.

5. I declare to all foreign banks that the deposits of the Shah and his family and all other thieves of the wealth of this deprived people (a partial list of these thieves has been drawn up) belong to the people. They constitute the embezzled wealth of the country, smuggled abroad. Banks must not permit these deposits to be withdrawn because competent authorities will soon open legal proceedings against those who made the deposits.[77]

6. I warn all members of both houses of the illegal Iranian Parliament to refrain from attending the parliament. If they do not, they will be called to account by the people.

7. I expect all members of the universities—now that the universities, those strongholds of the self-sacrificing student struggle, have been reopened—to continue voicing slogans against the corrupt regime and organizing demonstrations against the usurpatory government, the Shah, and the illegal Regency Council. They should not admit professors who are connected with the apparatus of repression and stifling or who support the corrupt regime. They should bar them from the university because of their crime of injuring the prestige and standing of the university.

8. I warn all those who have accepted membership in the illegal Regency Council that their illegal activity and their interference with the destiny of the country constitute a crime. They must immediately withdraw from the Council. If they do not, the responsibility for anything that may occur will be theirs.

9. The members of the Council of the Islamic Revolution are inside the country and their identity will soon be announced.

I pray God Almighty that He protect our people from the evil of domestic and foreign malefactors through His mercy, which encompasses all.

Declaration Upon Arrival at Tehran

Imam Khomeini gave this speech at Mehrabad Airport in Tehran, shortly after setting foot on Iranian soil for the first time in more than fourteen years. Source: Sayyid 'Abd ar-Rasul Hijazi, ed., *Majmu'a-yi Kamil az Payamha-yi Imam Khomeini* (Tehran, 1358 Sh./1979), pp. 2-3.

I THANK THE VARIOUS CLASSES of the nation for the feelings they have expressed toward me. The debt of gratitude I owe to the Iranian people weighs heavily upon my shoulders, and I can in no way repay it.

I offer my thanks to all classes of the nation: to the religious scholars, who have toiled with such devotion during these recent events; to the students, who have suffered so heavily; to the merchants and traders, who have undergone hardship; to the youths in the bazaars, universities, and madrasas of the country, who have shed their blood in the course of these events; to the professors, judges, and civil servants; to the workers and peasants. You have triumphed because of your extraordinary efforts and unity of purpose.

You have accomplished the first step toward a complete victory by removing Muhammad Riza, the chief traitor, from the scene. It is said that he is plotting certain intrigues abroad and that although his masters are keeping him at arm's length and refuse to admit him to their country, he is seeking the aid of treacherous rulers like himself. But his hopes are in vain after the fifty years of treason his family has committed and the more than thirty years of crime in which this traitor has himself engaged. He has exploited our country and made it more backward than it was before, destroyed our agriculture and ruined our land, and made our army subordinate to foreign advisers. Our triumph will come when all forms of foreign control have been brought to an end and all roots of the monarchy have been plucked out of the soil of our land.

The agents of the foreigners during the recent events have been trying desperately to restore the Shah to power, preserve the monarchy, or institute some equivalent form of government.

But they must know it is too late. Addressing them, I say that their efforts are in vain, and unless they submit to the will of the people, the people will soon put them in their places.

We must thank all classes of the nation. Victory has been attained by the unity of purpose not only of the Muslims, but also of the religious minorities,[78] and by the unity of the religious leaders and the politicians. Unity of purpose is the secret of victory. Let us not lose this secret by permitting demons in human form to create dissension in our ranks.

I offer again my thanks to all of you, and beseech God Almighty to foreshorten the arms of the foreigners and their agents.

Address at Bihisht-i Zahra

This speech, delivered at the cemetery outside Tehran where many of the martyrs of the Islamic Revolution are buried, is devoted chiefly to the questions of formal legality that were being raised in a hopeless effort to stem the tide of revolution. Source: *Majmu'a-yi Kamil,* pp. 10-17.

WE HAVE SUFFERED, SUFFERED GREATLY, during this recent period, but we have also gained certain victories that are, of course, great.

Women have lost their children; fathers have been bereft of their offspring; children have been orphaned. When my gaze falls upon some of those who have lost their children, a heavy weight bears down upon me that I can hardly bear. I cannot pay my debt of gratitude to our nation for all the losses it has suffered. I cannot adequately thank this nation, which has sacrificed all that it had for God's sake. It is God, Almighty and Exalted, alone Who must bestow on all their reward.

I offer my condolences to the mothers who have lost their children, and I share in their grief. I offer my condolences to the fathers who have lost their young offspring. And I offer my condolences to all the children who have lost their fathers.

Let us ask ourselves why our people have had to suffer these misfortunes. What was and is the claim of our people that, whenever it is raised, calls forth massacre, cruelty, and plunder in response? What has our nation demanded that deserves such chastisement? Our nation has insistently declared that this Pahlavi monarchy was illegal, was illegal from the time of its very foundation. Those who are of the same age I am will recall that at that time, the Constituent Assembly was convened at bayonet-point, without the least participation in its affairs by the people. The deputies were forced to vote for Riza Shah. The Pahlavi monarchy, therefore, was void from the outset. A monarchical regime is, in fact, contrary to all rational laws and precepts as well as human rights.

Let us suppose that an entire nation votes to make a certain individual its ruler. Insofar as the people have the right to deter-

254

mine their own destiny, their vote is valid for their own time. But what if a nation votes, even unanimously, to make the descendants of that individual rulers in perpetuity? Did our nation, say, fifty years ago, have the right to determine the destiny of subsequent generations?

The destiny of each generation must be in its own hands. For example, we were not alive at the beginning of the Qajar period. Let us suppose that the Qajar dynasty were founded in accordance with a referendum, and that the people had voted unanimously for Agha Muhammad Khan Qajar[79] to become their ruler, to be followed by the other Qajar monarchs. By the time we came into the world, Ahmad Shah[80] was ruling and none of us had ever seen Agha Muhammad Khan. If our ancestors had voted in favor of the foundation of the Qajar dynasty, would they have had any right to determine that Ahmad Shah should rule over us? The destiny of each generation is in its own hands. The nation as it existed one hundred or one hundred fifty years ago had the right to determine its own destiny, but it did not have the right to impose any particular ruler on us.

So let us suppose that this Pahlavi monarchy corresponded to the will of the people at the time of its establishment, and let us suppose further that the Constituent Assembly reflected the wishes of the people, and that the invalid, false institution of monarchy were correct and acceptable. All this would mean is that Riza Khan would be the ruler for the lifetime of those who voted him into power. But did anyone fifty years ago have any right to impose Muhammad Riza on us, in our time, as our ruler, though not many of us here were alive at the time of the decision?

The rule of Muhammad Riza, then, is illegal, first, because the rule of his father was also illegal, and the Constitutent Assembly was convened in his time at bayonet-point; second, even if we suppose the rule of Riza Shah to have been legal, those who put him in power had no right to determine our destiny. Are we the wards of our forefathers that they should have made decisions on our behalf eighty or one hundred years ago? In any event, even if the foundation of the Pahlavi monarchy had been legitimate and the Constituent Assembly were functioning legally at the time, our people are declaring today that they do not want this ruler. They are, in effect, voting against Muhammad Riza and the monarchical form of government, which is their right. The institution is therefore invalid.

Now let us examine the governments that have been appointed by Muhammad Riza and the Majlises we have had. The people have had no say in the choice of their representatives throughout the history of constitutionalism in Iran, with the exception of a few brief periods in which they were able to elect certain individuals of their choice. You know what kind of Majlis we have at present, and what kind of people are sitting in both the lower house and the Senate. I ask you who live in Tehran whether you had any role in determining those who are meant to represent you.

Do the majority of our people even know the names of those who are now sitting in the Majlis? They were appointed by force and without the knowledge of the people. A Majlis that has been appointed without the vote, consent, and knowledge of the people is, of course, illegal. Those who are now sitting in the two houses of the Majlis have no right to the salaries they draw; this is a usurpation of the property of the people for which they will be called to account.

As for the successive governments that have been appointed by the monarchy—a monarchy illegal both now and in the time of the Shah's father—they are illegal, just like the Majlis. Our nation has long been saying that it does not want Muhammad Riza Khan and the monarchy and that it wishes to determine its own future. Now it says in addition that the Majlis and the government are both illegal.

Can someone who has been appointed by an illegal Shah and an illegal Majlis be in any way legitimate? We tell him, "You are illegal and must go." We declare to everyone that not even he regards his own government as legal, because a few years ago, when he had not yet been appointed Prime Minister, he used to denounce the existing government as illegal.[81] What has changed in the meantime to make him regard his own government as legal?

The Majlis is illegal. Ask the deputies themselves whether the people appointed them. If any deputy claims to have been appointed by the people, we will have someone accompany him to his electoral district and inquire of the people there whether they recognize him as their representative and whether they did in fact appoint him. You can be sure that their answer will be negative.

Does a nation that loudly proclaims its government, its Shah, and its Majlis to be illegal and contrary to the *shari'a* deserve a vast cemetery filled with martyrs as its answer, here in Tehran as well as elsewhere?

Muhammad Riza Pahlavi, the vile traitor, has departed; after destroying everything, he has fled. In his time, only the cemeteries prospered; the country itself, he destroyed. The economy has been disrupted and ruined, and years of continuous effort by the whole population will be needed to restore it; the efforts of the government alone, or a single segment of the population, will not be enough. Unless the whole nation joins hands, our shattered economy cannot be restored.

You will remember that the Shah's regime carried out land reforms on the pretext of turning the peasants into independent cultivators, and that those reforms ultimately resulted in the complete destruction of all forms of cultivation. Our agrarian economy was ruined, and we were reduced to depending on the outside world for all our essential needs. In other words, Muhammad Riza enacted his so-called reforms in order to create markets for America and to increase our dependence upon America. We were forced to import wheat, rice, and chickens either from America or from Israel, which acts as an agent of America. In short, the so-called reforms constituted a blow that it will take us maybe as long as twenty years to recover from, unless all our people work hard, hand in hand.

Our educational system has been kept in a retarded condition, so that our youth cannot receive a complete education in Iran; after being half-educated at home, at the cost of great suffering, they are obliged to go abroad to complete their studies. We have had universities for about thirty-five years now, but because we have been ruled by a traitor, they have not been properly developed to meet the human needs of our nation.

That man destroyed all our human resources. In accordance with the mission he was given as the servant of foreign powers, he established centers of vice and made radio and television subservient to immoral purposes. Centers of vice operated with complete freedom under his rule. As a result, there are now more liquor stores in Tehran than there are bookstores. Every conceivable form of vice was encouraged.

Why was it necessary to make the cinema a center of vice? We are not opposed to the cinema, to radio, or to television; what we oppose is vice and the use of the media to keep our young people in a state of backwardness and dissipate their energies. We have never opposed these features of modernity in themselves, but when they were brought from Europe to the East, particularly to Iran, unfortunately they were used not in order to advance civilization, but in order to drag us into barbarism. The cinema is a modern invention that ought to be used for the sake of educating the people, but, as you know, it was used instead to corrupt our youth. It is this misuse of the cinema that we are opposed to, a misuse caused by the treacherous policies of our rulers.

As for our oil, it was given away to America and the others. It is true that America paid for the supplies it received, but that money was spent buying arms and establishing military bases for America. In other words, first we gave them our oil, and then we established military bases for them. America, as a result of its cunning policies (to which that man was also a party), thus benefited doubly from us. It exported weapons to Iran that our army was unable to use so that American advisers and experts had to come in order to make use of them.[82]

If the Shah's rule had (God forbid) lasted a few years longer, he would have exhausted our oil reserves in just the same way that he destroyed our agriculture. Then our people would have been reduced to total penury and would have been obliged to work for foreigners. It is on account of all these various forms of destruction and plunder that we have been crying out in protest against this man, and partly on account of them, too, that our young people have shed their blood.

Our young people have sacrificed their lives in order to be free. We have been stifled and repressed for fifty years. We have not had free press, radio, or television. Preachers have been unable to express themselves freely and congregational imams have been unable to exercise freely their function of guidance and exhortation. In fact, no class or segment of the population has been able to go about its business freely. Repression was particularly intense during the rule of Muhammad Riza, and it continues now under Bakhtiar, this feeble last gasp of the Shah's regime.

But his government and all those associated with it are illegal. If he and his colleagues persist, they will be counted as criminals who must be brought to trial. Yes, we will put them on trial.

I will appoint a government, and I will give this government a punch in the mouth. With the support of the people, and by-virtue of the acceptance the people have granted me, I will appoint a government.

This man, Bakhtiar, is accepted by no one. The people do not accept him, the army does not accept him, his friends do not accept him, he does not even accept himself. It is only America, which has sent an envoy to instruct the army to support him,[83] and Britain that recognize him. No segment of the population recognizes him, except the few ruffians he sends into the streets to make a noise on his behalf.

They say there cannot be two governments in one country. This is obviously true, but the government that has to go is the one that is illegal, and it is your government, Bakhtiar, that is illegal. The government I intend to appoint is a government based on divine ordinance, and to oppose it is to deny God as well as the will of the people.

This Bakhtiar must be put in his place. As long as I live, I will not let him and his associates gain a firm hold on power. I will never permit the former situation to be restored, with all its accompanying cruelty and oppression. I will never allow Muhammad Riza to return to power, for that is what they are planning to do. Yes, people, be alert, for the Shah has set up a headquarters where he is now and is establishing his contacts. They want to return us to the period when all we knew was repression and America swallowed up all of our wealth. We will never allow that to happen. As long as we are alive, we will never allow that to happen.

I ask God Almighty that He grant success to all of you, and I proclaim to all of you that it is our duty to continue this movement until all elements of the Shah's regime have been eliminated and we have established a Constituent Assembly based on the votes of the people and the first permanent government of the Islamic Republic.

Now I would like to offer my thanks to certain elements in the army, and to give some advice to the army as a whole.

Here is my advice. We want you in the army to be independent. We have toiled and suffered bloodshed, our young people have been killed, our honor has been besmirched, our religious scholars have been imprisoned and tortured. Part of our aim has been to make the army independent.

Army commanders, do you not want to be independent? Do you want to be the servants of others? My advice to you is to enter the ranks of the people and to add your voices to their demand for independence. The people want their army to be independent, not under the orders of American and other foreign advisers. They are making this demand on your behalf, so you too should come forward and say, "We want to be independent and to be rid of those advisers." But instead, you reward us by slaughtering the young soldiers on the streets who have joined the ranks of the people and thus saved the nation's honor as well as their own.[84]

We all extend our thanks and praise to the Humafars[85] and air force officers, as well as to all those who have fulfilled their religious and national duties in Isfahan, Hamadan, and elsewhere by joining the ranks of the people and supporting their Islamic movement. I thank them and invite all who have not yet joined the people to do so.

Members of the armed forces, Islam is better for you than unbelief, and your own nation is better for you than the foreigners. It is for your sake, too, that we are demanding independence, so you should do your part by abandoning this man. Do not think that if you do, we will slaughter you all. Other people behave that way. Look at the Humafars and officers who have joined us; they are treated with the utmost respect. We want our country to be powerful and to have strong armed forces. We do not wish to destroy our armed forces; we wish rather to preserve them so that they belong to the people and serve their interests, instead of being under the command and supervision of foreigners.

Peace be upon you, and also the mercy and blessings of God.

February 11, 1979

Martial Law Is Contrary to the Shari'a

This declaration was issued in Tehran shortly after the decisive confrontation had begun between the Islamic Revolution and recalcitrant elements in the armed forces. Source: *Majmu'a-yi Kamil*, p. 40.

COURAGEOUS PEOPLE OF IRAN, respected inhabitants of Tehran! As you know, it is my intention that the problems of Iran be solved peacefully, but since the regime of tyranny and oppression sees itself condemned by law, it has again resorted to crime and assaulted and slaughtered the courageous Muslims in Gurgan and in Gunbad-i Qabus.[86] In Tehran, the Imperial Guard has suddenly attacked elements in the air force that have joined the people, but with the aid of the courageous people, they have repulsed the attackers. I denounce this inhuman act of aggression by the Imperial Guard. It wishes to maintain the foreign domination of our country and to enable the plunderers to return by slaughtering their own brothers.

Although I have not given the order for sacred *jihad,* and I still wish matters to be settled peacefully, in accordance with the will of the people and legal criteria,[87] I cannot tolerate these barbarous actions, and I issue a solemn warning that if the Imperial Guard does not desist from this fratricidal slaughter and return to its barracks, and if the military authorities fail to prevent these attacks, I will take my final decision, placing my trust in God. The responsibility for whatever ensues will then belong to those shameless agressors.

If the aggressors retreat, I request the courageous people of Tehran to retain their state of readiness and to be alert for the strategems of the enemy and to preserve order and tranquillity. They should be fully equipped and prepared to defend Islam and the orders issued by the Muslim authorities.

As for the declaration of martial law, that is a mere trick. It is contrary to the *shari'a* and people should not pay it the slightest attention.

My dear brothers and sisters! Do not be anxious, for right will triumph, with the aid of God Almighty.

I ask God Almighty that He grant victory to the Muslim nation.

March 6, 1979

Address to a Group of Women in Qum

Imam Khomeini gave this address at his residence in Qum. Source: text provided by the Consulate-General of the Provisional Islamic Government of Iran, San Francisco.

GREETINGS WITHOUT LIMIT to the women of Iran! Peace be upon you, respected sisters. The mercy of God be upon you, lion-hearted women, whose noble efforts have delivered Islam from the fetters of enslavement to foreigners. Beloved and courageous sisters, you fought shoulder-to-shoulder with the men and ensured the victory of Islam. I thank you, women of Iran and women of Qum. May God and the Imam of the Age be pleased with you. Carrying your infants in your arms, you came into the streets and supported Islam with your ardent demonstrations. I have heard what happened in Qum and other cities; I have heard what happened on Chahar Mardan Street in Qum. I take pride in all the courageous deeds accomplished by the women of Iran, in Qum and other cities, for you have been in the vanguard of our triumph and have encouraged the men. We are all indebted to your courage, lion-hearted women.

Islam has particular regard for women. Islam appeared in the Arabian Peninsula at a time when women had lost their dignity, and it raised them up and gave them back their pride. Islam made women equal with men; in fact, it shows a concern for women that it does not show for men. In our revolutionary movement, women have likewise earned more credit than men, for it was the women who not only displayed courage themselves, but also had reared men of courage. Like the Noble Qur'an itself, women have the function of rearing and training true men. If nations were deprived of courageous women to rear true men, they would decline and collapse.

The laws of Islam are for the benefit of both man and woman, and woman must have a say in the fundamental destiny of the country. Just as you have participated in our revolutionary movement, indeed played a basic role in it, now you must also participate in its triumph, and must not fail to rise up again whenever it is necessary. The country belongs to you and, God willing, you will rebuild it.

In the earliest age of Islam, the women participated in wars together with the men, and we see that then as now the women fought shoulder-to-shoulder with the men, or even in front of them. They might lose their infants and children, but they would still resist the enemy.

We want our women to attain the high rank of true humanity. Women must have a share in determining their destiny. The repressive regime of the Shah wanted to transform our warrior women into pleasure-seekers, but God determined otherwise. They wanted to treat woman as a mere object, a possession, but Islam grants woman a say in all affairs just as it grants man a say. All the people of Iran, men and women alike, must repair the ruins that the previous regime has bequeathed to us; the hands of men alone will not suffice to accomplish the task. Men and women must collaborate in this respect.

There is one particular question to which attention should be paid. When women wish to marry, there are certain prerogatives they can stipulate for themselves that are contrary neither to the *shari'a* nor to their own self-respect. For example, a woman can stipulate that if her future husband turns out to be of corrupt moral character or if he mistreats her, she would possess the right to execute a divorce.[88] This is a right that Islam has granted to women. If Islam has imposed certain restrictions on both women and men, it is for the benefit of both. Similarly, just as Islam has granted man the right to divorce, it has also granted it to woman, on condition that the parties stipulate at the time of the marriage that if the husband behaves in a certain manner, the wife will have the right to execute a divorce. Once the man has accepted such a stipulation, he can never repudiate it. Apart from making it possible to include such a stipulation in the marriage contract, Islam forbids the husband to mistreat his wife; if he habitually mistreats her, he is to be punished and the *mujtahid* will grant the wife a divorce.

May God Almighty adorn all of you with dignity, health, happiness, and perfect faith and character.

Peace be upon you, beloved and respected ladies.

April 1, 1979

The First Day of God's Government

This declaration was issued in Qum on the occasion of the formal proc-lamation of the Islamic Republic of Iran. Source: *Majmu'a-yi Kamil,* pp. 135-136.

"We desired to grant Our favor to those that were op-pressed in the land, and to make of them leaders and the inheritors" (Qur'an, 28:4).

I OFFER MY SINCERE CONGRATULATIONS to the great people of Iran, who were despised and oppressed by arrogant kings through-out the history of the monarchy. God Almighty has granted us His favor and destroyed the regime of arrogance by His power-ful hand, which has shown itself as the power of the oppressed. He has made our great people into leaders and exemplars for all the world's oppressed, and He has granted them their just heri-tage by the establishment of this Islamic Republic.

On this blessed day, the day the Islamic community assumes leadership, the day of the victory and triumph of our people, I declare the Islamic Republic of Iran.

I declare to the whole world that never has the history of Iran witnessed such a referendum, where the whole country rushed to the polls with ardor, enthusiasm, and love in order to cast their affirmative votes and bury the tyrannical regime forever in the garbage heap of history. I value highly this unparalleled solidarity by virtue of which the entire population—with the exception of a handful of adventurers and godless individuals—responded to the heavenly call of "Hold firm to the rope of God, all together" (Qur'an, 3:103) and cast a virtually unanimous vote in favor of the Islamic Republic, thus demonstrating its political and social maturity to both the East and the West.

Blessed for you be the day on which, after the martyrdom of your upright young people, the sorrow of their grieving mothers and fathers, and the suffering of the whole nation, you have over-thrown your ghoulish enemy, the pharaoh of the age. By casting a decisive vote in favor of the Islamic Republic, you have established a government of divine justice, a government in which all segments of the population shall enjoy equal consideration, the light of divine justice shall shine uniformly on all, and the divine mercy of the Qur'an and the Sunna shall embrace all, like life-giving rain. Blessed for you be this government that knows no difference of race, whether between black and white, or between Turk, Persian, Kurd, and Baluch. All are brothers and equal; nobility lies only in the fear of God, and superiority may be attained only by acquiring virtues and performing good deeds. Blessed for you be the day on which all segments of the population have attained their legitimate rights; in the implementation of justice, there will be no difference between women and men, or between the religious minorities and the Muslims. Tyranny has been buried, and all forms of transgression will be buried along with it.

The country has been delivered from the clutches of domestic and foreign enemies, from the thieves and plunderers, and you, courageous people, are now the guardians of the Islamic Republic. It is you who must preserve this divine legacy with strength and determination and must not permit the remnants of the putrid regime of the Shah who now lie in wait, or the supporters of the international thieves and oil-bandits, to penetrate your serried ranks. You must now assume control of your own destiny and not give the opportunists any occasion to assert themselves. Relying on the divine power that is manifested in communal solidarity, take the next steps by sending virtuous, trustworthy representatives to the Constituent Assembly, so that they may revise the Constitution of the Islamic Republic.[89] Just as you voted with ardor and enthusiasm for the Islamic Republic, vote, too, for your representatives, so that the malevolent will have no excuse to object.

This day of Farvardin 12, the first day of God's government, is to be one of our foremost religious and national festivals; the people must celebrate this day and keep its remembrance alive, for it is the day on which the battlements of the twenty-five hundred-year old fortress of tyrannical government crumbled, a satanic power departed forever, and the government of the oppressed—which is the government of God—was established in its place.

Beloved people! Cherish and protect the rights you have attained through the blood of your young people and help to enact Islamic justice under the banner of Islam and the flag of the Qur'an. I stand ready to serve you and Islam with all the strength at my disposal during these last days of my life, and I expect the nation to devote itself similarly to guarding Islam and the Islamic Republic.

I ask the government that, fearing neither East nor West and cultivating an independent outlook and will, it purge all remnants of the tyrannical regime, which left deep traces upon all the affairs of our country. It should transform our educational and judicial systems, as well as all the ministries and government offices that are now run on Western lines or in slavish imitation of Western models, and make them compatible to Islam, thus demonstrating to the world true social justice and true cultural, economic, and political independence.

I ask God Almighty that He grant dignity and independence to our country and the nation of Islam.

Peace be upon you, and also the blessings and mercy of God.

Anniversary of the Uprising of Khurdad 15

This speech, given at Fayziya Madrasa in Qum, stressed the importance of the movement of Khurdad 15 as a turning point in Iranian history. Other concerns discussed here by Imam Khomeini were the essentially Islamic nature of the Revolution and the need for Westernized intellectuals to re-orient themselves to Islam and the people. Source: *Majmu'a-yi Kamil,* pp. 347-353.

WHY DID THE MOVEMENT OF of Khurdad 15 come into being? How did it start and how was it sustained? What is the present state of the movement, and what will its future be? Who brought this movement into being and who kept it going? Who is carrying it forward now, and in whom may we place our hopes? What was the aim of the movement of Khurdad 15? What is its present aim, and what will its aim be in the future?

Learn about the movement of Khurdad 15: what its aims were; who the people were who brought it into being, and who continued it; who the people are who might be expected to continue it now; and finally, who the people are who opposed it.

The movement of Khurdad 15 began here in this madrasa. On the afternoon of 'Ashura, a great meeting took place here, accompanied by speeches exposing the crimes of the government.[90] The sequel was the uprising that took place on Khurdad 15. It was an uprising that took place for the sake of Islam, in the name of Islam, and under the leadership of the religious scholars.

It was the same people present here today who created the movement of Khurdad 15. Not only did they create it; many of them also gave their lives for its sake. They rose up for the sake of Islam and created the movement of Khurdad 15. It was the same people who also kept the movement of Khurdad 15 alive and have continued it down to the present. It is also in them that we place our hope for the further progress of our movement and its full maturing.

Let us see who they are, these people who created the movement of Khurdad 15 and suffered the loss of 15,000 martyrs that day, not to mention those who rushed forward to greet martyrdom in other massacres; let us see what segment of society they represent. Yes, let us see what part of society it was that first created our movement and then advanced it to its present stage, that poured into the streets crying, *"Allahu akbar!"* and worked to destroy the great barrier of tyranny the regime had erected.

Those who did not participate in this movement have no right to advance any claims. Who are they that want to change the course of our nation now, and what are the groups that call for a change in direction? Who are they that wish to divert our Islamic movement from Islam? Some of them do not understand the realities of the matter; they are ignorant. Others consciously and knowingly are opposed to Islam.

Those who are ignorant must be guided to a correct understanding. We must say to them: "You who imagine that something can be achieved in Iran by some means other than Islam, you who suppose that something other than Islam overthrew the Shah's regime, you who believe non-Islamic elements played a role—study the matter carefully. Look at the tombstones of those who gave their lives in the movement of Khurdad 15. If you can find a single tombstone belonging to one of the non-Islamic elements, it will mean they played a role. And if, among the tombstones of the Islamic elements, you can find a single tombstone belonging to someone from the upper echelons of society, it will mean that they too played a role. But you will not find a single tombstone belonging to either of those groups. All the tombstones belong to Muslims from the lower echelons of society: peasants, workers, tradesmen, committed religious scholars. It was these people who brought the movement of Khurdad 15 into being, acting in obedience to Islam. Those who imagine that some force other than Islam could shatter the great barrier of tyranny are mistaken."

As for those who oppose us because of their opposition to Islam, we must cure them by means of guidance, if it is at all possible; otherwise, we will destroy these agents of foreign powers[91] with the same fist that destroyed the Shah's regime.

From Khurdad 15 until today, everything that has been accomplished has been by the activity of Muslims from the lower echelons of society, by their devotion and self-sacrifice. They are the ones who deserve to have their opinions heard as to what is to be done. The people who were abroad and have recently come back, those who were not in the ranks of the movement and have only recently joined it, have no claims on our movement and their opinions have no validity. The people who brought this movement into being, who defeated the great powers ranged against them, and who confront those powers still—they alone have claims on our movement.

Your opponents, oppressed people, have never suffered. In the time of the *taghut*, they never suffered because either they were in agreement with the regime and loyal to it, or they kept silent. Now you have spread the banquet of freedom in front of them and they have sat down to eat. If only they were to say, at least, "Why don't you join us?" But they say, "We are going to eat, not you! *We* are, not the clergy! *We* are, not any other class! Everything is for us; nothing is for Islam!" They want it all for themselves.

Xenomaniacs, people infatuated with the West, empty people, people with no content! Come to your senses; do not try to westernize everything you have! Look at the West, and see who the people are in the West that present themselves as the champions of human rights and what their aims are. Is it human rights they really care about, or the rights of the superpowers?[92] What they really want to secure are the rights of the superpowers. Our jurists should not follow or imitate them.

You should implement human rights as the working classes of our society understand them. Yes, they are the real Society for the Defense of Human Rights.[93] They are the ones who secure the well-being of humanity; they work while you talk. The workers and the peasants, the Society for the Defense of Human Rights—they work while you write. None of you are actively struggling to enable men to attain their real rights.

These classes alone are the ones who arose, first on Khurdad 15 and then during the Revolution. They are the ones who really care about humanity, for they are Muslims and Islam cares about humanity. You who have chosen a course other than Islam—you do nothing for humanity. All you do is write and speak in an effort to divert our movement from its course.

Muslim people of Iran! You have continuously shed your blood since Khurdad 15 down to the time of our return. Yes, you shed your blood, and I, who sit before you now, I also have no claims on our movement. It was you who shed your blood, who went forth to struggle and do battle with the regime; I also have no claims on our movement. I must serve you, not benefit from you by gaining some title. Let there be dust upon my head if I should wish to use you for the sake of acquiring some title! Let there be dust upon my head if I should wish to benefit from the blood that you have shed!

As for those in the upper classes who were neither active in the movement nor opposed to it, they also have no claims on it; but if they begin to serve the people now, they can acquire some standing. But as for those who want to divert our movement from its course, who have in mind treachery against Islam and the nation, who consider Islam incapable of running the affairs of our country despite its record of 1400 years—they have nothing at all to do with our people, and this must be made clear. Henceforth, it is the masses we need, not the classes that have separated themselves from the people.

Now is the time for Islam to be implemented. If we do not implement Islam and its ordinances with this Revolution, with this movement, when will we ever implement it? When will such a movement ever happen again? If this movement should (God forbid) subside and disappear, who would ever be able to mention the name of Islam again? If we do not implement the laws of Islam now, when will we implement them?

Those who say it is impossible to implement them now should tell us when it will be possible; if they are honest, they will say, "We will never want Islam." They should say openly, "We want this movement *minus Islam,*" in just the same way that they used to say, "We want Islam *minus the religious scholars.*"[94] If you do not implement the laws of Islam now, in full detail, you must give up all hope of ever being able to do so. Those who believe in Islam and whose hearts beat for the Qur'an must act decisively today.

The movement of Khurdad 15 came about, then, for the sake of Islam, and it was continued for the sake of Islam. We do not want anything other than Islam; Islam can be implemented at all times, and particularly at the present time.

Gentlemen, look at what you are now able to write and say. Understand that it is Islam that freed you from your fetters, Islam

271

that enabled you to return from abroad, Islam that made it possible for you to come out of your homes safely, Islam that set your pens free, Islam that gave you freedom of expression! And yet now you are against Islam!

The Muslims cannot endure the fact that although Islam and the blood of the Muslims set you free, you now rise up against Islam and write against Islam. That is gross ingratitude. God Almighty bestowed this bounty upon you; as a sign of gratitude, you should be loyal to Islam. Repent of what you have been saying and turn to Islam and the lower classes (that is, the classes you consider lower than yourselves, although in reality, they are higher).

Yes, those classes are the shining visage of Islam: the Most Noble Messenger looks upon them with favor, and they have God's protection. Join them and try to be like them; revise your views to accord with theirs.

How much you talk about the West, claiming that we must measure Islam in accordance with Western criteria! What an error! In gratitude for the bounty of liberty you have received, you should be loyal to Islam; that is my advice to you. In this very *madrasa*, I once gave some advice to the Shah; he didn't listen to me. On the afternoon of 'Ashura, I told him not to do anything that would cause the people to throw him out; he didn't listen to me, and the people did throw him out.[95]

You are all my brothers, whatever your class. It is not too late; come join the masses on their forward march! Not a single one of you is actually here at this gathering today, but come, join your voices to those of the people and give your loyalty to Islam, the Islam that has set you free! Be for Islam; whatever your sincere desire, it is contained in Islam; it is here in the corners of these madrasas.

Come and look at the way of life of those who live in these *madrasas*, and then compare it with that of those whose hearts allegedly pound for human rights (in reality, it is only their pens that are agitated!). Look at the way of life of the worker, the peasant, the tradesman! Show some concern for them! You do not show concern for them by picking up your pens and writing against Islam, supposedly in the name of human rights, and parading your qualifications as jurists! Did you ever spend anything out of your own pockets for the sake of this nation? Search your consciences and tell me!

Those whose hearts are truly beating for the needy and oppressed people of our country are the women of Qum, of south Tehran, and the poor quarters of other cities, those same people you regard as being "the lower classes"! They understand what human rights are all about and they act in accordance with their convictions; they donate their gold jewelry so houses can be built for the poor.[96] Add your efforts to theirs. I am not telling you to give money, but at least join them with your pens; put your pens in the service of Islam. Islam is beneficial to you; even if you do not believe in the hereafter, Islam is beneficial to your life in this world.

Do not oppose the religious scholars, for they are also of benefit to you—the committed religious scholars who live two or three to a room in the narrow cells of our madrasas. Their standard of living is similar to that of the slum dwellers on the edges of our cities, who are crowded, seven or eight people together, into some hole in the ground. They understand what human rights are all about better than we do! They are the people truly concerned about human welfare; they are the real Society for Human Rights, not you or I! Come then, show some concern for them and for the fulfillment of their rights.

This is my advice to the societies that meet once every few days to formulate their demands. I advise them not to make their course follow a path that diverges from Islam and the religious scholars. The power afforded the nation by the religious scholars is a God-given power; do not lose it. If you do, you will become nothing. It is the power of Islam, expressed in the exhortations of the religious scholars, that draws people into the streets to struggle for justice; do not subvert that power. God knows, I do not defend the religious scholars because I am a member of that class myself, but because I am convinced that it is they who can save the nation, and it is they whom the people are demanding.

It was the mosques that created this Revolution, the mosques that brought this movement into being. In the age of the Most Noble Messenger and for some time afterwards, the mosque was a place of political gatherings. The *mihrab* was a place not only

273

for preaching, but also for war—war against both the devil within man and the tyrannical powers without. This kind of war originates in the *mihrab*.

So preserve your mosques, O people. Intellectuals, do not be Western-style intellectuals, imported intellectuals; do your share to preserve the mosques. Jurists, start going to the mosques and preserving them and help to preserve their role. Preserve the role of the mosques so that our movement may achieve its aim and the country may be saved.

May God Almighty preserve our mosques for us, grant happiness to all our people, and guide those who are opposed to Islam.

September 24, 1979

Message to the Pilgrims

Written in Qum, this message is another exhortation to the Muslims of the world to join together in combat against imperialism. Source: *Jumhuri-yi Islami*, Mihr 3, 1358/September 25, 1979.

ABUNDANT GREETINGS AND INFINITE SALUTATIONS to all Muslims in the world, whether in the East or the West. Warm greetings to the pilgrims to the sacred House of God: may God grant them success!

It is undeniable and requires no reminder that the great religion of Islam, the religion of divine unity, destroys polytheism, unbelief, idolatry, and self-worship. It is the religion of man's essential nature, which liberates him from the bonds and fetters of material nature and from the temptations of demons in jinn and human form, both in his inner being and in his outward life. It is a religion that provides guidance for conducting the affairs of state and a guide to the straight path, which is neither Eastern nor Western. It is a religion where worship is joined to politics and political activity is a form of worship.

Now that Muslims from different countries of the world have set out toward the Ka'ba of their desires on the pilgrimage to God's House, so that this great act of worship decreed by God, this vast Islamic congress, is taking place at a blessed time and in a blessed place, the Muslims must strive not to content themselves with mere observance of form, but to benefit also from the political and social aspects of the pilgrimage as well as the devotional aspect. Everyone knows that no human authority or state is capable of convening such a vast gathering; it is only God's command that can bring about this great assembly. But unfortunately, the Muslims throughout history have never been able to make proper use of the divine power represented in this congress of Islam for the sake of Islam and the Muslims.

All assemblies of Muslims—for congregational prayer, Friday prayer, and especially the precious gathering of the hajj—have many political aspects. One of them is that through the coming together of religious leaders, intellectuals, and all committed

275

Muslims visiting God's House, the problems of the Muslims may be discussed and solved on a basis of consultation. Then, when the pilgrims return home to their respective countries, they may give reports at public meetings so that all may contribute to the solution of problems.

Another duty that must be fulfilled in this vast gathering is to summon the people, as well as all Islamic groups, to unity, overlooking the differences between the various Muslim groups. Preachers, speakers, and writers must undertake this vital step and attempt to bring into being a front of the oppressed and deprived peoples. Such a united front, proclaiming the slogan, *"La ilaha illa 'Llah,"* could then proceed to deliver the Muslims from their servitude to the diabolical powers represented by the foreigners, the imperialists and exploiters, and overcome all their problems on the basis of Islamic brotherhood.

Dear sisters and brothers, in whatever country you may live, defend your Islamic and national honor! Defend fearlessly and unhesitatingly the peoples and countries of Islam against their enemies—America, international Zionism, and all the superpowers of East and West. Loudly proclaim the crimes of the enemies of Islam.

My Muslim brothers and sisters! You are aware that the superpowers of East and West are plundering all our material and other resources, and have placed us in a situation of political, economic, cultural, and military dependence. Come to your senses; rediscover your Islamic identity! Endure oppression no longer, and vigilantly expose the criminal plans of the international bandits, headed by America!

Today the first *qibla* of the Muslims has fallen into the grasp of Israel, that cancerous growth in the Middle East. They are battering and slaughtering our dear Palestinian and Lebanese brothers with all their might. At the same time, Israel is casting dissension among the Muslims with all the diabolical means at its disposal. Every Muslim has a duty to prepare himself for battle against Israel.

Today our African Muslim countries are writhing beneath the yoke of American imperialism and other foreign powers and their agents. Muslim Africa calls out for help against its oppressors. Now, the philosophy of the hajj contains within it the answer to these cries for help. Our circling the House of God indicates that we seek aid only from God, and our stoning of the pillars[97] is in reality a stoning of demons, whether in jinn or human form. When you cast your stones at the pillars, vow to God that you will expel the superpowers—those demons in human form—from our beloved Islamic lands. Today the Islamic world is caught in the clutches of America. So convey to all Muslims in all continents of the globe this message from God: "Refuse all servitude except servitude to God."

O Muslims, followers of the school of *tauhid!* The ultimate reason for all the troubles that afflict the Muslim countries is their disunity and lack of harmony, and the secret of future victory will lie in unity and the creation of harmony. There is a verse in which God Almighty says: "Hold fast to the rope of God all together and fall not into disunity" (Qur'an, 3:103). Holding fast to the rope of God means creating harmony among the Muslims. Let us all act for the sake of Islam and the welfare of the Muslims and shun disunity, separation, and sectarianism, for these are the source of all our misfortunes and weaknesses.

I beseech God Almighty that He exalt Islam and the Muslims and grant unity to all Muslims in the world.

Address to Monsignor Bugnini, Papal Nuncio

Imam Khomeini gave this address in Tehran eight days after the occupation of the U.S. Embassy in Tehran by the Muslim Students Following the Line of the Imam, setting forth the demands and grievances of the Iranian people. Source: text supplied by the Embassy of the Islamic Republic of Iran, Washington, D.C.

IF OTHER AUTHORITIES HAD SOUGHT a meeting with me at this critical juncture in order to discuss the matter, I would not have granted their request. But given the respect that the Christian clergy and the Pope enjoy, I have acceded to this particular request, and I am indeed glad that the Pope has sent me a message, for it gives me an opportunity to bring certain matters to his attention. There is a question in the minds of myself and my people, and indeed in those of all oppressed peoples, whether Muslims or Christians or the followers of other faiths, and I would like to voice this question now.

The ears of thirty-five million Iranians, who suffered for fifty years beneath the yoke of imperialism and repression—particularly American imperialism, most recently under the direction of Mr. Carter—as well as the ears of millions of oppressed people throughout the world, have constantly been straining to hear some expression of sympathy on the part of the Pope, or at least some indication of paternal concern for the state of the oppressed, coupled with an admonishment of the tyrants and oppressors, or a desire to mediate between the oppressed peoples and those superpowers that profess to be Christian. But our ears have never heard any such expression of sympathy or concern. Our people were massacred for fifty years, and the best sons and daughters of our nation were thrown into inhuman prisons where they died under brutal tortures, yet the question of mediation never arose, nor did it ever occur to His Eminence, the Pope, to show any concern for our oppressed people or even to mediate with the plea that oppression cease.

Yet now he wishes to mediate, now that the young people of our nation, after long years of oppression and misery, have decided to hold in that nest of spies a few individuals who were spying on our nation and conspiring against it, or rather, against the whole region.

The proofs of their activity are extremely numerous, but the greatest proof is the fact that they reduced to powder, as far as they were able to, all the files and equipment they had. If those files and equipment had been of a purely diplomatic nature and not related to conspiracies against our people, there would have been no need for their destruction.

Now that the existence of a conspiracy has been proven to our nation, it unanimously supports the action of our youths (only a few perverted individuals do not support it). Their action represents the will of the entire nation, not the arbitrary whim of a small group.

It is a truly humanitarian desire that conspiracies directed against human welfare, against our Muslim countries and Iran in particular, should be uncovered; it is also the right of our people to have them uncovered. Embassies have no legal right to engage in espionage or conspiracy, but this place, as far as our experts have been able to determine, was a center for espionage and a center for conspiracy. How is it that it has now occurred to His Eminence, the Pope, to entertain the humanitarian impulse of intervening with us to make sure we do not mistreat those detained there?

Islam treats its enemies well, and our Muslim youths have treated them well and humanely, as far as I have heard; there is no cause for anxiety. As for their release, we must see what we want to do, what the nation wants to do. Is the desire of our nation illegal or inhuman? Is the act of our youths in occupying this center and preventing the conspiracy from being implemented a humane or an inhumane act?

What our nation wants is for that man who is now in the U.S., under whom it suffered for about thirty-seven years, who betrayed it continuously for thirty-seven years, who deprived our young people of freedom for thirty-seven years, who stifled our country and people with his all-embracing repression for thirty-seven years, who killed many people with his own hands or had them killed under his direction on Khurdad 15, and whose orders since then resulted in the killing of more than one hundred thousand people and the wounding and maiming of hundreds of thousands of others—what our nation wants is for that criminal under whom it has thus suffered to be returned to face a just trial.

If he is found guilty, the money he has stolen from us should be returned. Huge amounts of money have been taken out of the country by him and persons associated with him and now fill the banks in America and other Western countries. People of my age know, and those younger than us have heard from others or read in history, that when his father enacted his coup d'etat, he had nothing. He was an empty-handed soldier when he gained control of this country, but immediately, he began to confiscate the property of the people. He gained title to the best and most fertile land in Mazandaran, in the north of our country, by means of force and the pressure his agents exerted. Many who owned land, as well as many religious scholars who expressed themselves on the subject, were arrested, imprisoned, and sometimes killed.

I myself remember the massacre enacted in the time of Riza Shah at the Gauhar Shad mosque in Mashhad.[98] People of my age remember how this mosque, this center of Muslim worship and prayer, was assaulted and how a number of victims of oppression who had sought refuge there were massacred. When Riza Shah left Iran—or more accurately, when he was expelled—he stuffed as many of the crown jewels of Iran as he could into his numerous suitcases, only to have the English steal them from him on the high seas!

Then his rule came to an end and his son succeeded him—that is, the allies imposed his criminal son upon us, despite our unwillingness to accept him because of what we had suffered under his father. Since he owed his throne to the allies, he was obliged to put blindly at their disposal whatever they asked for. We have no time to enumerate all the acts of treachery he committed during his period of rule. We can give only a few examples of his so-called service to his country, in reality the mission entrusted to him by the allies. His mission became essentially to purchase arms and equipment from America in exchange for the oil he exported there, in order then to use the arms and equipment on their behalf and to build up bases for them! He gave them our oil and then built bases for them with the money he received!

The acts of treachery he committed during these last ten to fifteen years in particular—the slaughter and imprisonment of our young men and women—are too numerous to recount. During this period, we would have liked some foreign spiritual authority, particularly the supreme authority of the Christians, to have shown some concern for our defenseless people. I cannot believe that the Vatican was unaware of what was happening, and if our people ask me whether the Vatican was in agreement with all the crimes that were being committed, I will not know what answer to give them.

The Christian clergy know that the Noble Qur'an champions Jesus and Mary, the virtuous and chaste, and explicitly defends Mary against various unjust accusations. Indeed, the Qur'an goes so far as to champion the scholars, monks, and saints of the Christians.[99] This being the case, we would have welcomed a soothing expression of concern on the part of His Eminence, the Pope, or an attempt by him to discover why our nation has acted as it has. Let him ask Carter why he enabled a man like the Shah to keep ruling us; let him inquire of Carter why he has brought to America, under his protection, the man who blatantly committed so many crimes and acts of treachery for more than thirty years, and why he now wishes to hatch conspiracies with that man.

I am not surprised at Carter's antics, because he is a politician—not in the sense of healthy politics, but rather the sort of politics that Carter and his kind understand. He is willing to do anything—to commit any crime, to try any trick—in order to protect his personal interests, or what he imagines are the interests of his nation. His real concern is to prevent certain matters from becoming known by means of the people our youths are now holding.

But why is the Pope concerned? Why does he wish to intervene with an oppressed nation that wishes to uncover some small portion of the miseries it has suffered and thus enable other oppressed people to understand how they are being caused to suffer? If we were able to put this treacherous oppressor on trial in another country and bring before a foreign court all the manifold evidence of his criminal wrongdoing, we would certainly take the initiative in doing so. But it was here that he committed his crimes, here that all the relevant dossiers are to be found, and here that several million witnesses against him reside. He oppressed the peasants, he oppressed the workers, he oppressed the religious scholars, he oppressed the university students and teachers: all of them are our witnesses. We cannot possibly transport more than twenty million of our citizens abroad to testify against him.

In view of the respect we entertain for the Pope, however, we are ready for him, if the Shah is brought to Iran, to delegate whomever he wishes as representatives to observe the trial. The Shah could be tried in the presence of not only the Pope's representatives, but also those whom anyone else cares to send, even Carter, our worst enemy. The nation and I would abide by whatever verdict the court delivered.

The Pope should realize that this is not a question I can solve personally. I have no authority to impose anything on my people, for Islam does not permit me to act as a dictator. I follow the wishes of the people and I am bound to comply with whatever the people decide in this matter. As a servant of the nation, I may advance some humble request every now and then, but the solution of this matter does not lie in my hands. It lies in the hands of the people, and the people have declared their support for this act. As you may know, the radio has been reading out messages of support from different groups of people, and the messages are so numerous that it becomes tedious to listen to them.

In any event, our demand is a humanitarian one, dictated by the concern for humanity that is a characteristic of our Muslim nation. Since you profess Christianity, you too ought to follow Jesus Christ and become humanitarians. The same love of humanity that inspired Jesus Christ now impels our nation to demand an investigation of the Shah's crimes, with a particular view to discovering who it was that encouraged him in the commission of his crimes. It is thus that the world will come to know who the enemy of humanity is. Who was it that made the Shah devote all his power to the oppression of his people, commit all sorts of crime, and plunder our natural resources? If the answer to this question is known, it will be a salutary lesson for all people.

What conclusion, then, does the Pope wish to draw? I request him to contact Carter, who appealed to him, so that the whole matter may be investigated. Let the whole matter be explained, both here and abroad, and let them send their representatives. Then the Pope will have to decide whether it was just and proper for our people to be oppressed in this way, for all those massacres to be enacted, for the resources of our defenseless people to be plundered and hoarded in foreign banks, so that numerous city-dwellers, even here on the edge of Tehran, continue to go without housing, food, and work (of course, it is just possible that the Pope has not been informed of these things, in which case I am informing him now). Now, if despite all this, the Pope still feels we should arrange for the departure of those detained at the nest of spies without the Shah's being surrendered to us and without their agreeing to his being placed on trial, then let him announce this quite unambiguously. Naturally, we do not expect him to make such an announcement, for as a human being, he must be opposed to crimes such as those the Shah committed.

Our cause, in any event, is a legitimate one. It is intolerable to us that out of all the places in the world, the Shah should be taken to America, to be close to Carter. They have taken our criminal away from us and are keeping him. Hand the man over to us— that man who slaughtered our young people, who tortured them by burning them and sawing off their feet! Hand him over to us to stand trial! He will have a fair trial that can be attended by representatives from abroad. If what we say is untrue, let him come back and mount the throne again and all the people will obey him! But if it is the Shah and Carter that have spoken and acted unjustly, then use your moral influence to call Carter to account.

The Pope should realize that certain people claim to be Christians while acting in a manner contrary to the precepts of Jesus Christ, and they succeed in deceiving some of their own people. The Pope should show some concern for the honor of Christendom; if the policies of those individuals are carried out in the name of Christ and Christianity, the name of Christianity will be tarnished. The Pope should show some concern for all the oppressed people and their view of Christianity, and he should proclaim to all Christendom the crimes that Carter has committed and reveal his true identity to the world, just as we did with Muhammad Riza. Of course, our people knew the true nature of the Shah, but we still exerted ourselves to make sure that no doubt remained. If the Pope acts in similar fashion, we will be grateful to him.

As an oppressed nation, we request of him, then, that he save Christianity by condemning those leaders of the great powers who commit crimes while claiming to be Christian and acting in the name of Christianity. This is not good. Their conduct is not beneficial for Jesus (upon whom be peace) and it harms the reputation of all Christians. Let me inform the Pope that if Jesus Christ were here today, he would call Carter to account and deliver us from the clutches of this enemy of humanity. Since the Pope is the representative of Jesus, he must act in the same way that Jesus would. May God Almighty acquaint us all with our religious and divine duties so that we may become champions of the oppressed.

We hope that the Pope will show some concern for the state of our oppressed people and forgive us for being unable to comply with all his requests. As for his first request, concerning good treatment of those detained, the prisoners are already enjoing good treatment, and I would like you, as the Pope's representative, to go see them in order to inspect their living conditions and talk to them. Have no anxiety that they are being mistreated.

Of course, Carter is trying to do a number of different things; he is grabbing for anything, like a drowning man. First he tries to intimidate us with the threat of military intervention, and then he talks of imposing an economic embargo.

Unfortunately, a certain individual[100] (who calls himself an Iranian and even says, "I am an Iranian before I am a Muslim," although it is uncertain that he is either Iranian or Muslim) is requesting that Carter impose an economic embargo on Iran. This individual, who is now living in England, claims to be a nationalist, and his claim is proof of something I once said years ago. I said that the superpowers will often keep someone in reserve in a given country for twenty or thirty years, in order to use him as their servant at the proper time, and it will be part of his mission to put on the garb of a nationalist. So Bakhtiar associated with Musaddiq and claimed to be a nationalist, and after being held in reserve for twenty years, he finally saw the day his service was to begin. For many years, he had been a member of the National Front, and he claimed to be an Iranian before he was a Muslim (which itself is contrary to religion). But on the day his patrons wished to put him to use, they were not disappointed in their expectations. He took the place of the worst of God's creation,

Muhammad Riza, and started massacring the people in his stead. Ultimately, however, the army refused to obey his orders to carry out slaughters. This is the same person now calling for an economic boycott of Iran!

It is my duty to inform everyone, however, that we fear neither military action nor economic boycott, for we are the followers of Imams who welcomed martyrdom. Our people are also ready to welcome martyrdom today. Let us suppose that Mr. Carter were able to land his troops here—in reality, he can do no such thing— or even to launch a joint military expedition with other superpowers. We have a population of thirty-five million people, many of whom are longing for martyrdom. All thirty-five million of us would go into battle and after we had all become martyrs, they could do what they liked with Iran. No, we are not afraid of military intervention. We are warriors and strugglers; our young men have fought barehanded against tanks, cannons, and machine guns, so Mr. Carter should not try to intimidate us. We are accustomed to fighting and even when we have lacked weapons, we have had our bodies, and we can make use of them again.

As for economic pressure, we are a people accustomed to hunger. We have suffered hardship for about thirty-five or fifty years. Assuming that the Americans can impose an economic embargo on us by persuading all nations to sacrifice their own interests—which is nothing more than an idle dream, something that will never happen—we can always fast, or content ourselves with the barley and corn that we sow on our own land. That will be enough for us. We eat meat only one day a week, and in fact, it is not good to eat meat. If necessary, we can even restrict ourselves to one meal a day. So they should not try to intimidate us with economic pressure. If we are faced with the choice of preserving our honor or filling our stomachs, naturally we will prefer to go hungry and keep our honor.

Please convey my greetings to the Pope and tell him that he and I both, as men of religion, have a responsibility to give moral counsel. We ask that he assist our weak people by giving all the superpowers fatherly advice or by summoning them to account for their deeds.

New Year's Message

This message, delivered by Imam Khomeini in Tehran on the occasion of the Iranian New Year, is in the nature of a comprehensive review of the problems and dangers faced by the new order in Iran: Source: the pamphlet *Dau Payam-i Muhimm* (Tehran: Mujahidin-i Inqilab-i Islami, n.d.), pp. 1-14.

I OFFER MY CONGRATULATIONS to all the oppressed and to the noble people of Iran on the occasion of the New Year, which coincides with the completion of the pillars of the new Islamic Republic.[101]

God Almighty has willed—and all thanks are due to Him—that this noble nation be delivered from the oppression and crimes inflicted on it by a tyrannical government and from the domination of the oppressive powers, especially America, the global plunderer, and that the flag of Islamic justice wave over our beloved land. It is our duty to stand firm against the superpowers, as we are indeed able to do, on condition that the intellectuals stop following and imitating either the West or the East, and adhere instead to the straight path of Islam and the nation. We are at war with international communism no less than we are struggling against the global plunderers of the West, headed by America, Zionism, and Israel.

Dear friends! Be fully aware that the danger represented by the communist powers is no less than that of America; the danger that America poses is so great that if you commit the smallest oversight, you will be destroyed. Both superpowers are intent on destroying the oppressed nations of the world, and it is our duty to defend those nations.

We must strive to export our Revolution throughout the world, and must abandon all idea of not doing so, for not only does Islam refuse to recognize any difference between Muslim countries, it is the champion of all oppressed people. Moreover, all the powers are intent on destroying us, and if we remain surrounded in a closed circle, we shall certainly be defeated. We must make plain our stance toward the powers and the superpowers and demonstrate to them that despite the arduous problems that burden us, our attitude to the world is dictated by our beliefs.

Beloved youths, it is in you that I place my hopes. With the Qur'an in one hand and a gun in the other, defend your dignity and honor so well that your adversaries will be unable even to think of conspiring against you. At the same time, be so compassionate toward your friends that you will not hesitate to sacrifice everything you possess for their sake. Know well that the world today belongs to the oppressed, and sooner or later they will triumph. They will inherit the earth and build the government of God.

Once again, I declare my support for all movements and groups that are fighting to gain liberation from the superpowers of the left and the right. I declare my support for the people of Occupied Palestine and Lebanon. I vehemently condemn once more the savage occupation of Afghanistan by the aggressive plunderers of the East, and I hope that the noble Muslim people of Afghanistan will achieve victory and true independence as soon as possible, and be delivered from the clutches of the so-called champions of the working class.

The noble people should be aware that all our victories have been attained by the will of God Almighty, as manifested in the transformation that has occurred throughout the country, together with the spirit of belief and Islamic commitment and cooperation that motivate the overwhelming majority of our people.

The basis of our victory has been our orientation to God Almighty and our unity of purpose. But if we forget this secret of our success, deviate from the sacred ordinances of Islam, and embark on the path of division and disagreement, it is to be feared that God Almighty will withdraw His grace from us and the path will be open again for the tyrants to drag our people back into slavery by means of their satanic tricks and stratagems. Then the pure blood that has been spilled for the sake of independence and freedom, and the sufferings endured by old and young alike, would be in vain; the fate of our Islamic land would remain for all eternity what it was under the tyrannical regime of the Shah; and those who were defeated by our Islamic Revolution would treat us in the same way that they treat all the oppressed people of the world.

It is my God-given and religious duty, therefore, to impress certain things upon you and to assign to the President of the Republic, the Council of the Revolution, the government, and the security forces the responsibility for carrying them out. At the same time, I request the entire nation not to withhold from them all their wholehearted and ungrudging support, in accordance with their commitment to the Islam we all cherish.

I see that satanic counterrevolutionary conspiracies, aiming at promoting the interests of the East and the West, are on the rise; it is the God-given human and national duty of both the government and the people to frustrate those conspiracies with all the powers at their command. I wish to draw particular attention to several points.

1. This is the year in which security must return to Iran so that our noble people can pursue their lives in utter tranquillity. I declare once again my complete support for the honorable Iranian army. I stress that the army of the Islamic Republic must fully observe military discipline and regulations. It is the duty of the President of the Republic, whom I have appointed Commander-in-Chief of the Armed Forces, to admonish severely all those, irrespective of rank, who foment disorder in the army, incite strikes, neglect their duties, ignore military discipline and regulations, or disobey military commands. If they are proven to have committed any of these offenses, they should be immediately expelled from the army and prosecuted.

I can no longer tolerate any form of disorder in the army. Anyone who incites disorder in the army will immediately be denounced to the people as a counterrevolutionary, so that the nation may settle its accounts with any remaining vestiges of the criminal Shah's army.

Dear brothers in the army, you who turned your backs on the vile Shah and his plundering agents and joined the ranks of the people, today is the day for serving the nation, for serving Iran! With ceaseless efforts, devote yourselves to the task of defending this land against the enemies of Islam and Iran.

2. I declare once again my support for the Corps of Revolutionary Guards. I wish to impress upon them and their commanders that the slightest laxity in the fulfillment of their duties

is a punishable offense. If they act (God forbid) in such a way as to disturb the order of the Corps, they will immediately be expelled, and what I have said concerning the army applies equally to them. Revolutionary sons of mine, take heed that your conduct toward each other be inspired by affection and Islamic ethics.

3. The police and gendarmerie must also observe discipline. I have been informed that a remarkable laziness prevails in the police stations. The past record of the police is not good; they should therefore do their utmost to establish harmonious relations with the people, maintaining order throughout the country and regarding themselves as an integral part of society. A basic reorganization of the gendarmerie and police is envisaged for the future. In the meantime, the security forces must regard themselves as being at the service of Islam and the Muslims.

The explosions that have taken place in the south[102] deeply distressed me. Why have the police, the army, and the gendarmerie been unable to apprehend and punish a handful of the godless agents of a corrupt foreign regime that relies on America? Both those who commit these acts and those who direct them are corruptors on earth, and the penalties to which they are subject are clear. The Revolutionary Courts must act with the utmost decisiveness in order to root them out.

4. The Revolutionary Courts throughout Iran must be a model of the implementation of God's laws. They must try not to deviate in the slightest from the ordinances of God Almighty; observing the utmost caution, they must display revolutionary patience in fulfilling the judicial tasks entrusted to them. The Courts do not have the right to maintain their own armed forces, and they must act in accordance with the Constitution. An Islamic judicial system will gradually assume the responsibilities now fulfilled by the Revolutionary Courts, and in the meantime, judges must do their best to prevent all irregularities. If any judge (God forbid) deviates from the commands of God, he will immediately be exposed to the people and punished.

5. It is the duty of the government to provide the workers and laborers with all they need for productive labor. For their part, the workers should be aware that strikes and slowdowns not only tend to strengthen the superpowers in their hostility to the Revo-

lution, but also tend to transform into despair the hopes now placed in us by the oppressed of the world, who have risen in revolt in both Muslim and non-Muslim countries. As soon as the people learn that a strike is taking place at a factory in their town, they should proceed there immediately and investigate, identifying and exposing to the people all counterrevolutionary forces. There is no reason for the noble people of Iran to pay wages to a handful of godless individuals.

Beloved laborers, know that those who create a new disturbance every day in some corner of the country, whose only logic is that of armed force, are your determined enemies and wish to divert you from the course of the Revolution. They are potential dictators[103] who will not even grant anyone the opportunity to breathe if they ever attain power. Oppose them in all areas, denounce them to the people as your number-one enemies, and expose the ties that bind them to the aggressive East and the criminal West. It is the duty of the government to punish severely anyone who participates in their disruptive activities.

6. I do not know why the government has failed to proceed with its suspended plans for promoting the welfare of the people. It must immediately implement existing plans and adopt new ones in order to remedy the economic situation in our country.

7. Everyone must obey governmental authorities in government offices, and stern action is to be taken against those who fail to do so. Anyone who wishes to create a disturbance in any government office must immediately be expelled and denounced to the people. I am amazed at the failure of the government to appreciate the power of the people. The people are able to settle their accounts with counterrevolutionaries themselves and to disgrace them.

8. Confiscation of the property of miscreants by unauthorized individuals or courts lacking the proper competence is to be severely condemned. All confiscations must take place in accordance with the *shari‘a* and after a warrant has been obtained from a prosecutor or judge. No one has the right to intervene in these matters, and anyone who does so will be severely punished.

9. Land must be distributed according to the criteria of the *shari‘a*, and only the competent courts have the right to sequester

land after due investigation. No one else has the right to encroach on anyone's land or orchards. Unauthorized persons in general have no right to intervene in these affairs. They may place at the disposal of the competent authorities, however, any information they may have concerning the land, orchards, or buildings belonging to persons associated with the old regime who usurped the property of the people. Anyone who acts in defiance of Islamic and legal criteria will be subject to severe prosecution.

10. The Housing Foundation and the Mustazafan Foundation[104] must each submit a report balance sheet of their activity as soon as possible to acquaint the people with their revolutionary operations. The Housing Foundation must show how much it has accomplished, and the Mustazafan Foundation must provide a list of the movable and immovable property it has acquired throughout the country from persons associated with the Shah's regime, particularly from the Shah and his vile family and hangers-on, and account for what it has done with this property. Is it true that the Mustazafan Foundation has fallen into the hands of the wrong persons? If so, it must be purged, and it is religiously forbidden not to purge it. These two foundations must explain precisely why they have not been able to act more swiftly. If anyone has committed any offense in the name of the Mustazafan Foundation, it is the duty of the courts throughout Iran to take swift measures against him.

11. A fundamental revolution must take place in all the universities across the country, so that professors with links to the East or the West may be purged, and the university may provide a healthy atmosphere for cultivation of the Islamic sciences. The evil form of instruction imposed by the previous regime must be stopped, because all the miseries of society during the reign of that father and that son were ultimately caused by such evil instruction. If a proper method of education had been followed in the universities, we would never have had a class of university-educated intellectuals choose to engage in factionalism and dispute, in total isolation from the people and at a time of intense crisis for the country; they overlooked the sufferings of the people so completely that it was as if they were living abroad. All of our backwardness has been due to the failure of most university-educated intellec-

tuals to acquire correct knowledge of Iranian Islamic society, and unfortunately, this is still the case. Most of the blows our society has sustained have been inflicted on it precisely by these university-educated intellectuals, who, with their inflated notions of themselves, speak in a manner only their fellow so-called intellectuals can understand; if the people at large cannot understand them, too bad! Because the people do not even exist in the eyes of these intellectuals; only they themselves exist. The evil form of instruction practiced in the universities during the time of the Shah educated intellectuals in such a way that they paid no regard to the oppressed and exploited people, and unfortunately, they still fail to do so.

Committed, responsible intellectuals! Abandon your factionalism and separation and show some concern for the people, for the salvation of this heroic population that has offered so many martyrs. Rid yourselves of the "isms" of the East and the West; stand on your own feet and stop relying on foreigners. The students of the religious sciences as well as the university students must take care that their studies are entirely based on Islamic foundations. They must abandon the slogans of deviant groups and replace all incorrect forms of thought with the true Islam that we cherish. Let both groups of students be aware that Islam is an autonomous, rich school of thought that has no need of borrowings from any other school. Furthermore, let everyone be aware that to adopt a syncretic ideology[105] is a great act of treason toward Islam and the Muslims, the bitter fruits of which will become apparent in the years ahead. Unfortunately, we see that because of a failure to understand certain aspects of Islam correctly and precisely, these aspects have been mixed with elements taken from Marxism, so that a melange has come into being that is totally incompatible with the progressive laws of Islam.

Beloved students, do not follow the wrong path of university intellectuals who have no commitment to the people! Do not separate yourself from the people!

12. Another matter is that of the press and the mass communications media. Once again, I request the press throughout the country to collaborate, to write freely whatever they wish, but not to engage in conspiracies. I have said repeatedly that the

press must be independent and free, but unfortunately, I see some newspapers engaged on a course designed to serve the evil aims of the right and the left in Iran. In all countries, the press plays a fundamental role in creating an atmosphere that is either healthy or unhealthy. It is to be hoped that in Iran, the press will enter the service of God and the people.

Radio and television must also be free and independent, and they must broadcast all forms of criticism with complete impartiality, so that we do not again witness the kind of radio and television we had under the deposed Shah. Radio and television must be purged of all pro-Shah and deviant elements.

13. These days, the agents and supporters of the Shah are unleashing a campaign against the beloved religious scholars who were among the most militant segments of society in both the time of the deposed Shah and that of his father: they staged numerous uprisings against the corrupt regime to expose its true nature, continuously led the just struggles of our noble people, and guided them to victory. When the religious scholars embarked on their determined struggle against the treacherous Shah in the years 1341 and 1342 [1962 and 1963], he labelled our committed and responsible religious leaders "Black Reaction," because the militant religious scholars, with their deep roots in the souls of the nation, represented the only serious danger to him and his monarchy. Now, too, in order to crush the religious leadership, which is the very foundation of the independence and freedom of our country, the agents of the Shah are putting the word "reaction" in the mouths of some of our young people who are unaware of the true situation.

My beloved, revolutionary children! Insulting and attempting to weaken the religious leadership strikes a blow against our freedom and independence and against Islam. It is an act of treason to imitate the treacherous Shah and apply the word "reaction" to this respectable class of our population that has always refused to submit to either East or West.

Beloved sisters and brothers! Understand that anyone who regards the religious scholars as reactionaries is following the path of the Shah and America. By supporting the true and committed religious leaders, who have always guarded and protected this land, the noble nation of Iran is paying its debt to Islam and frustrating the covetous designs entertained on our country by historical oppressors.

At the same time, I wish to draw the attention of the respected religious scholars throughout the country to the possibility that the devils hostile to our Revolution may be spreading malicious propaganda among them against our beloved youth, particularly the university students. They should realize that it is our common duty today to ensure that all segments of society—particularly the university students and the religious leaders, who together constitute the intellectual resources of our nation—unite against satanic and tyrannical forces, advance our Islamic movement in unison with each other, and guard our independence and freedom as jealously as they would their own lives. In the time of the tyrannical regime of the Shah, it was the plan of the world-plunderers and their agents to create a division between these two important classes. Unfortunately, they succeeded, and the country was ruined as a result. Now they wish to implement the same plan again, and the slightest lack of vigilance on our part will lead to the ruin of our country again. It is my hope that in the year that is now beginning, all classes of the nation, in particular these two respected classes, will be fully conscious of the stratagems and conspiracies that are directed against us and frustrate those evil plans with their unity of purpose.

Finally, at the beginning of this new year, I seek God's mercy for the martyrs of the Islamic Revolution, and express my gratitude for the sacrifices they made. I also offer my congratulations to those they left behind, the mothers and fathers who reared those lion-hearted women and men. I also offer congratulations to those who were crippled or wounded when they were in the vanguard of our people's movement for the establishment of an Islamic republic. Our Islamic Revolution is indeed indebted to the sacrifices made by these valiant people. The people and I will never forget their courage and we will always cherish their memory.

I pray to God Almighty that He grant dignity and greatness to Islam and the Muslims.

Peace be upon you, and also the mercy and blessings of God.

The Meaning of the Cultural Revolution

This address concerning the reasons for the planned re-evaluation and reorganization of higher education was delivered in Tehran to an audience composed of Muslim students from the universities of Tehran. Source: *Kayhan-i Hava'i,* Urdibihisht 10, 1359/April 30, 1980.

GREETINGS TO THE GREAT NATION of Islam, greetings to all Muslims in the world! Greetings to the people of Iran! Greetings to the students of Iran's universities!

It is necessary for me to clarify what our aim is in reforming the universities. Some people have imagined that those who are calling for the reform of our universities and wish to make them Islamic regard every science as consisting of two sectors, one Islamic and the other non-Islamic, so that, for example, there is an Islamic mathematics and a non-Islamic mathematics, or an Islamic physics and a non-Islamic physics. On the basis of this assumption, they have protested that the sciences are not divisible into Islamic and non-Islamic. Others have assumed that the call for the Islamization of the unversities means that only *fiqh*, Qur'anic exegesis, and *usul*[106] would be taught there, that, in other words, the universities would adopt the same curriculum as the traditional madrasas. These ideas that some people hold, or pretend to hold, are erroneous. When we speak of the reform of the universities, what we mean is that our universities are at present in a state of dependence; they are imperialist universities, and those whom they educate and train are infatuated with the West. Many university teachers suffer from this infatuation, and they transmit it to their students, our young people. That is why we say that our universities in their present state are of no use to our people.

We have had universities in our country for fifty years now,[107] and throughout this period, the backbreaking expenditures that have been lavished upon them have been borne by our toiling masses. But we have been unable to attain self-sufficiency in any of the subjects taught in our universities. After fifty years of universities, when someone falls sick, many of our doctors will recommend that he go to England for treatment; we do not have doctors that can meet the needs of our people. We have had universities, but we are still dependent on the West for all that a nation needs.

It is for these reasons that fundamental changes must take place in the universities and it is in this sense that they must become Islamic. We do not mean that only Islamic learning should be taught in them, or that each science comes in two varieties, one Islamic and the other non-Islamic. But show us the achievements of our universities during their fifty years of existence! Our universities have served to impede the progress of the sons and daughters of this land; they have become propaganda arenas. Our young people may have succeeded in acquiring some knowledge, but they have not received an education, an Islamic education. Those who go to our universities to study do so in order to acquire a piece of paper and then become a burden to the people. The universities do not impart an education that corresponds to the needs of the people and the country; instead they squander the energies of whole generations of our beloved youth, or oblige them to serve the foreigners.

Teachers in our schools, as a class, have not conceived of their profession in Islamic terms; they have imparted knowledge, but not an education. Our university system, therefore, has not produced committed individuals, people concerned with the welfare of their country and prepared to overlook their narrow personal interests.

So, to repeat, we demand fundamental changes in our university system so that the universities come to serve the nation and its needs instead of serving foreigners. Many of our schoolteachers and university professors are now effectively serving the West by brainwashing and miseducating our youth. We are not rejecting modern science, nor are we saying that each science exists in two varieties, one Islamic and the other non-Islamic; this notion is attributed to us by some people out of malice or ignorance. Our universities lack Islamic morality and fail to impart an Islamic education; if this were not so, our universities would not have been transformed into a battlefield for ideologies harmful to the nation. If Islamic morality existed in the universities, these shameful clashes would not occur.[108] They reflect a lack of Islamic education and true understanding of Islam. The universities, then, must change fundamentally. They must be reconstructed in such a way that our young people will receive a correct Islamic education side-by-side with their acquisition of formal learning, not a Western education.

This is our aim, to prevent one group of our young people from being drawn to the West and another group to the East. We do not wish even one group among our university students and young people to aid those who are actively at war with us, who wish to impose an economic embargo on us.[109] If the Iranian people stand up to the West, we want our university students to join them in their resistance. Similarly, if the people take a stand against the communists, we want our university students to do the same.

Some of our young people have been simple-minded enough to assimilate the wrong education that was given by their teachers. As a result, now that we wish to carry out fundamental changes in the universities in order to make them independent both of the West and of the communist East, they oppose us. This is in itself an indication that our universities have not been Islamic or given our young people a proper education. Many of our university students not only lack an Islamic education, they also fail to pursue their studies; they spend all their time on sloganeering, false propaganda, and expressions of support for America or the Soviet Union. We want our young people to be truly independent and to perceive their own real needs instead of following the East or the West.

Those who are creating disturbances on the streets or in the universities and creating problems for the government and the nation are followers of the West or the East. In my opinion, they are mostly followers of the West, of America. For today it is the superpower America that we are confronting, and at a time when we need our youth to participate in this confrontation, we see them confronting each other instead and thus serving America. But we want to reconstruct our universities in such a way that our young people work for themselves and the nation.

Certain gentlemen sitting on the sidelines are raising all kinds of objections and imagine that the members of the Revolutionary

Council do not know what they are doing. They pretend, for example, that the Islamization of the universities rests on the assumption that the sciences are divisible into Islamic and non-Islamic varieties, so that we have Islamic mathematics and non-Islamic mathematics. Do they not know that some members of the Revolutionary Council hold doctorates and some are *mujtahids*?[110] The place for the strictly Islamic sciences is the traditional *madrasa;* the other sciences are to be taught at the university. However, the universities must become Islamic in the sense that the subjects studied in them are to be pursued in accordance with the needs of the nation and for the sake of strengthening it. The curricula that have been followed up to now at the universities have resulted in the gravitation of one part of our young people toward communism and another part toward the West. Some university professors, moreover, have prevented our young people from progressing in their various fields of study; being in the service of the West, they want us to remain in a state of perpetual dependence on the West. To Islamize the universities means to make them autonomous, independent of the West and independent of the East, so that we have an independent country with an independent university system and an independent culture.

My beloved listeners! We fear neither economic boycott nor military intervention. What we fear is cultural dependence and imperialist universities that propel our young people into the service of communism. We do not wish our universities to produce more people of the same type as those who are now objecting to the Islamization of the universities. They do not understand what is meant by making the universities independent and Islamic.

I support all that has been said by the Revolutionary Council and the President of the Republic concerning the necessity for a purge of the universities and a change in the atmosphere prevailing in them in order to make them fully independent. I request that all of our young people not resist or try to sabotage the reform of the universities; if any of them do so, I will instruct the nation as to how to respond.

I beseech God Almighty to grant happiness to the nation of Islam and to our young people, and I hope that our universities will be cleared of all elements of dependency, so that, God willing, we will come to have a university system based on Islamic morality and an Islamic culture.

Peace be upon you, and also the mercy and blessings of God.

Message to the Pilgrims

*Issued in Tehran, this is an important call to Muslim unity and the aban-
donment of ethnic and sectarian division. Of significance also are the
references to Iraq and its relations with the United States, and the laying
down of the four conditions for the release of the American hostages that
were formally adopted by the Majlis in November 1980.* Source: *Jumhuri-yi Islami,* Shahrivar 22, 1359/September 13, 1980.

GREETINGS TO THE VISITORS to God's Sacred House who have
gathered at the focal point of revelation, the place where God's
angels alight. Greetings to the believers who have migrated from
their own homes to the House of God. Greetings to all Muslims of
the world whose prophet is the Most Noble Messenger, the Seal
of the Prophets, whose book is the Noble Qur'an, and whose *qibla*
is the Exalted Ka'ba. Greetings to those who have turned away
from all forms of *shirk* toward the focal point of *tauhid,* who
have freed themselves from the fetters of slavery and obedience to
the idols installed in the centers of tyranny, imperialism, and satanic power, who have joined themselves to the absolute power of
God and the firm rope of *tauhid.* Greetings to those who have
grasped the sense of God Almighty's summons and set out, in
response, to His House.

Now it is necessary for me to bring certain matters to your
attention, free Muslims who have gathered at the site of revelation
in order to fulfill a duty that relates both to worship and politics,
so that you may be made aware of what is happening in the Muslim countries; what plans are underway to subjugate, exploit, and
dominate the Muslims; and what impure hands are engaged in
kindling the fires of division.

1. At a time when all the Muslims in the world are about to
join together and achieve mutual understanding between the
different schools of thought in Islam, in order to deliver their
nations from the foul grasp of the superpowers; at a time when
the arms of the Eastern and Western oppressors are about to be
foreshortened in Iran, by means of unity of purpose and reliance
on God Almighty—precisely at this time, the Great Satan has

summoned its agents and instructed them to sow dissension among the Muslims by every imaginable means, giving rise to hostility and dispute among brothers in faith who share the belief in *tauhid*, so that nothing will stand in the way of complete domination and plunder. Fearing that the Islamic Revolution of Iran will spread to other countries, Muslim and non-Muslim alike, and thus compel it to remove its foul hands from the lands it dominates, the Great Satan is resorting to another stratagem now, after the failure of both the economic boycott and the military attack. It is attempting to distort the nature of our Islamic Revolution in the eyes of Muslims throughout the world in order to set the Muslims at each others' throats while it continues its exploitation and oppression of the Muslim countries. Thus it is that precisely at the time Iran is waging a determined struggle to ensure the unity of all Muslims in the world on the basis of *tauhid* and true Islam, the Great Satan gives its orders to one of its pawns in the region, one of the dead Shah's friends, to obtain decrees from Sunni *fuqaha* and *muftis* to the effect that the Iranians are unbelievers. These pawns of America say that the Islam the Iranians talk about is different from their Islam. Certainly the Islam of Iran is different from the Islam of those who support the pawns of America, like Sadat and Begin, who extend the hand of friendship to the enemies of Islam and flaunt the commands of God Almighty, and who leave no lie and calumny unuttered in their efforts to create disunity among the Muslims. The Muslims of the world must be aware of these people who are attempting to spread dissension, and must frustrate their foul conspiracy.[111]

2. At a time when the superpowers are attacking Muslim countries like Afghanistan, inflicting pitiless and savage massacres on the Afghan Muslims who wish the destiny of their country to be free from foreign interference; at a time when America has a hand in every form of corruption; at a time when criminal Israel is unleashing a comprehensive onslaught against the Muslims in beloved Lebanon and Palestine, and is preparing to transfer its capital to Jerusalem and intensify and extend its crimes against the Muslims it has driven from their homelands; in short, at a time when the Muslims stand in greater need than ever of unity, Sadat, the traitor and servant of America, the friend and brother of Begin and the dead, deposed Shah, and Saddam, another humble servant

of America, are trying to sow dissension among the Muslims and will not hesitate to commit any crime their masters enjoin upon them in order to achieve their goal. America is engaged in continuous attacks on Iran, sending spies in the hope of defeating our Islamic Revolution and conspiring with Sadat to diffuse (by way of Iraq) lies and false propaganda concerning the leaders of the Islamic government. The Muslims must beware of the treason to Islam and the Muslims that these agents of America engage in.

3. One of the themes that the planners of disunion among the Muslims have put forward, and their agents are engaged in promoting, is that of race and nationalism. For years the government of Iraq has been busy promoting nationalism, and certain other groups have followed the same path, setting the Muslims against each other as enemies. To love one's fatherland and its people and to protect its frontiers are both quite unobjectionable, but nationalism, involving hostility to other Muslim nations, is something quite different. It is contrary to the Noble Qur'an and the orders of the Most Noble Messenger. Nationalism that results in the creation of enmity between Muslims and splits the ranks of the believers is against Islam and the interests of the Muslims. It is a stratagem concocted by the foreigners who are disturbed by the spread of Islam.

4. More saddening and dangerous than nationalism is the creation of dissension between Sunnis and Shi'is and diffusion of mischievous propaganda among brother Muslims. Praise and thanks be to God that no difference exists in our Revolution between these two groups. All are living side by side in friendship and brotherhood. The Sunnis, who are numerous in Iran and live all over the country, have their own 'ulama and shaykhs; they are our brothers and equal with us, and are opposed to the attempts at creating dissension that certain criminals, agents of America and Zionism, are currently engaged in. Our Sunni brothers in the Muslim world must know that the agents of the satanic superpowers do not desire the welfare of Islam and the Muslims. The Muslims must dissociate themselves from them, and pay no heed to their divisive propaganda. I extend the hand of brotherhood to all committed Muslims in the world and ask them to regard the Shi'is as cherished brothers and thereby frustrate the sinister plans of foreigners.

5. Part of the extensive propaganda campaign being waged apparently against Iran, but in reality against Islam, is intended to show that the Revolution of Iran cannot administer our country or that the Iranian government is about to fall, since Iran supposedly lacks a healthy economy, proper educational system, disciplined army, and armed forces ready for combat. Propaganda to this effect is put out by all the mass media of America and its allies, giving comfort to the enemies of Iran and Islam. This propaganda is actually directed against Islam, for they want to pretend that Islam in the present day is incapable of administering a country. The Muslims should study matters carefully, comparing the Iranian Islamic Revolution with non-Islamic revolutions. Our Islamic Revolution inherited a country that was completely dependent upon the outside world, that was ruined and backward in every respect. For more than fifty years, the Pahlavi puppet had dragged our country down, filling the pockets of the foreigners—particularly Britain and America—with the abundant wealth of our land, and awarding what little remained to itself and its agents and hangers-on. In short, it left us many problems to face. But by the blessing of Islam and our Muslim people, in the space of less than two years, we have voted on, approved, and put into practice all the measures necessary for the administration of the country. Despite all the difficulties that America and its satellites have created for us—economic boycott, military attack, and the planning of extensive coups d'etat—our valiant people have attained self-sufficiency in foodstuffs. Soon we will transform the imperialist-inspired education system that existed under the previous regime into an independent and Islamic education system. The armed forces, the Revolutionary Guards, the gendarmerie, and the police stand ready to defend the country and uphold order, and they are prepared to offer their lives in *jihad* for the sake of Islam. In addition, a general mobilization of the entire nation is under way, with the nation equipping itself to fight for the sake of Islam and the country. Let our enemies know that no revolution in the world was followed by less bloodshed or brought greater achievements than our Islamic Revolution, and that this is due entirely to the blessing of Islam. Do our enemies realize what they are saying? Is Islam supposed to be incapable of administering countries, the same Islam that for several centuries ruled over more

than half the populated areas of the globe, and that overthrew the governments of unbelief and oppression in less than half a century? Today our people are participating actively in the administration and organization of the country. The enemies of Islam are unaware—or pretend to be unaware—of the capacity of Islam to destroy the foundations of oppression and to establish in its place a just system of administration. The enemies of Islam—and even many of its friends—know nothing of the administrative ability of Islam and nothing of its political and social ordinances. Throughout history, in fact, since the earliest age of Islam, the true nature of Islamic rule has been abandoned and obscured. It must now be presented to the world anew through the efforts of all Muslims, particularly the scholars and thinkers, so that the bright visage of Islam will shine over the world like the sun.

Muslims the world over who believe in the truth of Islam, arise and gather beneath the banner of *tauhid* and the teachings of Islam! Repel the treacherous superpowers from your countries and your abundant resources. Restore the glory of Islam, and abandon your selfish disputes and differences, for you possess everything! Rely on the culture of Islam, resist Western imitation, and stand on your own feet. Attack those intellectuals who are infatuated with the West and the East, and recover your true identity. Realize that intellectuals in the pay of foreigners have inflicted disaster upon their people and countries. As long as you remain disunited and fail to place your reliance in true Islam, you will continue to suffer what you have suffered already. We are now in an age when the masses act as the guides to the intellectuals and are rescuing them from abasement and humiliation by the East and the West. For today is the day that the masses of the people are on the move; they are the guides to those who previously sought to be the guides themselves.

Know that your moral power will overcome all other powers. With a population of almost one billion and with infinite sources of wealth, you can defeat all the powers. Aid God's cause so that He may aid you. Great ocean of Muslims, arise and defeat the enemies of humanity. If you turn to God and follow the heavenly teachings, God Almighty and His vast hosts will be with you.

6. The most important and painful problem confronting the subjugated nations of the world, both Muslim and non-Muslim,

is the problem of America. In order to swallow up the material resources of the countries it has succeeded in dominating, America, the most powerful country in the world, will spare no effort.

America is the number-one enemy of the deprived and oppressed people of the world. There is no crime America will not commit in order to maintain its political, economic, cultural, and military domination of those parts of the world where it predominates. It exploits the oppressed people of the world by means of the large-scale propaganda campaigns that are coordinated for it by international Zionism. By means of its hidden and treacherous agents, it sucks the blood of the defenseless people as if it alone, together with its satellites, had the right to live in this world.

Iran has tried to sever all its relations with this Great Satan and it is for this reason that it now finds wars imposed upon it. America has urged Iraq to spill the blood of our young men,[112] and it has compelled the countries that are subject to its influence to boycott us economically in the hope of defeating us. Unfortunately, most Asian countries are also hostile to us. Let the Muslim nations be aware that Iran is a country effectively at war with America, and that our martyrs—the brave young men of our army and the Revolutionary Guards—are defending Iran and the Islam we hold dear against America. Thus, it is necessary to point out, the clashes now occurring in the west of our beloved country are caused by America; every day we are forced to confront various godless and treacherous groups there. This is a result of the Islamic content of our Revolution, which has been established on the basis of true independence. Were we to compromise with America and the other superpowers, we would not suffer these misfortunes. But our nation is no longer ready to submit to humiliation and abjection; it prefers a bloody death to a life of shame. We are ready to be killed and we have made a covenant with God to follow the path of our leader, the Lord of the Martyrs.

Muslims who are now sitting next to the House of God, engaged in prayer! Pray for those who are resisting America and the other superpowers, and understand that we are not fighting against Iraq. The people of Iraq support our Islamic Revolution; our quarrel is with America, and it is America whose hand can be seen emerging from the sleeve of the Iraqi government. God willing, our struggle will continue until we have achieved real independence, for, as I have said repeatedly, we are warriors, and for Muslims surrender has no meaning.

Neutral countries, I call upon you to witness that America plans to destroy us, all of us. Come to your senses and help us achieve our common goal. We have turned our backs on the East and the West, on the Soviet Union and America, in order to run our country ourselves. Do we therefore deserve to be attacked by the East and the West? The position we have attained is an historical exception, given the present conditions in the world, but our goal will certainly not be lost if *we* are to die, martyred and defeated.

I have said repeatedly that the taking of hostages by our militant, committed Muslim students was a natural reaction to the blows our nation suffered at the hands of America. They can be set free if the property of the dead Shah is returned, all claims of America against Iran are annulled, a guarantee of political and military non-interference in Iran is given by America, and all our capital is released. Of course, I have turned the affair over to the Islamic Assembly[113] for it to settle in whatever way it deems best. The hostages have been well treated in Iran, but the propaganda of America and its satellites has left no lie untold in this respect. At the same time, our beloved young people in America and England have suffered the worst kind of indignity as well as physical and psychological torture. No official in any international organization has defended those dear friends of ours, and no one has condemned America and Britain for their barbaric behavior.

I ask God Almighty that He grant all captive people freedom, independence, and an Islamic republic.

And peace be upon the righteous servants of God.

Notes

1. This condemnation of Nazi sympathies is directed not only against the author of the book being refuted, but also against Riza Shah, who cultivated an extreme nationalist ideology akin to Nazism.

2. Virtuous City: *Madina-yi Fazila*, a designation for the ideal political order that originated in Greek thought but was also used by Muslim philosophers, especially al-Farabi (259/872-339/950).

3. See Article 2 of the Supplementary Constitutional Laws of October 7, 1907.

4. This stipulation is also contained in Article 2 of the Supplementary Constitutional Laws.

5. In December 1928, Riza Shah imposed on the Iranian nation a Uniform Dress Law, which made it obligatory for men to wear a round peaked cap—similar to a kepi—which became known as the Pahlavi cap. This measure—like much else in his program of "reform"—was doubtless inspired by the example of Ataturk, who had, in November 1925, enacted the notorious Hat Law, which provided the death penalty for all who refused to don European headgear. See also p. 333.

6. In this and the following sentence, there is an allusion to two Persian idioms—to "rob someone of his hat" and to "place a hat on someone's head"—which mean, respectively, to rob someone in a cunning and unobtrusive manner, and to deceive someone in the same manner.

7. A railway linking the Persian Gulf with the Caspian littoral was built between October 1927 and August 1938, at an extremely high human and material cost. The railway project was more an extension of the royal ego than a rational response to economic need; it was thus a forerunner of similar projects initiated by Muhammad Riza in the 1970's.

8. In August 1919, Hasan Khan Vusuq ad-Daula, the Iranian Prime Minister of the day, concluded an agreement with Britain providing for employment of British military and civilian advisers in various branches of the Iranian government, with their salaries to be paid from a £2 million

loan imposed on the country by Britain. Since the effect of the agreement was to turn Iran into a virtual British protectorate, it aroused massive opposition in Iran and was never put into effect.

9. That is, Britain secured its control of Iran by installing Riza Shah in power. See pp. 215 and 333.

10. In late 1935, Riza Shah gave orders for strict enforcement of his newly promulgated decree requiring men to wear Western headgear. Police in Mashhad who sought to prohibit the wearing of turbans entered the mosque of Gauhar Shad, part of the shrine complex in that city, and joined by the infantry, they massacred several hundred people.

11. Ayatullah Hakim: more fully, Ayatullah Muhsin al-Hakim, a prominent *mujtahid* of Najaf, 1300/1883-1390/1970. He had a considerable following in Iran. On April 2, 1963, he sent a telegram to Imam Khomeini and other religious leaders in Qum condemning the repression to which they were subject and inviting them to migrate en masse to the Shi'i shrines of Iraq as a form of protest. See S.H.R., *Barrasi va Tahlili az Nihzat-i Imam Khomeini* (Najaf, n.d.), pp. 399-400.

12. The punitive drafting of religious scholars and students was officially inaugurated by a decree issued on April 21, 1963. See S.H.R., *Barrasi va Tahlili*, pp. 405-496. The Shah's regime continued sporadically to make use of this means of repression at least until 1970. See *Khabarnama* (Bulletin of the National Front), Mihr 1349/October 1970, p. 5.

13. In the early 1960's, oil deposits—less extensive than those of Khuzistan—were discovered at Saraja, near Qum.

14. A formal treaty with Israel appears never to have been concluded. Nonetheless, close working relationships were developed in a number of spheres—military, political, and intelligence—and Israeli leaders made frequent clandestine trips to Iran. See pp. 175-180, and p. 162, n. 153.

15. Umayyads: see p. 153, n. 38.

16. Yazid ibn Mu'awiya: see p. 164, n. 175.

17. The six-month old 'Abdullah was one of the three sons of Imam Husayn killed at Karbala. The other two were 'Ali and Ibrahim.

18. Bani Hashim: see p. 163, n. 166.

19. A reference to Qur'an, 14:24: "Do you not see how God sets forth a parable? A goodly word is like a goodly tree; its roots are firm in the ground and its branches reach up to the heavens." Shi'i exegetes have seen in the expression "a goodly tree" (*shajara tayyiba*) an allusion to

the Prophet's family. See Tabataba'i, *al-Mizan fi Tafsir al-Qur'an* (Beirut, 1390/1970), XII, 62-64.

20. *Maraji'*: plural of *marja'* (more fully, *marja'-i taqlid*), a scholar of proven learning and piety whose authoritative rulings one follows in matters of religious practice.

21. On January 26, 1963, the Shah organized a fraudulent referendum to obtain the appearance of popular consent to the six points of the so-called White Revolution.

22. Fatima, the Immaculate One: the sister of Imam Riza, the eighth Imam of the Shi'a. Her tomb in Qum is the center of the shrine complex.

23. Hajj Shaykh 'Abd al-Karim: that is, Hajj Shaykh 'Abd al-Karim Ha'iri; see pp. 13-14.

24. Burujirdi: see p. 15.

25. For the fulfillment of the prophecy implied here, see p. 272.

26. The Shah used the expressions "like an impure animal," "parasites," and "Black Reaction" in an angry and confused speech that he gave in Qum on January 23, 1963. For the text, see *Ittila'at*, Bahman 4, 1341/January 24, 1963.

27. This speech denouncing the granting of capitulatory rights to American personnel in Iran was delivered on the anniversary of the birth of the Prophet's daughter, which under normal circumstances would have been an occasion for rejoicing.

28. The Vienna Convention of 1961—amplifying and in part replacing annexes to the Treaty of Vienna of 1815—regulates the status of diplomatic personal exchange by its signatories.

29. *Marja'*: see n. 20 above.

30. A reference to attempts by the Shah's regime to create dissension among the religious leaders by using a small faction of Tehran *'ulama* who opposed—on allegedly religious grounds—Imam Khomeini's denunciations of Israel. See S.H.R., *Barrasi va Tahlili*, pp. 686-689.

31. Bandar 'Abbas: a port on the northern shore of the Persian/Arabian Gulf to which opponents of the regime were frequently banished because of its remoteness from all urban centers as well as its inhospitable climate.

32. Sayyid Hasan Mudarris: a religious leader who was active in opposing both Russian and British encroachment on Iran during and after World War I. He has been credited with formulating the theory of "negative balance" in Iranian foreign policy; i.e., the refusal of conces-

sions and privileges to all foreign powers. He also opposed the foundation of the Pahlavi dictatorship and was ultimately assassinated on the orders of Riza Shah in 1934. For an account of his life, see Ibrahim Khwaja Nuri, *Bazigaran-i 'Asr-i Tala'i: Mudarris*, new ed. (Tehran, 1359/1980).

33. "That wretch" presumably refers to the Prime Minister of the day, Hasan 'Ali Mansur, who was later assassinated by a young Muslim activist, Muhammad Bukhara'i, for his treacherous activities.

34. Amir 'Abbas Hoveyda served the Shah as Prime Minister with servile devotion from January 1965 until August 1977. He was executed on April 7, 1979 because of his key role in manifold crimes against the Iranian people, particularly his supervision of the activities of the security police SAVAK, which was an appendage of the Prime Minister's office (Interview of the translator with Ayatullah Khalkhali in Qum, December 21, 1979).

35. I.e., the Shah. The impersonal reference is more contemptuous than direct mention would have been.

36. A reference to the coronation ceremonies of 1967.

37. Military service for all female high school graduates was introduced in 1968.

38. *Al-Khutut al-'Arida:* a forty-page pamphlet by Egyptian writer Muhibb ad-Din al-Khatib, first published in Jidda in 1380/1960, which seeks to prove that the Shi'a do not constitute a school of thought within Islam, but rather an entirely separate religion. For a refutation, see Lutfullah as-Safi, *Ma'a 'l-Khatib fi Khututihi 'l-'Arida* (Qum, 1389/1969).

39. See p. 163, n. 161.

40. Masjid al-Aqsa: see p. 153, n. 37.

41. The attack that took place on Fayziya Madrasa was an insult to Imam Ja'far in that it was staged on Shavval 25, the anniversary of his martyrdom in 140/765.

42. Agha Muhammad Qajar: more fully, Agha Muhammad Khan Qajar, founder of the Qajar dynasty, which ruled Iran from 1785 until 1924. His most spectacular acts of savagery were the massacres he enacted at Kerman and Tiflis in 1795. Some inhabitants of the former city of Kerman escaped with their lives, only to be blinded under the personal supervision of the Shah.

43. Concerning the massacre at the mosque of Gauhar Shad, see n. 10 above.

44. The custom of building skull-pyramids appears to have been introduced into Iran by the Mongols. Among its most celebrated practitioners were Timur, who built a pyramid with the skulls of the people of Isfahan

in 1356, and Nadir Shah, an eighteenth-century monarch whose entire career of conquest was marked by atrocities.

45. The "good" monarch intended here is probably Nasir ad-Din Shah, who ruled from 1848 to 1896.

46. Because of the extreme poverty prevailing in southeastern Iran, impoverished families would sometimes sell their children into domestic slavery in Saudi Arabia and the Gulf Emirates.

47. For the text of this sermon, see Subhi as-Salih, ed., *Nahj al-Balagha* (Beirut, 1397/1967), pp. 48-50.

48. Ibn Ziyad: that is, 'Ubaydullah ibn Ziyad, governor under the Umayyad caliph Yazid. He participated in the battle against Imam Husayn at Karbala. He died in the year 67/686.

49. Hajjaj: that is, Hajjaj ibn Yusuf, governor and military commander under several of the Umayyad caliphs, 41/661-95/714. He was renowned for the cruelty he displayed on behalf of his masters in both Iraq and the Hijaz.

50. Muslim: a cousin of Imam Husayn who fought with him at Karbala and was martyred by the Umayyad forces.

51. Imam Ja'far as-Sadiq is said to have stated that knowledge and learning would one day disappear, like a snake into a hole in the ground, and would then reappear in Qum, whence it would spread out over the entire face of the earth. See Muhammad Husayn Razi, *Ganjina-yi Danishmandan* (Tehran, 1352 Sh./1973), I, 32-33.

52. The reference is to the sufferings endured by the Shi'i Muslims of South Lebanon as a result of continued Israeli attacks on the area.

53. The agent intended here may be President Elias Sarkis, installed in 1976 during the war in Lebanon.

54. After the Anglo-Russian invasion of Iran in August 1941, British Foreign Minister Anthony Eden made a statement conceding that Britain had engineered the rise to power of Riza Shah and promising that Britain would not repeat such gross intervention in Iranian affairs. The purpose of the statement was to mollify Iranian hostility toward Britain and to encourage collaboration with the occupying forces. It was first broadcast on BBC, and presumably repeated over Radio Delhi, where Imam Khomeini heard it. It was also publicized by British Information Services attached to the embassy in Tehran. See Peter Avery, *Modern Iran* (London, 1965), p. 228.

Confirmation of the British role in the origins of the Pahlavi dynasty is supplied by the memoirs of Major-General Sir Edmund Ironside, commander of the British forces in Iran. He wrote on February 23, 1921, the day of Riza Shah's coup d'etat: "I fancy that all the people think I engineered the coup d'etat. I suppose I did strictly speaking" (quoted in Denis Wright, *The English Amongst the Persians During the Qajar Period, 1787-1921* [London, 1977], p. 183).

55. See n. 21 above.

56. In March 1976, the Shah decreed a new official calendar of Iran. Until then, time had been reckoned from the migration of the Prophet from Mecca to Medina in the year 622 of the Christian era. The new calendar—known as the Imperial Calendar—took as its point of departure the foundation of the Iranian monarchy by the Achaemenid emperor Cyrus, fixed somewhat arbitrarily at 2,535 years ago. Imam Khomeini forbade the use of this anti-Islamic calendar, which was repealed by the Shah on August 27, 1978 as part of an effort to conciliate the rising forces of the Islamic Revolution.

57. Fayziya Madrasa was closed down by the Shah's regime in 1975. Thereafter, a succession of other madrasas in Qum became centers for the politically conscious activist elements among the religious scholars and students: Hujjatiya Madrasa, established in 1364/1945 by Ayatullah Hujjat (concerning whom, see p. 165, n. 186); Khan Madrasa, an establishment dating from the Safavid period; and Haqqani Madrasa, founded in 1384/1964 by the philanthropist whose name it bears. See Razi, *Ganjina-yi Danishmandan*, I, 44-47, 50, 58.

58. See also pp. 225 and 341.

59. See Qur'an, 3:46: "He [Jesus] shall speak to the people in the cradle and in maturity," words addressed by the angels to Mary, the mother of Jesus.

60. On June 23, 1908, Muhammad 'Ali Shah carried out a coup d'etat against the Majlis; the most effective military resistance to it was organized in Tabriz.

61. Zamzam: the spring of miraculous origin situated beneath the courtyard of the Ka'ba (God's House in Mecca). Kauthar: a spring in paradise referred to in Qur'an, 108:1.

62. Zuhhak: a villainous king in the mythical history of pre-Islamic Iran.

63. The Pahlavi regime glorified the pre-Islamic past of Iran and attempted to manipulate the symbols of Zoroastrianism as a means of subverting the Islamic identity of the nation. This policy was apparent not only in the change of the calendar (see n. 56 above), but also in the ceremonies marking the twenty-five hundredth anniversary of the monarchy,

especially the ludicrous episode in which Muhammad Riza addressed
the empty tomb of Cyrus, an episode that became the butt of countless
jokes in Iran.

64. For the text of the speech referred to, see *Kayhan*, weekly international ed., August 20, 1978.

65. The burning of the Cinema Rex was indeed exploited to the full
by almost the entire Western press, which not only accepted the government version of the incident with hardly any question, but also gave it a
continuous headline treatment it routinely denied the Shah's slaughter
of demonstrators in the streets of Iranian cities.

66. The diversionary voices referred to here probably sought to promote a compromise with the regime by assuring the retention of the
monarchy in exchange for promises of constitutional rule.

67. An alleged culprit by the name of Hashim 'Abd ar-Riza 'Ashur was
indeed found in Iraq and obligingly extradited to Iran in late August
1978. See *Guardian* (Manchester), August 29, 1978.

68. *Taghut:* see p. 154, n. 41.

69. On December 12, 1925, Articles 36, 37, and 38 of the Supplementary
Constitutional Laws, promulgated in October 1907, were changed to pro-
vide for the installation of the Pahlavi dynasty in place of the Qajars.
The change was ratified by what George Lenczowski, an academic apol-
ogist for the Pahlavi regime, has delicately termed "a specially called
Constituent Assembly" (*Iran Under the Pahlavis* [Stanford, 1978], p. 435).

70. In May 1978, for example, at the same time that unarmed demonstrators were being slaughtered in Tehran, Qum, and Tabriz, Britain
signed a protocol with the Shah's regime in preparation for a £750 million
defense contract. See *The Times* (London), May 11, 1978.

71. For example, on October 10—one day before this declaration—
Carter made the following remarks: "My own belief is that the Shah has
moved aggressively to establish democratic principles in Iran and to have
a progressive attitude towards social questions, social problems. This has
been the source of much of the opposition to him in Iran." *New York
Times,* October 11, 1978.

72. An allusion to Qur'an, 28:5: "We wish to grant our favor to those
who have been oppressed in the earth by making them leaders and making
them heirs."

73. It has been estimated that out of the thousands who were killed in
the massacre of Friday, September 8, 1978, more than two hundred were
children.

74. Imam Khomeini received a "vote of confidence" informally, from the numerous demonstrations throughout 1978 in which his leadership was invoked, and formally, from the first article of the declaration approved by a gathering of three million people in Tehran on December 10, 1978: "Ayatullah al-'Uzma, Imam Khomeini, is the leader of the people; his wishes are the wishes of the entire people, and this march constitutes a reaffirmation of the vote of confidence that has eagerly been given him several times over. . . ." *Khabarnama* [Bulletin of the National Front], No. 22 (Azar 1357/December 1978), p. 13.

75. Shortly after the Shah's departure from Iran on January 16, 1979, a tape began circulating in Iran that was believed to contain his farewell instructions to a group of high-ranking military officers. The instructions set out a number of stages whereby a powerful and rigorous military government could be installed.

76. In answer to a question posed to him at Neauphle-le-Chateau on December 20, 1978, Imam Khomeini stated that it was permissible to kill members of the armed forces in three cases: in self-defense, in punishing an officer who had been directly responsible for the slaughter of demonstrators, and in assassinating any major pillar of the regime.

77. In January 1979, employees of the Iranian Central Bank made a list available of persons who in the months just preceding had sent out of the country a total of more than $2 billion. The list was headed by Hushang Ansari, head of the National Iranian Oil Company, who had sent $68.5 million abroad (List circulated in the United States by the Muslim Students' Association [Persian-Speaking Group]).

78. Armenians participated in several of the mass demonstrations that took place in Tehran in December 1978 and January 1979. Among their slogans was: "Our religion is Christian; our leader is Khomeini." See 'Ali Kamali, *Inqilab* (Tehran, 1358/1979), p. 362. Jewish participation in the Revolution was led by the Tehran Society of Jewish Intellectuals, who published a weekly journal, *Tammuz.*

79. Agha Muhammad Khan Qajar: see n. 42 above.

80. Ahmad Shah: last of the Qajar monarchs, he reigned from 1909 to 1924.

81. The reference is, of course, to Bakhtiar. As a member of the National Front, he had previously denounced as illegitimate cabinets that were formed in the same way that his own was now—by royal fiat.

82. In September 1978, about 43,000 American personnel were working in Iran, including 32,000 in defense-related capacities. See Ahmad Faroughy,

"L'Armee iranienne, garante de la dependance," *Le Monde Diplomatique*, October 1978.

83. In January 1979, General Robert Huyser was dispatched to Tehran, allegedly to discuss with the Iranian military leadership the rescheduling of arms shipments to Iran. What was an obvious supposition at the time has since become indubitably clear: that his mission was in fact to investigate the feasibility of a military coup d'etat aimed at destroying the Revolution. See the article by the former U.S. ambassador, William Sullivan, "Dateline Iran: The Road Not Taken," *Foreign Policy*, 40 (Fall 1980), 175-186.

84. This happened, for example, in Masjid-i Sulayman on January 14, 1979, when six army cadets attempting to join demonstrations against the Shah's regime were shot to death by army regulars. *New York Times*, January 15, 1979.

85. Humafars: Air force technicians, the earliest group in the armed forces to join the ranks of the Islamic Revolution.

86. Gurgan and Gunbad-i Qabus: two cities in northeastern Iran.

87. What is meant here by "legal criteria" is not the laws of Pahlavi Iran, but rather a peaceful and agreed upon transition of power from Bakhtiar and the military to the provisional government named on February 6, 1979 by Imam Khomeini, a transition that would in itself be a source of legality.

88. The question of women's rights to obtain a divorce acquired currency after the Revolution when the Shah's "Family Protection Law" of 1967 was abolished. See also p. 154, n. 51, and p. 441.

89. As it turned out, the plan to form a Constituent Assembly that would draw up the definitive text for a new constitution was abandoned in favor of convening a numerically more limited Assembly of Experts, for which an election was held on August 3, 1979.

90. See pp. 177-180 for the text of Imam Khomeini's speech on that day.

91. The word translated here as "agents of foreign powers"—*va-bastaha*—does not imply that the individuals in question have formally enrolled themselves in the service of foreign powers. Rather, they are connected to those powers through their attitudes and way of thought, which tend to facilitate foreign domination.

92. Imam Khomeini probably has in mind here chiefly a resolution of the U.S. Senate on May 17, 1979 that deplored alleged violations of human rights in Iran.

93. An allusion to the Society for the Defense of Liberty and Human Rights, a body composed chiefly of jurists who objected to the activity of the Revolutionary Courts.

94. A slogan first put forward by the influential Islamic thinker and lecturer 'Ali Shari'ati (d. 1977), but put to a wider use that he probably intended by elements completely divorced from Islam.

95. See p. 178.

96. Shortly after the triumph of the Revolution, a fund was established to finance the construction of housing for the urban and rural poor. Contributions to it were soon forthcoming from all across the country.

97. On the tenth, eleventh, and twelfth days of the month of Dhu 'l-Hijja, the pilgrims cast stones at three pillars in the locality known as Mina that mark the site where Satan tempted Abraham to disobey God. This stoning of the pillars is a symbolic act of enmity against Satan and his forces.

98. See n. 10 above.

99. See Qur'an, 19:28-34 and 5:85-86.

100. The "certain individual" is Bakhtiar, who, from his exile in Paris, called for an economic embargo of Iran even before the United States imposed one. See *Le Monde*, November 10, 1979. Preliminary reports had indicated that Bakhtiar had found refuge in England, which he may indeed have visited in the fall of 1979. It later became apparent that he was in France.

101. Elections for the Majlis were completed in mid-March 1980, one week before the Iranian New Year; after the referendum on the new Constitution and the election of the President of the Republic, this was the third and decisive step in establishing the new political institutions.

102. A reference to acts of sabotage undertaken in Khuzistan by elements supported or infiltrated by the Baathist regime of Iraq.

103. The "potential dictators" are the leftist agitators who sought to infiltrate factories in order to promote the "class struggle."

104. The Housing Foundation was established in the Spring of 1979 in order to provide urgently needed housing for the poor. The Mustazafan Foundation is the successor to the Pahlavi Foundation, an organization founded by the Shah to administer and increase the vast estate of his family in Iran. The Pahlavi Foundation also existed as a fictitiously autonomous entity in the United States, serving as a finance and propaganda agent of the Shah's regime. Coming under new administration after the Revolution, the New York branch also became known as the Mustazafan

Foundation. Serious doubts have been raised not only as to the efficiency, but also as to the honesty with which the Housing and Mustazafan Foundations have been administered. It is to these allegations that Imam Khomeini is referring.

105. The "syncretic ideology" mentioned here is that evolved out of Marxist and Islamic elements by the Sazman-i Mujahidin-i Khalq ("Organization of People's Fighters"), which first emerged in 1960 for the purpose of waging a guerilla war against the Pahlavi regime. Although avowedly Islamic, the organization has drawn heavily on Marxist methods of social and economic analysis in the elaboration of its ideology and has sought to give a materialist interpretation to many verses of the Qur'an (see especially the anonymous works, *Shinakht* and *Takamul*). Initially, the organization enjoyed considerable support among the religious leaders, but a delegation that it sent to Najaf to obtain the endorsement of Imam Khomeini returned empty-handed. See the text of his speech on June 25, 1980, printed in *Junhuri-yi Islami,* Tir 5, 1359/June 26, 1980.

106. *Usul:* more fully, *usul ad-din,* the "principles of religion"; dogmatic theology.

107. Tehran University, the first to be established in the country, was opened in 1935.

108. A reference to clashes that took place at Tehran University in April 1980, when various political groups were ordered to end their occupation of certain buildings on campus. See *Jumhuri-yi Islami,* Farvardin 30, 1359/April 19, 1980.

109. The United States imposed a formal economic embargo on Iran on April 7, 1980, at the same time that it cut diplomatic relations.

110. Among the members of the Revolutionary Council holding doctorates were Mehdi Bazargan, Yadullah Sahabi, and Ibrahim Yazdi. Among the *mujtahids* were Ayatullahs Mutahhari (assassinated May 1, 1979), Musavi Ardabili, and Muntaziri. Ayatullahs Bihishti and Bahunar are both *mujtahids* and the holders of doctorates.

111. On the birthday of the Twelfth Imam, Sha'ban 15, which in 1980 fell on June 28, Imam Khomeini delivered a speech stressing the importance of the occasion. He pointed out in particular that it will be the mission of the Twelfth Imam, when he returns to the manifest plane, to inaugurate a universal rule of justice. The speech was immediately distorted by a number of Arab regimes to suggest that Imam Khomeini had somehow belittled the Prophet Muhammad. A number of them, led by Egypt, extracted statements from the compliant religious authorities in their countries to the effect that Imam Khomeini's statements were incom-

patible with Islam. See the remarks delivered at the Fourteenth Seminar on Islamic Thought, Algiers, by Sayyid Hadi Khusraushahi, clarifying both the intent of Imam Khomeini and the motives of those who attacked him, in *Ash-Sha'b* (Algiers), September 4, 1980.

112. This message was issued before the beginning of the Iraqi offensive against Iran on September 21, 1980. For some time, however, Iraqi forces had been harrassing Iranian border defenses, and the reference is to those activities. The statement here may also be a prediction of the full-scale war that was later launched by Iraq.

113. The National Consultative Assembly renamed itself the Islamic Consultative Assembly soon after it first met.

III

Interviews

THIRTY MILLION PEOPLE
HAVE STOOD UP

On December 29, 1978, Imam Khomeini granted Dr. Algar, the translator, the following interview at the modest suburban villa where he was staying in Neauphle-le-Chateau, near Paris. Of particular interest in his answers is the emphasis upon Shi'i traditions of rejecting illegitimate authority. Questions and answers have been translated from the transcript of the interview.

Why, in your opinion, has the Islamic movement of Iran reached a climax this year? We know that this movement has deep historical roots, but why has it now been transformed into a revolution on the threshold of victory, God willing?

There are, of course, various causes that I do not wish to mention, in addition to the reactions aroused by a certain newspaper article.[1] The religious scholars of Qum rose up in protest, and the government sought a confrontation with them. So the Muslim people joined the protest of their leaders and a massacre ensued. These events were followed by commemorative assemblies forty days after the death of the martyrs; these, in turn, produced further martyrs, and further commemorative gatherings.

As a result of this cycle of events, the people gradually lost their fear of the police. Whereas previously they had thought it impossible to confront the security forces, after one or two clashes they came to realize that confrontation was after all possible, and not the formidable task they had imagined.[2] So gradually, their fears and inhibitions dissolved, and they realized they could demonstrate and speak out against the Shah and the government.

Ceremonies of commemoration and mourning for the victims of the Shah on the fortieth day after their deaths spread throughout the whole country.

At the same time, the government continued to act with the utmost harshness, and the Shah persisted in his arrogance, thinking that no one could successfully oppose him. He could not digest the fact that the people were revolting against a dictatorship that had established complete control over the country, so he went on acting with unlimited cruelty. But the religious scholars gave the people guidance and leadership, which enabled them to resist, so that gradually, fears and inhibitions dissolved, and in the course of little more than a year, a concerted struggle against the Shah and his regime took firm root in the country, a struggle that is, of course, still continuing. The Shah is still killing the people, and they are still resisting. Frustrations had been building up in the people for fifty years, and it was only a matter of time until they exploded; the events of the past year or so provided the occasion for the explosion. Whenever repression is intensified to an extraordinary degree, the natural and inevitable result will be an explosion. Hence the revolutionary movement, which will continue until the Shah's regime is destroyed.

It appears that America will not easily give up its domination of Iran. Do you regard direct intervention by the United States as likely, and if so, how should this danger be confronted?

The measures taken so far to repress the movement of our people have all been the results of American intervention. First, they used these savages in the army without the open proclamation of martial law. Then they saw that that was not enough, so they had martial law proclaimed in twelve cities in Iran,[3] but still the people continued to resist bitterly. Not only was martial law imposed on American recommendation, but the so-called government of reconciliation, headed by Sharif-Imami,[4] was also an American ploy. Their next trick will be to install an allegedly popular and national government, but it too will probably last not more than a few days.[5] After that, they will probably attempt a military coup d'etat, but that also will not succeed.[6] All the plans of America, one after the other, have failed; they have no choice but to give up.

Have Islamic organizations in the Arab countries, Pakistan, Turkey, or elsewhere expressed their support for the movement in Iran?

No Muslim government has given us the slightest support, although individual citizens and groups have sometimes expressed their solidarity with us and denounced the cruelties to which we are subjected. As for the well-known Islamic organizations, none of them have offered us any support as far as I am aware, although minor groups, about whose exact nature I do not know very much, have expressed their sympathy toward us.

All the superpowers, together with the smaller nations that are subordinate to them, are opposing the Islamic movement in Iran, and as you have just said, no effective support for the movement is forthcoming from even the Islamic countries. What is the reason for this universal enmity toward the Islamic movement of Iran?

Certain countries are satellites of the Soviet Union and others are satellites of America—they obey America and follow its propaganda line. In addition, the rulers of these countries are afraid for themselves. Suppose they were genuinely independent and not subject to anyone's orders, not those of the Soviet Union nor those of America; they would still fear our movement. For seeing that an entire population has risen up against the Shah, despite all the power he has at his disposal, the rulers of Dubai, Kuwait, and so on naturally ask themselves, "How can we be sure the same thing will not happen to us?" Demands for an Islamic state are now being heard in Turkey as well, partly as a result of what is happening in Iran.[7] So the rulers of the Muslim countries are bound to oppose the movement in Iran for the sake of self-preservation, not only in the countries I have mentioned, but also in Pakistan and Afghanistan (of course, now there are additional factors in the case of Afghanistan).[8] All these rulers are afraid their own people will follow the example of Iran. This is true even of the Soviet Union; it is afraid that the same demands now being raised in Iran will be heard among the Muslims of the Caucasus and other parts of the Soviet Union.

In short, the rulers of the Muslim countries do not care about the slaughter that is going on in Iran; their only concern is to keep themselves in power and plunder their own people. So when they see an uprising taking place in Iran against that bandit, the Shah—an uprising that is, moreover, likely to succeed—they see their own interests in danger.

As for the superpowers, they see their dominance threatened not only in Iran, but in the rest of the world. So America directs those in its tutelage to oppose our movement, and the Soviet Union does likewise. This is true only of the governments, however, not the peoples; even if we have not received any effective support from the peoples of the Muslim countries, at least they have not opposed us.

When, God willing, an Islamic government is established in Iran, will it be part of its program to implement the provisions of Islamic law, whether immediately or in stages?

We will naturally proceed in stages, God willing.

You have said that the first stage in establishing an Islamic government in Iran will be to hold free elections under the supervision of trustworthy representatives of the people. Will parties participate in those elections or will candidates present themselves on an individual basis?

All parties will be free to exist in Iran, except those that clearly oppose the interests of the people, and the elections will also be free. Of course, we will make our recommendations to the people, which they may or may not follow.

It appears to be the case that at the present stage of the Islamic movement, many persons who are not bound to Islam by religious conviction have ranged themselves under the banner of Islam for the sake of overthrowing the Shah's regime, since Islam is the only power capable of defeating it. It is true that the general level of religious awareness on the part of the people has risen immeasurably, but do you anticipate that those who have now aligned themselves with the Islamic movement for political reasons will continue to follow the religious leadership in the future?

There are, of course, different political groups and factions. Some of them are definitely pro-Islamic and genuinely serving the cause. Others include both people sympathetic to Islam and others not sympathetic. And finally there are groups that are hostile to Islam, and those are a minority.[9]

In the past when uprisings occurred, in Tehran for example, they would be on a limited scale; they would not cover the whole country. And the question would be raised: were they led by the politicians or by the religious scholars (insofar as they were involved)? By the Muslims or the communists?

The question was justifiable then, but it no longer is. The present movement is an uprising that has brought together all segments of the population and all parts of the country. If you were to go to some village in Iran now, or some remote mountain community, you would hear the same things being said there that are being said in Tehran (those who have travelled around the country have reported this to me). Everywhere the goal is the same: an Islamic government. It is possible, of course, that some people understand and accept the principle of an Islamic government without knowing the details of its functioning, but what is certain is that the whole of Iran—including townspeople, peasants, tribesmen, and mountaineers—is unanimously proclaiming its demand for an Islamic government. There may be people who are supporting this demand out of opportunism, but given the proportions that the movement has now attained, they will be unable to play any disruptive role.

Suppose we have a few thousand communists in the country. What can they do in the face of this human tide, this thirty million who are defying the Shah's huge army—baring their breasts against his bullets and fighting with bare hands against his tanks while they cry out their demand for Islamic government? Could ten thousand communists oppose this thirty million, let alone dominate them?

For all his power, the Shah is proving unable to withstand them, these Muslims who defy him on the streets and in the bazaars. A total of four hundred thousand troops are ranged against them; tanks, cannons, and machine guns are brought up to massacre them on the streets. But the people have continued to resist. Someone is killed, and immediately a *fatiha*[10] is recited for him. While the *fatiha* is still being recited, someone else is killed and a *fatiha* is recited for him, but the struggle goes on without interruption. That is the way it is in Iran now. How could such a country ever go communist?

The Shah has always sought to convince people that if he goes, the communists will take over; if he goes, the country will fall apart; if he goes, the country will be occupied by foreigners. That is all nonsense. A nation of thirty million or more has stood up and defied tanks and machine guns. If the Soviets or the Americans come marching in, they will be met with the same defiance. But presumably, they are too intelligent to attempt such an escapade. In any event, the fear that a communist or Marxist party might take over the country is completely idiotic.

I am aware that one of your aims is to assure unity among the Muslims, to bring together the followers of different schools of thought that exist in the Islamic world. During last Muharram, at exactly the same time that the people of Iran were fighting heroically to gain freedom, independence, and Islamic government, we saw, unfortunately, Sunnis and Shi'is fighting each other in India. What suggestions do you have for abolishing these ancient and harmful prejudices?

Our method is one of education and guidance. We are doing our best in this respect, in accordance with the means at our disposal. It will be a lengthy process, however. The Muslim peoples must become acquainted with the fundamental ordinances of Islam. Ignorance exists on both sides, among Sunnis and Shi'is alike, and it is as a result of this ignorance that clashes and enmity have arisen.

Certainly these divisions did not exist in the earliest age of Islam.

The Islamic movement in Iran can be said to be the only truly vital Islamic movement now existing in the entire Islamic world. Why is it that in countries other than Iran, we see stagnation of various degrees?

The Shi'i school of thought, which is the prevalent one in Iran, has had certain distinguishing characteristics from the very beginning. While other schools have preached submission to rulers, even if they are corrupt and oppressive, Shi'ism has preached resistance against them and denounced them as illegitimate. From the outset, Shi'is have opposed oppressive governments.

In countries other than Iran, where either there are no Shi'is or the Shi'is are in the minority, the earlier traditions of submission to the rulers have prevailed. The rulers are obeyed as the legitimate holders of authority (*ulu 'l-amr*[11]).

According to Shi'i belief, only the Imams or those who act on their behalf are the legitimate holders of authority; all other governments are illegitimate. This belief has been expressed throughout history in Shi'i uprisings against different governments. Sometimes it was possible to resist; at other times, it was not. If the Iranian people are now rising up against the Shah, they are doing so as an Islamic duty.

Many Sunnis, however, may regard this rebellion against oppressive government as incompatible with Islam; for example, we find the Azhar[12] opposing us and condemning the Iranian people. That is because of the belief that even an oppressive ruler must be obeyed, a belief that is based upon an incorrect interpretation of the Qur'anic verse concerning obedience.[13]

In contrast, we Shi'is, who base our understanding of Islam on what we have received from 'Ali (upon whom be peace) and his descendants, consider only the Imams and those whom they appointed to be legitimate holders of authority. This view conforms to the interpretation of the Qur'anic verse on authority made by the Prophet himself.[14]

This is the root of the matter: Sunni-populated countries believe in obeying their rulers, whereas the Shi'is have always believed in rebellion—sometimes they were able to rebel, and at other times they were compelled to keep silent.

What effect will the triumph of the Islamic movement in Iran—which, God willing, is not far off—have on the people of neighboring countries and the people of the Middle East as a whole?

Doubtless it will gradually have an effect, but I do not know when.

According to the news I receive, the situation is changing in Iraq, particularly among the young; things are no longer the way they used to be. It may be that when the people of Iraq see the progress made by the Revolution of Iran, they will begin their own movement. Of course, at places in Iraq where Sunni *fuqaha* enjoy influence, this may not be feasible, but where this factor is not present and the masses are free to decide, they will not endure the treatment they are receiving from the Iraqi government. The Sunni youth do not accept the teaching of their *fuqaha* that one must obey the government, so they too may rise up in revolt. The likelihood is greater in areas of Shi'i population.

In Turkey, as I have already said, demands are also being raised for an Islamic government.

An Islamic government is, in fact, the desire of all Muslims, but the conduct of certain Sunni *fuqaha* is delaying the realization of this desire.

Is it possible, in your opinion, that Iran's neighbors will become bases for exerting pressure on Iran after the triumph of the Revolution?

Could there be worse pressure than a fully equipped army of 400,000 men inside the borders of the country? Will our neighbors be able to exert more pressure upon us than the Shah's army? Of course they will not, and sooner or later, they will realize that they are bound to fail. They probably will try to exert pressure upon us, but their efforts will lead nowhere.

THE RELIGIOUS SCHOLARS
LED THE REVOLT

A year to the day after the interview conducted in Neauphle-le-Chateau, Imam Khomeini granted the translator a second interview, which took place at his residence in Qum. The first question posed—concerning the central issue of the position held by the religious leadership in the new political system—was answered in such detail that no time remained for other questions. The Persian text of this interview was published in the Tehran daily newspaper Jumhuri-yi Islami, *on Day 12, 1358/January 2, 1980.*

It is apparent to everyone that the militant religious scholars, led by yourself, have played an important role in the Islamic Revolution. One of the factors enabling them to play this role has no doubt been the independence they have enjoyed vis-a-vis the state, an independence that was often complete. Now that, as a result of the Revolution, an Islamic government has come into being in Iran, will the religious scholars continue to function as a separate institution, or will some form of merger take place between them and the state? The latter possibility is suggested by the fact that certain religious scholars have already assumed executive functions.

You know that under the former regime, and also under the other monarchies that existed throughout Iranian history, not to mention the other forms of government in different parts of the world that contravened divine law and the principle of *tauhid*, the laws enforced were manmade laws, the product of the human mind. Whatever the specific form of government in each case, the laws enforced all had that common characteristic, and they were generally inspired by a desire to dominate the people. Of course, it occasionally happened that laws were put into effect for the sake of assuring order in society and the liberty of the people. But if we are looking for a government that is based on the principle of *tauhid* and follows divine law, it is to Islam that we must turn. If such a government did exist before Islam, examples of it must be extremely rare.

The sole determining principle in a government based on *tauhid* is divine law, law that is the expression of divine will, not the product of the human mind. Now in the first age of Islam— an age nearer to us in time, of course, than that of the earlier prophets—such a government existed. It was at first weak and limited in scope, and then later it ruled over vast areas, but insofar as it was Islamic and did not pursue any aims other than those of Islam, its ruling principle was always divine law, or God Himself. The government was the government of God. The prophets and those who succeeded them did not introduce anything of their own devising; their sole aim was to implement divine law. In certain matters of detail, they naturally had recourse to measures of their own, but as far as fundamental matters were concerned—those aspects of government that have to exist in every country—they followed divine law. The Messenger of God (peace and blessings be upon him), who is of course our exemplar, never enacted a single judgment or executed a single law in opposition to God's decree; on the contrary, he executed God's law.

There is a great difference between all the various manmade forms of government in the world, on the one hand—whatever their precise nature—and a divine government, on the other hand, which follows divine law. Governments that do not base themselves on divine law conceive of justice only in the natural realm; you will find them concerned only with the prevention of disorder and not with the moral refinement of the people. Whatever a person does in his own home is of no importance, so long as he causes no disorder in the street. In other words, people are free to do as they please at home. Divine governments, however, set themselves the task of making man into what he should be. In his unredeemed state, man is like an animal, even worse than the other animals.[15] Left to his own devices, he will always be inferior to the animals, for he surpasses them in passion, evil, and

330

rapacity. As originally created, man is superior to all other beings, but at the same time, his capacities for passion, anger, and other forms of evil are virtually boundless. For example, if a person acquires a house, he will begin to desire another house. If a person conquers a country, he will begin plotting to conquer another country. And if a person were to conquer the entire globe, he would begin planning the conquest of the moon or Mars. Men's passions and covetousness, then, are unlimited, and it was in order to limit men, to tame them, that the prophets were sent. If this animal that has broken its bridle is allowed to roam freely outside all recognizable bounds, if it is left to itself and no attempt is made to train it, it will desire everything for itself and be prepared to sacrifice everyone to its desires. The prophets came to tame this unbridled beast and to make it subject to certain restraints. After taming it, they showed it how to achieve the perfections that constitute its true happiness, and here it is not a question of this world and the natural realm only. In the prophets' view, the world is merely a means, a path by which to achieve a noble aim that man is himself unaware of but that is known to the prophets. They know what the final destiny of man will be if he continues in his unfettered state, and they also know how different it will be if man is tamed and follows the path leading to the noble rank of true humanity.

All the concerns that, taken together, form the objective of most governments are but a path or a means in the view of the prophets. For them, the world cannot be an objective or a point of orientation, but only a path of ascent leading to the rank of true humanity. If a person embarks on this path, he will attain true happiness. The happiness he may enjoy in this world will not be confined to it, for his ultimate goal is a world that lies beyond the present one. The prophets have seen that world, which is unknown to us because it is beyond the range of sensory perception.

So the prophets came, first, to tame the forces of anger, passion, and evil that are present in man, and then to guide him on the path of ascent to which those forces are in opposition. Unfortunately, there were many obstacles in their way and they rarely succeeded in attaining their goal. For men are inclined by their very natures to passion, anger, and evil, and even those who do wish to tame those forces within themselves face all kinds of opposition and impediment. But whatever salvation or blessing does exist in the world is the result of the exertions of the prophets. Within the limits that were set for them, and as far as the rays of their teaching extended, they were able to impose certain bounds on the evil forces present in man. Their task was extremely difficult, but whatever good does exist in the world proceeds from them. If we were to exclude the prophets from the world, it would collapse, and everyone would see what chaos would ensue. It was the prophets who were responsible for imposing some limits on man, and whatever good and blessedness exist in this world are their work.

Islam has taken all the dimensions of man into consideration and provided for them. The law of Islam is restricted neither to the unseen realm nor to the manifest dimension, in the same way that man himself is not restricted to a single dimension. Islam came to fashion true and complete human beings, complete in all their dimensions. It did not cultivate exclusively either the spiritual dimension of man, which would have fostered in him an aversion to the natural realm, or the natural dimension, which would have made him satisfied with the natural realm. The natural dimension is the means, and the spiritual, the end. Stated differently, it was the task of the prophets to reform the natural dimension of man in order that it might become the means of his ascent.

Unfortunately, true Islam lasted for only a brief period after its inception. First the Umayyads[16] and then the Abbasids[17] inflicted all kinds of damage on Islam. Later the monarchs ruling Iran continued on the same path; they completely distorted Islam and established something quite different in its place. The process was begun by the Umayyads, who changed the nature of government from divine and spiritual to worldly. Their rule was based on Arabism, the principle of promoting the Arabs over all other peoples,[18] which was an aim fundamentally opposed to Islam and its desire to abolish nationality and unite all mankind in a single community, under the aegis of a state indifferent to the matter of race and color. It was the aim of the Umayyads to distort Islam completely by reviving the Arabism of the pre-Islamic age of ignorance, and the same aim is still pursued by the leaders of certain Arab countries, who declare openly their desire to revive the Arabism of the Umayyads, which is nothing but the Arabism of the Jahiliyya.[19]

The Umayyads and their successors in Islamic history did not allow men to grasp the true nature of Islam, in particular, Islamic government. As we have said, government is a means, a lower state that leads to a higher state, but the Umayyads and their successors prevented people from grasping even this lower state. It must be stated that throughout Islamic history, as a result of various kinds of distortion, Islam remained unknown among men.

This was particularly true during the last fifty years. You may be too young, but I witnessed it all during the past fifty years, from the coming to power of Riza Khan through a coup d'etat down to the state of our country just before the Revolution.

It was the British who put Riza Khan in power, as they later admitted themselves in a broadcast over Radio Delhi,[20] and when he disobeyed them, they carried him off to a place of their own choosing.[21]

In the beginning, he sought to employ Islam as a weapon against Islam by doing things designed to please the Muslims. The martyrdom of the Lord of the Martyrs (peace be upon him) is important in Iran, so Riza Khan used to devote much attention to attending *rauzas*,[22] and it is said that he used to go barefoot to *takiyas*[23] where *rauzas* were being held. He thus succeeded in gaining popularity, although his true aim was to acquire a weapon to use against the people. Once his government was firmly established, he began to carry out his instructions (of course, his own inclinations may have coincided with his instructions, and some of what he did was in imitation of Ataturk).[24] Now he reached for the weapon of unbelief, and the first thing he planned to do was to root out every trace of Islam in Iran. How was this to be done? One way was to take away the religious assemblies to which the people were so attached and to destroy them—the assemblies where the struggle of the Lord of the Martyrs was commemorated, which had such great moral value for the people. Riza Khan banned *rauzas* throughout Iran; no one could organize a *rauza*, not even if only a few people were to be present. Even in Qum, which was then, as now, the center of the religious institution, there were no *rauza* assemblies, or if there were, they had to be held between dawn and sunrise. Before the first call to prayer, five to ten people would gather for a brief talk and commemoration of Karbala, and when the call to prayer was sounded, or very soon after, they had to disperse. Sometimes informers were present, and when they turned in their reports, all who had attended the meeting were arrested.

Worse than that, and striking a more damaging blow to the foundations of Islam, was Riza Khan's plan to destroy the religious institution completely. He began by removing the religious scholars' turbans from their heads and forbidding turbans to be worn. Some government officials would say that not more than six people in all Iran should be permitted to wear turbans, but they were lying since it was their intention to abolish the turban entirely. The goal was to destroy the religious scholars as a class.

Those instructing Riza Khan in these measures had seen for more than a century that whenever they wished to inflict some loss on the people, the religious scholars had stood in their way. For example, when the British had more or less conquered Iraq, they saw a great religious leader, the late Mirza Muhammad Taqi Shirazi,[25] oppose their aims and rescue the independence of Iraq. Earlier, his teacher, Mirza Hasan Shirazi,[26] had saved Iran from the British by uttering a single sentence. In short, they saw the religious leaders as troublesome elements that prevented them from attaining their goals, which were primarily to gain access to the natural resources and minerals of the East and to turn our cities into markets for their goods, so that we would be reduced to the dependent status of consumers.

They realized that in order to deprive our people of the leadership that made it possible for them to concentrate their forces against foreign domination, religious scholars as a class had to be destroyed. The religious leaders had consistently served as defenders of Islam and the laws of Islam, sometimes with success, as in the case of Mirza Hasan Shirazi, whom all Iran followed, and sometimes with failure.

In more recent times, when Muhammad Riza embarked on his satanic rule, he imitated his father by professing loyalty to Islam initially and using Islam as a weapon. For example, he commissioned a printing of the Qur'an, visited Mashhad once or twice a year, and prayed upon occasion. He wanted to deceive the people, and indeed he did succeed in deceiving some of them. But gradually he came to feel there was no longer any need for deceit, and he began to rule by pure force and, at the same time, to rob the people of all their wealth and resources. As you know, it was impossible to breathe freely in Iran. All the newspapers and magazines, as well as the radio and television, served him and opposed the people. Many people were silenced and imprisoned, and the resources of the nation were plundered.

But at the same time, Muhammad Riza made loud claims about having "A Mission to Serve the Country," even writing a book with that title,[27] and conducted a propaganda campaign about the alleged progress the nation had made. Everyone knew those were lies. Everywhere in Iran there is still poverty and wretchedness; conditions for the common people are so miserable that they do not even have homes. The people that live right on top of our oil deposits are suffering from hunger and thirst, and cannot even clothe themselves adequately. I once passed through the region of Ahvaz and its surrounding villages by train, and I remember seeing barefoot people—adults and children—rushing up to the train to beg for a mouthful of food. Vast oil resources lay beneath them, but the wealth those resources produced went elsewhere—into the pockets of foreigners, particularly the Americans. In return, America gave us the military bases it constructed for itself in our territory. That is, it took back the money it had paid for our oil and used it to build military bases for itself; this is one of the worst adversities it inflicted upon us. In addition, there were the burdensome contracts and agreements they imposed on us: none of them benefited our nation; on the contrary, they increased the domination of Iran by America.

As a result of all this, our people came to feel desperate. Many were forced to spend their lives in prison or banishment, and indeed, in a certain sense, everyone was a prisoner, because government agents were always watching to make sure that no one uttered a word of protest. If you or someone like you had come to Iran, it would have been impossible for him to conduct an interview on these matters, or even say a few words.

The people were feeling desperate and waiting for some voice to be raised in protest so that they could join in.

That voice was raised in Qum on Khurdad 15.[28] During the months just before it, the city's religious scholars were beginning to voice their opposition to the regime, and various events ensued that culminated in the great uprising of Khurdad 15. That uprising was suppressed by a huge massacre. I was in prison at the time and did not know what was happening, and even when I was released from prison, I was under house arrest. Nonetheless, people found ways to inform me that 15,000 were killed and an indefinite number arrested. People were reduced to such a state that life no longer meant much to them. They had to live out their lives in the shadow of evil. Fathers and sons watched each other suffer; so did husbands and wives. In short, the life of the people was harsh and difficult, and they again began to wait for a spark of deliverance.

Khurdad 15 had been such a spark, and although it was put out, the people were not entirely defeated. They continued to await a favorable opportunity for resuming their struggle, until finally there began the series of events that started two years ago.

The people were ready for revolution: they were dissatisfied with their government and discontented with their lives, and—most importantly—God had brought about a spiritual transformation in them. The essence of this transformation, which still persists to some extent, is that people began to yearn for martyrdom, just as they had done in the earliest age of Islam. Look at the demonstrations that are still taking place; you will see people wearing shrouds and proclaiming their readiness for martyrdom. Mothers who have lost children come to me and ask me to pray that one or two more of their children may be martyred. Young people, both men and women, also ask me to pray that they may become martyrs. This, then, is a spiritual transformation being wrought in our people by God's will.

In addition, the whole nation was unanimous in its dissatisfaction. Muhammad Riza had done nothing to satisfy any segment of the population. He cared only for the upper echelons of the army and the security forces; he despised everyone else. He took no account of anyone: not of the civil service, nor the army (its lower ranks, that is), nor the bazaar, nor the mosque, nor the religious institution, nor the university. In fact, that was his greatest mistake: he regarded the people as nothing.

The people, then, were united in their dissatisfaction, and when the demand for an Islamic republic was raised, no one opposed it. The whole country in unison demanded the foundation of an Islamic republic and the abolition of the monarchy, and since the people were strengthened by divine support, they reached their goal despite the support and protection that were being extended to Muhammad Riza by various powers, great and small —particularly America and Britain (unfortunately, the governments of most Muslim countries adopted their attitude).

Once the people had shattered the great barrier of tyranny and driven out Muhammad Riza, the factional interests of certain groups came to light and differences began to appear.

It is possible that many of those differences were created by hidden hands and manipulated in such a way as to undermine the strength of the nation.

The strength of the nation has been concentrated in two particular principles, and it is exactly these that have come under attack. One is unity of purpose, and the other, the demand for an Islamic republic.

Certain elements did all they could to oppose the establishment of the Islamic Republic. For example, they said it would be enough to have a republic; to speak of Islam in this connection is quite unnecessary.[29] Others said, "We want a 'democratic republic,' not an Islamic one," and others—the least offensive of them all—spoke of a "democratic Islamic republic."

Our people would not have any of this. They said, "We understand what Islam is, and we understand what a republic means. But as for 'democratic,' that is a concept that has constantly changed its guise throughout history. In the West it means one thing, and in the East, another. Plato described it one way, and Aristotle another way. We don't understand any of it. And why should something we don't understand appear on the ballot form for us to vote on? We understand Islam and we know what it is—namely, justice. We know how rulers in the first age of Islam like 'Ali ibn Abi Talib exercised rule, and we also know that the word 'republic' means voting, and that we accept. But as for 'democratic,' we won't accept it even if you put it next to 'Islamic.' "

Even apart from this, as I said in an earlier talk, to juxtapose "democratic" and "Islamic" is an insult to Islam. Because when you place the word "democratic" in front of "Islamic," it means that Islam is lacking in the alleged virtues of democracy, although Islam is, in fact, superior to all forms of democracy. To speak of a "democratic Islamic republic" is like speaking of a "justice-oriented Islamic republic." That is an insult to Islam because it suggests that justice is something extrinsic to Islam, whereas it is the very substance of Islam.

So the people did not accept these various alternative formulae. Certain writers and intellectuals still continued to insist that the word "Islam" should not be used in the designation. We decided that their hostility toward Islam must mean that they had been dealt a blow by Islam; we related this, in turn, to the fact that the superpowers had been deprived of their control over our oil by a nation that was crying out, "Islam!" It was in the interest of the superpowers that the word "Islam" be deleted from our form of government, and thus, that the mainstay of our Republic be denied. The mainstay of any government must be its people; it if lacks the support of its people, it cannot be a true government, or enjoy stability and permanence. So, certain elements were insistent that our government be deprived of its main source of support—popular devotion to Islam.

Of course, they are still trying to be insistent, although now in a different way. Now it is said that the Constitution is not a "popular" constitution, and that it has many problems.[30] The fact is that this Constitution was approved by the elected representatives of the people and then submitted to a popular vote in the referendum, and it is only a small minority—whose leadership and aims we know well—that seeks to oppose the desires of the whole nation. The conclusion is inescapable that this minority wants to see the former state restored so that it can regain its former interests. Islam dealt it a blow, so it does not want to see Islamic government take firm hold.

Throughout the different stages of the Revolution, the religious leaders played the primary role. Of course, others also took part—university professors, intellectuals, merchants, students—but it was the religious leaders who mobilized the whole people.

In every region there are three or four mosques, presided over by a religious scholar whom the people believe in. I have always advised the Iranian people not to overlook the impregnable fortress that the religious leaders provide for them, and I have particularly advised the intellectuals who might desire the independence of their country that the religious institution constitutes a great barrier to foreign domination, and its loss would leave them powerless.[31]

If the religious scholars were eliminated from this movement, there would not have been a movement. The people do not listen to anyone else. They do not listen to the intellectuals. Political parties, unless they are Islamic, cannot gather more than a thousand or so members, and the people will not listen to them. However much the party leaders try to attract their attention, the people say to themselves, "They're talking nonsense."

It is this group alone, the religious leaders, who are capable of arousing the people and inspiring them to self-sacrifice. Your remark that they have played a great role is quite true, although of course individual religious leaders have different degrees of influence according to their status. But in proportion to the scope of his influence, each has his words heeded by those who comprise his audience. People understand that he seeks their well-being; if they follow him, they will attain true happiness, and even if they are killed, they will die martyrs.

So it was the religious leaders who mobilized the people all over Iran, and it was from the mosques that the people set out behind their preachers and leaders to participate in demonstrations.

I ask all the factions of the people—including those who regard themselves as nationalists[32]—to protect the religious leaders. God is protecting them; the nationalists should also do so, and be careful not to lose them. You see some people today wanting to drag them into discussions in order to weaken them, but it is not in the worldly or the religious interest of these people to do so.

It is not my intention to proclaim the whole class of religious scholars free from blemish, or to say that anyone who wears a turban is a virtuous, upright, and pious person. I am not making any such claim, nor is anyone else. But those who oppose the religious scholars are not opposing the bad ones who may exist among them; they are opposing the good ones, those who have influence on the people. If their opposition were directed against evil elements among the religious scholars, their aim would be justified; such elements must be purged (I accept this, and the purge will take place at the appropriate time). But when our nation is in a state of upheaval in the aftermath of a revolution, when it is beginning successfully to confront the problems that always exist under such circumstances and that have been especially acute in our case, when it is facing the enmity of a superpower, indeed of all superpowers—it is not the time to endanger this great support of the nation, the element that is capable of mobilizing the people. It may be that we have a grievance against a particular religious leader, or objections to another, but this is not the time to pursue these matters. The problem must be solved gradually.

I do not know whether you are familiar with this story.[33] Once a man went into his garden and saw a *sayyid*, an *akhund*,[34] and an ordinary man busy stealing his fruit. Addressing the ordinary man, he said, "Well, that gentleman's a *sayyid*, a descendant of the Prophet, so never mind. And his friend is one of the religious scholars; he's most welcome to whatever he wants. But what do you have to say for yourself?" With the assistance of the *sayyid* and the *akhund*, the owner of the garden bound the hands and feet of the ordinary man. The he sat himself down and said to the *akhund:* "The *sayyid* is a descendant of the Prophet, and it's not proper to quarrel with a descendant of the Prophet, but let me hear what you have to say. How do you justify your coming here to steal, despite your turban and beard?" And with the aid of the *sayyid*, he tied up the *akhund*. There remained now only the *sayyid*. He asked the *sayyid*, "Did your ancestor ever tell you to steal?" seized him, and bound him also, hand and foot.

The strategy the opponents of the religious scholars are following is like that of the owner of the garden. They say, "What do the *akhunds* think they are doing? What is all this 'akhundism'?[35] The country must not fall into the hands of the *akhunds*." Do they imagine that the *akhunds* want to take over the country and do whatever they like with it? That is not it at all. Those who speak about "akhundism" really wish to separate the people from the *akhunds* so that the people are deprived of this great resource, just as they were in the time of Riza Shah. Their plan is to begin with the lower-ranking religious scholars, and then to move gradually higher until there is no one left and the whole class is completely destroyed. They want to take away from the people this class that is able to diffuse Islam in the world, to propagate it and give it outward expression. The basic object of their hostility is Islam itself.

As for your question concerning the future role of the religious leaders and scholars, their function is to guide the people in all matters. Attempts were made in the past to separate the religious leaders from the people, which meant, in fact, a separation of religion from politics.

As you know from your studies, Islam is a religion whose divine precepts have a political dimension. Sermons given at Friday prayer and on the occasion of festivals; congregational prayer; the pilgrimage with its vast assemblies at Mecca, Muzdalifa, Mina, and 'Arafat—all these are political matters. Of course, they are acts of worship, but politics and worship are intermingled in them. Attempts were made to separate Islam and religion from politics; people were told, "The emperor has his rightful place, and the *akhund* has his. Why should the *akhund* concern himself with what Riza Shah is doing to the people? Let him go attend to his prayers. What is it to the *akhund* that back-breaking agreements are imposed on the country? Let him draw his cloak about himself and go to the mosque for prayers. After all, he's quite free to pray for anything he wants there; no one is going to stop him."

I do not believe that Jesus held the views on this question of religion and politics that are now attributed to him.[36] Could Jesus ever have taught people to accept oppression? All the prophets, including Jesus, were sent to root out injustice, but later, institutions arose that distorted the nature of religion. This happened also in the case of Islam; in every age, there were attempts to prevent its correct implementation.

So yes, the religious scholar will have a role in government. He does not want to be the ruler, but he does want to have a role. On this question of the presidency, there were proposals made to me, some of which even originated in the universities, that the President ought to be a religious leader, and I realized that that was because no one else would be trusted in the role. But I said, "No, the religious scholar does not wish to be President himself; he wishes instead to have a role in the presidency, a supervisory role.

He will exercise this role on behalf of the people. If the government begins to misbehave, the religious scholar will stand in its way."

Now the Constitution makes some provision for the principle of the governance of the *faqih*.[37] In my opinion, it is deficient in this regard. The religious scholars have more prerogatives in Islam than are specified in the Constitution, and the gentlemen in the Assembly of Experts[38] stopped short of the ideal in their desire not to antagonize the intellectuals! In any event, only part of the principle of the governance of the *faqih* is present in the Constitution, not all of it. Given the contingencies with which Islam has surrounded the operation of this principle, it cannot harm anyone. Particular attributes have been set down as necessary for the "holder of authority" (*vali amr*) and the *faqih,* and they are attributes that prevent him from going astray. If he utters a single lie, or takes a single wrong step, he forfeits his claim to governance. The whole purpose of the clause in the Constitution relating to the governance of the *faqih* is to prevent tyranny and despotism. Those who opposed the Constitution said that it instituted a form of tyranny, but how can that be? Whatever we do, it is always possible that some despot will come along in the future and try to do whatever he wants, but the *faqih* who possesses the attributes mentioned in the Constitution cannot, in the very nature of things, be a tyrant. On the contrary, he is just, not in the limited sense of social justice, but in the more rigorous and comprehensive sense that his quality of being just would be annulled if he were to utter a single lie, or cast a single glance at a woman past the degrees that are forbidden. Such a person will not act wrongly; on the contrary, he will seek to prevent others from acting wrongly. Justice,[39] in this sense, has not been made an essential qualification for the President; it is possible that he might wish to do something wrong, in which case the *faqih* will prevent him. If the head of the army tries one day to go beyond his functions, the *faqih* has the legal right to dismiss him. The most valuable part of the entire Constitution is that which relates to the governance of the *faqih;* those who oppose it are acting out of either ignorance or self-interest.

The religious scholars do not wish to become Prime Minister or President, and indeed it is not in their interest to do so. They do, however, have a role to play, a role that has always existed, even though they were pushed aside. Now God has given them the opportunity to fulfill this role as a result of the deeds wrought by our people: they rose up in revolt, and the religious scholars assumed their role. The role that they have is one of supervision, not of assuming executive positions without the proper expertise. It would make no sense, for example, for a religious leader to become the commander of a battalion if he is ignorant of military science. The expertise of the religious scholar lies in the area of Islamic law, that law which, if properly executed, secures us all our goals; and if he sees any mistake being made or any deviation from Islamic law occurring, he will move to prevent it.

This supervisory role is subject to particular conditions and principles to which we are bound. In addition, we are bound to follow the expressed wishes of the people. Once a religious leader has a role in government, he will not permit the President or the Prime Minister to practice oppression. Any power center that wishes to go beyond its bounds he will prevent from doing so. Any act tending toward dictatorship or the curbing of freedom he will also prevent. If the government wishes to conclude an agreement with a foreign power that brings about a relationship of dependence, the religious scholar will prevent it.

In summary, the religious leaders do not wish to be the government, but neither are they separate from the government. They do not wish to sit in the Prime Minister's residence and fulfill the duties of premiership, but at the same time, they will intervene to stop the Prime Minister if he takes a false step. The principle of the governance of the *faqih*, then, is a noble one, conducive to the welfare of the country. Once implemented, it will lead to the fulfillment of the hopes of the people.

Notes

1. I.e., the defamatory article published in the official Iranian press on January 8, 1978. See p. 19.

2. This statement is not, of course, intended to minimize the massive force and brutality employed by the Shah's regime against the Iranian people. It means rather that the Shah's regime was no longer seen as invincible once the people became imbued with the spirit of martyrdom and became prepared—and even eager—to pay the heavy price of their freedom.

3. This proclamation came in May 1978.

4. Sharif-Imami was installed as Prime Minister on August 27, 1978, and replaced on November 6 by General Ghulam Riza Azhari.

5. This prediction of Imam Khomeini came true with the installation of Shahpur Bakhtiar as Prime Minister on January 4, 1979; his tenure of the position, nominal toward the end, lasted a little more than a month.

6. See p. 315, n. 83.

7. The reference is in part general: to the rise of various Islamic movements in Turkey in the 1970's; and in part particular: to the events that took place in the southeastern Turkish city of Kahramanmaras shortly before this interview was conducted. During these events, the cry of "Islamic Turkey!" was raised. For a full account and analysis of the happenings in Kahramanmaras, see the Turkish Islamic weekly *Tevhid*, No. 4 (n.d.), pp. 13-16.

8. The movement for the foundation of an Islamic state in Afghanistan had already begun in the time of the monarchy. Its earliest stages are generally associated with the name of 'Abd ar-Rahim Niyazi, who died in 1971 while in prison (see his obituary in *Shar'iyat*, the journal of the Faculty of Theology of Kabul University, III No. 2 [Saratan 1350/July 1971]). The "additional factors" referred to are, of course, the Marxist coup d'etat in Kabul of April 27, 1978 and the ever-increasing Soviet intervention in Afghan affairs it brought in its wake.

9. Among the pro-Islamic groups would presumably be included Nihzat-i Azadi-yi Iran ("Iranian Freedom Movement"), a group formed in 1962 as an offshoot of the National Front; among groups containing both pro- and anti-Islamic elements, the National Front; and among those hostile to Islam, Marxist organizations like the Sazman-i Fida'iyan-i Khalq ("Organization of the People's Devotees") and the Tudeh Party.

10. *Fatiha:* the opening chapter of the Qur'an, recited as a funerary prayer over the dead.

11. This expression is drawn from Qur'an, 4:59.

12. The Azhar: the foremost institution of religious learning in Egypt. It has also enjoyed considerable prestige in other Muslim countries, despite its subservience to the state. Echoing Sadat's infatuation with the Iranian monarchy and hostility to the Islamic Revolution, the Azhar has several times lent its dubious authority to condemnation of the Revolution in general, and the person of Imam Khomeini in particular. See also p. 317, n. 111.

13. "O you who believe, obey God, and obey the Messenger and the holders of authority from among you" (4:59). It is true that a number of classical Sunni authorities including Mawardi (d. 450/1058), Ghazali (d. 505/1111), and Ibn Taymiya (d. 728/1328) attempted to legitimize both the hereditary caliphate and the usurpation of power by military dynasties, by means of their political theories. Their theories were in large part, however, an attempt to palliate the evil effects of a situation they saw no hope of changing. What is indisputable is that the influence of those theories has far outlived the circumstances that produced them and it continues to affect the political attitudes of Sunni Muslims, although it is now diminishing.

14. See pp. 77-78.

15. Cf. Qur'an, 25:44: "They [those who take their own passions for gods] are like cattle: indeed, they are more seriously astray."

16. Umayyads: see p. 153, n. 38.

17. Abbasids: see p. 153, n. 39.

18. A striking example of the "Arabism" of the Umayyads was provided by Hajjaj ibn Yusuf, governor of Iraq, when he forbade all non-Arab Muslims to lead the prayer in the cities under his jurisdiction. See Ibn 'Abd Rabbih, *al-'Iqd al-Farid* (Cairo, 1359/1940-1369/1950), II, 233.

19. Jahiliyya: the period of ignorance of divine guidance in the Arabian Peninsula that was brought to an end by the coming of Islam. Among the Arab leaders who wish to revive the Arabism of the Jahiliyya, the Baathist

rulers of Iraq are no doubt those whom Imam Khomeini had in mind primarily. He had been exposed to their capricious rule during his exile in Najaf. A fundamental point of Baathist ideology is the primacy of race over religion as the proper focus of loyalty and identity; see Michel 'Aflaq, *Fi Sabil al-Ba'th* (Beirut, 1963).

20. See p. 311, n. 54.

21. The British transported Riza Shah first to Mauritius and then to Johannesburg, where he died on July 26, 1944.

22. *Rauza:* see p. 164, n. 170.

23. *Takiya:* a building used for commemorative assemblies during the month of Muharram.

24. The two irreligious dictators met in 1934 when Riza Shah paid an official visit to Turkey. Among the measures Riza Shah enacted in imitation of Ataturk were the cultivation of an extreme form of nationalism, the imposition of sartorial "reforms" designed to make his subjects resemble Europeans, and the attempt to purge the Persian language of Arabic loanwords, with the substitution of neologisms that were frequently ludicrous. During his visit in 1934, Riza Shah evidently spent most of his time playing poker with his host and the British ambassador in Ankara. See Lord Kinross, *Ataturk* (London, 1964), p. 462.

25. See p. 162, n. 157.

26. See p. 162, n. 155.

27. The ghostwritten autobiography of the Shah (*Mission For My Country*) that appeared in a number of languages in 1961.

28. See p. 17.

29. The reference here is to arguments advanced by various non-Islamic elements before the referendum of March 29-30, 1979 in which the Iranian people were asked to choose between monarchy and an Islamic republic as their form of government. The referendum yielded a 98% majority in favor of an Islamic republic.

30. After a period of formal discussion in an elected Assembly of Experts, as well as informal discussion in the press and public media, the Constitution of the Islamic Republic of Iran was submitted to a referendum December 2 and 3, 1979 and approved by an overwhelming majority. The allegedly problematic aspects of the Constitution relate chiefly to the respective functions of the Leader (see Articles 107 to 112) and the President, and the interrelation between divine and popular sovereignty.

31. See, for example, the speech given on the sixteenth anniversary of the uprising of Khurdad 15, on pp. 268-274.

32. "Nationalists" refers to those individuals who propagate a secular nationalism and present themselves as the heirs of Dr. Muhammad Musaddiq.

33. This story is to be found, in slightly different form, in the *Masnavi* of Jalal ad-Din Rumi, where the three thieves are a Sufi, a *faqih*, and a sayyid (see *Masnavi*, II, lines 2167-2211). The ultimate source of the story appears to be the *Jawami' al-Hikayat* of 'Aufi, the seventh-/thirteenth-century litterateur. See Badi' az-Zaman Furuzanfar, *Ma'akhiz-i Qisas va Tamsilat-i Masnavi* (Tehran, 1347 Sh./1968), pp. 67-68.

34. *Akhund:* see p. 150, n. 5.

35. Akhundism: a word coined to designate the allegedly excessive role played by the religious scholars in Islamic society. It was used in particular by the terrorist group Furqan that assassinated a number of close associates of Imam Khomeini in 1979. See the preface by Hamid Algar to Ali Shari'ati, *Marxism and Other Western Fallacies: An Islamic Critique*, trans. R. Campbell (Berkeley, 1980), pp. 9-10.

36. See also Imam Khomeini's remarks addressed to the Papal Nuncio, on pp. 278-285.

37. Chapter Eight is devoted to this subject (see *Constitution of the Islamic Republic of Iran*, trans. Hamid Algar [Berkeley, 1980], pp. 66-69).

38. The Assembly of Experts that revised the draft constitution and drew up the text that was finally approved was elected on August 3, 1979 and completed its work on November 15, 1979.

39. Concerning the particular meaning that "justice" bears in this context, see p. 152, n. 21.

IV

Lecture on the Supreme Jihad

In late 1972, Imam Khomeini delivered a second series of lectures in Najaf, again to an audience of students of the religious sciences. The lectures were recorded, transcribed, and published the following year under the title Mubaraza ba Nafs ya Jihad-i Akbar *("The Struggle Against the Appetitive Soul, or the Supreme Jihad").*

This second series served in many ways as a counterpart to the first, delivered in 1970 on the subject of Islamic government. Whereas the first series dealt mainly with the institutional, political, and legal aspects of Islam, the second is primarily concerned with the moral purification and spiritual advancement that must be joined to political activity in order to make it Islamically valid and effective. The reader may recall that it was initially as a lecturer on ethics and gnosis that Imam Khomeini acquired renown in Qum; these lectures are one reminder that this dimension of his activity has never been displaced by the tasks of political struggle and leadership.

The extract we have chosen (pp. 71-98 of the original text) is part of a commentary on a passage from the "Invocations of Sha'ban," a litany recited by all the Imams during the month of Sha'ban. Imam Khomeini always concluded his lectures on ethics in Qum with a sentence from this litany (see Muhammad Razi, Asar al-Hujja [Qum, 1332 Sh./1953], II, 45), which also occurs in one of his lectures on the opening verses of the Qur'an (see p 420): "O God, grant me total separation from other-than-You and attachment to You, and brighten the vision of our hearts with the light of looking upon You, so that they may pierce the veils of light and attain the fountainhead of magnificence, and our spirits may be suspended from the splendor of Your sanctity." This litany has held an important and constant place in the spiritual life of Imam Khomeini, and that one sentence of it in particular may be regarded as a kind of personal motto.

THE FOUNTAINHEAD
OF MAGNIFICENCE

WHEN MAN ORIENTS HIMSELF to other-than-God, veils of darkness and light envelop him. All the worldly affairs that cause man to devote his attention to the world and become unaware of God Almighty give rise to veils of darkness; indeed, all corporeal realms become a series of such veils. But when worldly affairs lead man to orient himself to reality and aspire to the hereafter—which is the realm where man is to be ennobled—the veils of darkness are transformed into veils of light. Total separation from this world is achieved when all veils, both those of darkness and those of light, have been drawn or torn aside, allowing man to enter the divine hospice that is the "fountainhead of magnificence."[1] That is why the Commander of the Faithful petitions God Almighty in his famous invocation for the vision and luminosity of heart—so that penetrating the veils of light, he may attain the fountainhead of magnificence.

But one who has not penetrated even the veils of darkness— one whose whole attention is directed to the natural world, who (God forbid) has completely turned away from God, and who is completely unaware of what lies beyond this world, the realm of spirituality—is subjugated to nature. He will never reach the stage of refining himself, of creating spiritual, inner motion and energy within himself and casting aside the black veils that overshadow his heart. He remains at a standstill at the lowest of the low, the outermost of the veils of darkness ("Then We sent him down to the lowest of the low," Qur'an, 95:5), whereas the Lord of the World has created man in the highest station and rank: "Truly We created man in the fairest of forms" (95:4). Anyone who follows the desires of his carnal self and devotes his attention exclusively to the dark world of nature from the first day that he attains consciousness of himself, never thinking that apart from this dark and polluted world another place and abode may exist—such a person is completely caught up in veils of darkness, and serves as an illustration of the verse: "He inclined to the earth, and followed his own vain desires" (7:166). With his heart polluted by sin and enveloped in veils of darkness, and his constricted spirit distanced from God Almighty by the abundance of his sin and rebellion, and his intelligence and eye, which otherwise would have been capable of seeing the truth, blinded by his servitude to passion and his worship of the world, he will never be able to escape from the veils of darkness, let alone penetrate the veils of light and become fully absorbed in God. Even if such a person does not deny the station of the *awliya*[2] and does not regard the intermediate realms, the bridge of Sirat,[3] the return to God's presence, resurrection, the reckoning and judging, paradise and hellfire as mythical, he will nonetheless, as a result of his sins and attachment to the world, gradually come to deny these truths and to refuse to acknowledge the stations of the *awliya*.

Occasionally you encounter a person who has knowledge of these realities but does not believe in them. The washer of the dead does not fear the dead, for he is very certain that the dead have no power to harm or injure him; even when alive, with spirit still joined to bodily shell, they were quite harmless, and now their shells are empty of spirit. Those who fear the dead do so because they have only knowledge of these truths, not certain conviction. Similarly, men have knowledge of God and the Day of Requital,[4] but do not have full belief in them; the heart is unaware of what the intellect has perceived. They know by means of rational proofs that there is a God, a return to His presence, a resurrection; but the proofs may themselves come to serve as a veil over their hearts, preventing the light of faith from shining upon them, so that God Almighty might bring them forth out of the darkness and shadows and into the realm of light and brilliance: "God is the Protector of those who believe; He brings them forth from the darkness into the light" (2:257). The one whom God the Protector has brought forth from darkness into light will no longer sin. He will not backbite, he will not engage in false accusation, he will not feel envy toward his Muslim brothers and, with luminosity in his heart, he will attribute no value to the world and all it contains. Thus the Commander of the Faithful (upon whom be peace) said: "If I were offered the world and all that it contains on condition that I steal a barley husk from the mouth of an ant, I would not accept it."[5]

But some of you trample everything underfoot, and even slander the great ones of Islam. While other people may slander and abuse the corner grocer, there are some who rudely insult and make false accusations against the *'ulama*.[6] The reason for this is that their faith has not yet firmly taken root: they do not believe in the existence of punishment for their deeds and conduct.

'Ismat[7] derives, in fact, from the perfection of faith. The *'ismat* of the prophets and the *awliya*, for example, does not mean that Gabriel has taken them protectively by the hand (though, of course, if Gabriel were to have taken Shimr[8] by the hand, even he would never have sinned). Rather, *'ismat* is the product of faith. If a man believes in God Almighty and with the eye of his heart sees Him as clearly as he sees the sun, it is impossible for him to commit any act of sin or rebellion against Him. The fear of a powerful presence will always deter man from falling into sin.

As for the *ma'sumin* (upon whom be peace), not only were they created out of a pure substance, but they also constantly perceived themselves to be in the presence of God Almighty, Who knows and encompasses all things, as a result of their ascetic exercises and the acquisition of luminosity and noble virtues. They had complete faith in the meaning of *"La ilaha illa 'Llah,"* believing that all persons and things except God are destined to perish and cannot play any role in the destiny of man: "All things shall perish but His face" (28:88). If a man has certain faith that all the realms of creation, seen and unseen, are a form of divine presence and that God Almighty is present everywhere and watches over all things, given this awareness of God's presence, as well as the enjoyment of God's gifts, is it at all possible that he will commit sin? A person will not commit sin or do anything shameful in the presence of a perceptive child; how is it that he will do so in the presence and awareness of God Almighty and have no fear or hesitation in committing crime of all kinds? It is because he believes in the presence of the child but does not believe in the divine presence, although he may have knowledge of it. Indeed, as a result of the multiplicity of sins that have blackened and darkened his heart, he can no longer accept the truths of religion; he considers it improbable that they are true and correct. In fact, it is not necessary that a person have certain faith; it is enough that he regard the promises and threats set down in the Noble Qur'an as probably true and revise his conduct so that he ceases his unrestrained and carefree sinning.

If you regard it as likely that there is a wild beast along the route you are to travel and that it may harm you, or that an armed bandit is lying in wait for you, you will decide not to take that route; you will stop and think things over. Is it possible that someone would regard it as likely that hellfire exists, as well as the prospect of burning in it eternally, and still commit offenses against God? Someone who knows God Almighty to be present everywhere and watching over all things, who perceives himself to be in the divine presence, who believes that there will be requital for his words and deeds, that an accounting and recompense will take place, that every word he utters in this world, every step he takes, and every deed he performs is being recorded and registered, that God's angels are watching him vigilantly, recording all his words and deeds—is it possible that such a person will undauntedly continue to sin?

The problem is that people do not consider these truths to be even likely. The conduct, manners, and behavior of certain people clearly indicate that they see the existence of any world beyond the natural world as improbable, for to view it simply as probable would be enough to deter them from many evil deeds.

How much longer do you wish to continue your sleep of neglect, to remain immersed in evil and corruption? Fear God and the consequences of your deeds; wake up from your sleep of neglect. You have not yet awakened and taken the first step on the path of wayfaring, for awakening is the first step. Yes, you are asleep. Your eyes are open, but your hearts are deep in sleep.[10]

If your hearts were not intoxicated with sleep and black and rusted with sin, you would not be able to continue so tranquilly and heedlessly with your wrong deeds and words. Were you to think a little about the hereafter and the places of horror it contains, or to reflect on the heavy duties and responsibilities you bear, you would take these matters more seriously.

You have another world ahead of you; there is resurrection and a return to the divine presence awaiting you. You are not like other creatures who face no return. Why do you not take heed? Why do you not awaken and come to your senses? Why do you engage so nonchalantly in backbiting and slandering your Muslim brothers, or cheerfully listen to others doing it? Are you at all aware that the tongue that is now busy backbiting will be trodden underfoot by others on the Day of Resurrection? Do you know that the backbiter will be devoured by the dogs of hellfire?[11] Have you ever reflected on the evil consequences of all these disputes, all this enmity, envy, pessimism, selfishness, pride, and arrogance? Do you know that the outcome of all these vile and forbidden things is hellfire, and that (God forbid) they may earn you an eternity there?

May God preserve man from affliction by diseases that are without pain, for while diseases that cause pain impel man to seek a cure, to go to a doctor or the hospital, a disease without pain remains unfelt and is therefore more dangerous; it is often too late when a man finally learns of his disease.

Diseases of the spirit are of this type. If they involved pain, it would be something of an advantage; one would be impelled to go seek a remedy or cure. But what is to be done, for these dangerous diseases produce no pain? The disease of arrogance and selfishness, for example, causes no pain. Other sins, too, corrupt the heart and the spirit without causing any pain, and indeed these diseases not only cause man no pain but even appear pleasurable to him. Sessions and circles devoted to backbiting are very lively and enjoyable! Self-love and love of the world, which lie at the root of all sin, are also very pleasurable. The dropsy sufferer will be destroyed by water, but he continues to drink it with enjoyment until his very last breath. If a person derives pleasure from a disease, and moreover, it entails no pain, he will never seek to be cured of it. However much he is warned that the disease will prove fatal, he will not believe it.

Once a man is afflicted with the disease of worshipping this world and desiring his own passions, and his heart is completely immersed in love of this world, anything that does not pertain to this world will disgust him. He will (God forbid) become hostile to God, to God's servants, to His prophets, *awliya*, and angels; he will feel rancor and hatred toward them. When the angels, upon God's command, come to take his soul, he will feel strong disgust and repulsion because God and His angels are about to separate him from his beloved, this world and the things of this world. Thus he may depart this world in a state of enmity and hostility to God. One of the great men of Qazvin[12] (may God have mercy upon him) related that he once went to the bedside of a dying man. In the last minutes of his life, the man opened his eyes and said: "No one has done me the wrong that God is now doing! What anxious care I lavished on my children while bringing them up, but now He wants to separate me from them! What wrong could be greater than this?" If man does not remedy his state and detach himself from the world by ridding his heart of love for it, it is to be feared that he will surrender his soul with a heart full of resentment and hatred toward God and His *awliya*. Evil and dangerous consequences such as these await man, who, though the noblest of creatures, still may come to suffer an ignoble fate. Is the man who abhors all restraint the noblest of creatures or, in reality, the worst?

"By the Age! Verily man is in a state of loss, except those who believe and perform good deeds, and enjoin truth upon each other, and enjoin patience upon each other" (103:1-3). In this *sura*, the only persons exempt from a state of loss are those believers who performed good deeds; that is to say, deeds that are in conformity with the spirit. But you see that many of the deeds men perform are in conformity with their bodies instead, and there is no question of their enjoining truth and patience upon each other.

If it seems that love of the world and self-love are about to gain dominance over you and prevent you from perceiving truths and realities and devoting your deeds more fully to God, and about to hinder you from enjoining patience and truth upon each other, then indeed you are in a state of loss; you will have lost both this world and the hereafter. For you have renounced your youth, you have nothing of this world, and in addition, you will be deprived of the blessings of paradise and the bounties of the hereafter.[13] It is true that there are others who will not be admitted to God's paradise; the gates of His mercy will be closed to them and they will remain eternally in hellfire. But at least they will have enjoyed this world and its goods. The same cannot be said of you.

Beware lest (God forbid) love of the world and self-love begin to increase in you to the point where Satan is able to take away your faith. It is said that all the efforts of Satan are devoted to this one goal; all his wiles and exertions, by day and by night, have as their purpose to snatch away men's faith. No one ever gave you a guarantee that you would retain your faith permanently. Your faith may only have been given to you on trust, so that in the end, Satan will succeed in taking it from you and you will leave this world full of hostility toward God Almighty and His *awliya*. You will have enjoyed God's blessings for a whole lifetime, seated at the banquet of the Imam of the Age (may God hasten his appearance), but when you surrender your soul, you will be (God forbid) without faith, and an enemy to Him Who has provided for you.

If you have any tie or link binding you to this world in love, try to sever it. This world, despite all its apparent splendor and charm, is too worthless to be loved, particularly if one is deprived of what it has to offer.[14] What do you possess in this world that makes you so attached to it? All you have are these mosques, *mihrabs*,[15] *madrasas*, and the corners of your cells. Is it true that you compete with one another for these mosques and *mihrabs*, creating division among yourselves and corruption in society? Even if you did enjoy a prosperous and comfortable life, like the worldly, and (God forbid) spent your life in enjoyment and pleasure, in the end you would perceive that it all passed like a pleasant dream, while the heavy penalties you incurred would remain with you forever. What value does this transient and seemingly sweet life (supposing that it is indeed spent pleasantly) have when compared to infinite torment? For the torment suffered by those attached to this world is indeed sometimes infinite.

Those attached to this world are mistaken when they imagine that they are in possession of it and its various benefits and advantages. Everyone looks upon the world through the aperture of his own environment and place of residence, and imagines that the world consists of what he possesses. But this corporeal world is vaster than man can even imagine, let alone traverse or possess. Despite all the adornments with which He equipped it, God has never looked upon this world with mercy, according to a certain tradition. We must see, then, what the other world is upon which God, Almighty and Exalted, did look in mercy, and what the "fountainhead of magnificence" is to which He is summoning man.

It is true that man is too petty a being to understand fully what the "fountainhead of magnificence" is. But if you purify the intention with which you perform your acts of worship, make your deeds truly righteous, rid your hearts of self-love and ambitiousness, lofty stations and elevated degrees await you. Compared to the rank God Almighty has prepared for His righteous servants, the whole world with its false allure counts as nothing. Strive, then, to attain those lofty stations and if you are able, try to advance to such a point that even those lofty stations and elevated degrees become a matter of indifference to you, so that you do not worship God for their sake, but rather call upon Him as befits His glory, prostrating yourselves before Him. It is then that, penetrating the veils of light, you will have attained the "fountainhead of magnificence."

Given your present conduct and deeds, and the path you are following, will you ever be able to attain that station? Will it be easy to escape divine punishment and evade the terror and the fire of hell? Do you imagine that the tears of the Imams and the lamentations of Imam Zayn al-'Abidin Sajjad[16] (upon whom be peace) were merely for the edification of others? Despite all their spirituality and the high rank they had attained, they wept in fear of God and knew how difficult and dangerous the path was that lay before them. They were aware of the difficulties, hardships, and hazards that attend the crossing of the Bridge of Sirat, which joins this world to the hereafter and which passes over hellfire. They were conscious of the world of the tomb, the intermediate world, resurrection and its terrors. They were therefore never at peace, and constantly took refuge in God from the severe punishments of the hereafter.

What provision have you made against these overwhelming terrors and punishments? What path of salvation have you found? When do you intend to begin reforming yourselves? If you do not begin purifying yourselves now while you are young and possess the energy of youth, enjoying full control of your capacities without suffering from physical weakness, how will you be able to do so when you are old: when you are prey, body and soul, to weakness, apathy, and cold; when you have lost your willpower, resolve, and ability to resist; and when the weight of sin and rebellion against God has further blackened your heart? With every breath and step that you take, with every passing moment of your life, the task of self-reform becomes more difficult, and darkness and corruption increase. As man's age advances, the obstacles to his happiness increase, and his strength to resist them decreases. So when you reach old age, your chances for success in purifying and reforming yourselves and attaining virtue and piety are small. You will be unable to repent, for repentance is not accomplished simply by saying, "I turn to God in repentance"; it requires regret and firm resolve to abandon sin, and such regret and firm resolve are impossible for persons who have engaged in backbiting and slander for fifty or seventy years, whose beards have grown grey in the commission of sin. Such people will be caught up in sin to the end of their lives.

The young should not neglect this task, for one day the dust of old age will whiten them and their beards (I have reached old age and know well what difficulties and miseries it brings). While you are still young you can accomplish something. While you still have the energy and willpower of youth, you can ward off from yourselves passionate desires, worldly longings, and animal wants. But if you do not begin to reform yourselves in youth, it will be too late in old age.

The heart of the young is pure and subtle; the corrupt impulses within it are weak. But as man's age advances, the roots of sin in his heart become firmer and stronger until it becomes impossible to pluck them out. According to a certain tradition, "The heart of man is at first like a mirror, pure and luminous. Whenever he commits a sin, a black spot appears on it, and the more he sins, the more the black spots increase until the whole of the heart is blackened, and neither a day nor a night will pass without his sinning against God." When one reaches old age, it is difficult for a man to restore his heart to its original state.

If (God forbid) you do not reform yourselves, and you depart this world with blackened hearts, with eyes, ears, and tongues polluted by sin, how will you meet God? How will you return to Him the divine trust, polluted and stained, that was given to you pure and spotless? These eyes and ears that you possesss, this hand and tongue that are at your command, these limbs and members that enable you to live, were all utterly pure and whole when they were given you as trusts by God Almighty. If they have now been polluted by sin, made vile by the commission of forbidden acts, you will be asked when you wish to return them, "Is this the way in which a trust is kept? Is this the state the trusts were in when We gave them to you? Is this the same eye that We gave to you, the same heart that We gave to you? Were all these other limbs and members so polluted and filthy?" What answer will you give to these questions? How will you meet your God after thus misusing the trusts He has given you?

You are young, but you have sacrificed your youth in order to study the religious sciences, even though it will not greatly benefit you from a worldly standpoint. If you devote your precious time and the spring of your youth to the cause of God and a sacred, precise aim, you will not lose anything. On the contrary, your welfare in this world and the hereafter will be assured. But if you continue in the state I now observe among you, you will have wasted your youth, and the choice part of your life will have been squandered. In the next world you will be called to a severe accounting by God. If the punishment for your deeds of corruption is not confined to the next world, you will also suffer various grave misfortunes in this world and be plunged into a whirlpool of disaster.

Notes

1. A phrase from the Supplications of Sha'ban. The passage in which it occurs is quoted in full in Imam Khomeini's fifth lecture on the opening chapter of the Qur'an; see p. 420.

2. *Awliya:* those who possess the quality of intrinsic *vilayat* (see p. 155, n. 63 above). In Shi'i belief, they are the foremost among the prophets and the Twelve Imams who succeeded to the Prophet Muhammad. In the present context, it is primarily the Imams that are meant, but we have retained the word *awliya* because it indicates primarily their spiritual rank, whereas the word *imam* designates their function of leadership.

3. Sirat: the narrow bridge in the hereafter that leads to paradise.

4. Day of Requital: the Day of Judgment.

5. *Nahj al-Balagha,* ed. Subhi as-Salih (Beirut, 1397/1967).

6. This reprimand is directed to some of Imam Khomeini's younger followers among the students of the religious sciences in Najaf for excessive ebullience in their hostility to passive and apolitical religious leaders like Ayatullah Khu'i. Apart from its impropriety, their behavior tended to further the plans of the Shah's regime to create two warring camps in the religious establishment. Imam Khomeini—both in Najaf and in Qum—was scrupulous in his determination to prevent this from happening.

7. *'Ismat:* see p. 156, n. 67.

8. Shimr: the Umayyad general who martyred Imam Husayn during the battle at Karbala.

9. *Ma'sumin:* see p. 162, n. 154.

10. Cf. the tradition of the Prophet: "People are asleep; when they die, they awaken."

11. See the traditions quoted by al-Ghazali in *Ihya' 'Ulum ad-Din* (Cairo, n.d.), III, 138-141.

12. Qazvin: a city in northwest Iran.

13. The audience this lecture addresses—the religious students—has given up its youth by submitting to the moral regimen and material hardship of the madrasa life.

14. This sentence, and others similar to it in content, should not be taken to imply a deprecation of the world as an arena for striving to attain divine pleasure or as a vast system of divine signs. It is not a call to other-worldliness, as Imam Khomeini's whole life makes plain. The "world" that is being condemned here is the aggregate of earthly attachments and goals to which a man assigns absolute and quasi-divine value. This is made explicit in the second lecture on Surat al-Fatiha; see p. 388.

15. *Mihrab:* the niche in the mosque indicating the direction of the Ka'ba (God's House in Mecca), the point of orientation for worship.

16. Imam Zayn al-'Abidin Sajjad: the fourth of the Twelve Imams. He was the only son of Imam Husayn to survive the massacre at Karbala. He spent the rest of his life in Medina, dying there in 95/712. He composed a book of fifty-seven prayers known as the *Sahifa-yi Sajjadiya,* which is one of the major Shi'i manuals of prayer.

V

Lectures on Surat al-Fatiha

After the triumph of the Revolution in February 1979, Ayatullah Taleghani gave a series of televised lectures on the interpretation of the Qur'an, under the title Qur'an dar Sahna *("The Qur'an on Stage"). They proved immensely popular. After his death on September 10, 1979, the program was suspended until Imam Khomeini consented to give the following five lectures on* Surat al-Fatiha *(or* Surat al-Hamd, *as it is called in Iran), the opening chapter of the Qur'an.*

Although he never proceeds beyond the second verse of the chapter (and engages in what appear to be numerous lengthy digressions), the designation "On Surat al-Fatiha" is appropriate. The point of departure and return is always the opening chapter, and more importantly, the wide range of subjects evoked illustrates the fact that the chapter contains the whole of Islam compressed within it—that it is "the mother of the Book," as the Prophet designated it.

Surprisingly, no carefully edited text of the lectures has yet been published in Iran. Our translation is based upon a collation of two versions: one containing the first four lectures, printed by the Muslim Women's Movement (Nihzat-i Zanan-i Musalman) *as pamphlets 11 and 21 in their series of ideological publications; and the other from the daily newspaper* Jumhuri-yi Islami, *on Days 1, 10, 15, 22, and 29, 1358/December 22 and 31, 1979 and January 5, 12, and 19, 1980. Both versions are marred by numerous orthographical and other errors, particularly in the first two lectures. It did prove possible to construct a usable text, however, and although the translation may not correspond word for word in all cases to the original remarks of Imam Khomeini, it accurately conveys their sense.*

1

EVERYTHING IS A NAME OF GOD

THE INTERPRETATION OF THE QUR'AN is to be the topic for a few lectures I have been asked to give. The interpretation of the Qur'an is not an easy task for someone like myself. Throughout history the eminent scholars of Islam, both Sunni and Shi'i, have written numerous books on this subject, and their efforts have, of course, been most valuable. But each of them wrote from the standpoint of his own specialization and skill and could interpret only a certain aspect of the Qur'an, and do that much only imperfectly.

For example, commentaries have been written over the centuries by such mystics as Muhyi'd-Din ibn 'Arabi,[1] 'Abd ar-Razzaq Kashani (author of *Ta'wilat*),[2] and Mulla Sultar 'Ali.[3] Some of these commentators wrote well from the standpoint of their specialization and skill. But what they wrote is not commensurate to the Qur'an; it represents only a few pages or aspects of the Qur'an. Tantawi,[4] Sayyid Qutb,[5] and others like them interpreted the Qur'an in a different way, but their work too does not represent a complete interpretation of the Qur'an with respect to all of its meanings; again, it is concerned only with a single aspect of the Qur'an. There are other commentaries still that do not belong to either of these groups; for example, the *Majma' al-Bayan*,[6] which we Shi'is use, is a good commentary that includes the views of both Sunni and Shi'i exegetes, but it, too, is not exhaustive.

The Qur'an is not a book that someone can interpret comprehensively and exhaustively, for its sciences are unique and ultimately beyond our understanding. We can understand only a given aspect or dimension of the Qur'an; interpretation of the rest depends upon the *ahl-i 'ismat*[7] who received instruction from the Messenger of God. Recently, people have appeared who, without the slightest qualification for interpreting the Qur'an, try to impose their own objectives and ideas upon both the Qur'an and the Sunna; even a group of leftists and communists now claims to be basing themselves and their aims on the Qur'an.[8] Their real interest is not the Qur'an or its interpretation, but trying to convince our young people to accept their objectives under the pretext that they are Islamic. I emphasize, therefore, that those who have not pursued religious studies, young people who are not well grounded in Islamic matters, and all who are uninformed concerning Islam should not attempt to interpret the Qur'an. If they do so nevertheless for the sake of their own goals, no one should pay any attention to their interpretations. One of the things that is forbidden in Islam is interpretation of the Qur'an according to personal opinion, or attempting to make the Qur'an conform to one's own opinions. Let us suppose that one man is a materialist and tries to make every verse in the Qur'an conform to his materialist notions, while another is concerned exclusively with spiritual matters, so that every part of the Qur'an he encounters will be interpreted in the light of his preoccupation. They both represent extremes and attitudes that are to be avoided.

In interpreting the Qur'an, then, we are subject to certain restrictions. The field is not open for anyone to try to impose on the Qur'an any idea that enters his head and then tell people, "*This* is the Qur'an." Now if I say a few words concerning certain verses of the Qur'an, I do not in any way claim to be expounding their ultimate meaning. What I say represents a possibility, not a certainty; I do not say, "This, and nothing else, is the true meaning."

Because I have been asked, then, to say a few words on these subjects, I will speak briefly every few days or once a week, for a limited period, concerning the opening chapter of the Qur'an or one of the last chapters, for neither I nor other people have time for a detailed interpretation of the Qur'an. I will briefly set forth some of the noble verses of the Qur'an, and I repeat that what I have to say is based on possibility, not certainty.

I will begin with the blessed Sura of Praise:

I take refuge in God from Satan the accursed. In the Name of God, the Compassionate, the Merciful. Praise belongs to God, the Lord of the Worlds.

It is probable that this phrase, "In the Name of God," at the beginning of all *suras* of the Qur'an is syntactically connected to the verses that follow it. It is sometimes said that the phrase is connected to an implied statement that follows upon it, but it seems more likely that it is connected to the *sura* itself. So we understand the Sura of Praise in this sense: "In the Name of God, the Compassionate, the Merciful, praise belongs to God."

A name is a sign. Names are given to people and assigned to things in order to provide them with a sign by which they may be recognized and to distinguish them one from another. The names of God are also signs, signs of His Sacred Essence; and it is only His names that are knowable to man. The Essence Itself is something that lies totally beyond the reach of man, and even the Seal of the Prophets,[9] the most knowledgeable and noble of men, was unable to attain knowledge of the Essence. The Sacred Essence is unknown to all but Itself. It is the names of God that are accessible to man. There are, however, different levels for understanding those names. We can understand them at certain levels, but comprehension at other levels is reserved for the *awliy* i,[10] for the Most Noble Messenger and those whom he has instructed.

The whole world is a name of God, for a name is a sign, and all the creatures that exist in the world are signs of the Sacred Essence of God Almighty. Here some people may reach a profound understanding of what is meant by "signs," while others may grasp only the general meaning that no creature comes into existence by itself.

It is a rationally self-evident proposition, intuitively understood by every human being, that no being can come into existence by itself—no being for which it is possible both to exist and not to exist. For such a being to come into existence, there must be a being that exists by virtue of its essence, that is, a being from whom existence cannot be withdrawn, unlike other beings for whom it is possible both to exist and not to exist. These require that something external to them bring them into existence.

There are those who say that infinite space existed from the very beginning and that within this infinitude, forms came into existence, followed first by vapors and gases and then by forms of life. It is against the dictates of reason, however, that a thing would change into something other than itself without the action of an external cause. Such a cause is always needed for the transformation of one thing into something different, as for example when water freezes or boils. If the temperature did not pass below zero or above one hundred degrees (both of these being external causes), the water would remain just as it is. Likewise, an external cause is required to make water stagnate.

Equally, anyone who reflects a little will regard it as rationally self-evident, and assent to the proposition, that in the case of a thing that may exist or not exist, its non-existence as opposed to its existence does not require a cause. But its transformation from a contingent being that does not exist to a contingent being that does exist is inconceivable without a cause.

As for the proposition that all beings in the world are a name and a sign of God, any rational person can understand it in the general sense, in light of our foregoing discussion of causality. But to attain a real understanding of the matter, we must realize that here it is not a question of naming something or someone in order to render it knowable to other-than-itself, as, for example, when we attach a name to a lamp, a car, or a man. For God is a being that is infinite, that possesses the attributes of perfection to an infinite degree, and that is subject to no limitation. A being that is unlimited in this manner cannot be contingent, for it is in the nature of a contingent being to be limited. If there is no limitation in the existence of a thing, then, reason dictates that it cannot be other than the absolute and necessary being that possesses all forms of perfection, for once a being lacks a single form of perfection, it becomes limited and thus contingent. The difference between contingent and necessary being is that the latter is infinite in all respects and constitutes absolute being, whereas the former is, in its nature, finite. If it turns out that all of the attributes of perfection are not present to an infinite degree in the being we thought necessary, it is no longer regarded as necessary, but instead as contingent.

Now if we take necessary being as the origin and source of all other being, the beings that come into existence as a result of its origination inherently represent the aggregate of its attributes. These attributes, however, exist in different degrees, and the highest degree is that wherein all the attributes of God Almighty are contained, to the extent that it is possible for a word to subsume them. This highest degree of the attributes is represented by the Supreme Name,[11] which consists of the name or the sign that contains, however defectively, all the perfections of God Almighty. Although it is defective with respect to God, it is perfect with respect to all other beings. Beings that are subordinate to the Supreme Name also possess perfection, but to an inferior degree, one limited by their inherent capacity. The lowest degree is represented by material beings, which we imagine have neither knowledge of any form of perfection nor the capacity to acquire it. This belief is not true, however, and is caused by our being veiled from the truth. These beings, which are lower than man and the animals and are deficient, still have the divine perfections reflected in them, but to a degree dictated by their inherent capacity. They even have perception, the same perception that is present in man. "There is naught but glorifies and praises Him, but you understand not their glorifying" (17:44).

Since it has been considered impossible for material beings to have perception, it has been said that they are an example of static glorification, although the verse just quoted does not indicate this. We know that it cannot be a question of such glorification because they are material beings subject to causes. Traditions describe certain material beings as engaging in glorification, for example, the pebbles that were held in the hands of the Most Noble Messenger.[12] Their glorification of God was a kind inaudible to your ear or mine, and their language and speech were different from ours, yet it still involved perception, perception to a degree dictated by the inherent capacity of the pebbles. It may be that men, who possess the higher degrees of perception and regard themselves as the source of all perception, have wished to deny all perception to other orders of being. It is true, of course, that those orders do not possess the same high degree of perception, but we, too, are veiled from full perception of the truth. Because of those veils, we are not fully aware, and because we are not fully aware, we imagine many things not to be that are. It is simply that you and I are alien to them. Today many things are becoming known that previously were not. For example, although the vegetable realm was formerly thought to lack consciousness, it is now said that a certain kind of sensor can pick up sounds from the roots of a tree when they are immersed in boiling water. I do not know if this is true or not, but it is certain that the whole world is alive and in ferment.

Everything is a name of God. You, too, are names of God; your tongues are names of God, you hands are names of God. When you praise God, saying, "In the Name of God, praise belongs to God," your tongue is a name of God as it moves. When you get up to go home, you cannot separate yourself from the names of God: you go in the name of God, and you are the name of God; the movements of your heart are the names of God, and the movements of your pulse are the name of God. The winds that are blowing are the name of God.

This is a possible meaning of the noble verse we have cited, as well as others where mention is made of the name of God. Everything is a name of God; conversely, the names of God are everything, and they are effaced within His being.

We imagine that we have some independence, that we are something in and of ourselves. It is not so. Were those rays of absolute being that every instant create us with an expression of the divine will and a manifestation of God to cease for a second, all beings would instantly lose their state of existence, reverting to their original state of non-existence, for their continued existence depends on His continued manifestation.

It is by means of God's manifestation that the whole world has acquired existence; that manifestation, or light, is the origin and essence of being. "God is the light of the heavens and earth" (24: 35), and conversely, the heavens and earth are His light or manifestation; the light of all that exists is from God. Whatever emerges from potentiality into actuality, whatever appears in this world, is light, for the characteristic of light is to appear and be visible. Man appears and is visible, and is light; the animals are light;

all beings are light, the light of God. "God is the light of the heavens and the earth"—that is, the existence of the heavens and earth is from light and from God. So destined to effacement in the divine being are the heavens and earth that the verse says, "God is the light of the heavens," not "The heavens are illumined by God," which would imply a certain mode of separation. "God is the light of the heavens"—that is, they are nothing in and of themselves, and there is no being in the world that possesses independence. By "independence," we mean here a being's leaving the stage of contingency and advancing to that of necessity, which is impossible, since God Almighty alone is the necessary being. Therefore, when God says, "In the Name of God, praise belongs to God," or "In the Name of God, say, 'God is One' " (112:1), the meaning probably is not so much that we are to say, "*In* the Name of God, the Compassionate, the Merciful," as "*With* the Name of God," where your speaking is a name of God.

Notice, too, that the Qur'an says, "Whatever is in the heavens and earth glorifies Him," not "Whoever is in the heavens and earth. . . ." Whatever exists on earth and in the heavens glorifies God by means of the name that is His manifestation. All beings share in this manifestation; all motion that takes place derives from it, and all that occurs in the world proceeds from it. Since all things proceed from Him and return to Him, and no being has anything in and of itself, there can be no question of the independent possession of anything. Is there anyone who can say, "I have something in and of myself," that is, "Independently of the light that is the origin of my being, I have something"? What you have is not yours; even the eye you have is not yours. It came into being through His manifestation. The praise and laudation we offer in concert with all other beings is with the name of God and by the name of God; it is for this reason that God has said, "In the Name of God."

The name God (*Allah*)[13] is a comprehensive manifestation; it is a manifestation of God Almighty that embraces all other manifestations, including those of Compassionate and Merciful. To put it differently, the name of God (*Allah*) is a manifestation of God, and the names Compassionate and Merciful are, in turn, manifestations of that manifestation. God, the Compassionate One, created all beings with mercy and compassion, and existence itself is mercy. Even the existence bestowed on creatures known to be evil is mercy, universal mercy that embraces all beings; all beings are mercy.

The name God (*Allah*), then, is the fullest and most complete manifestation; it is a comprehensive name and manifestation. The Essence of God Almighty does not Itself have a name: "He has neither name nor trace."[14] As for the names Compassionate and Merciful,[15] they too are manifestations; they are means whereby the name God (*Allah*), which combines all perfections in itself, becomes apparent. God has mentioned these two names here because mercy, which has the two aspects they express, pertains to His Essence, whereas the attributes of anger and revenge are secondary.[16]

"In the Name of God, the Compassionate, the Merciful, praise belongs to God." All praiseworthy qualities and perfections, all instances of praise and laudation that exist in the world, pertain to Him and are for Him. When a person eats a meal and praises it, saying, "What delicious food that was," he is praising God even without knowing it. Similarly, if we say of someone, "What a good man he is, what a philosopher, what a scholar!" this expression of praise also belongs to God, even if we are unaware of it. Why is this? Because the philosopher and scholar in question has nothing in and of himself; all that he has is a manifestation of God. If someone has come to perceive something, it is a perception that is a manifestation of God. Likewise, the thing perceived is a manifestation of God; everything is from God. People may imagine that they praise a carpet, for example, or a certain individual, but there is no praise that is uttered that is not for God. For when you praise someone, you do so on account of something he has, not on account of something non-existent, and whatever that person may have is from God. So whatever praise you utter belongs to God.

The meaning of *al-hamd*, which we translate as "praise," is generic; it includes all forms and instances of praise, the essence of praise. All belongs to God. We think we praise Zayd or 'Amr,[17] we think we praise the light of the sun or the moon, but that is because we are veiled from full perception of the truth. We imagine we praise a particular person or thing, but when the veil is removed, we see that all praise belongs to Him and the manifestation we are praising is a manifestation of Him. "God is the light of the heavens and the earth." Whatever good exists has come from Him; whatever perfection exists has come from Him. Everything and everyone that we praise is a manifestation of God and they were all created by means of a manifestation. We imagine that we act independently, but God said to the Most Noble Messenger, "When you cast the dust, you did not cast it; rather God cast it" (8:17);[18] that is, your casting the dust was a manifestation of God. Similarly: "When they swore allegiance to you, they swore allegiance to God" (48:10);[19] the hand of God's Messenger is a manifestation of God, but since we are veiled from full perception of reality, we do not recognize it as such.

The only persons who have such a perception are those who received direct instruction from God. I do not have the certainty such instruction bestows, but I can say that one may assume that the expression "In the Name of God" is syntactically connected with *al-hamd* ("praise"), meaning, "With the Name of God, all praise, all laudation, belongs to God and is His manifestation, because He draws it all to Himself in such a way that nothing remains for other-than-Him." Even if you wish to, you cannot praise other-than-God; your praise will revert to Him. If you imagine that you are praising something other than God, that is only because you do not know its true nature. However much you try to speak of other-than-God, you cannot; there is nothing to be said in praise of other-than-God, for other-than-God is nothing but deficiency.

By this I mean that all things that exist have two aspects: an aspect of existence and an aspect of deficiency. The aspect of existence is light; it is free from all deficiency and pertains to God. The other aspect, the negative aspect or that of deficiency, pertains to us. Now no one can praise the negative; it is only the affirmative—existence and perfection—that can be praised. There is only one perfection in the world and that is God, and there is only one beauty and that is God. We must understand this, and understand it with our heart. If we understand it, not with words or speech, but with our heart, it will suffice us. It is easy to state this truth, but to convey it to the heart and understand it there is difficult. One may say freely, in words, that hellfire exists, and even be convinced of it. But believing is different from being intellectually convinced. Proofs can be adduced, but the reality of belief has nothing to do with proofs.

The quality of *'ismat*[20] that exists in the prophets is the result of belief. Once one truly believes, it is not possible for one to sin. If you believe that someone is waiting with drawn sword to behead you if you utter a word against him, you will also become sinless after a fashion, for loving your life, you will never defy the swordsman. If someone believes that if he backbites with so much as a single word, he will be punished in the hereafter by having his tongue grow as long as the distance is between him and the subject of his backbiting; if he further believes that the backbiter is fed to the dogs of hell, that fiery dogs will devour him, not with a devouring that has a beginning and end, but one that continues indefinitely in hellfire—if he believes this, he will never engage in backbiting.[21] If (God forbid) we decide to engage in backbiting, it is because we have not believed in the existence of hellfire. A person who believes that all his deeds will assume an appropriate form in the next world, good if the deed is good, evil if it is evil, and that he will be called to account, will necessarily abstain from sin.

We must believe that the backbiter will be called to account, and that paradise awaits the believer and the doer of charitable deeds. We must believe this, not read it in a book or comprehend it with our reason, because there is a great difference between rational perception and belief with the heart (by heart, of course, I do not mean this physical heart).[22]

Men may rationally perceive something to be true, but since they do not believe in it, they will not act in accordance with it. Only when they believe in it will they act in accordance with it. Faith consists of this form of belief that impels man to action. Merely knowing about the Prophet is of no use; one must believe in him. Likewise with God: establishing proofs of God's existence is not enough; man must have faith, must believe in his heart and submit to Him. Once faith comes, everything else follows. If man believes that a certain being originated this world, that man will be called to account at a later stage, that death is not the end of all things, but a transition from a deficient realm to a perfect one, such belief will protect him from all sin. The only question remaining is, How should he believe? The answer is indicated in the Qur'an: "In the Name of God, praise belongs to God."

Again let me stress that the sense I am discussing is possible, not certain; and part of the possible meaning I am suggesting is that if man believes that all expressions and instances of praise belong to God, *shirk*[23] will not penetrate his heart.

As an example, if you hold to this belief, and wish to compose a panegyric for a prince, you will understand that it really pertains to God, because the prince is a manifestation of God. You will be praising that manifestation, because all praiseworthy qualities belong to God. If the prince arrogantly beats the drum of kingship, it will be because he does not know himself; he does not know that he is nothing. "One who knows himself knows also his Lord."[24] If a person understands and believes that he is nothing, that all that exists is He, he will have come to know his Lord.[25]

Our fundamental problem is that we know neither ourselves nor God, and we believe neither in ourselves nor in God. That is to say, we do not believe that we are nothing and that everything is from Him. As long as this belief is not operative, all that the Qur'an has sought to establish will be ineffective.

In our egoistic obstinacy and mutual enmity, we still say, "I possess such-and-such qualities, but you do not." All the empty claims to leadership and so on arise out of enmity, and enmity can exist only when man has his attention fixed on himself. All the disasters that afflict man derive from his love of self, but if he were to perceive the truth of the matter, he would understand that his self does not belong to him. True love of self, therefore, is love of other-than-self, but it has been mistakenly regarded as self-love. This error destroys man; all the miseries we suffer arise from this misguided love of the self and desire for its exaltation. This desire leads men to death and destruction; it carries them off to hellfire, and it is the source of all sin. When man fixes his attention on himself and desires everything for himself, he becomes the enemy of anyone who stands in his way, and grants others no rights. That is the source of all our miseries.

It may be for this reason—to make it clear that everything is God's and that man has nothing in and of himself—that God begins the Qur'an by saying, "Praise belongs to God." In other words, we cannot say that only some praise belongs to God and not other praise; I cannot praise you without praising God. "Praise belongs to God" means that all expressions of praise, together with the very essence and notion of praise, belong to God and are His. You may imagine that you are praising something other than Him, but this verse removes the veil from this question and many others that are related.

The whole point is to believe in this verse; if one believes that all forms of praise belong to God, all forms of *shirk* will be negated within the heart.

When he said, "Throughout my entire life I have never committed *shirk*,"[26] that was because he had intuitively perceived the truth, had experienced it with his conscience; it was not something he had been taught, but a truth he had experienced. Proofs are not very effective. They are good, of course, and even necessary, but they are a means by which you are able to perceive something with your reason, as a preliminary to believing in it by means of inner exertion.

Philosophy itself is a means, not an end; a means for you to convey truths and forms of knowledge to your reason through proofs. That is its sole scope. It has been said, "Those who seek proofs have wooden legs."[27] This means that the leg of rational proof is wooden, while the leg that conveys man and actually enables him to walk is his knowledge of himself as a manifestation of God; it is the faith that enters his heart and his conscience.

When a man achieves such belief, he should always be aware that there are higher degrees of belief still for him to attain.

Let us not be satisfied merely to read the Qur'an and study its interpretation. Let us read every topic and every word of the Qur'an with faith. For the Qur'an is a book that purposes to reform men, to restore them to the state in which God created them by means of His Supreme Name. God is everything in man, although he does not understand that. The Qur'an wishes to advance man from the defective state in which he finds himself to the higher state that befits him. This is the purpose for which the Qur'an has been revealed and all the prophets have been sent: to take man by the hand and deliver him from the deep pit into which he has fallen— the pit of egohood, the deepest of all pits—and to show him the manifestations of God, that he may forget all other-than-God.

May God grant that we attain such a state. And may peace be upon you, and also God's mercy and blessings.

MIGRATING TO GOD AND HIS MESSENGER

LAST TIME I DISCUSSED the possibility that the expression "In the Name of God," in every *sura* that it heads, is syntactically connected to the *sura* itself, or to the first part of its subject matter. For example, in the Sura of Praise, the meaning that emerges is "praise in, or by, the name of God." The same expression, then, has a different meaning in each *sura*, for in each case it relates to the particular topic that opens the *sura*.

In the Sura of Praise, it is connected with the word "praise," and it indicates the name by which praise is achieved, and the name is a manifestation of God. In the case of another *sura*, that of Unity (112), for example, the sense of the expression changes to indicate the name that is appropriate to the statement: "Say, 'He is God, One.' "

It is also specified in *fiqh*,[28] that if one wishes to recite more than one *sura*, a single recitation of the expression "In the Name of God" at the very beginning is not enough; the phrase must be repeated at the beginning of every *sura*. The reason for this is that the precise sense and function of the expression varies on each occasion. Were this not the case, each occurrence would be identical with the next. Indeed, some people have said that the expression does not form part of the *sura* except in the Sura of Praise, where it has been included in the *sura* because of its blessedness. That is not true, however.

At present we are concerned with the Sura of Praise, and here the expression is connected with the word praise that immediately follows it. This yields the probable meaning that "praise" (*al-hamd*)—meaning all instances of praise, by whomever uttered

—is accomplished by the name of God; it is the name itself that produces the utterance. All the limbs and members of man's body are names, and whenever man engages in praise, the praise takes place through God's name. Each individual constitutes a different name of God, or the manifestation of a different name.

Notice that there are many differences between the divine agent—which is the agent of existence—and natural agents.[29] One distinctive characteristic of that which emerges from the Divine Principle, which we know as the divine agent, is that in some sense, it is reabsorbed or destined to be reabsorbed into its origin; it has no reality or independence of its own. In order to understand this better, you may compare the relation of the divine agent to the Divine Principle with that of the rays of the sun to the sun. This is not an exact comparison, but it is true insofar as the rays of the sun have no independence with respect to the sun, and the divine agent similarly lacks independence with respect to that Principle of Absolute Good from which its existence is derived—that is, it cannot come into existence or remain in existence independently. If the rays of existence are withdrawn from a being for a single instant, it will not be able to subsist for a single instant, for just as it depends on the Principle in order to come into existence, it also depends on It in order to remain in existence. Having no standing of its own, then, it is reabsorbed into the Principle.

This being the case, the manifestation of God's names is, in a sense, identical with the names themselves. "God is the light of the heavens and the earth"—the light is the manifestation of God, not God Himself, but the manifestation has no existence apart from the Principle from which it derives; it is reabsorbed in It since it possesses no independence. It is in this sense that we are to understand: "God is the light of the heavens and the earth."

Returning to "praise" (al-hamd), we see that the definite article has a generic sense, and connecting it with the expression "In the Name of God," which precedes it, we concluded that every instance of praise, by whomever it is uttered, takes place by means of the name of God. The name of God is both the one who praises and that which is praised; from a certain point of view, they are one and the same, the instance of manifestation and the general principle of manifestation. When the Prophet (upon whom be peace and blessings) said, "You are as You praise Yourself to be," or on another occasion, "I take refuge in You from You," part of what is indicated is that the one who praises is effaced in the One Who is praised. It is as if God were praising Himself, therefore. No one else enjoys any real existence that enables him to say, "*I* am praising Him"; it is He who praises Himself.

Another possibility is that the definite article in *al-hamd* is not generic in the sense of "praise" being a category applicable to many individual acts. Instead, the sense may be that nature, in its very essence, is deprived of all the characteristics of praise, and that praise resists all individuation. "In the Name of God, the Compassionate, the Merciful, praise belongs to God" then comes to mean that praise is without individuation and is absolute. This second interpretation is the exact opposite of the first in that the praise we utter does not truly pertain to God, and only that praise pertains to Him that He Himself utters. The praise offered by others is limited and individuated, but He is unlimited. Limited praise cannot pertain to the Unlimited, since it contradicts His nature.

We said previously that nothing can be praised except God. You imagine that you praise someone's handwriting, but in reality you are praising God. You imagine that you praise the light, but in reality you are praising God. You imagine that you praise a scholar, but in reality you are praising God. Whatever praise is uttered, no matter who utters it, reverts to God, because there is no perfection in the world that is not His and no beauty in the world that is not His. Created things are nothing: if the divine manifestation is taken away from them, nothing of them remains; it is by means of that manifestation that they exist. All things are the manifestation of God, and are light. Since there is no perfection other than God's, for it is a manifestation of God, and since it is this manifestation that is being praised, other-than-God cannot, in the very nature of things, be praised. There is no perfection other than His, the perfection of His Essence and His attributes. All the perfections that exist in the world are His perfections made manifest; praise of those perfections, therefore, is praise of Him.

According to the second possibility (which is no more than that), "praise" (*al-hamd*) does not mean all instances of praise, but absolute praise, praise without any condition or limitation. The praise in which we engage is individuated; it is limited, among other things, by the intention with which we utter it. We have no access to God in His absoluteness in order to praise Him correspondingly. When you say, "Praise belongs to God (*al-hamdu lillah*)," you have not fully perceived His reality in order to praise Him. Any praise that you utter relates not to Him, but to His manifestations.

Here again, the second possibility contradicts the first. According to the first possibility, all instances of praise necessarily are praise of Him. According to the second, however, no instance of praise can be praise of Him except His own praise of Himself. If it be the case, the meaning of "name" in "In the Name of God, praise belongs to God" cannot be what we suggested—that you are a name, and everyone else is a name. Instead, the name of God comes to be the unlimited manifestation of the Absolute, a sign of the unseen, and it is by means of this name alone that God is praised; that is, He praises Himself by means of Himself. The manifestation praises the One Who makes manifest.

All of this, then, represents another possibility. On the one hand, "praise" (*al-hamd*) may mean all instances of praise; on the other, it may mean absolute and undifferentiated praise. The first possibility is that all instances of praise cannot relate to other-than-God, and the second is that no praise, being limited, can relate to God, Who is absolute. This second possibility means further that absolute and undifferentiated praise is His by means of the name that is appropriate to Him.

A third possibility mentioned by some people is that the expression "In the Name of God" is not connected to the *sura* at all, but relates only to the manifestation of being. That is, whatever comes into existence does so by means of the name of God; the name is the origin from which the manifestation of all beings derives.

It may be possible to connect this interpretation with the tradition that says, "God created will by means of itself, and He created other things by means of His will." Here, will represents the first manifestation of God, created "by means of itself" (that is, without any intermediary), and everything else came into being by means of the will. Similarly, according to our third possibility —which rejects any syntactic connection between "In the Name of God" and the *sura*, but connects it instead to something outside the *sura*—"In the Name of God, the Compassionate, the Merciful" is the means whereby things attain existence.

Those who have examined the Qur'an using the method of the grammarians have suggested that the sense of "In the Name of God" is: "I seek God's aid," or something similar. Now even if that is the meaning, still the concept of name must be present, whether or not they are aware of it, for whoever seeks God's aid does so by the invocation of His name; he cannot do so without it. This does not mean that "In the Name of God" is a simple verbal formula of invocation; for the "Name of God" means His manifestation in all things, and the one who seeks God's help, invoking His name, is in fact seeking His aid by means of His manifestation. All things are by means of His manifestation, so that this interpretation, too, refers matters back to God.

So much for the syntactic relationship of "In the Name of God." As for the sense of "name," I have already said that it is the sign of the thing that it names. Whatever you may imagine to exist, its name is a manifestation or sign of it.

Not all names are equal in this respect. There are names that are signs in the fullest sense of the word, and others that function at a lower degree. All things are signs and manifestations, manifestations of the name, but to different degrees.

There is a tradition that states: "We are the Most Beautiful Names";[30] that is, the Supreme Name manifests itself as the Most Noble Messenger and the Immaculate Imams, those who have attained the degree of advancement from deficiency to perfection, who have liberated themselves from nature and all things. They are not like us, who are still in the pit and have not even begun to walk on the path. They have left the pit and are advancing on the path; they have migrated.

"When anyone leaves his home, migrating to God and His Messenger, and is then overtaken by death, it is incumbent on God to reward him."[31] One possible meaning of this tradition is that the migration referred to is a migration from the self toward God, and the home mentioned is man's selfhood. There is a class of men who have left their dark home of egohood and migrated from it, "migrating to God and His Messenger," and they are then "overtaken by death"—that is, they reach a point where there is no longer anything of themselves: absolute death. Their reward is incumbent upon God; there is no question of any other reward, neither paradise with its bounties nor anything else, save God Himself. If a person departs from the home of egohood and migrates to God and His Messenger (migrating to the Messenger being a form of migrating to God), and then reaches a state where he is "overtaken by death," where nothing remains of his self and he sees all things as coming from God—if he engages in such a migration, then it is incumbent upon God to reward him.

There is a class of people who have accomplished this: they have migrated in this way, and attained their goal (although in another sense their migration is continuing[32]), and it has become incumbent upon God to reward them. There are others who have migrated but not yet reached the goal of being "overtaken by death." And then there is still another group—to which you and I belong—that has not even begun to migrate.[33] We are still caught up in the darkness; we are captives in the pit of attachment to the world, to nature, and, worst of all, to our own egos. We are enclosed in our home of selfhood, and all that exists for us is our selves. Whatever we want, we want for ourselves. The thought of migrating has not even occurred to us; all our thoughts are devoted to this world. We do not return to God the trust of the strength and energy He has put in us,[34] but expend all of it for the sake of this world. As time goes on, we become more and more distant from our point of origin, that place toward which we are supposed to migrate.

According to a tradition, the Prophet was once seated with his Companions when suddenly they heard a noise. They asked him what it was and he told them, "Once a stone fell into hellfire, and now, seventy years later, it has reached the bottom, making the sound you just heard." By this the Prophet was referring to a man who had sinned for seventy years and just died. I, too, have traveled in the same direction, but for eighty years, not seventy; and you have, too, for differing numbers of years. I hope that henceforth you will travel in the opposite direction.

Anything that afflicts us is caused by our love of self, our egoism. There is a well-known saying: "The most hostile of your enemies is your self, enclosed between your two sides."[35] Your self is worse than all your enemies, worse than all idols. It is, in fact, the chief of all idols, compelling you to worship it with a greater force than that of all other idols. Until one breaks this idol, one cannot turn to God; the idol and God, egoism and divinity, cannot coexist within you. Unless we leave this idol temple, turn our backs on this idol, and set our faces toward God Almighty, we will in reality be idolators, even though we may outwardly worship God. We say "God" with our tongues, but our selves are what is in our hearts. When we stand in prayer we say, "You alone do we worship and from You alone do we seek help,"[36] but in reality it is our selves that we are worshipping. I mean that we are exclusively concerned with ourselves, and desire everything for ourselves.

All the problems besetting the world, including wars, arise from this egoism. True believers will not go to war with each other; if war breaks out between two people, they must realize that they are not believers.[37] When there is no belief, but only attention to self, concern for the self and its desires, then trouble arises. I want this seat for myself and you want it for yourself; conflict arises, for these desires are incompatible. I may want a carpet for myself, or some position of leadership, which you desire equally for yourself, so that a dispute ensues between us. Someone wants to rule a country himself; another harbors the same desire, so war breaks out between them. All the wars that take place in the world are wars between opposing egos.

The *awliya* are exempt from this egoism, and no war takes place among them. If they were all gathered together, neither strife nor dispute would occur among them, for they are all devoted entirely to a single aim, God, and nothing remains of their selfhood that might cause them to pull in different directions. But we are trapped in a pit in darkness of the worst kind, the darkness of egoism. Yes, we are caught in a dark pit of egoism. We are preoccupied with ourselves and our own desires, and while we are willing to consider harm for others if it is to our benefit, we refuse to accept what is proper and right if it threatens our interests. We also believe immediately whatever we think is to our benefit, but refuse to believe anything contrary to our interests.

All human sufferings are caused by egoism of these and other forms; people pull in different directions dictated by their own selfish desires. As long as matters continue this way, there will be no question of worshipping God, but only the self.

Who can escape this temple of the self, this idol-temple that is situated within man himself? Man needs a helping hand from the world of the unseen to reach him and lead him out. It is precisely for this purpose, to lead man out of his idol-temple, that all the prophets have been sent and all the heavenly books revealed. They have enabled man to shatter the idol and begin worshipping God.

The prophets all came to make this world a divine world after it had been a satanic world, a world governed by Satan. It is Satan that is ruling us, too; we follow him, and our vain desires are a manifestation of him. As long as that great Satan that is our un-redeemed soul exists within us, whatever we do will be done in egoism. We must destroy the government of Satan within us.

When we migrate to the teachings of the prophets and the *awliya,* turn our backs on egoism, we will have begun to emerge from the pit. Some will even succeed, while still in this world, in reaching a stage that is now beyond our imagination—that of non-being, of being effaced in God. We must desire to make this migration from egoism, and be prepared to struggle in order to migrate.

The Prophet said, "You have now returned from the lesser *jihad;* the greater *jihad* still remains as a duty for you."[38] All forms of *jihad* that may be waged in the world depend on this greater *jihad;* if we succeed in the greater *jihad,* then all our other strivings will count as *jihad,* and if not, they will be satanic. Some who waged *jihad* may have been given simply a slavegirl as their just reward, whereas others who made the migration to God received God as their reward.

There are different categories of deeds. The deeds of the *awliya* are completely different from our deeds because of the source from which they spring. It is said of the Commander of the Faithful, for example, that a single blow struck by him during the Battle of the Ditch[39] was better than all the deeds of worship performed by both men and jinn. Part of the explanation is, of course, that the blow he delivered that day to kill an enemy was struck during a confron-tation between Islam and all the forces of *kufr;*[40] if Islam had been defeated on that day, it would have been destroyed. The other part of the explanation, however, lies in his pure intention, sincerity, and absorption in God. Was this not the same Commander of the

Faithful who once rose from the breast of an enemy he was about to kill, because the man spat in his face and he feared that his deed might be diminished by egoism? When such meticulous concern for the right motive inspires a deed, the spirit of that deed will indeed exceed all possible acts of worship, for it is that spirit that makes worship truly worship. Polytheists and monotheists, those who worship idols and those who do not, may resemble each other outwardly. Abu Sufyan[41] used to pray, and Mu'awiya[42] even used to lead the congregation in prayer. These outward appearances are of no value in themselves. What elevates prayer is the spirit that animates it. If that spirit is present, prayer ascends to the divine presence and itself becomes divine.

But we engage in worship for our own sakes. At most, if one of us is very good, he engages in worship for the sake of paradise. But take away paradise and see how many people will be left praying! One should aspire to the state of the Commander of the Faithful, who was "enamored of worship and embraced it."[43] There is no question of paradise for him; he is unaware of it, having died, or been "overtaken by death." Since he no longer has any consciousness of the self, paradise and hell are equal in his view. His worship and praise are devoted exclusively to the Essence of God Almighty, for he has recognized God as deserving to be worshipped. This is the degree of a person who is "enamored of worship"; he worships God because He deserves to be worshipped.

This, then, is the first step: to quit your home of egoism, to take a step in the direction of God. We must awaken from our sleep, for it is only the animal dimension of our being that is now awake; the human dimension is sound asleep.

"People are asleep, and when they die they awaken."[44] And when they awaken, they ask themselves what the sense was of their chaotic lives. But it is too late, for "Hellfire surrounds the unbelievers" (Qur'an, 9:49). Even now it surrounds them, but drugged by nature, they are unaware of it and fail to take heed. When the effects of the drug wear off, they see that they are surrounded by flames and are being borne off to hell, whether they like it or not.

Yes, we must wake up while there is still time, and embark on the straight path under the guidance of the prophets. The prophets, without a single exception, all had as their mission the reformation of man. Both justice and injustice arise from men's deeds, and the purpose of justice, therefore, is to transform the unjust into the just, the *mushrik*[45] into the believer. So the person who, if left to his own devices, would have headed for the deepest pit of hellfire will listen and obey when he is shown the path he must take.

We have not yet set out on this path, not even begun on our migration, despite the seventy or eighty years we have lived. But you young people are better able to refine your souls; you are closer to the spiritual realm than the elderly, and the roots of corruption within you are still weak and undeveloped. But if you postpone your task of self-reform, those roots will grow stronger and firmer with every passing day. Do not leave it, then, until old age; begin now. Make your lives conform to the teachings of the prophets; that is the starting point. One must follow the path they have indicated—it is they who know where the path lies; we do not. They are physicians and know the path to true health; if you desire health, you must follow their path.

Gradually, you must extricate yourself from the demands of your ego; naturally, this cannot be achieved all at once. All our worldly hopes and desires will be buried with us, and all this incessant attention to the self will work to our disadvantage. For all that can remain in the hereafter is what belongs to God: "What is with you will perish, and what is with God will remain" (16:96). Man has what is "with himself" and he also has what is "with God." What is "with himself" is all that comes from his preoccupation with himself, and it will inevitably perish. But whatever he has that relates to God, what is "with God," will remain by virtue of the divine name Eternal (*Baqi*).

So let us strive to extricate ourselves from the situation in which we find ourselves. Those who fight in *jihad* against the external enemy never fear superior numbers, for the Prophet said that he would never turn back even if all the Arabs united against him. His cause was the cause of God, and the cause of God can never be defeated, nor is there any turning back from it.

Those who engaged in *jihad* in the first age of Islam advanced and pushed forward without any regard for themselves or their personal desires, for they had earlier waged a *jihad* against their selves. Without the inner *jihad*, the outer *jihad* is impossible. *Jihad* is inconceivable unless a person turns his back on his own desires and the world. For what we mean here by "world" is the aggregate of man's aspirations that effectively constitute his world, not the external world of nature with the sun and the moon, which are manifestations of God. It is the world in this narrow, individual sense that prevents man from drawing near to the realm of sanctity and perfection.

May God grant us success in emerging from the pit and following the path of the prophets and the *awliya*, for it is they who have been "overtaken by death." And may peace be upon you.

3

VEILS OF DARKNESS,
VEILS OF LIGHT

IN ORDER TO UNDERSTAND some of the questions I have been discussing, it is necessary to understand the nature of the relation of God to creation. We may understand this relation to a certain degree with the help of proofs we have learned to recite parrotlike (since what lies beyond proof is inaccessible to us). The relation of God to creation is not like that linking one creature to another; for example, father to son or son to father, where it is a question of two independent beings standing in relation to each other. The relationship of the rays of the sun and the sun itself is of a higher order, but again it concerns two beings linked to each other. Of a higher order still is the relation linking the faculties of the soul to the soul, but this relationship of the auditory, visual, and other faculties and the soul is still marked by a certain separation and multiplicity. The relation that links all beings to their principle, God Almighty, cannot be regarded as similar to any of the foregoing.

There are expressions in both the Qur'an and the Sunna indicating the true nature of this relationship. For example, "His Lord manifested Himself to the mountain" (7:143), or this phrase from the Prayer of Simat[46]: "By the light of Your face, which You manifested to the mountain, causing it to crumble." Both expressions indicate that the nature of God's relation to creation is one of manifestation. The same thing is indicated by the verse: "God takes souls at the time of their death" (39:42), for it means that God takes the life even of the person who is apparently killed by another, and by the verse: "When you cast the dust you did not cast it; rather God cast it" (8:17), which states the matter explicitly.

God's relation to His creation, then, is one of manifestation and light. If we understand this, even on the basis of proof repeated parrot-fashion, it will assist us in understanding many matters in these noble verses.

According to the first possibility we suggested, "praise" (*al-hamd*) means the sum total of instances of praise and is infinitely multiple, and the sense of "name" in the expression "In the Name of God" is correspondingly multiple. Whatever praise is uttered cannot but revert to God Almighty, for it is the manifestations that are being praised, and they are God's. The manifestation of God is of a higher order than that of the sun through its rays, or that of the soul through its auditory and visual faculties. Praise belongs to the manifestations, and the corresponding multiple names belong to Him.

The second possibility we advanced was that "praise" means absolute praise and, contrary to the first possibility, no praise uttered by a praiser can relate to God. It relates only to His manifestations, and cannot be absolute. However, insofar as all forms of multiplicity are effaced in that absolute being, again it can be said that any praise that is uttered pertains to Him. The difference here is between the vantage point of multiplicity and that of unity. According to the former, no praise uttered can pertain to the absolute being, and according to the latter, all instances of praise pertain to Him, given that multiplicity is effaced in unity.

The two interpretations of the verse differ completely. If praise is generic, meaning the sum total of instances of praise, then "name" in the expression "In the Name of God" also means in effect, "the sum total of multiple names," so that every being is a name. But if we hold to the other interpretation of "praise," then the sense of "name" also changes. Each name will differ and be marked by multiplicity. The name *Allah* becomes a manifestation of God Almighty in multiplicity and differentiation.

According to the first possibility, the Supreme Name is a manifestation of God's Essence in beings, and the names Compassionate and Merciful are a manifestation of the acts of His Essence. The same is true of the name Lord of the Worlds. But according to the second possibility, which regards "praise" as meaning absolute and unrestricted praise, praise belongs only to the name *Allah*, while the names Compassionate, Merciful, and

Lord of the Worlds are subsumed within the Essence for which the Supreme Name stands, instead of being manifestations of that Essence.

All of the foregoing depends on inductive reasoning, as employed in the higher forms of philosophy. It is, however, totally different from what the *awliya* experienced and came to witness directly after traversing the stages of spiritual wayfaring.

The *awliya* cannot convey their witnessings to men. It was also necessary that the Qur'an descend, come down to a level where it would be able to address humanity, trapped in its fetters and the pit of misguidance. The tongue of the Prophet was tied; he could not convey reality to men except by descending to their level of perception. The Qur'an has seven or seventy levels of meaning,[47] and the lowest of those levels is the one where it addresses us. For example, God Almighty makes Himself known to us by invoking the camel: "Do they not look upon the she-camel, to see how it was created?" (88:17). The sun, the heavens, the earth, and man himself are similarly invoked.

This inability of men to comprehend was a source of sorrow to the prophets. Their tongues were all tied, and Moses (upon whom be peace) prayed to God: "O Lord, expand my breast for me, make my task easy and loosen the knot on my tongue" (20:25). There were knots confining the prophets' tongues or their hearts in the sense that they were unable to convey to men the realities they had experienced and the way in which they had experienced them. The realities were ineffable, but the prophets tried to convey something of them to us by means of parables and symbols.

If God makes Himself known to us by invoking the camel, it is obvious that we exist on a very low level, in fact on the same level as the animal itself, and that the knowledge we are capable of attaining is extremely deficient.

Let us examine the Qur'anic narrative concerning Moses. "When his Lord manifested Himself to the mountain, He made it as dust and Moses fell down in a swoon" (7:143). That is, Moses was overwhelmed by his Lord, and passed beyond the levels of perception to which we are limited. But then he said: "Show me, that I may look upon You"(7:143). Moses, a great prophet, asked to see God with his own eyes; that is, he asked for a mode of vision, involving seer and seen, that is unattainable for us with respect to

God. Although he had advanced to the point of receiving direct address from God, he said: "My Lord, show me that I may look upon You." The answer came: "You shall not see Me" (7:143). The probable meaning of this response is: "As long as you are Moses, as long as you are you, you shall not see Me." But God did not leave Moses without any hope, and told him to look instead at the mountain. What was the mountain? Was the mountain that received the divine manifestation denied to Moses Mount Sinai? If there had been people on the mountain that day, would they have seen the manifestation, perhaps in the form of bright sunlight? "Look upon the mountain, and when the mountain subsides you shall see Me" (7:143). What is meant by the mountain subsiding is probably its dissolving into dust as a result of the divine manifestation. As for the mountain itself, it is probably a symbol for the egoism of the human soul, traces of which still persisted in Moses. When God reduced the mountain to dust by His manifestation, all egoism perished and Moses attained the station of death: "Moses fell in a swoon."

All this is a story for us; what others have witnessed and experienced directly is conveyed to us in the form of a story, the story of Mount Sinai, because we are still imprisoned in the darkness. The manifestation itself appears to have been in the form of light seen by Moses on Mount Sinai, and insofar as it was capable of being perceived by the senses, others too would have seen it. Likewise, when Jibra'il, the Trusted Spirit, recited the Qur'an to the Most Noble Messenger, those present also heard it. But the seeing and hearing were as if from afar.[48]

The prophets are like men who have seen a dream that they cannot describe; their tongues are tied, and those around them are deaf. They are unable to speak and we are unable to hear; rather they do speak, but not for us. We understand only those things that are comprehensible to us. The Qur'an is everything: it contains exoteric material, legal injunctions, as well as narratives whose inner sense we cannot understand; we understand and benefit from their outer aspects only. Full benefit can be drawn from the Qur'an only by the man to whom it was addressed—the Messenger of God.[49] All others are deprived of such complete benefit unless they attain it by means of instruction from him, as was the case with the *awliya*.

The Qur'an indicates that it descended to the Prophet: "The Trusted Spirit descended with it to your heart" (26:193). The Qur'an underwent a descent to the Prophet by means of the Trusted Spirit so that it might be received by him at his station. In the same connection, God says: "We sent it [the Qur'an] down on the Night of Power" (97:1); that is, "We sent it down in its entirety to the Prophet on the Night of Power, in the form of a manifestation." First, the Qur'an was in the keeping of the Trusted Spirit, and then it underwent a descent in order to enter the heart of the Prophet.

The Qur'an descended, then, from level to level, from degree to degree, until finally it assumed a verbal form. The Qur'an is not verbal in substance; it does not pertain to the audiovisual realm; it does not belong to the category of accidents. It was, however, "brought down" so that we, the dumb and the blind, might benefit from it to the extent of our ability. But as for those who can benefit more fully, their understanding of the Qur'an is different, and their orientation to the principle from which the Qur'an has descended is different. When the manifestation of God Almighty emerges from the unseen and descends to the world of nature or bodies, there is a vast distance separating this lowest degree from the infinite realms of the unseen, and beyond them, the first appearance of that manifestation. There is a correspondingly vast distance separating our perception from that of those superior to us, at the pinnacle of whom stand the *awliya* and the prophets of God.

Moses, then, witnessed a divine manifestation when his Lord manifested Himself to the mountain. The Prayer of Simat[50] also makes reference to this manifestation in the phrase "by the light of Your face which You manifested to the mountain." A different form of manifestation is referred to in the verse: "O Moses, I, verily I am God" (28:30); here the tree is the vehicle for the manifestation. All these statements referring to manifestation are true, and represent different aspects of manifestation. But if we wish to learn the Qur'an, what are we to do? Matters like these can neither be taught nor learned in their deepest sense.

When we wish to study the Qur'an and its interpretation, we have recourse to the commentaries currently in use that contain indications likely to be of use to deaf and blind persons like ourselves. The Qur'an contains everything, but only he who was addressed by it fully understands it. The high degree of that person is indicated in the verses: "The Trusted Spirit descended with it [the Qur'an] to your heart," and "We sent it [the Qur'an] down on the Night of Power." The visionary experience indicated in these verses cannot be shared by anyone else. It is not a question open to rational proof or demonstration, but a question of immediate perception of the unseen; no one else can attain it by any means, whether by unveiling[51] or by vision of the soul, the intellect, or the heart. It was only the heart of the world—the heart of the Prophet—that was vouchsafed that perception, as "he who was addressed by the Qur'an."

He is unable to convey what he has perceived except by clothing it in words and symbols. How can you make the blind understand what the light of the sun is? What language, what words can you use? Light is something that dispels darkness; how can you make one who has never seen light understand what it is? There is, then, a knot tying the tongues of the prophets, and there are knots tying the ears of those who hear them.

The difficulties of the Most Noble Messenger were greater than those of the other prophets in this respect. To whom could he convey those dimensions of the Qur'an that had descended upon his heart, except the one whom he had appointed to be his successor in every respect?[52] He is reputed to have said: "No other prophet was vexed as I have been." If this tradition is authentic, it may be that part of its meaning relates to the Prophet's inability to convey fully what he had experienced, or to find anyone to convey it to. It grieved him that although what he had experienced was greater than what all the earlier prophets had experienced, he was unable to convey it to everybody as he wished to. Imagine the sorrow of a father who wishes to make his blind son understand what the sun is; what could he possibly say that would convey to him the meaning of light? All he has available to him are verbal formulae that may even serve as a barrier to understanding.

It has been said that "Knowledge is the thickest of veils," for pursuit of knowledge causes man to be preoccupied with rational and general concepts and hinders him from embarking on the path. The more knowledge increases, the thicker the veil becomes, and the scholar may come to imagine that the knowledge he has achieved rationally represents everything. For man is arrogant as long as his skin contains him, and any branch of learning he has studied and mastered he regards as the sum total of perfection. The *faqih* imagines that there is nothing but *fiqh;* the mystic, that there is nothing but mysticism; the philosopher, that there is nothing but philosophy; and the engineer, that there is nothing but engineering. In each case, they imagine that science consists exclusively of what they have learned, observed, and experienced, and that nothing else should be regarded as knowledge.

Knowledge, once seen in this way, becomes the thickest of all veils, until what was meant to be a guide on the path serves as a hindrance. The knowledge that was intended to guide man now denies him guidance. That is the case with all formal learning: it may veil man from what he should be. Whenever learning enters an unpurified heart, it induces egoism in it and holds it back, and the greater the weight of accumulated knowledge, the greater its harmful effects. Seed that is sown in brackish, stony ground will never yield fruit. When veils keep a heart from the perception of truth, a heart that has not been purified, that does not fear the name of God, it will shrink back from contemplating philosophical matters as if they were a snake, even though philosophy is merely a branch of formal learning. The philosopher, in turn, will shrink back from mysticism, and even the mystic will shrink back from what lies beyond him. For all branches of formal learning consist of transmitted verbal formulae.

At the very least, therefore, we ought to strive to purify ourselves so that formal learning does not completely bar our access to God or prevent us from remembering Him. This, too, is an important concern: our lack of knowledge should not cause us to be heedless of God, or induce such arrogance in us that we fall away from the source of all perfection. This arrogance is to be seen in all learned people, whether concerned with the physical and natural sciences, the sciences of the *shari'a*, or the rational sciences. If the heart is not purified, learning brings arrogance, and it is precisely arrogance that hinders man from setting out toward God. When the scholar studies, he is completely absorbed in his study, but when he prays, he is not present in his prayer. A friend of mine (may God have mercy upon him) used to say: "I have forgotten; let me pray so maybe I can remember."[53] When such men pray, it is as if they were completely absent from the prayer: they do not direct their attention to God and their hearts are elsewhere. They might be attempting to solve some academic problem, so that what was meant to be an aid in attaining the goal now holds them back.

There are the sciences of the *shari'a*, of Qur'anic interpretation, of *tauhid*,[54] but, placed in an unprepared and unpurified heart, they become like fetters and chains tying one down. The sciences and concerns of the *shari'a* are all a means, a means for proper action, and action, in turn, is a means for attaining the ultimate goal, which is the awakening of the soul and its emergence from the dark veils that envelop it. Even then, the soul will find itself facing veils of light, for: "God has seventy thousand veils of light and of darkness." Veils of light are no less veils for being composed of light, but *we* have not even emerged from the veils of darkness; we are thoroughly entangled in veils. What is to become of us? Learning has had entirely negative effects on our souls. All the sciences of the *shari'a* as well as the rational sciences (which are also called the "abstract" sciences; i.e., sciences that have no objective existence) are intended as means for attaining the goal, but instead, each of them has come to serve as a hindrance. It is no longer a question of learning, but of a dark veil, an obstacle in the path of man preventing him from attaining that goal for the sake of which all the prophets came: to lead man forth from this world, out of the darkness, and to convey him to the realm of absolute light. The prophets wanted to immerse man in that absolute light, to merge the drop with the ocean (this image, of course, is not exact).

It is for this purpose that all the prophets were sent. All true knowledge and objective reality belong exclusively to that light; we are all non-beings, and our origin is that light. All the prophets were sent to deliver us from the darkness and convey us to the absolute light, freeing us from both the veils of darkness and those of light. The science of *tauhid* may itself turn into a veil. It establishes proofs for the existence of God Almighty, but simultaneously veils man from God and prevents him from becoming what he should be. The prophets and the *awliya* did not depend on proofs; they knew the proofs but never cared to use them to establish the existence of God. The Lord of the Martyrs said, addressing God

Almighty: "When were You ever absent? It is blind eyes that have failed to see Your presence."

The point of departure is "arising" (*qiyam*), as is enjoined in this Qur'anic verse: "I admonish you to do one thing: to arise for God" (34:46). Those who have analyzed spiritual wayfaring, for example, Shaykh Abdullah Ansari in this *Manazil as-Sa'irin*,[55] have regarded this "arising" as the first stage on the path. (It may not be a stage at all, however, but rather a preliminary, followed by the stages.) First there is an admonition, an injunction, coming from someone who has attained the goal himself and is instructed by God to summon men to arise. It all starts with this "arising for God." Man begins to move for the sake of God, to remain still for the sake of God—to awaken from his sleep. In this verse, it is as if an order is being given to tell the sleeping and heedless to arise for God's sake and to embark on God's path. We have not heeded this simple injunction and have therefore been unable to set out on that path. We prefer instead to follow our own paths; that is true even of the best of us.

This admonition is directed to us, not to the *awliya;* they are a different breed of men and have already attained the goal. We too will be taken in that direction; no one can say that we are here to stay. The angels empowered over all our faculties are taking us in that direction, and have been doing so ever since we entered the natural realm. But we will go burdened by darkness and veils.

Love of the self is the source and origin of all sins and errors, together with love of the world. This love may sometimes cause a man, even though he is a worshipper of the One God, to leave the world with resentment and hatred in his heart if he believes that God has taken something from him. It is said that when a man is about to depart from this world, the demons that do not want him to leave it a believer will display to him all the things he loves. A student of the religious sciences, for example, might be attached to a book. They will bring the book to him and say, "Unless you renounce your belief, we will burn this book." They will threaten others in a similar way with their children or whatever they may be particularly attached to.

Do not imagine that it is necessarily the wealthy who are regarded as worldly. It is possible, for example, that someone might own vast estates but not be worldly,[56] while a student might possess only a book and yet be quite worldly. The criterion is attachment, the ties that bind man to things. These ties may make man an enemy of God when he sees them being severed at the end of his life, so that he then leaves the world in a state of enmity toward God. So, curtail your attachments; we will leave this world whether or not we are bound in affection to something. Maybe you are attached to a book you own and maybe you are not, but in either case the book is yours and what is important is that you make use of it. Likewise, maybe you are attached to the house you live in and maybe you are not, but again, the house is yours, and what is important is that you make use of it. So curtail your attachments, or even eliminate them if possible. What afflicts man is his attachments, and they, in turn, arise out of his love of self. Love of the world, love of leadership, love of authority, love for a particular mosque, all these are forms of attachment to the world, a series of veils that envelop us. Let us not sit and discuss the state of others, but let us pay attention to our own situation. Let us see how strong our attachments are to our possessions, and whether what we find objectionable in others also exists in us.

Were it not for this self-love and arrogance, man would never find fault with others. When some of us do so, it is because in our love of self, we see ourselves as perfect and purified and others as full of defects and faults. You know of that poem—I do not wish to recite it—in which someone condemns a certain woman and she replies: "I am indeed all that you say, but are you truly all that you seem?"[57] We pretend to society that we have come to the madrasa to study the *shari'a* for the sake of God, and that we are part of God's army. But are we really what our outward appearances proclaim us to be? All too often, our inner reality does not conform to our outer appearance but instead contradicts it.

What is this if not hypocrisy? Is it not hypocrisy to proclaim one's religiosity without being religious, as Abu Sufyan[58] did? It is also hypocrisy to pretend to possess certain qualities without in fact doing so. All of these are different forms of hypocrisy.

We must forgo this world, then, and avoid the attachment to it that arises from love of self. But let it not be said that the prophets have summoned us only to the hereafter, not to this world. For while they did indeed summon men to an awareness of the

hereafter, they also established justice in this world. The Most
Noble Messenger was a being close to God, but because of his
perpetual involvement in this world, he is reported to have said:
"My heart is clouded, and I seek pardon of God seventy times a
day."[59] Interacting with men at a lower level than himself clouded
his heart, for he was meant to be constantly in the presence of
his Beloved. Even if the person who came to him was a truly good
man prompted by the desire to ask a question, still he prevented
the Prophet from remaining uninterruptedly at the level where
he wished to be. Naturally, the Prophet submitted to the necessity
of such interaction with men and regarded those who came to
speak to him as manifestations of God. Nonetheless, he was prevented from remaining constantly in the presence of his Beloved,
and thus he said: "My heart is clouded, and I seek pardon of God
seventy times a day."

Preoccupation with the faults of others is a veil that we must
remove. Let us at least strive to be what we appear to be, not something else. If there are marks of constant prostration on our fore-
heads suggesting that we are laboring for God's sake, let us shun
all hypocrisy in our prayer. If we present ourselves as very saintly,
let us not accept interest or deceive people, and so on.

The idea that the spiritual sciences discourage people from
activity is untrue. The man who taught these sciences to the people
and who was more versed in their truths than anyone, after the
Messenger of God, took up his pickaxe and went about his work
immediately after receiving the allegiance of the people.[60] There is
no contradiction between spirituality and activity. Those who
would dissuade people from engaging in supplicatory prayer and
dhikr[61] on the pretext of involving them more fully in the world
do not understand how matters lie. They do not know that it is
precisely prayer and the like that make man become a true human
being so that he may conduct himself toward the world as he
ought. It was, after all, the prophets who established justice in
this world, while they were engaged in meditation and dhikr.

The same was true of those who rose up against tyrants; look,
for example, at the prayer made on the Day of 'Arafa[62] by Husayn
ibn 'Ali (upon whom be peace). Prayer and dhikr are the beginning of all things, for if man practices them correctly, they cause
him to turn toward the origin of his being in the unseen and to

strengthen his attachment to it. Not only does this not deter him from activity, it even produces in him the best of activity, for he comes to understand that his activity should not be for his own sake but for the sake of God's bondsmen, and that his activity should be service to God.

Those who criticize the books of prayer do so out of ignorance. The poor people do not know the way these books make true human beings out of men. The prayers that have been handed down from the Imams, like the Invocations of Sha'ban,[63] the Prayer of Kumayl,[64] or the Prayer of the Lord of the Martyrs (upon whom be peace) on the Day of 'Arafa, all contribute to the making of true human beings. The person who recited the Invocations of Sha'ban was also the same one who drew his sword to go into battle against the unbelievers. Indeed, according to tradition, all the Imams recited the Invocations of Sha'ban, something that is not recorded concerning any other prayer.[65] These prayers lead man out of the darkness, and once he has emerged, he wields his sword for God's sake, fights for God's sake, and rises up for God's sake. These prayers do not deter man from labor and activity, as those people imagine for whom the world consists exclusively of personal desires, while everything else becomes "abstract." Sooner or later they will come to realize that what they thought was abstract is objective and real, and vice versa. Books of elevating sermons and prayer—*Nahj al-Balagha,*[66] *Mafatih al-Jinan,*[67] and the like—all offer support for man in his efforts to become a true human being.

Once a man has become a true human being, he will be the most active of men. He will till the land, but till it for God's sake. He will also wage war, for all the wars waged against unbelievers and oppressors were waged by men absorbed in the divine unity and engaged in the constant recitation of prayer. Most of those who fought with the Most Noble Messenger (upon whom be peace and blessings) or with the Commander of the Faithful (upon whom be peace) were men devoted to countless acts of worship.

The Commander of the Faithful not only stood in prayer at the beginning of a battle; he would also continue his prayer in its midst. Once someone asked him a question concerning the divine unity just as a battle was about to begin, and he proceeded to answer it. When another person objected, "Is now the time for such things?" he replied, "This is the reason that we are fighting Mu'awiya, not for any worldly gain. It is not our true aim to capture Syria; of what value is Syria?" It was not the aim of the Prophet or the Commander of the Faithful to capture Syria and Iraq, but rather to make men into true human beings, and to free them from the clutches of oppressors. This they did because they were reciters of prayer, not in spite of that fact. Look at the Prayer of Kumayl, which has been transmitted from the Commander of the Faithful, and reflect on the fact that it was composed by a man who wielded the sword.

At one time, it was the practice to burn the books of prayer in order to deprive people of them. That vile person Kasravi[68] set aside a day on which books relating to mysticism or supplicatory prayer would be brought in for burning. They fail to understand what effect supplicatory prayer has on the souls of men; they do not realize that it is the reciters of prayer who perform all virtuous and blessed deeds. Those who recite prayers and engage in *dhikr*, even in a weak and parrotlike manner, will benefit to a certain degree, and to that degree they will be better off than those who abandon prayer and invocation. Similarly, the person who performs his daily prayers, even at a low level of awareness, is better than the person who does not; he will be purer of soul, and at least will not engage in theft, for example. Look at the statistics on crime and see how few crimes have been committed by students of the religious sciences in comparison with other people. See how few *mullas* are guilty of theft, drunkenness, or other offenses. Of course there are some persons who have infiltrated the religious institutions, but they are not given to prayer or other forms of worship; they have merely assumed the guise of the *mulla* for the sake of worldly benefit. As for those who are given to reciting prayers and fulfilling the outward duties of Islam, they have either no criminal records or relatively few. They are a support for the order of the world.

We must not, then, dismiss supplicatory prayer or dissuade our young from engaging in it. There are people who would do so on the pretext of bringing the Qur'an into greater prominence, but supplicatory prayer is a path to understanding the Qur'an, a path we must not lose. The notion that the Qur'an alone should be recited, to the total exclusion of supplicatory prayer and *hadith*, is an insinuation of the devil. Once we exclude supplicatory prayer and *hadith,* we will lose the Qur'an itself. Those who wish to set aside *hadith* in order to promote the Qur'an are incapable of promoting it, and likewise, those who say, "We do not want supplicatory prayer, only the Qur'an" are incapable of acting in accordance with the Qur'an.

All these notions are insinuations of the devil designed to mislead our young. But our young must ask themselves which group has served society better—those who cultivate the *hadith* and engage in supplicatory prayer and *dhikr,* or those who have abandoned them all, claiming to be devoted exclusively to the Qur'an. It is the believers, those who supplicate and remember God and perform their prayers regularly, that have performed virtuous and charitable acts and established institutions to aid the weak. Those who could afford it have also established madrasas and hospitals.

These forms of devotional practice, then, must not be banished from our people. On the contrary, let us encourage the people to turn increasingly to God through them. Quite apart from the fact that they help man in his movement toward absolute perfection, they are of benefit to society. For the person who devotes himself to prayer will not disturb lawful public order, nor will he engage in thievery, and prevention of theft is more beneficial to society than apprehension of a thief once a theft has already been committed. Suppose that half the members of society engage in supplicatory prayer, *dhikr,* and so forth; this means that half of society will be abstaining from sin. The merchant, for example, will not be stealing from his customers. But those who take their guns to go lie in wait on mountain passes and shoot people are strangers to prayer and invocation.

Society is trained and educated, then, by means of these supplicatory prayers, as God and the Most Noble Messenger have indicated: "Say: 'Were it not for your supplicatory prayer, your Lord would not pay you heed' " (25:77). Those who claim to be devoted to the Qur'an should realize that the Qur'an itself exalts supplicatory prayer and exhorts men to engage in it. God tells them that if it were not for their calling upon Him, He would not pay any attention to them. Those who claim to reject supplicatory prayer on the authority of the Qur'an are rejecting the Qur'an, for the Qur'an says: "Call upon me in prayer, that I may answer you" (40:60).

May God make us devotees of supplicatory prayer, devotees of *dhikr,* and devotees of the Qur'an, if He so wills.

4

HE IS THE OUTWARD
AND THE INWARD

ANOTHER MATTER THAT EMERGES from what we said on previous occasions is that the *ba* in *Bismillah* ("In the Name of God") is not a causative *ba*, as the grammarians would put it. There can be no question of cause and effect with respect to God's action. God's action is best described in terms of manifestation, for that is the term the Qur'an itself uses in the verse: "His Lord manifested Himself to the mountain" (7:143), and implies in the verse: "He is the First and the Last, and the Outward and the Inward" (57:3). Manifestation implies a relationship of a different mode than that of cause and effect, which would presuppose an inclination on the part of the Divine Essence toward creation.

Therefore, we must either interpret causality broadly enough to accommodate manifestation, or say flatly that the *ba* in *Bismillah* is not a causative *ba*. *Bismillah* has the sense of "by means of the name of God," "by means of His manifestation," and in conjunction with *al-hamdu lillah*, it means: "Praise belongs to God by means of His name." It is not that the name is a cause of which praise is the effect (to the best of my recollection, the expression "cause and effect" does not occur anywhere in the Qur'an or the Sunna). Rather, it is an expression used by the philosophers. The terms we encounter in the Qur'an are "manifestation" and "creation."

Another point to be mentioned, and one that is the subject of a certain tradition, is the dot under the *ba* of *Bismillah*. It is referred to in a particular tradition attributed to the Commander of the Faithful (upon whom be peace). The authenticity of the tradition is uncertain, and there are some indications that it has been falsely ascribed to him. In any event, he is reputed to have said: "I am the dot under the *ba*."[69] If the tradition is authentic, we can take the dot to mean "absolute manifestation," the first individuation, which consists of *vilayat* in its essential meaning; i.e., universal *vilayat*.[70] The first individuation or absolute manifestation, in turn, may be understood as the highest degree of being, corresponding to universal *vilayat*.

There are also a number of questions connected with the sense of the word "name." One is that the name sometimes stands for the Divine Essence; it is the comprehensive or Supreme Name, of which the names Compassionate and Merciful are the manifestations. *Allah* is the supreme name, the first manifestation standing for the Essence, and the other names represent nominal manifestation. The Essence also has other manifestations, notably active manifestations, which are said to relate either to the oneness (*vahidiyat*)[71] or the will. These terms should be noted.

Many divine names are mentioned in the last three verses of *Surat al-Hashr:* "He is God, other than Whom there is no god, the Knower of the manifest and the unseen; He is the Compassionate, the Merciful;/He is God, other than whom there is no god, the Sovereign, the Sanctified, Peace, the Guardian of Faith, the Preserver of Safety, the Mighty, the Irresistible, the Supreme. Glorified be God above the partners that they attribute to Him!/He is God, the Creator, the Evolver, the Bestower of Forms" (59:22-24).

We see three possible categories of names mentioned in each of these verses. In the first, the name *Allah* stands for the Essence, and the names that follow it are apposite to the Essence. In the second, the name *Allah* stands for the manifestation of the Essence by means of the attributes, and the names that follow it correspond to that. While in the third, *Allah* stands for the active manifestation of the Essence, and the names following it are again correspondent. To put it differently, there are three forms of manifestation: the manifestation of the Essence to the Essence, the manifestation through the names, and the manifestation through the acts.

"He is the First and the Last": this may mean that the existence of all that lies between first and last is negated; there is only He. Again, "He is the Outward and the Inward": that is, whatever is manifest is He, not from Him. There are different degrees of manifestation, but the manifestations are not separate from the Manifestor. This is difficult to conceive, but once a person has grasped it, it is easy for him to assent to it.

Allah may also be a name indicating the manifestation of the Essence through the attributes, and if that is the case, it is a comprehensive (*jami'*) manifestation. This does not contradict the first two possibilities; it is compatible with both of them, although they are mutually incompatible. The compatibility is due to the absence of separation between the degrees of manifestation.

We are, of course, passing over these matters very rapidly without discussing them fully, but there is a further matter to which I must draw attention. Sometimes we attempt to gauge reality in accordance with sensory perception; at other times, we view it in accordance with 'reason; and at still other times, we contemplate it with our heart. Beyond the vision of the heart, there is also the possibility of witnessing.[72] Generally, however, we rely on rational perception and the weighing of proof, and even according to this usual method, we can recognize that all reality can be reduced to the Sacred Essence and Its manifestations.

There are three categories of manifestation then—the manifestation of the Essence to the Essence, the manifestation through the attributes, and the manifestation through the acts—that may be indicated in the verses cited above. They also yield the meaning that in the face of God Almighty, nothing exists; in the face of absolute being, nothing can exist.

If we understand this through rational perception, we can examine ourselves and see whether we have conveyed it to our hearts, where it can be converted into faith; whether we have assimilated it by means of spiritual wayfaring, for it to be converted into gnosis; and whether we have attained states even beyond that.

Regardless of the mode and degree of our perception, reality remains what it is. And the reality is this: there is nothing other than God Almighty; whatever is, is He. The manifestation is not only His; it is also He. There is no exact image that can be evoked in this respect; the object that casts a shadow together with the shadow itself is imprecise and defective. A preferable image would be the ocean and its waves. The wave has no separate existence with respect to the ocean; it is the ocean, although one cannot say the converse, that the ocean is its waves. Waves come into exist-

ence only through the motion of the ocean. When we consider the
matter rationally, it appears to us that both the ocean and the
waves exist, the latter being an accident with respect to the former.
But the truth of the matter is that there is nothing but ocean; the
wave is also the ocean. This world is also like a wave with respect
to God.

This image, too, is inevitably defective, of course. When we
attempt to understand these matters in accordance with our limited perception, we are bound to have recourse to general images
that enable us to grasp the concepts involved. The next stage is to
establish the truth of those concepts by means of rational proof.
And if we wish to establish the truth of the statement that there
exists only the Essence and Its manifestations, that there is only
pure and absolute being, being without qualification, we say
that if being is subject to any limit or defect, it is not absolute being; absolute being is that in which there is neither defect nor
individuation. And since there is neither defect nor individuation
in absolute being, it must be the entirety of being, not lacking in
any respect. All of its attributes are absolute, not individuated:
compassion, mercy, divinity—all these are absolute.

Once light or being is absolute and undifferentiated, it must
include all perfections within itself, since the loss of a single perfection entails individuation. If there is even a single point of
deficiency in the Divine Essence, it will mean that a point of being
is absent; being will no longer be absolute, and becoming deficient, it will also become contingent and no longer necessary,
for necessary being is absolute perfection and beauty. Therefore,
when we regard the matter using the imperfect method of rational
proof, we conclude that *Allah* is the name for the Essence of absolute being, Which is the source of all manifestations. It contains
all the names and all the attributes and is absolute perfection, perfection without individuation. This perfection cannot lack anything, for if it did, it would no longer be absolute but contingent,
however high the degree of relative perfection that it might still
enjoy. It is said that "Pure being is all things, but is not a single
thing among them."[73] That is, it is all things, not by means of
individuation, but in absolute perfection.

In addition, since the names are not separate from the Essence,
all that applies to the name *Allah* must also apply to the name

407

Compassionate. Once Compassionate becomes absolute perfection, absolute mercy must also possess all the perfections of being, for otherwise it would not be absolute.

"Call upon *Allah* or call upon the Compassionate; however you call upon Him, His are the Most Beautiful Names" (17:110). All the Most Beautiful Names are present in all the attributes of God Almighty in absolute fashion. This being the case, there can be no question of boundaries between the name and the thing named, or between one name and another name. The Most Beautiful Names are not like the names that we apply to things, each in accordance with different perceptions that we have. For example, we speak of light and manifestion, but light and manifestation are not two separate aspects of the same reality: manifestation is identical to light, and light to manifestation. Absolute being, then, is absolute perfection, ánd absolute perfection means the possession of all attributes in absolute fashion, in such a way that no separation among them is conceivable.

The foregoing represents a process of rational argument. A certain mystic is reputed to have said, "Wherever I go, I find this blind man with his stick." By the blind man he meant Avicenna, and the sentence as a whole means that whatever he[74] attained by means of visionary experience, Avicenna attained by means of rational argument. He was blind, but had a stick—that is, rational argument—and supporting himself on that stick, he advanced to the same place that the mystic had reached through witnessing.

The mystic rightly described us who depend on rational argument as blind, for even after expounding the divine unity, absolute unity, and establishing by means of argument that the principle of being is absolute perfection, we are still dependent on our rational proofs and sit outside the wall of proof we have erected without being able to see. We may, of course, convey the result of our arguments to the heart by means of strenuous effort, so that the heart, in turn, comes to perceive that "Pure being is all things." The heart is like an infant that must be fed slowly and carefully, with small morsels. One who has reached a rational perception of the truth by means of proof and argument must gradually inculcate it to the heart, spelling it, as it were, letter by letter and constantly repeating it.

Once the heart has perceived that pure being is the sum total of all perfection, it will have attained faith. When the fruit of rational perception is conveyed to the heart through constant effort and repetition, the heart begins to read the Qur'an itself and to learn the truths contained in it. It will come to believe that "There is no one in the house but the owner of the house."[75]

This still represents the degree of faith, and even the degree of "tranquillity of the heart"[76] is inferior to what the prophets attained. Witnessing is superior to all of these, as Moses witnessed the beauty of God Almighty that He made manifest upon the mountain. After thirty- and then forty-day periods of vigil, Moses left the house of his wife's father, Shu'ayb, and set out with his wife and children. He said to his wife: "I perceive a fire" (20:10), and the fire that he saw was completely invisible to his wife and children. "[I will go to the fire] and bring you back a burning brand" (20:10): that is, "I will convey to you a manifestation of the fire." When Moses approached the fire, a voice called out to him from the fire that was enveloping the tree: "Verily I, I am God" (20:12). That is, Moses now witnessed what the blind man with his staff could not see, and what the mystic could only see with his heart.

These words that I am speaking and you are hearing fall far short of the reality. Other than Moses, no one could see the light emitted by that fire, just as when revelation came to the Prophet, no one could understand what it was. Who could understand the descent of the Qur'an—it all its thirty parts[77]—to the heart of the Prophet, when ordinary hearts would have been incapable of bearing the burden?

The heart has special properties; it is for this reason that the Qur'an descended to the heart. The Qur'an is a mystery, a mystery within a mystery, a mystery veiled and enveloped in mystery. It was necessary for the Qur'an to undergo a process of descent in order to arrive at the lowly degree of man. Even its entry into the heart of the Prophet was a descent, and from there it had to descend still further in order to become intelligible to others. But man, too, is a mystery, a mystery within a mystery. All we see of man is his outward appearance, which is entirely animal and maybe even inferior to other animals. Man, however, is an animal endowed with the aptitude of becoming human and attaining perfection, even absolute perfection, of becoming what is now inconceivable for him and transcending existence.

The Qur'an and man, then, both represent a series of mysteries. There is also a mystery pertaining to the outer world, the world of nature—namely, that you cannot perceive the essence of bodies but only their accidents. Our eyes see color and other visible qualities; our ears hear sounds; our sense of taste experiences flavor; and with our hands we feel the external dimensions of an object. But all of these are accidents. Where is the body itself to be found? When we wish to define something, we mention its width, its depth, and its length, but these too are accidents. If the body in question has the power of attraction, that is likewise an accident. Any attributes you may·use in your attempt to define it are accidents. Where, then, is the body itself? The body itself is a mystery, the shade or reflection of a higher mystery. It is the shadow cast by the unity of the Divine Essence, for the names and attributes of all that exists are the same names and attributes of the Essence that are made manifest to us. Were it not for the names and attributes, the world itself would be part of the unseen.

One meaning of "the unseen and the manifest"[78] may be that the world of nature itself comprises unseen and manifest sectors. The unseen sector is that which is unseen and imperceptible to us, for whenever we wish to define a thing, we speak only of its attributes, names, effects, and so on. Man's ability to perceive the thing that is a shadow of the absolute mystery is necessarily defective, unless it happens that he has advanced by means of *vilayat*[79] to the point where the manifestation of God Almighty, in all its dimensions, has entered his heart. This mystery exists in all things; the unseen and the manifest are everywhere commingled.

"The unseen," of course, may also mean the world of the angels, the world of the intelligences, or the like. These too comprise an inner mystery and an outer appearance, hiddenness and manifestation, as is implied in the expression: "He is the Outward and the Inward" (57:3). Wherever there is outwardness, there is also inwardness, and wherever there is inwardness, there is also outwardness.

All the names of God Almighty, then, participate in all the degrees of being, and each name is all of the names. It is not the case, for example, that the name or attribute Compassionate stands in contradistinction to the name Merciful, or to the name Avenger. All of them possess everything: "However you call upon Him, His are the Most Beautiful Names" (17:110). All the Most Beautiful Names belong to the Compassionate, as they belong, too, to the Merciful and to the Eternally Self-Subsistent. It is not as if one of the names relates to one thing, and another relates to something else. Were this the case, the name Compassionate would indicate a particular aspect or degree of God Almighty distinct from other aspects, and the Essence of God Almighty would then become a compendium of aspects. That is impossible for absolute being; it is not divisible into aspects. Absolute being is Compassionate *qua* absolute being, and it is also Merciful *qua* absolute being. God is Compassionate with all of His Essence, and Merciful with all of His Essence, and Light with all of His Essence; He is *Allah*. His being Compassionate is not something separate from His being Merciful.[80]

There are those who ascend by means of gnosis to the point where a complete manifestation of the Essence enters their hearts —not, of course, this physical heart, but the heart where the Qur'an descended, the heart where Jibra'il alighted, the heart that is the point of departure of revelation. That manifestation contains all other manifestations within itself; it is the Supreme Name. The Messenger of God himself is also the Supreme Name made manifest, for it has been said: "We are the Most Beautiful Names."

We began tonight's talk by discussing the question of causality and pointing out that the relation of God to His creation is not one of simple causality. Indeed that relationship cannot be stated adequately, but only indicated by various approximate images. We also discussed the sense of the "dot under the *ba*," always supposing the tradition in question to be authentic. Then we spoke of the various forms of manifestation: the manifestation of the Essence to the Essence, the manifestation of the Essence to the attributes, and the manifestation of the Essence to beings. This last constitutes our beings. To have recourse to another metaphor, imagine one hundred mirrors positioned so that the light of the sun is reflected in each. From one point of view, you might say that there are a hundred lights—one hundred separate, finite lights, each in a mirror. All of them, however, are the same light, the same manifestation of the sun visible in a hundred mirrors. Let me repeat that the image is approximate.

The manifestation of God Almighty takes place by means of individuations, which is not to say that the individuation is separate from the manifestation or light. When light manifests itself as an act, the concomitant is individuation. "Name" in the expression "In the Name of God, the Compassionate, the Merciful" means the name of the Essence, and the name *Allah* is the manifestation of the Essence that includes all manifestations. Compassionate and Merciful are part of this same comprehensive manifestation; they do not refer to separate things. *Allah*, Compassionate, and Merciful are like three names for the same entity. There is but one manifestation: He is *Allah* with all His Essence, Compassionate with all His Essence, and Merciful with all His Essence. It is impossible that this not be so, for if it were not, God would be limited and thus contingent.

As I said previously, "In the Name of God, the Compassionate, the Merciful" is syntactically connected to: "Praise belongs to God." We may therefore paraphrase the two expressions taken together as follows. "All instances of praise belong (or absolute praise belongs) to the comprehensive manifestation of *Allah*, Who with the entirety of His Essence is also Compassionate and Merciful." If one takes the second form of manifestation—that of the Essence to the attributes—the name indicating comprehensive manifestation is equivalent to absolute will; all things occur by means of it, by means of the name *Allah*. Finally, if we consider manifestation through the acts, the name *Allah* as a comprehensive manifestation will be equivalent to reality. To summarize, then, the name *Allah* is the name indicating the comprehensive manifestation within the Essence itself, with respect to the attributes, and with respect to the acts.

There is much else to be said concerning the names Compassionate and Merciful, but we must be brief. I hope we all feel that the discussion of these matters is necessary. Some people in their hearts totally deny all the concerns of mysticism and gnosis. He who lives at the level of an animal cannot believe that anything exists beyond his bestial state. We, however, must believe in the validity of these concerns, and the first step toward advancing beyond our present state is to refrain from denying them. A person should not deny whatever he is ignorant of. It was Avicenna who said: "Whoever denies something without proof forfeits the attribute of humanity."

Just as the affirmation of something depends upon proof, so, too, does its denial. To deny is different from to confess ignorance. There are certain hearts that are given to denial; they deny everything they are unable to perceive and thereby "forfeit the attribute of humanity." A person must have proof in order both to affirm something and to deny it. Otherwise he must say: "I do not know; it may be so." Anything you hear, regard as possible; it is possible that it might be, and also possible that it might not be. But why should we engage in denial, when our hands cannot reach beyond this world, and what they have touched is only a small part of this world? What we know of this world is very limited; many things of which we were ignorant a hundred years ago have now become known, and others will become known in the future. We who have not been able to comprehend fully the world of nature and man—why should we deny what has been granted to the *awliya?* Certain hearts are predisposed to denial, hearts that are entirely deprived of the penetration of truth and light. A person with such a heart will not say, "I do not know"; he will say instead, "It is not true." He will accuse the mystics of talking nonsense, whereas in reality, he is veiled from the perception of what they are saying. The same concerns that the deniers label "nonsense" are also to be found in the Qur'an and the Sunna, although the deniers would not dare admit it.

Such denial is a type of unbelief, although not, of course, unbelief as defined by the *shari'a.* It is unbelief to deny what one is ignorant of. All the misfortunes that beset man arise out of his inability to perceive reality and his consequent denial of it. Unable to attain what the *awliya* have attained, he denies it and falls prey to the worst form of unbelief.

The first step to take is to refrain from denying what is in the Qur'an and the Sunna, what the *awliya* have said, what the mystics and philosophers have said, within the limits of their perception. (There are some who go so far in their denial as to say: "I will not believe unless I can dissect God with this knife.") Let us at least not deny what the prophets and the *awliya* have said, for unless we take this first step, we cannot take the second.

413

Denial does not allow the denier to pursue anything unless it lies immediately in front of him. If a person wishes to emerge from the dark abode in which he is caught, he must at least grant the possibility that all these matters are true, for otherwise he will remain a prisoner behind the wall of denial. Let him pray to God that He unfold a path before him, a path that leads where he must go, for it is God alone Who can unfold the path.

Once a man ceases his denial and beseeches God for a path, a path will gradually open itself up before him, for God will not refuse him. Let us, then, at least attain the stage of not denying what is contained in the Qur'an and the Sunna. There are some who claim to believe in the Qur'an and the Sunna, but deny whatever it contains that lies outside their perception. They do not express their denial outright with respect to the Qur'an and the Sunna, but if someone begins to speak on the mystical matters contained therein, they will begin to talk nonsense and deny the truth of what is said. Such denial deprives man of many things. It prevents him from attaining the state needed to set out on the path; it is an obstacle that bars his way.

I recommend to all of you, then, that you at least grant the possibility that what the *awliya* attained and experienced is true. You might not declare openly, "It is possible"; but do not make a downright denial and say, "It is all nonsense"; for if you do, you will not be able to set out on the path. So, remove this obstacle.

I hope that we may remove this veil of denial from our hearts and ask God Almighty to acquaint us with the language of the Qur'an. For the Qur'an has been revealed in its own distinct language, and we must become familiar with that language. The Qur'an possesses everything. It is like a vast banquet that God has spread out in front of all humanity and that everyone partakes of according to his own appetite. The sicknesses of the heart deprive man of his appetite, but if his heart is healthy, he will partake of the banquet according to his appetite. The world, too, is a vast banquet and all creatures partake of it according to their needs and capacities: some are content with mere grass, others eat fruit, and still others aspire to more elaborate nourishment. Man partakes of this banquet of being in one way when he is at the animal level, and in another way when he has risen above it. So, too, with the Qur'an: everyone partakes of its banquet according to his own capacities and appetite. The highest share is reserved for the one to whom it was revealed: "The only person who truly knows the Qur'an is he who was addressed by it." We should not despair, though, but rather should take our own share of the banquet.

The first step is to stop imagining that nothing exists except nature, and that the Qur'an was revealed exclusively to discuss matters of nature and society. To imagine this is to deny prophethood, for the Qur'an was revealed to make men into men, and all matters of worldly and social concern are means to this end.

Worship and prayer are also means to this end, the end of eliciting the true nature of man and making it manifest, of bringing it forth from potentiality into actuality. Natural man should become divine man in the sense that everything pertaining to him should become divine; whatever he looks at he will see as God. All the prophets were sent to assist man in attaining this goal. They did not wish to establish a government or administer the world as an end in itself, although this was part of their mission, for even the animals have a worldly existence and administer their part of the world.

Those who have eyes to see with know that justice is an attribute of God Almighty, and so they strive to establish a government of justice and to ensure social justice. But this is not their ultimate aim; it is merely a means for advancing man toward that goal for the sake of which all the prophets were sent.

May God Almighty support us and grant us success in all things.

5

THE SAME THING IN DIFFERENT LANGUAGES

BEFORE PROCEEDING, I WOULD LIKE to raise a point, which you might find useful or even necessary.

The disagreements that occur between the visionary and the scholar are caused by their failure to understand each other's languages, for each has his own distinctive way of expressing things. I do not know whether you have heard the story of the three people —one a Persian, one a Turk, and the other an Arab—who were discussing what they should eat for lunch. The Persian said, "Let us eat *angur*"; the Arab said, "No, let's have *'anab*"; and the Turk said, "As for me, I would prefer *uzum*." Now all three words mean "grapes," but since they did not understand each other's languages, they argued until each of them had to fetch what he desired and they realized they had all wanted the same thing.[81]

Different languages express the same thing in different ways. The philosophers, for example, have their own language and terminology; so do the mystics, the *fuqaha*, and even the poets. The *ma'sumin*[82] (upon whom be peace) also have their own language, and we must examine the language of each of the other four groups to see which is closest to the language of the *ma'sumin* and also to that of the Qur'an. The matter to be expressed is the same: no rational human being who believes in the divine unity will disagree that God Almighty exists and that He is the origin of all existence: all creatures are the outcome of this origin. No rational person will believe that a man dressed in jacket and trousers, or in turban and cloak, could be God; such a man is a created being. When it comes to interpreting the relationship of God and His creation, however, and choosing terms to express it, disagreements arise. Let us see, then, why the mystics express matters in a certain way, what prompts them to do so.

It is my intention to reconcile the various groups, of course, and to point out that they are all saying the same thing. I do not wish to justify all the philosophers, all the mystics, or all the *fuqaha*. As the saying goes, "There's many a cloak that deserves the fire,"[83] and the members of each group frequently may deserve criticism. Conversely, within each group there have been many pure individuals, and the disagreements that have arisen have been caused by the failure to comprehend each other's terminology. For example, within the madrasa, the Akhbaris[84] and the Usulis[85] have denounced each other as unbelievers, even though their concerns and beliefs are identical.

The philosophers, or some of them, use terminology like "cause of causes," "primary cause," "secondary cause," "causality," and so forth. This dry terminology of "causality," "cause and effect," "principle and derivative" was especially used by the pre-Islamic philosophers, but our *fuqaha* have also made free use of it, although, at the same time, they speak of "Creator" and "creation." Then there are certain mystics who use a different terminology, such as "manifest," "manifestation," and the like. Let us see why they use those terms, and why the terms also occur in the usage of the Imams (upon whom be peace), who also refrain from speaking of "causality," although they do mention "creation." Why is it that the mystics refrain from using the terminology of the philosophers or common usage, and instead express matters differently?

To speak of cause and effect means that one being—the cause—brings another being—the effect—into existence, so that on the one hand, we have the cause, and on the other, the effect. What do we mean by "on the one hand . . . and on the other"? Is there a spatial difference between the cause and the effect, as there is with the sun and its light? The sun possesses the light, insofar as the light emerges from it and is its manifestation, but the sun is a substance located in one place, and its light is another substance located in another place, although it is the effect produced by the sun. Can we speak of the Essence of the necessary being acting as cause in the sense of natural causation, as when, for example, fire causes heat or the sun causes light, where the effect in both cases is spatially separated from the cause? Can we say that the Supreme Principle is separate from other beings, or that they are spatially and temporally separate from Him?

As I said before, it is difficult to imagine fully the nature of abstract being, particularly the Supreme Principle of all being, God Almighty, and the manner in which He holds all being in His sustaining embrace.

What is meant by the Qur'anic saying: "He is with you wherever you are" (57:4)? Does "with you" imply some type of physical presence?

Phrases like this have been used in the Qur'an and the Sunna because they are the closest approximation to a reality that cannot be fully expressed. It is extremely difficult to understand the concepts of Creator and created. God Almighty is the Creator and we are created by Him, but does this involve a spatial difference, and what is the nature of the relationship of the Creator and His creation? Does it resemble the relationship of fire and the effect it creates, or that of the soul and its visual, auditory, and other capacities? The latter provides a more adequate parallel than any other image, but it still does not fully correspond to the sustaining embrace of all beings, for that embrace means that there is no place in creation where He does not exist.

"Were you to let a rope descend to the nether parts of the earth, . . ."[86] you would find God there. This and similar traditions are not intended to point out a literal truth, that God Almighty is restrictively located in a certain place like a contingent being, like one of us dressed in turban and cloak. No rational person would make such a statement.

Expressions implying a location for God Almighty are merely attempts to make the relationship of the Creator and creation comprehensible. It may happen, however, that someone not fully conversant with these matters might say of a certain thing: "This is God." It is for this reason that the philosophers, including the Muslims, have said: "Pure being is all things, but is not a single thing among them."

This statement is not a contradiction, despite its appearance, because pure being rejects all deficiency and possesses all perfection, whereas discrete beings are all deficient. If pure being were then to become identified with a discrete being, it would become deficient, whereas it is complete and exempt from all deficiency. Being exempt from all deficiency, it is impossible that it should lack a single perfection, and every perfection found in every being therefore comes from it and is its trace or manifestation. When that manifestation exists in the essence in simple (as opposed to compound) form, it is the totality of perfection and the essence of all perfection.

The statement that pure being is "all things" means, then, that it is all perfection, and the statement that it is "not a single thing among them" means that it is free of all deficiency. That pure being is all things should not be taken to mean that you and I are pure being, for pure being is "not a single thing among them," and it alone is the totality of perfection.

There are some who, failing to understand matters properly, have quoted in this connection the saying: "Colorlessness fell prey to color." The verse in which this saying occurs is not at all related to the matter under discussion, which is the nature of reality. Instead, the verse concerns a war or dispute that arose between two men; but failing to understand the statement, people have regarded it as blasphemous.[87]

The verse it occurs in seeks to answer the question of why wars arise in the world. What is meant by "color" in this verse is "attachment," another expression that occurs in the usage of some poets, as, for example, in the phrase "who is free of all that takes on the color of attachment."[88] As for "colorlessness," it means lack of attachment to anything in the natural realm. When such attachment no longer exists, dispute and war will vanish. All disputes that arise derive from the covetous attachment of two or more adversaries to the natural realm; the adversaries necessarily oppose each other in everything.

The poet means that the primordial disposition of man is free of color, and when this color does not exist, dispute will also not exist. If Pharaoh had been, like Moses, without the color of attachment, no dispute would have arisen between the two, and if all the people in the world were prophets, no dispute would ever arise. Disputes arise out of competing attachments. But colorlessness "fell prey to color": man's primordial disposition, free of the color of attachment, fell prey to attachment, and discord arose. Were it not for the color of attachment, Pharaoh would have made peace with Moses.

This is the true sense of the verse, one that relates to two separate beings that are at war with each other, not to the nature of reality or the relation of the Creator to creation.

Some people, who have failed to understand the true meaning of certain terms and expressions used by the mystics, have gone so far as to declare them unbelievers. But let us see whether these concepts and terms do not also occur in the prayers of the Imams (upon whom be peace).

In the Invocations of Sha'ban,[89] which were recited by all the Imams (something true of nó other prayer or invocation), we read as follows: "O God, grant me total separation from other-than-You and attachment to You and brighten the vision of our hearts with the light of looking upon You, so that they may pierce the veils of light and attain the fountainhead of magnificence, and our spirits may be suspended from the splendor of Your sanctity. O God, make me one of those who answer You when You call, and who cry out at Your splendor."[90] What is meant by these pleas? What did the Imam mean by "total separation from other-than-You and attachment to You"? Why did he petition God for this form of spiritual advancement? He pleads: "Brighten the vision of our hearts." What could this mean if not a form of vision enabling man to look upon God Almighty? As for piercing "the veils of light" and attaining "the fountainhead of magnificence," and our spirits being "suspended from the splendor of God's sanctity," this is none other than the state that the Qur'an describes Moses as having attained, and none other than the effacement and vanishing of which the mystics speak. Similarly, the process of "attaining" the fountainhead of magnificence is precisely the same as the "attaining" to which the mystics refer.[91] As for "the fountainhead of magnificence," it is, of course, God Almighty; since all magnificence derives from Him, He is its fountainhead.

The terminology used by the mystics, then, is consistent with the Qur'an and the Sunna, and for this reason, the concept of manifestation they employ is to be preferred to the constricting notions of causality used by the philosophers. "Creator" and "creation" are the terms employed in common usage, but "manifestation" is also preferable to them since it more closely approximates what is an ineffable reality. One may easily assent to the relation of God to His creation, but to imagine it is extremely difficult. How can we imagine a being that is present everywhere, that is both hidden in things and manifest in them? Indeed, God is the cause of creation, but to say that is not enough, for God is present in all things; in their outward and inward aspects, "There is naught that is without Him." There is no way that such truths can be fully expressed in words; all that is possible is, for those who have the capacity, to petition God for the immediate experience of reality, as in the Invocations of Sha'ban.

The differences that exist in terminology, then, are no reason for one group to denounce the other as unbelievers, or for that group to respond by denouncing its accusers as ignorant.

We must first understand what is being said, and in the case of the mystic, we must comprehend the inner state that prompts him to express himself in a certain way. Light may sometimes enter his heart in such a manner that he finds himself saying, "Everything is God." Remember that in the prayers you recite, expressions occur like "the eye of God," "the ear of God," "the hand of God," and all of these are in the same vein as the terminology of the mystics. There is also the tradition to the effect that when you place alms in the hands of the pauper, you are placing them in the hands of God. Then, too, there is the Qur'anic verse: "When you cast the dust, you did not cast it; rather God cast it" (8:17). What does it mean? That God cast the dust instead of the Prophet? That is the literal meaning, which you all accept, but those who experience the reality that is indicated in this verse cannot see matters in the same way, and are bound to express themselves differently. Nonetheless, you will find the expressions they use throughout the Qur'an and especially in the prayers of the Imams. There is no reason to regard them with suspicion. We must understand why they express themselves in their particular, distinct way, and why they have deliberately abandoned the common usage of which they are certainly aware.

They have insisted on doing this out of a refusal to sacrifice reality to themselves, and instead, they have sacrificed themselves to reality. If we understand what such persons are attempting to say, we will also understand the terms that they use, which are, after all, expressions derived from the Qur'an and the traditions of the Imams. None of us has the right to say of a certain person or thing, "This is God," and no rational person would accept such a claim. However, one may perceive a manifestation of God that is completely impossible to express other than by formulations such as this, which occurs in a prayer concerning the *awliya:* "There is no difference between You and them, except that they are Your servants, whose creation and dissolution lies in Your hands."

All expressions are necessarily inadequate, but those of the Qur'an and the Sunna come closer to conveying the truth than all others. Not everyone, of course, is able to comprehend and correctly employ these expressions. There have been some persons, however, who, having a complete and exact mastery of all the sciences, would talk about the manifestation and visage of God. Some of them were my contemporaries, and I was closely acquainted with them.

So make peace with those given to the use of a certain terminology. I repeat, it is not my wish to defend any category of persons as a whole, or to generalize concerning them. For example, when I speak of the religious scholars, I do not mean that they all possess a given set of attributes. What I wish to make clear is that no class should be rejected as a whole, and that no one should be denounced as an unbeliever merely because he uses the language of the mystics. First, see what he is saying and then try to understand it; if you do, I do not think you will deny its truth. Bear in mind the parable with which I started: the difference between *'anab, angur,* and *uzum* is the same as that between "causality," "creation," and "manifestation."

This problem of terminology is caused by the difficulty of discussing a being who is everywhere but is not identifiable with any object, although we do encounter the terms "hand of God" and "eye of God," as for example in, "God's hand is over their hands" (48:10). In what sense is God's hand over their hands? Clearly, in a supramaterial sense, but beyond that we can say very little. In just the same way that God Almighty is exalted beyond commingling with men or substantially conjoining with anything, so, too, He is exalted beyond our fully comprehending a single one of His manifestations. Even His manifestations in their ground are unknown to us. We still believe and do not reject, and we hope that those matters occurring in the Qur'an and the Sunna that we believe in will be made accessible to us.

God says in *Surat al-Hadid:* "He is the First and the Last, the Outward and the Inward," and also, "He is with you wherever you are." According to a certain tradition, full comprehension of these expressions, as well as the rest of this *sura's* first six verses, is reserved for those who shall come at the end of time. And who among us understands even what is meant by "the end of time"? Probably not more than one or two people in the entire world.

The important point to be noted is that Islam does not merely consist of its ordinances. Ordinances are secondary, not the essence of religion, and the essence should not be sacrificed to the secondary. Once the late Shaykh Muhammad Bahari,[92] on seeing a certain person approach, said: "He is a just and unbelieving person." We asked how this could be. He answered: "He is just in that he acts according to the stipulations of the law, but he is an unbeliever because the god he worships is not God."

There is also the story in tradition of an ant who thought God had two feelers, for in his self-love, he regarded the possession of two feelers as the mark of perfection! The ant is also mentioned in the Qur'an, in the verse, "At length, when they came to the valley of the ants, one of the ants said to its fellows: 'O ants! enter your dwellings lest Solomon and his troops destroy you, for they are unaware.' So Solomon smiled, amused at her speech" (27:18-19). The common ant that we see everywhere regarded Solomon, then, as unaware. Similarly the hoopoe said to him: "I have compassed territory that you have not compassed" (27:20). Now Solomon was a prophet, and one of his companions had brought the throne of Bilqis to him "in the twinkling of an eye" (27:40). (This was something unprecedented: was it some form of communication, or was the throne destroyed and then recreated?) It is also said in a certain tradition that another of the companions of Solomon knew one letter of the Supreme Name. Nonetheless, the hoopoe said to Solomon, who had companions of this rank and whose commands were obeyed by all orders of being, that *he* was aware of matters unknown to Solomon.

We find certain scholars, however, whose rank is obviously less than that of Solomon, denying the validity of mysticism and thus depriving themselves of a form of knowledge. It is regrettable.

When I first went to Qum (soon after the religious teaching institution had been established),[93] the late Mirza 'Ali Akbar Hakim[94] (may God have mercy upon him) was still alive. A certain pious individual (may God have mercy upon him, too) said: "See the level to which Islam has fallen; the doors of Mirza 'Ali Akbar are open to receive students." For some of the *'ulama,* among them the late Khwansari[95] and the late Ishraqi,[96] would go to Mirza 'Ali Akbar's house to study mysticism with him. Now Mirza 'Ali Akbar was a very worthy man, but when he died, there was so much suspicion about him that a preacher found it necessary to testify from the *minbar* that he had seen him reading the Qur'an. This greatly disturbed the late Shahabadi.[97] It is regrettable that some of the *'ulama* should entertain those suspicions and deprive themselves of the benefits to be gained from studying mysticism. Similar attitudes prevail toward philosophy, which is actually very straightforward. Now if the *'ulama* in question had achieved the same goal that is common to all the groups, such disputes would not have arisen. Those who wear cloaks and turbans and denounce the mystics as unbelievers do not understand what they are saying; if they did, they would not denounce them.

The whole problem is caused by differing terms and expressions. Some people find that the language of causality does not correspond to reality. For as I have repeatedly said in the course of these talks, the name is not separate from the thing named. The name is a manifestation, not a sign comparable to a milestone. The term most suggestive of the relation of creation to God, although still inadequate, is the Qur'anic term *aya.*[98]

The Qur'an is like a banquet from which everyone must partake in accordance with his capacity. It belongs to everyone, not to any particular group; there is a share in it for everyone. The same is true of the prayers of the Imams (upon whom be peace). They are replete with mystical insight and may be regarded as the tongue or interpreter of the Qur'an, interpreting those aspects of it that lie beyond the reach of other men. People should not be dissuaded from the recitation and study of these prayers; no one should say, "We wish to confine ourselves to the Qur'an." It is by means of these prayers that people make the acquaintance of God, and once they do so, neither the world nor their own selves will be of value in their eyes any longer, and they will set to work for God. Those who recited these prayers and experienced the states reflected in them were the very ones who wielded the sword for God's sake. The Qur'an and prayer are not separate from each other. Would it occur to anyone to say, "We have the Qur'an, so we no longer need the Prophet"? The Qur'an and the Prophet belong together, and they shall never be separate. Those who wish to bring about such separations—the Qur'an from the Imams, the Imams from their prayers—even going so far as to burn books of prayer, are motivated by the error that invariably befalls those who try to venture beyond their innate limits.

Kasravi,[99] for example, was a historian well-versed in history and also a good writer. But he became arrogant and went so far as to claim prophethood. He laid aside the prayers of the Imams completely, although he continued to accept the Qur'an. Unable to rise to the level of prophethood, Kasravi brought prophethood down to his own level.

The mystics, the mystically inclined poets, and the philosophers are all saying the same thing, although they use different idioms. The poets have their own terminology and idiom, and among them, Hafiz[100] has his own peculiar mode of expression.

If I make repeated use of the same expressions—"manifestation" and so forth—do not object that I have mentioned them already; they must constantly be repeated. Once a group of merchants came to see the late Shahabadi (may God have mercy upon him), and he began to speak to them on the same mystical topics that he taught to everyone. I asked him whether it was appropriate to speak to them of such matters and he replied: "Let them be exposed just once to these 'heretical' teachings!" I too now find it incorrect to divide people into categories and pronounce some incapable of understanding these matters.

A subject for further discussion would be "the Compassionate, the Merciful," as it occcurs both in the *Bismillah,* and in the third verse of the *Sura,* in particular whether the two attributes in the expression *Bismillah* describe the name or *Allah.*[101]

Notes

1. Muhyi'd-Din ibn 'Arabi: a master of theosophic Sufism, 560/1165-638-1240. His influence came to permeate the intellectual and spiritual life of virtually the entire Muslim world. The complete but relatively concise commentary on the Qur'an attributed to him appears in fact to have been written by a later Sufi, 'Abd ar-Razzaq Kashani; nonetheless, it very clearly bears the stamp of Ibn 'Arabi's thought. In addition, manuscripts survive of partial but more detailed commentaries. See Suleyman Ates, *Isari Tefsir Okulu* (Ankara, 1974), pp. 177-191.

2. 'Abd ar-Razzaq Kashani: prolific Sufi author, d. 730/1330. Most of his work bears the imprint of Ibn 'Arabi's influence. His best-known work is the Qur'an commentary entitled *Ta'wilat*, which has been wrongly ascribed to Ibn 'Arabi. See Ates, *Isari Tefsir Okulu*, pp. 204-211.

3. Mulla Sultan 'Ali: more commonly known as Sultan'alishah, a scholar and Sufi, 1251/1835-1327/1909. He belonged to the Gunabadi branch of the Ni'matullahi order. His commentary on the Qur'an, *Bayan as-Sa'ada fi Maqamat al-'Ibada*, was completed in 1311/1893 and first published three years later.

4. Tantawi: that is, Tantawi Jauhari, an Egyptian scholar, 1287/1871-1358/1940. His commentary on the Qur'an, *Tafsir al-Jawahir*, is marked by rationalizing tendencies.

5. Sayyid Qutb: leader of the Muslim Brethren in Egypt, 1324/1906-1386/1966. He was martyred by the regime of Jamal 'Abd an-Nasir, which accused him of conspiracy against the state, a charge it was unable to substantiate in court. He was a skillful and influential writer and his commentary on the Qur'an, *Fi Zilal al-Qur'an*, is widely read in the Arab world. It places particular emphasis on the relevance of the Qur'an to the contemporary problems of the Muslim world, as well as on its structural coherence. Parts of the commentary have been translated into Persian under the title *Dar Saya-yi Qur'an*. His work on social justice in Islam, *al-'Adalat al-Ijtima'iyya fi 'l-Islam*, has been made available in Persian translation and has enjoyed popularity in Iran.

426

6. *Majma' al-Bayan:* more fully, *Majma' al-Bayan li 'Ulum al-Qur'an,* one of the most voluminous and authoritative Shi'i commentaries on the Qur'an, written by Shaykh Abu 'Ali Amin ad-Din Tabarsi (d. 548/1153), who also wrote a number of shorter works on Qur'anic exegesis. See Muhammad 'Ali Mudarris, *Rayhanat al-Adab* (Tabriz, n.d.), IV, 36-41.

7. *Ahl-i 'ismat:* those possessing the quality of *'ismat* (see p, 156, n. 67), viz., the Prophet, his daughter Fatima, and the Twelve Imams. Obviously, the instruction that the Imams received from the Prophet in the interpretation of the Qur'an was not given to them directly (except in the case of 'Ali, the first Imam). What is meant, rather, is that the Imams inherited from the Prophet a certain body of teaching concerning the interpretation of the Qur'an, which they enriched as they transmitted it.

8. See p. 317, n. 105.

9. Seal of the Prophets: an epithet of the Prophet Muhammad, in whom prophethood reached its culmination and perfection.

10. *Awliya:* see p. 361, n. 2.

11. The Supreme Name is generally held to be the name *Allah,* which is supreme in that it relates to the Essence and all other names are subsumed within it.

12. See al-Qadi 'Iyad, *ash-Shifa bi Ta'rif Huquq al-Mustafa* (Damascus, n.d.), I, 577-578.

13. Given the special qualities of the name *Allah* that are under discussion here, qualities that are absent from all other designations of God, we leave it untranslated.

14. Arabic expression of unknown provenance.

15. The names Compassionate (*Rahman*) and Merciful (*Rahim*) relate to different aspects of divine mercy. The former manifests itself through the provision that God makes for the material necessities of all creatures by placing appropriate forms of sustenance in the world and equipping them with bodily senses and organs. Since the manifestation of this name makes no distinction between believer and nonbeliever, worshipper and sinner, rainfall may be regarded as its outward symbol. The name Merciful is manifested through the sending of revelation and guidance and the granting of salvation in the hereafter; only those who believe in religion and follow it benefit from this manifestation. See al-Ghazali, *al-Maqsad al-Asna fi Sharh Ma'ani Asma'i 'Llah al-Husna,* ed. Fadlou Shehadi (Beirut, 1971), pp. 65-70.

16. An allusion to the tradition: "My compassion has outstripped My anger," a celebrated *hadith qudsi* recorded by Bukhari, Muslim, Ibn

Maja, and others. The sense is that mercy is intrinsic to the Essence and thereby has primacy over anger.

17. Zayd and 'Amr: two paradigmatic names commonly used in grammatical and legal discussions.

18. This verse was revealed with reference to the Battle of Badr, the first engagement of the Muslim community in Medina with its enemies in Mecca, which took place in the second year of the Islamic era. In the course of the battle, the Prophet cast a handful of dust in the direction of the enemy, miraculously inducing panic in them. The statement that in reality it was not the Prophet but God Who cast the dust means that the Prophet, emptied of personal volition, was a pure instrument for the accomplishment of a divine act.

19. In the sixth year of the Islamic era, a group of Muslims swore allegiance to the Prophet at Hudaybiya. When they placed their hands on the hand of the Prophet as the outward sign of their pledge, his hand was a "manifestation of God" because obedience to him was equivalent to obedience to God (see Qur'an, 4:80: "Whoever obeys the Messenger obeys God," and p. 78).

20. 'Ismat: see p. 156, n. 67.

21. Backbiting (ghiba) is defined as mentioning behind the back of another a fault that he may possess but that one would not mention in his hearing. This practice is severely condemned in Qur'an, 49:12, where it is compared to eating the flesh of one's dead brother.

22. In addition to the physical heart (often termed qalb sanubari, "pineal heart"), there is a subtle heart that stands in an indefinable relationship to it and serves as the organ of faith and inner vision.

23. Shirk: see p. 154, n. 42.

24. A tradition of the Prophet.

25. The statement that "everything that is, is He," as well as similar formulations elsewhere in these lectures, should not be understood in a pantheistic sense. It does not mean that God is coextensive with His creation, so that creation enjoys divinity, but rather that other-than-God does not exist: He is the sole reality and the sole existence.

26. An utterance probably of the Commander of the Faithful, 'Ali ibn Abi Talib.

27. A celebrated hemistich from the Masnavi of the great Sufi poet Maulana Jalal ad-Din Rumi (604/1207-672/1273). The complete line reads: "Those who seek proof have wooden legs; wooden legs are very infirm" (Book I, line 2128).

28. *Fiqh:* see p. 157, n. 81.

29. Divine agent: *fa'il-i ilahi,* "that which makes the thing caused (*ma'lul*) emerge from utter non-existence into existence, which bestows perfection without losing it, and from the scope of whose being and the radiation of whose light none may escape" (Mulla Hadi Sabzavari, *Sharh-i Manzuma,* eds. M. Muhaqqiq and T. Izutsu [Tehran, 1348 Sh./1979], p. 185).

30. Tradition ascribed to Imam Ja'far as-Sadiq.

31. For a similar interpretation of this verse by the Sufi 'Ayn al-Quzat Hamadani (d. 526/1137), see *Namaha-yi 'Ayn al-Quzat Hamadani,* eds. 'A. Munzavi and 'A. 'Usayran (Tehran, 1350 Sh./1972), II, 24.

32. In the other sense, their migration is continuing because given the infinity of the divine being, there is no question of His constituting a destination that sooner or later may be reached.

33. Imam Khomeini's inclusion of himself in the group of those who have "not even begun to migrate" should be taken neither as an accurate description of his state nor as formal self-deprecation. Instead, it is an expression of genuine humility and, at the same time, self-identification with his audience for didactic purposes.

34. Cf. Qur'an, 4:58: "God commands you to return trusts to their possessors."

35. A tradition recorded by Bayhaqi.

36. Qur'an, 1:5.

37. These remarks should not be taken to imply a total disavowal of war. They are intended rather to condemn the wars that arise from two competing egoisms, which disregard divine norms, not the wars waged by truth against falsehood or the wars the Islamic state may find itself compelled to wage. For clarification, see the discussion of the conflict between Moses and the Pharaoh on pp. 419-420.

38. The lesser *jihad* is the struggle against the visible enemy in the battlefield, and the greater or supreme *jihad* is the ceaseless war man is called upon to wage against his lower self. See p. 349.

39. Battle of the Ditch: a battle fought in the fifth year of the Islamic era against the Meccan polytheists and their allies who sought to conquer Medina. The battle was so called because of the ditch dug around the city as a defensive measure. See also p. 160, n. 123.

40. *Kufr:* see p. 153, n. 40.

41. Abu Sufyan: the leader of the Meccan opposition to the Prophet for many years who later accepted Islam when it became apparent that

the Muslims were about to conquer Mecca. He died during the caliphate of 'Uthman, at the age of 88.

42. Mu'awiya: see p. 158, n. 101.

43. This phrase, the source of which we have been unable to identify, is quoted by Imam Khomeini in Arabic.

44. A tradition varyingly attributed to the Prophet and to Imam 'Ali.

45. *Mushrik:* one who is guilty of *shirk* (see p. 154, n. 42).

46. A prayer attributed to the fifth and sixth Imams. Its recitation is particularly recommended during the last hours of Friday. For the text of the prayer, see Shaykh 'Abbas Qummi, *Mafatih al-Jinan* (Tehran, n.d.), pp. 95-100.

47. Cf. this tradition of the Prophet: "The Qur'an has been revealed on seven levels (*ahruf*), each having an outer and an inner meaning, and 'Ali ibn Abi Talib has knowledge of both."

48. See Jalal ad-Din as-Suyuti, *al-Itqan fi 'Ulum al-Qur'an* (Cairo, 1370/1951), I, 39 ff.

49. The Prophet was not only the transmitter of the Qur'an to mankind at large but also its primary recipient: certain aspects of its meaning were reserved for him alone.

50. See n. 46 above.

51. Unveiling: *kashf,* immediate awareness of those unseen matters that lie beyond the dark and light veils of God's creation.

52. I.e., 'Ali ibn Abi Talib. The phrase "in every respect" obviously does not mean that he succeeded to the prophetic function of the Messenger, but rather that he inherited full political authority as well as a unique competence to understand and interpret the Qur'an. See n. 47 above.

53. That is, the mind of this man would wander so uncontrollably during prayer that he might accidentally remember something he had forgotten.

54. The science of *tauhid:* that discipline of theology which seeks to establish the divine unity and related doctrines by means of rational argument.

55. Shaykh 'Abdullah Ansari: a prolific Sufi author, 396/1006-481/1089. A scholar of great literary skill and spiritual insight, he wrote in both Persian and Arabic. For the relevant passage in his *Manazil as-Sa'irin* ("The Stages of the Wayfarers"), see pp. 16-17 of the edition published in Cairo in 1954 by S. de Laugier de Beaurecueil, together with the *sharh* ("commentary") of 'Abd al-Mu'ti al-Iskandari. The commen-

tary defines "arising" as: "awakening from the slumber of neglect and emerging from the pit of apathy."

56. This statement is not intended to sanction "vast estates," but merely to emphasize that the essence of worldliness is attachment to possessions, not the mere owning of them.

57. An allusion to one of the celebrated quatrains of 'Umar Khayyam (412/1021-515/1122):

> A shaykh once said to a whore: "You're drunk,
> And held each night in a different embrace!"
> Said she: "O shaykh, I am indeed all that you say,
> But are you truly all that you seem?"

58. Abu Sufyan: see n. 41 above.

59. A similar interpretation of this "clouding" of the Prophet's heart is to be found in the celebrated seventh-/thirteenth-century Sufi compendium *Mirsad al-'Ibad*, by Najm ad-Din Razi (p. 326 of the Tehran edition of 1352 Sh./1973).

60. I.e., 'Ali ibn Abi Talib.

61. *Dhikr:* inducing or maintaining a state of awareness of God, especially by means of the vocal or silent recitation of His Supreme Name.

62. Day of 'Arafa: the ninth day of the month of Dhu 'l-Hijja, when all the pilgrims participating in the hajj must be present at the plain of 'Arafa outside Mecca. For the text of the prayer that Imam Husayn recited on this day, see Shaykh 'Abbas Qummi, *Mafatih al-Jinan*, pp. 350-369, and for a translation of it, see William C. Chittick, *A Shi'ite Anthology* (Albany, N.Y., 1980), pp. 93-113.

63. Invocations of Sha'ban: see p. 349.

64. The Prayer of Kumayl: a prayer taught to Kumayl ibn Ziyad, a close associate of Imam 'Ali, by the Imam. Its recitation is particularly recommended during the early hours of Friday. For the text, see Shaykh 'Abbas Qummi, *Mafatih al-Jinan*, pp. 83-90

65. See introductory note by Shaykh 'Abbas Qummi, *Mafatih al-Jinan*, p. 213.

66. *Nahj al-Balagha:* a collection of sermons, addresses and epistles attributed to 'Ali ibn Abi Talib. It was compiled by Sayyid Sharif Razi in the fourth/tenth century.

67. *Mafatih al-Jinan:* the standard manual of Shi'i devotion, containing the supplicatory prayers of the Imams, as well as formulae for recitation at particular times or during visitation of the tombs of the Imams. Its compiler, Shaykh 'Abbas Qummi, was a scholar of vast learning who died

in Najaf in 1359/1940.

68. Kasravi: more fully, Ahmad Kasravi, an Iranian historian, 1306/1888-1364/1945. In a series of controversial works, he attacked both Sufism and Shi'i Islam as sources of superstition and national retardation (see his *Sufigari* and *Shi'agari*). He also attempted to propagate a "pure Persian" language, replacing all Arabic loanwords with coinages of his own, and a pseudo-religion he called Pak-Din ("the pure religion"). He was assasinated in 1945 by Navvab Safavi, founder of the Fida'yan-i Islam, an organization dedicated to the installation of an Islamic polity in Iran. See also p. 425.

69. The sense of this tradition (which may not be authentic) is connected to another tradition, which states: "All that is in the revealed books is in the Qur'an; all that is in the Qur'an is in Surat al-Fatiha; all that is in Surat al-Fatiha is in *Bismillah;* all that is in *Bismillah* is in the letter *ba;* all that is in the letter *ba* is in the dot beneath it." See Isma'il Haqqi al-Burusawi, *Ruh al-Bayan* (Istanbul, 1389/1969), I, 10.

Correlating the two traditions, we conclude that 'Ali ibn Abi Talib was a compressed manifestation in human form of the truths of revelation.

70. Concerning universal *vilayat*, see p. 155, n. 63.

71. *Vahidiyat:* oneness as it pertains to the divine attributes; the unity that pervades the multiplicity of the divine attributes and assures the coherence of their manifestation in creation.

72. Witnessing: *shuhud*, the witnessing of God that excludes any awareness of self and that takes place through the agency of God Himself, not by means of any organ of vision, whether outer or inner.

73. This sentence is quoted by Imam Khomeini in Arabic. We have not been able to identify its origin.

74. We are unable to identify the mystic intended here. It may be Abu Sa'id ibn Abi 'l-Khayr (350/967-440/1049), a contemporary of Avicenna, who was paid a visit by the great philosopher in about 403/1012. Abu Sa'id and Avicenna were closeted together for three days, at the end of which Avicenna's pupils asked him his opinion of the mystic. He replied: "All that I know, he sees." Similarly, the disciples of Abu Sa'id asked him for his evaluation of Avicenna. He answered: "All that I see, he knows." See Muhammad ibn Manavvar, *Asrar at-Tauhid* (Tehran, 1348 Sh./1979), pp. 209-211.

75. A dictum frequently quoted in mystical texts, meaning that the purified heart becomes a receptacle for the divine presence.

76. "Tranquillity of the heart": an allusion to Qur'an, 13:28: "Is it not by the remembrance of God that hearts attain tranquillity?"

77. In addition to the division of the Qur'an into *suras* of differing lengths, there is also a purely quantitative division into thirty equal parts.

78. "The unseen and the manifest": the two realms of creation mentioned in numerous verses of the Qur'an that subsume all orders of being.

79. *Vilayat:* See p. 155, n. 63.

80. That is, although the two names are separate in meaning (see n. 15 above), they do not designate separate "aspects" of God, which would be to introduce division into the divine being; instead, each name pertains to the entirety of the Essence.

81. This celebrated story is taken from the *Masnavi* of Jalal ad-Din Rumi, where the Persian, the Arab, and the Turk are joined by a Greek who expresses a preference for *istafil*. See *Masnavi*, II, lines 3681-3686.

82. *Ma'sumin:* those possessing the quality of 'ismat (see p. 156, n. 67 above); i.e., the Prophet, Fatima, and the Twelve Imams.

83. In this saying, the cloak (*khirqa*) serves as a symbol of the Sufi, particularly the one who puts his trust in outward appearances.

84. Akhbaris: a school of Shi'i law that holds to a narrow reliance on the Qur'an and the Sunna of the Prophet and the Imams, rejecting secondary sources of law. It was largely displaced in Iran toward the end of the eighteenth century, but it continues to exist in the Shi'i communities of Kuwait, Bahrayn, and the Qatif region of Eastern Arabia.

85. Usulis: the adversaries of the Akhbaris. They hold that the *faqih* may legitimately apply rational exertion to the solution of legal problems. The Iranian religious scholars have been overwhelmingly Usuli since the late eighteenth century. For an account of the disputes between the Akhbaris and Usulis, see Hamid Algar, *Religion and State in Iran, 1785-1906* (Berkeley, 1969), pp. 33-36.

86. The first part of a tradition of the Prophet, indicating the universal presence of God.

87. "Colorlessness fell prey to color": a quotation from Jalal ad-Din Rumi, *Masnavi*, I, line 2467: "When colorlessness fell prey to color,/a Moses came into conflict with a Moses." The meaning is that Pharaoh, in his primordial nature free of attachment and color (and therefore himself "a Moses"), became colored by attachment and thus the antithesis of Moses. The erroneous interpretation of the verse that Imam Khomeini is seeking to correct sees "colorlessness" as pure being and "color" as things in their multiplicity.

88. See Hafiz, *Divan*, eds. Furughi and Ghani (Tehran, n.d.), p. 37. The complete line reads: "I am a slave to the aspiration of him who is free of all that takes on the color of attachment."

89. See p. 349.

90. See Shaykh 'Abbas Qummi, *Mafatih al-Jinan*, p. 216.

91. "Attaining" (*vusul*) the ultimate degree of proximity to God; being with God, with neither absorption nor separation.

92. Shaykh Muhammad Bahari: presumably a contemporary of Imam Khomeini during his years of study at Qum.

93. See the introduction to this anthology, p. 14.

94. Mirza 'Ali Akbar Hakim: also Yazdi, one of Imam Khomeini's teachers of philosophy, and himself the foremost pupil of the celebrated Mulla Hadi Sabzavari (1212/1797-1295/1878). He died in 1344/1925. See Muhammad Razi, *Asar al-Hujja* (Qum, 1332 Sh./1953), I, 216.

95. Khwansari: see p. 165, n. 188.

96. Ishraqi: more fully, Mirza Muhammad Taqi Ishraqi, a celebrated scholar and preacher, 1313/1895-1368/1949. He used to include political comment in the sermons he gave in Qum; he was also the father of Imam Khomeini's son-in-law, Hujjat al-Islam Shihab Ishraqi. See Razi, *Asar al-Hujja*, I, 135-137.

97. Shahabadi: more fully, Mirza Muhammad 'Ali Shahabadi, a master of both the religious and the rational sciences, 1292/1875-1369/1950. He spent the years between 1347/1928 and 1354/1935 teaching in Qum, where Imam Khomeini was among his foremost students. See Razi, *Asar al-Hujja*, I, 217-219.

98. *Aya:* sign. Cf. Qur'an, 41:53: "We shall show them Our signs (*ayat*) on the horizons and in their own selves"; that is, God has placed in man's cosmic environment and within his own being indications of His reality.

99. Kasravi: see n. 68 above.

100. Hafiz: the supreme master of Persian lyrical poetry, 726/1325-792/1390. His verse is marked by a rich interplay between different levels of meaning—mystical and profane, personal and political.

101. This fifth lecture was in fact the last in the series that Imam Khomeini delivered.

APPENDIX:
Legal Rulings

Like other religious authorities of the Shi'i Muslims, Imam Khomeini has compiled—or allowed to be compiled under his supervision—a collection of rulings on a wide range of topics covered by the shari'a. Unique to Imam Khomeini, however, is the inclusion in his collection of rulings explicitly political in nature. Of particular interest in relation to Islamic Government *are these extracts from two sections of his collection of rulings, added, at varying times after 1963, to the original edition. We have retained the original headings. The number introducing each ruling refers to the serial numbering of the whole collection.* Source: *Tauzih al-Masa'il,* n.p., n.d., pp. 454-456, 460-463.

Enjoining the Good and Forbidding the Evil

(2793) If some evil innovation appears in Islam, such as the evil actions undertaken by governments in the name of Islam, it is the duty of everyone, particularly the *'ulama,* to proclaim the truth and to denounce the falsehood [in question]. If the silence of the *'ulama* [in such cases] is liable to discredit them or to arouse suspicion concerning them, they must proclaim the truth in whatever way possible, even if they know it will have no [practical] effect.

(2795) If the silence of the *'ulama* will tend to strengthen the oppressor, gain support for him, or encourage him to engage in further impermissible actions, it is the duty of everyone to proclaim the truth and denounce the falsehood [in question], even if it has no practical effect.

(2797) If the entry of the *'ulama* into the state apparatus of the oppressor will prevent the occurrence of corruption and evil, it is their duty to accept such a [state] position, unless acceptance entails in its turn a greater form of corruption, as, for example, the weakening of popular trust and confidence in the 'ulama. In such cases, it is forbidden.

(2798) It is not permissible for the 'ulama and congregational imams to accept posts in religious schools administered by the state and the Department of Endowments, whether their stipends, together with those of the students of the religious sciences, are paid by the state, by the people, or out of the religious endowments, even if the endowment [used for this purpose] pertains to the school in question. For the intervention of the state in these and similar matters is preparatory to the destruction of the fundamental principles of Islam at the orders of the imperialists; similar measures have been enacted in all Muslim states, or are about to be enacted.

(2799) It is not permissible for students of the religious sciences to enter state institutions that have been established under the name of religious institutions, such as religious schools in which the state interferes, which have been taken away from their rightful administrators by the state, or whose administrators have been brought under the influence and control of the state. Any money given to the students by the Department of Endowments or with its approval is unlawful.

(2800) It is not permissible for students of the religious sciences to enter schools that are administered by turban-wearers and congregational imams who have been appointed by or at the suggestion of the state, whether the syllabus has been drawn up by the state or by the administrators, who are agents of the tyrannical state, for such schools form part of a plan for the obliteration of Islam and the ordinances of the Noble Qur'an.

(2801) Those who enter institutions established by government decree while wearing the dress of the 'ulama must be shunned by the Muslims and religious people; all dealings with them must be refused. They are to be regarded as lacking in justice.[1] It is not permissible to pray behind them; divorces recorded by them are invalid; the share of the Imam[2] (upon whom be peace) and that of the sayyids[3] must not be given to them, and if it is, it does not constitute a fulfillment of the obligation. If the persons in question are preachers, they must not be invited to preach; and no one should participate in meetings where those people preach on government instructions, diffusing falsehood and propagating the anti-Islamic government programs.

(2803) The assumption of various positions by those turban-wearers who are the agents of the oppressors produces great harm and corruption, the effects of which will gradually become apparent. Therefore, the Muslims must not pay any heed to the excuses they offer for accepting their positions, and it is the duty of the 'ulama to expel them from their centers of the religious institution. It is also the duty of the 'ulama, the students of the religious sciences, the respected preachers, and all classes aware of the treacherous plans of the foreign agents to identify and expose those sinful and corrupt people and to warn the people against the evil they represent.

(2825) If the evil [that is to be forbidden] is of a kind accorded great importance by the Sacred Legislator, one that He in no wise wishes to occur, it is permissible to prevent it by any means possible. If someone wishes to kill another, for example, in the absence of legal justification, he must be prevented. If the killing of the wronged party cannot be prevented except by killing the wrongdoer, then it is permissible, even necessary, to do so. It is not necessary to seek permission from a *mujtahid.* Care should be taken, however, to resort to other means of prevention that do not involve killing wherever possible. If one exceeds the necessary amount [of violence], he becomes a sinner and is subject to the penalties inflicted on the aggressor.

Questions of Defense

(2826) If the enemy attacks the lands of the Muslims or their borders, it is the duty of all Muslims to defend them by any means possible, including the sacrificing of one's life and the expenditure of one's wealth. With respect to this matter, there is no need to seek permission from a *shari'a* judge.

(2827) If the Muslims fear that the foreigners have drawn up a plan to conquer their lands, whether directly or by the intermediary of their agents acting outside or inside the country, it is their duty to defend the Islamic lands by any means possible.

(2829) If it is feared that foreigners will gain control over the lands of the Muslims by expanding their political, economic, or commercial influence, it is the duty of the Muslims to defend their lands by any means possible and to destroy the influence of the foreigners as well as their domestic agents.

(2830) In the case of political relations between Muslim states and foreign states, if it is feared that the foreigners will gain control of the Islamic countries, even if that control is purely political and economic, it is the duty of the Muslims to oppose such relations and to force the Islamic states to sever them.

(2831) With respect to commercial relations with foreigners, if it is feared that the bazaar of the Muslims will suffer economic damage and the country will be reduced to commercial and economic slavery, such relations must be severed, and the Muslims are forbidden to engage in commerce of this type.

(2832) If the establishment of relations, whether political or commercial, between one of the Muslim states and foreigners is contrary to the interest of Islam and the Muslims, such relations are not permissible and if a Muslim government moves to establish such relations, it is the duty of the other Muslim governments to compel it, by any means possible, to sever relations.

(2833) If certain heads of state of Muslim countries, or certain members of either house of the Majlis, permit foreigners to expand their influence, whether that influence is political, economic, or military, [in a manner] contrary to the interests of Islam and the Muslims, they automatically forfeit their posts—whatever their posts may be—by virtue of this treason, even if it is supposed that the post [in question] was legitimately obtained. Furthermore, it is the duty of the Muslims to punish them by any means possible.

(2834) [The establishment of] commercial and political relations with states like Israel that are the tools of the tyrannical superpowers is not permissible and it is the duty of the Muslims to oppose such relations in any way possible. Merchants who establish commercial relations with Israel and its agents are traitors to Islam and the Muslims, and they are aiding in the destruction of the ordinances of Islam. It is the duty of the Muslims to discontinue all dealings with those traitors, whether they are governments or merchants, and to compel them to repent and renounce their relations with such states.

Miscellaneous Questions

(2835) Laws that have passed, or are now passing, the two houses of the Majlis on the orders of agents of the foreigners (may God curse them), in clear contradiction to the Noble Qur'an and the Sunna of the Prophet of Islam (peace and blessings upon him and his family), are null and void with respect to Islam and invalid with respect to the law. It is the duty of the Muslims to shun those who impose [such laws] and those who vote [for such laws] in any way possible, and to discontinue all intercourse and transactions with them. They are criminals, and anyone who acts in accordance with what they have voted [into law] is a sinner and an offender.

(2836) The law that has recently passed the two houses of the Majlis (which [in their present composition] are illegal and contrary to the *shari'a*) on the orders of the agents of the foreigners, the law designated the "Family Law,"[4] which has as its purpose the destruction of the Muslim family unit, is contrary to the ordinances of Islam. Those who have imposed [this law] and those who have voted [for it] are criminals from the standpoint of both the *shari'a* and the law. The divorce of women divorced by court order is invalid; they are still married women, and if they marry again, they become adulteresses. Likewise, anyone who knowingly marries a woman so divorced becomes an adulterer, deserving the penalty laid down by the *shari'a*. The issue of such union will be illegitimate, unable to inherit, and subject to all other regulations concerning illegitimate offspring. All of the foregoing applies equally whether the court itself awards the divorce directly, orders the divorce to take place, or compels the husband to divorce his wife.

(2837) It is the duty of the *'ulama* (may God Almighty support them) to protest forcefully against laws such as this that are void from the standpoint of both Islam and the law; they should not seek to gain the favor of the true criminals by pretending that lower-ranking officials are responsible for executing the orders of the opponents of Islam. For attempts of this kind tend to clear the true criminal of responsibility and encourage him in his destruction of God's ordinances. It is the duty of all Muslims to resist these laws, which threaten religion, worldly welfare, and family life; which provide for their defenseless daughters to be dragged off into military service; and which seek to nullify the efforts of the prophets and the *awliya* (peace and blessings upon them all). They must express their abhorrence of these anti-Islamic laws, refuse to act in accordance with them, and defend the ordinances of Islam by any means possible lest they become afflicted (God forbid) with the black and hideous future that the agents of imperialism (may God curse them) plan for Islam and the Muslims.

Notes

1. "Justice" is used here in the technical sense defined on p. 152, n. 21.

2. Share of the Imam: *sahm-i imam,* monies paid to the Imam, or, in the period of his occultation, to the *'ulama,* for charitable disbursement.

3. *Sayyids:* descendants of the Prophet Muhammad through his daughter Fatima and Imam 'Ali.

4. The "Family Protection Law" of 1967 virtually abolished all provisions of the *shari'a* relating to marriage and divorce and gave the courts wide discretionary powers in granting and withholding divorces.

INDEX

MORE ABOUT KPI BOOKS

If you would like further information about books available from KPI please write to

> The Marketing Department
> KPI Limited
> Routledge & Kegan Paul Plc
> 14 Leicester Square
> London WC2H 7PH

In the USA write to

> The Marketing Department
> KPI Limited
> Routledge & Kegan Paul
> 9 Park Street
> Boston
> Mass. 02108

In Australia write to

> The Marketing Department
> KPI Limited
> Routledge & Kegan Paul
> 464 St. Kilda Road
> Melbourne
> Victoria 3004

KPI